BLACK AND WHITE ON WALL STREET

JOSEPH JETT

WITH SABRA CHARTRAND

BLACK AND WHITE ON WALL STREET

THE UNTOLD STORY OF THE MAN WRONGLY

ACCUSED OF BRINGING DOWN

KIDDER PEABODY

WILLIAM MORROW AND COMPANY, INC. / NEW YORK

Library of Congress Cataloging-in-Publication Data
Jett, Joseph.
      Black and white on Wall Street : the untold story of the man
wrongly accused of bringing down Kidder Peabody / Joseph Jett with
Sabra Chartrand. — 1st ed.
            p.   cm.
      ISBN 0-688-16136-7
      1. Jett, Joseph.   2. Kidder, Peabody & Co.—Employees—Biography.
3. Insider trading in securities—United States.   4. Securities
industry—corrupt practices—United States.   I. Chartrand, Sabra.
II. Title.
HG4928.5.J48   1999
332.6'092
[B]—DC21   98-33335
                                                                CIP

Printed in the United States of America

First Edition

1   2   3   4   5   6   7   8   9   10

BOOK DESIGN BY JO ANNE METSCH

www.williammorrow.com

To my father, who forged my will;
to my mother, may I never lose your gentleness;
to Pizarro and Yvette, who sheltered me through childhood's storms

CONTENTS

AUTHOR'S NOTE

N THE SPRING of 1994, I was forced out of my job as a top bond trader at Kidder, Peabody & Co. and charged with masterminding one of the largest securities scams in Wall Street history. The book you are about to read is my personal accounting of the events that led to my ouster. For the last five years, Kidder Peabody and its parent company, General Electric, have harnessed unlimited resources and an array of lawyers, public relations experts and the media to tell their side of the story. From the day the story broke, Kidder and GE have insisted I was a rogue trader who acted completely alone in perpetrating an enormous fraud right under the noses of Kidder's and GE's top executives. But after years of investigation and lawsuits, no criminal charges have been brought against me.

This book is my attempt to set the record straight by telling my side of the story. Kidder's former executives would prefer that the events that occurred in the struggle for power and money at the firm remain behind closed doors. But they are central to understanding how a moneymaking trading strategy went sour. Some of them are overtly racist. As you will read, people at Kidder and elsewhere on Wall Street dismiss my account as a ruse. But with this book, I've tried to tell my story as accurately and honestly as I can recall it. I believe that I was wrongly accused and made the scapegoat for a culture in which racism remains rampant, and greed is the only currency of value. It is my hope that this book will allow the public, finally, to understand that as well.

PART
ONE

GROUND ZERO

UST BEFORE FIVE o'clock in the morning on a Monday in early
April, I opened my eyes to a soft gray light filtering through the
skylight of my loft. Darkness and quiet filled the corners of the vast
room. I lay still in bed, feeling, for a few seconds, the beginning of
a day like any other. I always rose before dawn because the bond
markets in Tokyo and London had already been open for hours.
But then I remembered the letter, and that today was already quite
different. I got out of bed, running through a mental list of the
bond traders who worked for me. Nearby was the only other furniture in the loft, a couch, a table where I ate and worked, a TV
on the floor. Robotically I reached out and switched on the television. I was preoccupied, deciding which of my traders to take with
me to my new job.

The letter lay on the table. Should I go to the office and confront
my boss, Edward Cerullo? I would demand severance pay and my
deferred benefits package. Kidder, Peabody & Co. owed me several
million dollars. I rummaged through my closet, searching for a
T-shirt. Every day, after hearing the overnight business news on
TV, I would call Tokyo, then London, then make a pit stop at the
office to turn on the computers before heading to a Wall Street
gym. I'd work out and get back to my desk before most of my
colleagues were out of their pajamas. I'd adopted my predawn habits from my father, who learned his as a U.S. Army sergeant in
Korea and demanded that my brother, sister and I be out of bed

every day of our childhood in time for his personal reveille. Even as a kid, I knew that I could get a lot done before dawn, while the less-disciplined burrowed in their warm beds.

I found a T-shirt, only half listening to the early Hong Kong news report. Instead, I wondered: Should I confront Cerullo face-to-face, or just have a lawyer handle it? If Cerullo is mad at me now, he'll really be angry when he discovers that the best people on his Government Bond trading desk have jumped ship with me. Too bad. Twelve hours ago, I had run that desk at Kidder Peabody, a blue-chip investment firm. My lips twitched with a small smile. Raiding Kidder of its best traders would not only ensure a top-notch team for me, but would also leave Kidder floundering. It would take the firm months to rebuild the team I'd so carefully cultivated. And it'd never replace me.

It didn't matter that I had no idea where my new job would be. The letter on the table, hand delivered by a messenger the night before and telling me I'd been fired, was inconsequential. It just gave me a reason to plan for the future. I'd have a new job before the end of the week. This would be my chance to jettison some of the deadwood among my traders. I wouldn't offer to take everyone. I wanted a powerful, daring, moneymaking team. I'd devoted the last two years to hiring smart people and creating a competitive desk where everyone worked long, hard hours. It hadn't been like that at all when I joined Kidder, but I drove my traders relentlessly, and in the end, we'd jelled into a cohesive, proficient team, and my people liked the money they earned. I was determined to leave behind anyone who was disloyal, who spent too much time and energy on rumormongering, backbiting and politicking. Politicking had cost me my job.

I'd lost it in the most recent round of fighting among managers at Kidder. In fairness, Kidder was no different than any other Wall Street firm. Jockeying for power was endemic on the Street, because power meant money. Careers, reputations, personal lives were fair game, and they were trashed every day. To be successful you kept moving, kept watch behind you, to the sides and ahead. Survival required supreme confidence. Doubt meant weakness. I never doubted myself.

Four of us worked for Edward Cerullo, all vying for his approval, his backing, his largesse with the purse strings. Though they never said so, the other three managers were probably also vying for his job. I said so—I was openly determined to oust Cerullo and take his place. The balance of power among the four of us shifted constantly, depending on who was in favor, which meant who was making the most money for Cerullo. For over a year, that had been me. I'd been anointed more often than I could count as a rising star, a golden boy, an heir apparent. So I had enemies. I was locked in a war of personalities, work style and goals. I was a formidable foe, because I didn't care about winning friends. I wasn't about to accommodate anyone, to compromise my methods or objectives. I knew I had enemies; I also knew they couldn't defeat me.

I understood that being fired was not defeat. I'd always known that either I'd oust Cerullo, or that he, or one of the other managers, would oust me. Being fired meant losing a battle, not the war. I'd explained this often to my parents. My father was my mentor, my inspiration and the yardstick against which I measured my life, and we talked on the phone a couple of times every week. I'd warned him and my mother more than once that I was about to be fired. When the messenger bore the letter to my door on Sunday evening, I saw it as little more than another salvo in my battles at Kidder. I'd fire back. I'd take the best traders with me. Then I would take the bond business away from Kidder. I had allies, a strategy and weapons of my own. The war was far from over.

If the letter made that Monday different from others, in many ways it meant more of the same. Or so I thought as I got dressed. When the ground shifts, opens up and swallows someone, the wrench that knocks them off their feet also stuns. When reality is altered, it isn't apparent as it's happening. Awareness and clarity come only later. I got up that Monday assuming the world remained ordered as I knew it, however chaotic and vicious that order had been. I prepared to lock horns with my adversaries. But I charged and bucked at thin air, my opponents out there but unreachable. By Friday I would begin to understand why. Reality had simply shifted, and would never be the same.

The first jolt came as I pulled the T-shirt from my closet. The TV was just background noise, but suddenly an anchorman's voice emerged clearly from the babble. My ears picked up his offer of a special report on the trading scandal at Kidder Peabody. I focused on the screen as it cut to a commercial, standing still, holding the T-shirt, until the anchorman returned. "Wall Street brokerage Kidder Peabody has announced it's fired the head of its Government trading desk for creating a scheme of phantom trades," he intoned. "The consequences will be a $350 million charge that will show up Tuesday on parent company GE's earning results."

The anchorman cut to a reporter, who had a guest, a stocky, dazed-looking man with gray hair and glasses whom I didn't recognize. His square face was pale, his striped sports shirt didn't match his suit coat, and with no tie, he looked as if he had dressed in a hurry. As soon as I heard his name I knew it—Dennis Dammerman, chief financial officer of General Electric. General Electric was the parent corporation that owned Kidder Peabody.

"I've been in this job for ten years, and this is the first time I'd had to surprise investors in terms of quarterly earnings release, and we don't like it." I gaped at the screen, opening my mouth to protest just as the TV guy voiced the same incredulity. "It does bend the bonds of credibility to think that one man could do this all on his own," the reporter said. Dammerman looked at his fingernails.

"Certainly, certainly some back-room controls were circumvented," he said with less conviction, "and to do that, he had to have the, uh, knowing or unknowing cooperation of people in place to, uh, impose those controls." GE had suspended six others "who are close to the activity and the extent of their involvement has yet to be determined." My mind immediately supplied the names—the six had to include Edward Cerullo, the chief of the Fixed Income department, and the managers I feuded with: David Bernstein, Charles Fiumefreddo, J. J. McKoan, Mel Mullin. My trading strategy was *our* trading strategy—based on computer software written by Mullin, devised and taught to me by Bernstein, analyzed and approved by Fiumefreddo and directed by Cerullo.

"We spent a good deal of the weekend talking with the people we thought were necessary to talk to," Dammerman said. Who did he mean? He never said, preferring to reassure viewers that none of GE's investors had lost money. The reporter said GE had "already gone to great lengths to say that Jett's trades were internal, that retail and institutional clients were not affected." Dammerman drove the point home. "This was an isolated area, the systems were unique because it was government trading and there's no reason to believe that there should be any other area involved."

I glanced at a window. It was barely light out. How long had GE been at work on this? Long enough, clearly, for the anchors and reporters to adopt GE's tone. An anchorman announced that GE's chief executive officer, Jack Welch, was "damn mad," and then said that Kidder was planning its next step. The anchorman turned to his co-anchor with a smile. "You can rest assured that with Jack Welch damn mad, they're going to do something!" he chuckled.

Fascinated, I flipped channels. My name dominated the morning news. Few of the reports contained caveats, and none mentioned trying to reach me for my side of the story. On another business news show, the anchorwoman stated flatly that "Kidder Peabody is firing the head of its Government trading desk for his involvement in a scheme that created phantom trades and inflated profits." The charges were lobbed as if they were inherently true—phantom trades, bogus trades, fictionalized trades, inflated profits, fraud. The word "fraud" snagged my attention, and I laughed out loud, a bark of relief that rose from deep in my chest. I relaxed. Fraud was such a far-fetched charge that I immediately dismissed the entire TV blitz. On Wall Street, the term "fraud" usually meant an attempt to hide a bad trade. If a bond trader bought a bond only to see its price drop like a stone, he could pretend he never made the purchase. It happens often enough. It's called "hiding the ticket." Traders are supposed to fill out a purchase ticket for every trade. But if the trader hesitates, and then the price drops, the temptation to destroy or hide the ticket can be great. No ticket means the trade never happened. Of course, it's illegal.

But the losses Dammerman blamed on me did not arise from any hidden tickets. Every trade was properly recorded. Every one was conducted in the open. Most of them were so massive—hundreds of millions of dollars at a time—that hiding them would have been like hiding an elephant under a doormat. GE couldn't be serious; the traders on my desk would never back up such a story. All they had to do was talk about their daily tasks and the trades we conducted. Then there were the extra data processors who'd been hired to handle the overload in the back office. They could describe the trades they'd spent hours inputting into the computer. The idea that anything had been hidden, that any duplicitous action or fraud had occurred, was ludicrous. All these allegations had to be nothing more than posturing from GE. I turned away from the TV. I shouldn't have. It meant I wasn't listening closely when at the end of an interview, with a slight smile, Dammerman added almost sheepishly: "Yes, there is talk of suing Mr. Jett, and going after him any way we possibly can."

CLEARLY, IT WAS pointless to go to the office and have it out with Cerullo. He was no longer there either. I pulled on the T-shirt. So the truth was finally out. We'd lost huge amounts of money in recent weeks at Kidder, that much was certainly true. I knew why, and now GE must have discovered it as well. Our department had been systematically underreporting how much of GE's capital we were using to play the market. As our parent company, GE was our money tree. We took money from GE, used it as collateral to borrow billions of dollars, then invested and hopefully profited from those loans. But GE, and its mercenary CEO, Jack Welch, in particular, had an intense love-hate relationship with Kidder. Welch had bought an 80 percent stake in Kidder in 1987, a decision that very publicly blackened the eye of a man who believed his own publicity about his uncanny business savvy. He invested $650 million in Kidder at precisely the worst time, at the very end of the greed-and-glitter 1980s and the onset of the demise of Wall Street. Welch was loath to throw good money after bad; soon GE constantly nagged Kidder to use less of its money and limit our ratio of capital to loans. We ignored the pleas. Instead, we constantly used more of GE's money than we were allowed and overextended ourselves through borrowing. We got away with it because we just didn't tell GE exactly how much of its money we were using at any given time. We used a technicality to keep two sets of books; the lower balance sheet we showed to GE, the higher sheet we kept to ourselves. GE could call that fraud, but it wasn't illegal. It wasn't why we'd lost $350 million, and it certainly didn't amount to a "trading scandal." My boss, Ed Cerullo, knew that. He'd had a plan, a secret ambition to wrest Kidder away from GE. We'd embarked on the balance sheet manipulation to hide assets from GE because it was critical to Cerullo's dream of escaping GE ownership. Cerullo ordered us to keep GE in the dark. So where was he now? What exactly was GE angry about? I realized I was mumbling aloud to myself. Who could I call to find out what was going on? Who was left standing?

I could only wait. No one would arrive in the office until 7:30 or 8:00. None of the senior managers would show up until 10:00. Picking up the TV remote control, I started channel surfing, mesmerized by a revolving display of anchormen and women, all naming me a fraud, a scam artist, a rogue trader. All of them noted that GE had been about to announce record earnings for the last quarter, and every channel reported that now GE would be forced to post a loss. Profits were down $350 million, one reporter said. GE stock dropped $2 a share when the market opened. Still holding the remote, at some point I sat down on the couch, not noticing the hours pass or the rising sun slowly fill the loft with brighter light.

Ringing broke my concentration. It was after seven. I picked up the phone, surprised to hear one of my neighbors. "Joseph, I just wanted to tell you there's a crowd of reporters downstairs. When I walked out of the building they thought I was you and asked for comments." I'd forgotten there was an outside world. A few minutes later, my apartment buzzer started ringing; shouting came over the intercom: "Mr. Jett! We know you're up there! Come down and talk to us! It's for your own good!"

The buzzer rang every few minutes, the same loud male voice shouting the same demands. They knew I was in the apartment. I couldn't hide. But then, why should I? I'd respond somehow. I decided to write a statement, take it downstairs and read it to the reporters. Certainly I'd seen that on TV often enough. But each effort ended in a wad of paper at my feet. Each explanation of what happened at Kidder was too verbose, each wandered off into digressions about my three-year career. My trades were too complicated and too dependent on detailed understanding of the bond market. Concentration was difficult with the buzzer ringing constantly. I needed a short, crisp statement of the trades and my innocence. Most important, I wanted to make it clear that I handled $30 billion of GE's money. How could I hide trading on that scale? I wanted to go downstairs and say: "I traded nine percent of GE's assets, and GE says it had no idea what I was doing?"

Finally I decided my statement sounded clear and sensible. I practiced reading it aloud, then changed into an expensive, hand-tailored suit. In the elevator, my foot tapped nervously. From the lobby I could hear the voice of the guy shouting into the intercom as I paused to calm myself. Taking a deep breath, I pulled the door open. A blaze of lights erupted, blinding me. I could feel a crowd surge forward and I blinked, trying to make out shapes of people in front of the lights. For a second or two I couldn't see anything but the glare. My vision cleared in time to see the group begin to relax, break up and retreat. Directly in front of me the face and hair of a young blond woman emerged from a silhouette as the lights dimmed. She was thrusting a large microphone toward my face. Suddenly it fell limp in her hand, the metal stem dangling for a second from its cord as she looked at me blankly, slightly exasperated. Then she, too, turned away. All the lights were off, no one was looking at me anymore, and I heard the now familiar voice resume shouting. Behind me, the guy was wedged behind the lobby doors, pressing again on the buzzer: "Mr. Jett, Mr. Jett! We know you're in there! Come down and talk to us!"

I pushed through what was left of the milling crowd and started walking toward the corner, shaking with the rage rising in my chest. Reality had shifted under my feet again, only this time the jolt was all too familiar. I wanted to turn around and bellow: "I *am* Mr. Jett!" Instead I kept walking. The crowd of reporters let me go. They were looking for Joseph Jett, Harvard graduate and multimillionaire Wall Street bond trader. They weren't looking for a black man.

ALL THE ANGER I'd felt toward Kidder Peabody and GE, and all the nervousness I'd felt about reading my statement, disappeared and was replaced by shock that left me almost breathless. They didn't know who I was. The man they saw wasn't Joseph Jett—because in their minds the man they saw couldn't possibly be him.

I walked to the corner, incensed at the judgment forced on me again. It had been a long time since that had last happened. I'd chosen Wall Street as a career precisely to avoid being judged by the color of my skin. Wall Street is a meritocracy—all anyone cares about, all that is ever measured, is the bottom line. How much money you make. Color, gender and age don't matter when it comes to profit. My parents' lives in the South of the 1950s had been poisoned by racism, as a child I'd been teased and repudiated by light-skinned black playmates and schoolmates, and as an adult I'd been judged and found wanting by whites all too often because of the color of my skin. After it all, I'd chosen Wall Street for its very avaricious environment. As long as a trader worked the phones skillfully and made money, no one cared about skin color. I'd worked in that meritocracy long enough that I'd almost forgotten the gut wrench that came with being put in my place. Almost. The feeling of being kicked in the stomach was too familiar.

I walked to Bubby's Cafe on the next corner, at Hudson Street, bought a newspaper and sat at a table in the window. I could see the front stoop of my brick building, the sun glinting off its tall, arched loft windows and delicate iron fire escapes. For the next hour I watched the crowd of reporters rush every white man who came or went from the lobby. I looked down at *The New York Times*. I'd made the front page. Now I knew I needed a lawyer. Back on Hudson, I stopped at every phone booth, searching for the Yellow Pages. I asked for a phone book at a magazine kiosk. There were pages and pages of meaningless names. I handed the book back, exasperated. I went into a bookstore at the corner of Broad Street. At home I had a volume about Wall Street called *The Predator's Ball*. Lawyers were named in it; books like that seemed a place to start. I bought *Barbarians at the Gate*, *Den of Thieves*, and *Greed and Glory on Wall Street*.

I walked home, striding right past the crowd of reporters with my bookstore bag, saying, "Do you mind?" to the ones blocking the stairs to my building. On my stoop there were fewer reporters, but the ones who'd stuck it out still paid no attention to me. The intercom shouter was gone. The blond TV reporter was still there. A handful of photographers remained. They hardly glanced at me. In my loft, I scanned the book indexes, made a list of lawyers and started calling, beginning with Michael Milken's attorney. An aide of his came to the phone and immediately said: "Look, we're counsel for General Electric." I dialed again and again. Over and over I heard the same reply: "We work for GE." "We work for RCA." "We work for NBC," or another subsidiary of GE. One lawyer said, "Look, I read the *Times* story, I work for GE and you're barking up the wrong tree." Another told me, "Wish I could help you, but you're dog meat." A third was kinder. "We're counsel for GE, but let me give you a name." I called the referral and that lawyer said, "You're right, I'm not counsel for GE, but I sure as hell hope to be. It wouldn't be a wise career move to go up against them."

Every lawyer seemed to have read the *Times* story on the commuter train to work. They'd already decided I was guilty. I needed a break, and I knew I needed to talk to my parents. Even though they were forewarned, I wasn't looking forward to the call. My mother, a teacher, and my father, an accountant and independent businessman, had rigorous expectations of their three children. I didn't like to worry them. But I knew that Mops and Pops read *The New York Times*, and that they'd have seen the television reports.

I tried to joke. "Send lawyers, guns and money," I quipped. But they knew that I was upset, and I could tell that they were as well. My father's reply was curt and typical of him: "Do what you have to do. Have you found a lawyer?"

I hesitated. "A lot of these lawyers work for GE."

"Make sure you find a good attorney," Pops said.

"They're saying fraud . . ." my mother started. I called her by our family nickname.

"Mops, I'm not worried about this, just because they're accusing me of fraud," I told my mother and father, who were on separate extentions at home in Ohio. "If they'd just accused me of losing money, it would be one thing. But they've accused me of fraud, that means I hid something. I've got to tell you, that's like accusing someone of hiding the ocean. Everyone there knows that we were ordered to do these trades.

"I don't know if Cerullo is involved," I said. I tried to explain that the whole drama probably revolved around Cerullo's plan to hide the size of Kidder's assets from GE. That effort, I guessed, had spun out of control. "If they're saying fraud against me, that's one thing, but if Cerullo is involved, then they're talking about the whole team."

"Well, make sure you find a good lawyer," my father repeated before hanging up.

I still hoped that I wouldn't have to do anything. Several traders worked for me; I had several managers at my level and above me. Each of them was as involved in my trading strategy as I was. At some point, they'd be forced to explain what our trading desk had been doing. GE might not like it, but the notion that I was somehow a lone criminal would evaporate. Yet the day was passing with no word from anyone at Kidder. Early evening passed in restless rambling around my loft. The reporters were still camped downstairs. Finally one of my traders, Joe Ossman, called me at home. If I was close to anyone, it was Ossman—whom everyone at Kidder called Joey-o—and another trader, Elizabeth Cavanaugh. Ossman had been suspended, he said, along with another trader, Jeff Unger, and two managers, David Bernstein and Charles Fiumefreddo.

But not our department chief, Ed Cerullo.

"Bastard," I groaned over and over. "Joey-o, can you find out whether Bernstein and Fiumefreddo are going to tell the truth about the trades?"

They'd all been called to the office on Sunday, Ossman said. My chief traders—Joey-o, Cavanaugh and Unger—had sat down with a guy none of them had seen before. He was Gary Lynch, and he turned out to be a former chief enforcement officer of the Securities and Exchange Commission. Now he was GE's hired gun. He quizzed everyone as part of his investigation of Joseph Jett and the $350 million loss, Joey-o told me. Then he'd ordered everyone to come to work on Monday, where they'd all been stuck in a room together. They'd sat there all day with nothing to do, Joey-o said, except play cards and imagine the worst. Unger whimpered a lot, and Bernstein sat silent and stoic.

TUESDAY MORNING MY landlord called, asking bluntly, "Where do you keep your money?" Mine was in a cash management account at Kidder. Many people on Wall Street banked their money with their firms; some companies even required it. It prevented investments that might derive from inside information. I hadn't thought about it until my landlord asked: "Do you have access to your account?"

I loped down the stairs of my apartment building and out the front door, past the clutch of reporters and went immediately to the nearest cash machine. It ate my card. Back home, I called Bank One in Ohio. My account, the girl informed me, had been frozen. "They control the account," she said. "It's under Kidder Peabody control because it's under Kidder's name. If they want to freeze the money, they can. We suggest you see your attorney."

The account contained over $4 million. I'd invested my mother's retirement money with Kidder, and it was in there as well. My parents used one of my ATM cards for their living expenses. Their card was confiscated the same day. I couldn't touch a penny of the money I'd earned and deposited over the last three years.

* * *

MY ANSWERING MACHINE filled up with messages from journalists. I didn't call them back. Instead, I called more lawyers. I met one attorney who said he had contacts at Kidder, but he and his associates were dismayed to learn that I had no money. When I got home, I found a letter from the New York Stock Exchange, summoning me to appear before an investigative panel on the coming Thursday. I looked at the delivery date on the FedEx package. The NYSE had posted this letter on Saturday, the day before I was fired. Investigative panels like this one normally took months to convene, I knew. Why had they started forming this one the day before my firing, and how had they pulled it together so swiftly?

ON WEDNESDAY I asked the NYSE for an extension. At the very least, I needed time enough to find a lawyer. The panel wasn't particularly encouraging: one woman and five middle-aged white men who looked just like the middle-aged white male managers at Kidder and GE, all six chosen to investigate a scandal at a firm that paid dues to their organization. Going in, I had little expectation of independence, and even less after one of the panelists shouted at me to answer his questions. When I couldn't, the panel suspended my license to trade. Since I didn't trade stocks, it made little difference to my ability to buy and sell bonds. But the suspension effectively blackballed me on Wall Street.

I wasn't comfortable with the criminal lawyer I'd met, but only he had been willing to talk to me. We met again, this time with one of his partners, a civil attorney. The civil attorney told me he'd been contacted already by David Bernstein, one of my Kidder managers. Then he asked how much money I had, saying he'd represent me if I could pay, but that he'd throw in with Bernstein if I couldn't. The criminal lawyer assured me that Gary Lynch, GE's hired gun, was an old personal friend. He put in a call to see if Lynch and I couldn't sit down and talk. Lynch told the criminal lawyer to send me over for a talk; the lawyer asked whether that would mean I'd get my money back. I didn't like the tone of these negotiations at all. The civil attorney didn't care whether he represented me or Kidder, as long as he got paid. The criminal lawyer seemed willing to turn me over to Lynch and GE so long as he got his money, too. Lynch sent his answer via mail—a letter informing me that twenty-four hours before, on Tuesday, GE had filed suit against me, accusing me of fraud and demanding that I be required to return my salary and bonuses, and pay damages of $370 million to Kidder.

The plot was thickening too quickly. Desperate for an attorney, I called old friends, former Wall Street colleagues, classmates from MIT and Harvard. One friend suggested her sister-in-law's father, who in turn suggested a colleague who might help me. On Wednesday evening, Gustave Newman came to my apartment.

I watched the TV news as I waited. Tom Brokaw broadcast yet another story about the Kidder trading debacle on the NBC nightly news. This time, however, my picture appeared on the screen. It was a 1987 photo from the Harvard Business School yearbook—I still had a mustache and goatee. The correspondent told the country that I was from Wickliffe, Ohio, and that I'd earned $9 million in salary and bonuses in 1993. NBC flashed a synopsis of my crimes on the screen: "Making phantom trades of government bonds . . . ," "entering fictitious trades into company computers . . . ," "appearing to create huge profits . . ." It didn't escape my notice that it was NBC—owned by GE—that plastered my face and hometown on network television. My freedom to come and go was now over, but for a fleeting second I almost smiled for the first time all week. Those reporters and photographers camped out on my doorstep, the ones who for days had watched with apathy as I came and went—surely they'd be apoplectic when they saw my picture.

Newman arrived. He didn't ask many questions about the trading strategy. Instead, he wanted to hear about working at Kidder. I told him my story and admitted that I was broke, all my money in a frozen Kidder account.

"You've been railroaded," he said at the end. "I won't let you down, but if you lie to me . . . I'll. Drop. You. And everyone will know why."

THE PHONE WOKE me at four in the morning on Thursday, not an entirely ungodly hour for my parents. But Mops was crying. Reporters had been camped up and down our street since the night before. They'd found my parents' house in Wickliffe, and ever since had been trying to interview them and every single neighbor on the block. My mother hadn't slept all night.

"No matter what has happened, you know that I support you. I'll always support you. But I have to know. Please tell me. Please tell your Mops. Did you do what they are saying?"

My mother had never questioned me before. I assured her the news reports were lies. If GE's accusations had become so compelling, so convincing that my own mother doubted me, then I was in real trouble. Up to then, I hadn't said a word to any reporter. I'd made no effort to speak out or defend myself. None of my traders had spoken out. All anyone had heard was GE's version of events. Now I knew that GE was winning converts.

I'd talked every day to Joey-o, and now I wanted to call a press conference of my own. Joey-o could appear and back me up. Even though I was tired, I got up to make a list of how to explain that my trades were aboveboard. I'd spent three hours with Gus Newman the night before. He'd grilled me as if I were on the witness stand, asking not about the trading strategy, but about the people at Kidder, about who knew what about my trades and when they'd known it, and about what evidence I had to support my claims.

In the end, he said he believed me, and that he was not concerned that I couldn't pay him immediately. Since he had agreed to represent me, I thought Newman should be at the press conference, too. I lost track of time working on the list, but was jerked back to the present when someone began banging on my front door, kicking and hitting the panel with a force that shook the heavy fire door. I froze, my heart pounding. Paparazzi—somehow one of the more aggressive photographers had gotten into the building. The hammering increased and the door seemed about to buckle; then a slamming noise like a sharp retort echoed through the loft. I recognized the sound of the trapdoor in the hall that led to the roof. The relentless banging continued. A flicker of movement above my head caught my eye and I jumped away from the skylight. Someone was crawling around on the window. Through the cloudy glass I could see a vague shape. He rattled the window catch, and then leaned on the panes. I saw his hands clearly. He held a gun.

I called the police.

Twenty minutes later, a cop appeared at my door. They'd caught two men who had scaled my building. But they wanted to bring them up to my apartment. I stood in my doorway, surprised, uncertain, until the cop returned with two sweaty, heavyset men in gray suits. One flipped open a wallet to reveal an FBI badge. Agents from the Securities Fraud area, they said, as I hung on to the doorknob and stared, mute and apprehensive. The agent explained that they were investigating the charges of fraud at Kidder Peabody, but they didn't want to question me yet. Instead, they hoped to persuade me to deal with them—and not with the Securities Exchange Commission or the New York Stock Exchange. I was already wary of the SEC and the NYSE, but I also had a black man's natural suspicion of cops. And of these FBI agents in particular. After all, one of them had just been on my roof, prying my glass skylight with one hand while holding a gun in the other. Ironically, they didn't need to persuade me that I stood a better chance of a fair investigation with law enforcement than with the clubby members of any Wall Street arbitration panel. The agents persisted, urging me to "talk to us and cooperate with the U.S. Attorney's Office, not the SEC or the New York Stock Exchange. They're not independent, they won't give you a fair hearing."

I knew enough not to say anything to the agents. Instead, I called Gus Newman. It was Friday, and he'd been my lawyer for only a few hours. I told him about the FBI's offer. He asked to speak to one of the agents.

"Thanks for coming to see Mr. Jett. Now please get the hell out of his apartment."

IF ANYONE HAD asked about my state of mind that week after I was fired, I would have looked them in the eye for a long, silent moment and then told them that I had no regrets about anything I'd done at Kidder, and that I would prevail over my enemies simply by being tougher, more disciplined and more resilient than they. I had no doubts about myself. It was not in my nature to hesitate. I could not be cowed. I cared not at all about other people's opinions.

It was the only manner of man I knew how to be, and it was a reflection of the man who raised me. When I was a boy, my father was resolute in his effort to teach my older brother, sister and me what it took for blacks to succeed in America. Our only hope, he believed with absolute certainty, was in economic independence. Black communities and black people had to understand and exploit capitalism. Only when success, power and inclusion could be determined on an economic scale would blacks have true freedom. My father taught me to worship hard work and discipline, for they had an almost mythical power to vanquish racism, prejudice, discrimination. Stress the numbers, he taught. Numbers were cold, hard, color-blind facts. Top grades. Bottom-line profits in business. Votes at the ballot box. If you had any one of these, skin color didn't matter. No one could argue with your success, no one could hold you back. The numbers said it all. Numbers were objective. Numbers were facts on the page.

He was ruthless and unforgiving in his pursuit of objective independence for blacks, and merciless in instilling the lesson in his children. He was harsh, blunt and unapologetic with us, and with our friends and neighbors. He didn't care what anyone thought about him, only that he spread his message. As a result, people didn't like him, they didn't understand him, and they feared his obsessions. As a child I often hated my father, but I loved him, too, and struggled to please him. Along the way, I became very much like him. In my soul I knew that only through merit would I succeed in life, that only through merit did I deserve success. It didn't matter what anyone thought of me, as long as I could point to good grades and a profitable career. The numbers on the bottom line would determine whether I was a success, not my personality, and certainly not my skin color. If my numbers were better than the next guy's—be he white, Asian or black— then truly I would have overcome.

I took this philosophy to its natural conclusion. For my career, I had to choose a profession where the only measure of success was in the numbers. Wall Street and I seemed a perfect match. Of course, I was wrong about this, but I wouldn't know that until it was too late.

First, however, I turned to another of my father's credos in the week after my firing. When I was a boy, my father practiced what he preached, starting local businesses and leading a nonprofit inner-city entrepreneurial project. Usually his businesses failed. As a result, we were often poor, but sacrifice and self-discipline only galvanized my father further. We always knew when the dark periods began because my father would declare: "I'm going to ground zero." It was Cold War slang he'd picked up in the army, when ground zero referred to the epicenter of a nuclear blast where nothing was left standing. It meant that our entire family would hunker down for a long, harsh stretch of time, with nothing but our own fortitude to see us through.

In the weeks after Kidder fired me, those words came unbidden to my mind over and over. Only this time it was my voice, my determination: "I'm going to ground zero."

THE PROMISED LAND

W E TRACE MY father's family to a slave called Fred Lattimore, but I know little about him other than his name. Both sides of my family hail from Alabama, so we assume that is where Fred slaved on a plantation and settled after the Civil War. He chose a barren, hardscrabble farm community not far from Montgomery. Fred's two children, a boy and a girl, were born into freedom sometime between the end of the war and the early 1870s. His son, Benny, refused to call himself Lattimore because it was the name of his father's master, a white man who also owned and raped Benny's mother. Benny himself was very fair-skinned. One day he walked away from the family home and was never heard of again. Most relatives believed he'd gone north and was living there, passing as a white man.

Benny's sister, Sarah Lattimore, was my great-grandmother. Unlike her brother, Sarah was dark, and slender and strikingly beautiful. She married William Jett, a sharecropper whose family name was probably Jeeter, after the white landowner whose acreage he farmed. Sometime in the 1880s, my family began calling itself Jett. No one remembers why. Sarah and Will lived in a rough-boarded, small shack surrounded by a square of hard-packed, lifeless dirt. After their son, Jesse, was born, Sarah went to work as a maid for a family called Hern, and her fate followed her mother's. Mr. Hern evidently could not resist her beauty, and raped her. He then forced her to be his mistress, raping her for years. Hern would appear whenever he wanted at Sarah's small boarded house. When he arrived, visitors had to leave. Sarah's husband, Will, had to leave. Everyone left but Sarah. Eventually she gave birth to a daughter, Ada. Will refused to have anything to do with the light-skinned baby because she was Hern's child. Hern, in his own way, provided for the girl. He continued to force himself on Sarah, but now also brought dresses and presents for the little girl. When Ada was a teenager, Hern saw to it that she had the best clothes. He kept tabs on her friends. She was forbidden to socialize with black boys. Ada herself was fair, with blue eyes, but she had distinctively black features. Only fair-skinned young men, the sons of other plantation masters, could court her. Nearly every family had part-white half brothers and sisters, the children of local landowners. These light-skinned Negroes formed a separate, upper-class society. They attended their own churches, ones reserved for "yellow," or light-complected Negroes. White landowners like Hern encouraged this, but the black community also enthusiastically embraced this hierarchy of skin tones. When she grew up, Ada adopted her mother's maiden name, calling herself Ada Lattimore. Her birth certificate backed up this claim—it listed Sarah as her mother and Fred Lattimore, her grandfather, as her father.

Will and Sarah Jett had five children together in addition to their first son, Jesse. My grandmother, Willie Mae, was born around 1908, though even she never knew her exact birth date. Next came Elizabeth, called Little Sister most of her life. My parents and I called her Big Mama because by the time I was born, she was immense. (Nearly everyone had a nickname. Elizabeth married a man called Rooster. At a family reunion in 1985, I asked Rooster, who was then eighty years old, where he got the name. "I was a cocksman of world renown," the spry old man quipped. "I covered every woman in Montgomery.") Porter was the third child, and there were two others whose names were forgotten after they were killed in a flood in the 1920s. By that time, Ada had moved north, where she, too, passed for white. She learned about the flood, but was told that her whole family had been killed. Believing them all dead, she had no reason to keep in touch with home. She lost contact for years.

In the late 1920s, Sarah's oldest daughter, Willie Mae Jett, met Johnny Chester, a full-blooded Indian from Florida. An orphan, Chester's parents had died during a forced march through the South. Tribal land in the Everglades had been seized in the early 1900s and the Indians were forced to walk through Florida and Georgia, and into Alabama. After his parents' deaths, a black woman adopted Chester and his sister. Chester did odd jobs and seasonal agricultural work, but his main talent was apparently for drinking. In 1930, Willie Mae and Johnny Chester had a son, James. Chester never lived with Willie Mae and their son and had no hand in raising him, and Willie Mae told the boy little about his father. The child didn't even meet his father until he was eleven years old and had a job at the local soft drink bottling plant. One day the old Indian dropped by and introduced himself to the boy. By that time, Willie Mae had been drinking heavily for years, too. She had a well-paying job as a nanny for a white family, but she lived in a Montgomery slum and was careless with James, her only child and my father. She married twice more, and when she wasn't married, had countless boyfriends. The summer James was three, Willie Mae took him to the country and left him at the sharecropper's cabin with her mother, Sarah. When she came to collect the boy in the fall, James threw a tantrum and refused to leave. He remembered his mother's place in Montgomery as smelly, dirty, hot and frequented by too many strangers. The farm was clean and pleasant. His cousin, Findlay, who was his age, and his uncle Porter, nicknamed Shug (short for sugar) and not much older than he, lived with Sarah, too. The three boys were like brothers. So Sarah told Willie Mae to leave her child in the country for two more weeks. Those two weeks turned into the rest of my father's childhood. He didn't leave his grandmother's house until he joined the navy.

Though the country was better than a city slum, my father grew up in the same rough shack his grandmother had lived in all her adult life, without running water or electricity. The only convenience was an outhouse a few paces away. The hard-packed dirt yard was always dry and dusty, cluttered with goats and chickens. The first summer that my father took his children back home, my brother, sister and I gaped at the primitive shanty. It looked exactly like a set from a favorite 1970s movie about poor black sharecroppers, *Sounder*. Imagining our father spending his childhood and youth in such squalor simply boggled our minds. We couldn't get over the fact that people petted and cooed over a goat in the morning and slaughtered and ate the same animal for dinner. To this day, whenever I think of my father's upbringing, I realize I've never known true hardship. Only black people lived in the area, and throughout his childhood, the closest my father came to a white man was seeing one on a horse in the distance. When that happened, he'd turn and head in the opposite direction.

MY MOTHER'S FAMILY fared better. Her grandfather, Henry Albert, was a black landowner. He worked his farm in summers, and in winters traveled to Mobile to sign on with a bridge construction crew. As a result of his industry, he was well off, and my grandmother, Alberta, was born into a comfortable family. But it wasn't always a happy one—Henry died of pneumonia when my grandmother was about eight years old. As an adult, Alberta worked as a maid and married a man named Joseph Todd in 1930. I would be named for this grandfather. Todd inherited several acres of land from his father in Hope Hull, also near Montgomery, but he was a cement layer by trade. Unfortunately, as a worker he was unreliable. He was obsessed with golf, of all things, and would often stop by the local golf course before work. If someone asked him to caddie, he'd skip work for the day. He was a gifted golfer, and yearned to play professionally. But in the twenties and thirties, the only way a black man could get into a golf club was as a caddie, or a waiter, or other menial worker. Tournaments were for whites only. There were no black clubs, no public courses that allowed blacks, no black championship circuit—no place for Todd to compete. Caddying was as close as he would ever come, a fact that left him angry and bitter. He started drinking, and soon the money he earned from cement laying and caddying was not making it home. Worse, he took up gambling. He bet on golf— not just on games, but on how far he could hit a ball, how many strokes a hole would require, or on any wager anyone suggested or he could dream up. He often risked all of his meager salary, and often lost, usually when his opponents plied him with alcohol.

In 1933, the first of Alberta and Joe Todd's five daughters was born. The girl baby was named Golden Annette Todd—because she was born fair-skinned and her parents hoped that by permanently honoring her with the name Golden on her birth certificate, the girl would remain light-skinned as she grew. She was fair enough to be baptized in the local "yellow" church. Joe and Alberta were too dark to aspire to belong to this church, but they had ambition, and got in on the strength of their daughter's skin color. For years they attended the church, with Alberta often carrying Golden in her arms like a shield to ward off the stares and whispers of the light-skinned parishioners. But Golden did not grow up fair. Another sister, Caroline, was born light, but a third sister, Dorothy, was dark. (The sisters would have both light and dark children of their own.) One Sunday, when Golden was seven, the congregation sang a hymn called "Only for the Yellow." The Todd family was booed and hissed out of the church, and never went back. Golden never forgot the shame and embarrassment of that day, and as soon as the Todds joined a black church, the little girl changed her name to Juanita, after an aunt. Juanita is my mother.

As Todd's eldest child, Juanita was often sent to search local bars, speak-easies and gambling joints for her father. It was her job to find him and bring him or at least some of his money home before he spent all of his pay. But he seldom came home when he was supposed to, preferring the watering holes where everyone knew him and he was the life of the party. My mother's childhood was punctuated by feast-or-famine economics—the family either had a lot of money from one of my grandfather's big gambling wins, or none at all when he was losing steadily. Eventually his financial irresponsibility cost him the farm he'd inherited. When he fell behind on property taxes, the land was confiscated. Todd developed a twofold hatred for government—over the loss of his land and over the institutional racism that thwarted his golf career.

When my mother was about twelve years old, her father heard that blacks could play golf freely in Europe. He abandoned his family completely then, moving to Europe to compete professionally. Word came back that he won and earned money. From Europe Todd was drawn to the sunny golf courses, casinos, and nightlife of 1950s Cuba. He bought property there with his winnings, and stayed until his land was confiscated after the Cuban revolution. He fled to Miami and joined the Bay of Pigs invasion, but was shot and captured. Todd recovered, and was sent to work in the sugar fields on a Cuban prison chain gang. The cane repeatedly sliced his legs, and since medical care for prisoners was miserable, he developed gangrene. Cuban doctors amputated his legs. After that, he was useless as a worker, so he was released from prison and deported to the United States. Unable to work, or to play golf or caddie, Todd turned to panhandling. He'd park his wheelchair in the corner of a Mobil gas station lot in Jacksonville, Florida, and beg coins from passersby and motorists.

In 1972, my uncle Bud, a navy officer, was driving through Florida and stopped for gas. Chatting with the attendant, Bud mentioned that he was headed for home in Alabama. "You should talk to that old man over there, he's from Alabama, too," the attendant said, nodding toward a figure slumped in a wheelchair. My uncle and the old man talked for a few minutes, mentioning hometowns, forgotten neighbors and long-lost relatives. They were startled to discover that my uncle's wife, Caroline, and her sister, Dorothy, shared the same names as two of the old man's daughters. It took my shocked uncle Bud several minutes to grasp that the crippled old man before him was his long-lost father-in-law.

Two years later, at a family reunion in Alabama, I met the grandfather for whom I am named for the first time.

MY FATHER FINISHED ninth grade in a one-room school in Union Springs, Alabama. At eleven, he had met an Indian named James Chester, Sr. After that, he'd sometimes see Chester on the dusty lanes of the town. People would point to the Indian and say, "There goes your daddy." Later, when he joined the navy, the military demanded a copy of his birth certificate. Only then did my father discover that two facts he'd accepted as true all his life were wrong—his birthday and his last name. The birth date on his certificate was not one he recognized, and his family name was entered as Jett.

At eighteen, my father, James, joined the navy. Only then did he realize how brutal was his life in the South, how subhuman his existence. While stationed in Guantanamo Bay, he discovered that a black man could walk freely in Cuban towns, go to cafes and stores and movies without fear or harassment or color barrier. For the first time, he felt like a man. For the first time, he wasn't a second-class citizen. Moreover, ordinary people treated him with respect when they saw his uniform. It gave him an identity. A few black sailors outranked white sailors, and military hierarchy required them to treat those blacks according to rank, not skin color. Pops had never experienced anything like that before. In 1951, when he was twenty-one, and after three years in the navy, Pops decided the military would be his new home. After release from the navy, he joined the army.

The war in Korea was just beginning, and Pops knew he'd be sent there. Before he left, however, someone set him up on a date with a co-ed at the Alabama State College for Negroes, a girl named Juanita Todd. My mother was a determined student, working toward a degree in sciences and planning to be a teacher, and she was very particular about the men she dated. But James Jett was a smart, disciplined man in a classy-looking uniform. And he was a sergeant, a rank respectable enough for her. When my father left for Korea, they began writing the letters they would exchange throughout the war.

My father trained as a paratrooper and was promoted to master sergeant, one of the few blacks to reach that rank. President Harry Truman had just decided to integrate the military, a momentous social decision that would have an indelible impact on young blacks like my father. But while integration was good, Pops noticed that its immediate implementation was not. The army responded to integration by treating black troops like cannon fodder. They were usually poorly trained and sent more often to the front battle lines than white troops. When my father had only minimal paratroop training, he was ordered to parachute into the front lines.

A student of history, Pops believed that the army was convinced that blacks were cowards by nature, that any black soldier sent into battle would turn and run. He blamed this conviction on Teddy Roosevelt, who had written disparagingly about the black soldiers at the battle of San Juan Hill. Those soldiers had been part of the first assault, and Roosevelt later wrote that the second wave of troops had had to shoot the blacks retreating in fear. My father knew that Chinese soldiers believed black-skinned people were ghosts, a superstition similar to one held by Native Americans in the Old West. In the wars over America's Indian lands, slaves and later black soldiers—called Buffalo Soldiers—were sent into battle first to scare the Indians.

My father was one of a handful of black master sergeants given command of white soldiers. For a time he led a troop of mostly Hispanic soldiers, with some blacks and a few white men. My father named his sons after two of his Hispanic soldiers—my brother is Pizarro and I am Orlando Joseph. His troop seemed always to be on point, well ahead of the other troops. A white private named Blair ferried commands from the white lieutenant who gave Pops his maneuvering orders. Blair was also from Montgomery, and during one battle, my father's troop was moving forward and did not know that the rest of the army had halted until a runner reached them with the message. They found themselves far out front and pinned down under enemy fire. In a foxhole that night, Blair and my father talked about Alabama and home, and forged a friendship of sorts. It was the first time my father chatted as an equal with and befriended a southern white man.

The war was a pivotal experience for Pops. Halfway around the world from home, he had respect from his peers and authority over white men. He spent his leave in Japan and learned to speak Japanese. He came back to the U.S. convinced that the military was an essential stepping-stone toward equality and progress for blacks. Later, though he never insisted that my brother and I join the army, he constantly encouraged us to consider enlisting. The army held more value than college to my father. When my brother, Pizarro, dropped out of college and joined the army, my father had no objection.

Pops wanted to reenlist when his first tour in the army was up in 1953. But he'd asked my mother to marry him, and she refused to do so if he was going to go back to Korea. So Pops took money from the GI bill and finished his high school education. In August 1954, Juanita Todd and James Jett were married. My father wanted to continue his education at a vocational electronics school, but there wasn't a single one in Alabama that accepted blacks.

While studying for his high school degree, Pops heard that several of his former soldiers had been killed in Korea, including Private Blair. So he was shocked later that year to see Blair on a Montgomery corner. The street crossed from the white to the black neighborhood, with a movie theater midblock marking the unofficial border. Thinking Blair might have news of other soldiers, Pops tried to catch his eye, but the white man turned toward his friends. "Private!" Pops shouted. Blair spun around and spat: "You don't talk to me that way. You don't give me orders. You're just a nigger."

My father was stunned. He was well known in the neighborhood, respected for his army record. To be dressed down in the street, in front of friends and strangers, by a man he thought he knew, enraged him. He lunged toward Blair, but some black men put their hands on his arms and shoulders and guided him away. After that, my father chafed at acting the part of the deferential black. He looked for trouble. When he and my mother tried to vote, they were accused of being uppity. With each like incident, my father longed to retaliate with physical violence. His friends began warning him to get out of Alabama.

My father's cousin, Findlay, had moved to Cleveland when my father joined the army. My mother's half-white aunt Ada lived there, too. Findlay urged Pops to come to Cleveland before he got himself in serious trouble. But my mother was reluctant to leave her people. She was very close to her family, and she wanted her children to grow up near their relatives. My father, however, was determined to leave the South. He couldn't take the Jim Crow discriminations anymore, the everyday insults at water fountains, bathrooms, restaurants and on buses. Only when my brother, Pizarro, was born in May of 1955, did my mother agree to go. My parents did not want their son to grow up with the racism that had poisoned their lives. Years later, my father would remember what he told my mother at the time: "No son of mine is going to grow up here, not even for five minutes."

My father went to Cleveland in July, ahead of my mother and their baby, to look for a job. He worked packing boxes and on the loading bay of a cheese factory. He signed up for an aptitude test, and it showed he had ability in bookkeeping and accounting. He took night classes in business, and in the fall, earned an associate's degree and landed a job as an account- ant at the East Ohio Gas Company. My mother and Pizarro arrived in Cleveland in September, moving in with her aunt and uncle. Ada had lived in Cleveland for years, working in a good-paying job restricted to whites only. She was found out and fired when she married a "high yellow" black man. Accepting that she was black made Ada want to find her family again. Since her relatives were already in the North, my mother felt slightly better about leaving home for Cleveland. She and Pizarro lived with Ada and her husband until Pops could afford to rent a small apartment just after the new year in 1956.

FOR MY PARENTS, leaving the South also meant leaving behind another unwanted legacy—their fatherless, shattered homes. They were determined to break the cycle of poverty and instability that plagued both their families.

In Cleveland my mother used her college science degree to land a job as a hematology lab technician, where she drew and tested blood. She also enrolled in night school, working toward a teaching certificate. My mother started teaching high school science, and in 1956 my sister, Yvette, was born. Two years later, I followed. Both of us were born at a local Catholic hospital because it had a reputation of treating black patients better than the other hospitals in Cleveland. But the North was far from perfect. When my mother was in labor with me, a white woman came into the ward with a twisted ankle. She insisted on a bed with privacy, so to make room for her, my mother's bed was pulled into a hallway. Workmen were sweeping when my father arrived to find my mother, in labor, breathing dust and debris in the public hall. Enraged, he began arguing and shouting and was nearly thrown out of the hospital. Incensed, Pops called a black attorney he knew, and together they forced the hospital to give my mother a room.

We lived in an ugly corner of the city until I was about three years old, when a man was shot dead on the sidewalk near our home. My parents moved to a top-floor apartment in a two-story house on 143rd Street. The house's owners, the Bledsoes, lived downstairs. The apartment is the first home I really remember. My mother was adamant about good manners and discipline, and her three children were trained to be quiet and obedient. We were always circumspect in our talk and play, always respectful of adults, always quiet in front of company, always neatly dressed and lined up at attention. We were "good kids," and the Bledsoes, a heavyset couple, often complimented us on being such a "lovely family." Shortly after we moved, my grandmother, Alberta, arrived to take care of us while my parents worked. A thin, tiny woman standing only about five feet two, my grandmother lived with us off and on for several years, taking turns with my aunts in helping care for us. We loved our aunts, who had all studied at the Alabama State College for Negroes and become schoolteachers, but we absolutely adored our grandmother. As the baby, I was especially attached to her.

My mother read to us constantly. Our favorite books were the *Adventures of . . .* series by Thomas Burgess. We had to hear a chapter every night before bed, or there would be a cacophony of wailing. We would pile on the bed, and as the youngest I'd always get a favorite spot in the crook of Mops's arm, to hear the *Adventures of Buster Bear* or of Old Man Possum, Peter Rabbit, Happy Jack the Grey Squirrel, Chatterer the Red Squirrel, Reddy the Fox and Granny Fox. My favorite was Old Man Coyote, because he was wily and had a thousand voices.

In 1962, when I was nearly five, my parents had saved enough money for a down payment on a plot of land in Wickliffe, a little country village outside Cleveland. My father was determined to buy the land for one reason: The property title carried a covenant forbidding its sale to Negroes. We wouldn't have been the first blacks in the village; two other families already lived up the street. Their arrival had led white homeowners to insert racial covenants into their deeds. Pops immediately hired lawyers and dug in his heels for a protracted fight. The white owners caved, and my parents bought the land for about $15,000 and built a house.

Wickliffe was rural, and our house was surrounded by open land and farms. An elderly World War I veteran kept goats, pigs and chickens in his yard just up the street. Right after we moved into our new home, my grandmother, Alberta, died, and her passing prompted our family's first trip into the Deep South. We piled into a bulbous, light blue sedan and drove to Alabama for Grandma's funeral. It was 1963, and I was five years old when I crossed the Mason-Dixon line for the first time. Suddenly I was aware of the color of my skin. We slept in the car because we couldn't find motels that allowed blacks. We drove for hours to find a restaurant where we could eat. But my most vivid memory is of stopping at a gas station because my mother desperately required a bathroom. The clerk refused her request— the bathrooms were for whites only. Instantly belligerent, Pops argued heatedly with the attendant while my mother pleaded that she could just go into the woods behind the station. The attendant would not budge. My eight-year-old brother and I walked into the trees with our mother, and I have a vivid memory of holding her shoulder while she crouched among the bushes to relieve herself. All my life, that picture has come unbidden into my mind, as clear as if it were yesterday. My father sputtered with rage as we climbed back in the car, yelling at the top of his voice, "I'll kill him, I'll kill him!" as my mother insisted, "Just go, let's just go," refusing to let Pops go back into the gas station, and for the rest of the afternoon, refusing to let him turn the car around to confront the attendant. All the while, we children cowered in the backseat, terrified and crying until Pops began to yell at us. We had never been so scared, never seen our father so angry, and we had never known him to be so powerless.

After that, everyone had to "hold it" until we could find a black rest area. We could cry and beg for a bathroom, but Pops steadfastly refused to pull over. He wouldn't even allow Pizarro and me to pee on the side of the road. The more we cried, the angrier he grew. He refused to submit to humiliation. He'd simply yell: "You will wait until we get somewhere we can go." We'd pull off the highway and drive down unknown roads, looking for black faces like clues to safety. We'd stop at black five-and-dime stores and ask to use their bathroom. We kids took to peering over the back of the front seat, watching the road for cues. A Howard Johnson was good, they'd let us use their facilities. Gas stations were bad—they'd take our money for gas, but not let us inside the building. Often we'd get lost, and then the ordeal of finding our way back to the right road would prolong the search for a bathroom or food. We learned that federal highways usually had facilities that allowed blacks, but if we were on a state road, our chances of finding a place to stop were virtually nil.

My grandmother's funeral was the first time we went back to Alabama, and only other funerals could get us back there again. My parents had no desire to go, and after that first trip my brother, sister and I hated the place. We always drove, first in the big 1950s sedan, and later in a dark red Dodge Dart. My father insisted on driving for long stretches, with my mother navigating. But she had no sense of direction, and we always got lost. As we got older, our visits became more unpleasant. We children decided that our down-home cousins still lived like slaves. My brother and sister noticed it first: Our cousins, who would mouth off and sass each other and black adults, would become timid supplicants when a white person spoke to them. Suddenly all they could say was yassir, yass'm. Even the proximity of a white person would cow them—their heads seemed to droop automatically, and they wouldn't look white people in the eye. I remember making a boyish vow that once I grew up, I'd never set foot over the Mason-Dixon line. And I didn't, until the mid-eighties, when my distant cousin Alonzo Babers, a grandson of my father's uncle Porter—the one called Shug—won two gold medals in track and field at the 1984 Olympics. These victories awakened a family pride in the youngest generation and set off a new tradition of family reunions.

My first taste of the South made me aware of my color. But in Wickliffe, I also realized that my family was different. Most of the residents were working-class people of Italian or Slavic origin. There were a few black families, but nowhere near as many as in our old neighborhood in Cleveland. Pizarro and Yvette had the hardest adjustment. They were already in school, and the switch from the inner-city school where they'd earned good grades to the more challenging suburban school was difficult. In their Cleveland school, Pizarro and Yvette had been among the smart kids. In Wickliffe, they fell behind. My mother, a teacher, grilled them with flashcards to help them catch up. I was more fortunate—since I started kindergarten in Wickliffe, the school system there was the only one I'd ever known.

We watched TV and news events, and I had already learned to evaluate white people, such as government leaders, based on what my parents told me about how they treated blacks. When President John F. Kennedy was shot, I was shocked and saddened because I knew that he had been good for blacks. My grandmother, Willie Mae Jett, had told me so, and she cried on the day he died. I remember knowing George Wallace by name and sight, and hating him. I remember that my father said that even though President Lyndon B. Johnson was a champion of the civil rights movement, he wasn't trustworthy because he came from Texas. But then my father had trouble with civil rights as a whole from its very beginning, because the movement was pacifist. The army—which my father routinely said he always regretted leaving—had shown Pops that equality had to come from within, from a black man's sense of duty to himself, his discipline and his achievements. In the 1950s and early 1960s, virtually all of the young men in my father's family had found a way out of poverty and discrimination through the military. Pops believed that the lesson learned from this was that blacks had to look inward for strength. The civil rights movement, he felt, put too much emphasis on changing how whites treated blacks. He felt that blacks should use their inner strength and determination to gain a foothold in society, and use capitalism to build an economic base that would force society to grant them equal rights. Only through capitalism, economics and business could blacks earn the respect of whites.

What are we doing for ourselves? my father would always demand to know. How are we behaving? And in answer, he'd say that the behavior of blacks was far short of what it should be, and this meant that as a people we were letting ourselves down. He grew up with little contact with white men, but saw too many black men who drank, did not work and did not properly care for their families. The exception was his aunt Elizabeth's husband, Rooster. Rooster had been something of a surrogate father, and he hired my father, Findlay and Shug to help harvest his crops and care for his farm animals. From a very young age, my father watched Rooster labor on his farm and learned the value of working odd jobs after school. He knew that he was contributing to the household. He saw other kids doing nothing in the afternoons, while from the age of nine, he, Findlay and Shug were expected to work. Those formative experiences later formed the basis for the earliest philosophical and political mantra I remember from my father: "Don't expect the civil rights movement to get white people to change. Blacks have to do for themselves. Most blacks very seldom interact with whites. You have to take care of your community, your neighborhood, you have to have the values that will allow you to be a success. You don't have to be around whites, or anywhere near whites, just be prepared to work and take care of yourself."

Around this time, the world first became aware of Martin Luther King, Jr. My earliest impressions of Dr. King were that he looked like my father—they were the same age, and both had the same almond-shaped eyes and a similar jawline. We would see Dr. King on television and in news clips, and we watched broadcasts of the marches. Living in the North, however, we felt removed from the outrages of racism and the daily thoughts and discussions of the civil rights movement. However, Dr. King and the movement are seared into my memory most vividly, because it was during a nonviolent peace march in Alabama that I saw most clearly my father's agony over his race. We watched the rally on television, transfixed by the grainy, black-and-white images of clean-cut Negro men and dignified women marching resolutely through the city streets. Then suddenly there were dogs, and fire hoses, and billy clubs flying, and hundreds of harmless, innocent people were slammed against brick walls by the torrents of water, chased and mauled by snapping German shepherds, beaten as they tried desperately to escape policemen run amok. The world seemed turned upside down, and hell was on our TV, and no one could do anything about it. No laws, no rights could protect those marchers, people who looked just like us. It was a terrifying sight for my brother and sister and me, but not nearly as terrifying as what happened next in our own living room. As the violence raged on TV, my father jumped out of his chair. Startled, we looked around, and I saw tears streaming down his face, a wild, lost expression in his eyes. My heart stopped and I forgot the TV. I watched as Pops, shaking, kicked the wall over and over, then pounded on it until his hands were bruised, and after that smacked his head against the plaster. In a voice filled with agony he cried, over and over: "Why don't they fight back? Why don't they fight back? Why don't they fight back?"

PIZARRO YOU ALL

I N MY FIRST day of kindergarten, a group of white children clustered around me, touching my hair. I was an oddity, but then some of them were odd to me, too. I was assigned to a little desk, and a girl in a hat came and sat right in front of me. When she removed her hat, I jumped up, shouting: "She has red hair! She has red hair!" I'd never seen such fiery carrot-colored hair in real life. As a punishment for disrupting the class, I spent part of the day sitting on a garbage can in a corner.

After the first introductions, the distinctions were forgotten and kids in Wickliffe played together. I was popular in school because I was big and athletic and a natural leader—settling squabbles, choosing the games we would play at recess. I loved school until the fourth grade. I remember all my teachers vividly—in kindergarten, it was Miss Monich; in first grade, Mrs. Andrus; and in second grade, Miss Monich again. In the third grade I had Miss Tretnick. She decided the class would take turns reading aloud from *Huckleberry Finn*. As we went around the room, she asked me to read the part of Nigger Jim. I loved to read, and was good at it, and I basked in the attention of this special role. After three days I began to realize that the other kids read whatever part of the book we happened to be on when they were called, but I always read Nigger Jim. And even though I'd been born and raised in Ohio, Miss Tretnick liked me to read it with a southern accent. I sensed from the way the character talked that there was something negative about him, something shameful. All the white kids seemed to know that Nigger Jim was a lowly character. Then a boy called me Nigger Jim during recess. I don't think either of us knew what he meant by it, but we got into a fistfight just the same. On the fourth day of reading, when Miss Tretnick called on me to read Nigger Jim, she said: "You don't mind, do you?" I realized that I did. I felt like I was helping perpetuate a bad image. We stopped reading from *Huckleberry Finn*.

The same year, my brother began to get into racial fights in his sixth-grade class. That year, there was a surge of new black children in school. Wickliffe was becoming known as a good place for black families to buy a house, and people were moving out from Cleveland. The streets surrounding ours filled up with black families. A new development opened up, on a new street called Kennedy Drive, and every home was owned by a black family. On Robindale, the street directly behind ours, the top half of the street slowly became black, while the bottom half remained white. Suddenly racial distinctions began to surface, and the first manifestation was separation. Some white families on Robindale literally moved down the block to be on the white end.

Pizarro, Yvette and I talked, acted and dressed just like the white kids in our school. We were also naïve, docile suburban kids. The new black kids from Cleveland had their own distinctive speech and culture, and they were tough and wary. The older white kids were afraid of them, and Pizarro and Yvette were forced to take sides. Pizarro's sixth-grade teacher, Mrs. Skaggs, had a policy of lining up her students, two by two, boys and girls holding hands, to walk to lunch, recess or the bathroom. But she wouldn't allow Pizarro to hold hands with any white girl. Instead, he walked at the end of the line, alone. My father went to talk to her about this, and she explained that she assigned Pizarro to the back of the line because she could rely on him to keep the other kids in order. My father pointed out that she made her only other black student walk alone at the front of the line, thereby segregating the black kids. Soon my brother and sister were coming home from school with stories about racial fights, most of them the result of black and white children taunting one another. A big fight erupted on the playground when Cassius Clay changed his name to Muhammad Ali.

I escaped most of these tensions in the third grade. But I was very aware of the new students, anyway. When they first arrived, I was eager for more black classmates. Soon, though, they just embarrassed me. We read aloud in class nearly every day, and I was devastated to discover that none of these new black kids could read well. Their schooling in Cleveland had been poor, and most sounded like first-graders. The white children laughed when they stumbled through a passage. I sat at my desk, tense, waiting for my turn just so I could show how well a black child could read. I became very competitive. One day Miss Tretnick took me aside and asked me to help two of the new black students, Don Ingram and Terry "Pumpkin" Steplight. The three of us formed a separate reading group in the back of the room, with me tutoring the two black children while Miss Tretnick taught the rest of the class at a different level.

Pizarro and Yvette didn't want to be different from the other black kids. Instead, they pretended they couldn't or didn't want to read. They competed less, and their grades began to slip. Our parents reacted with panic, and assaulted Pizarro and Yvette with a battery of flashcards, relentless homework and strict rules about which neighborhood kids they could play with. Concerned that the new black families were not demanding academic excellence from their children, Pops called a neighborhood meeting of black parents. When friends of Pizarro and Yvette came to our house, Pops interrogated them about their schoolwork and behavior. Those who were unruly troublemakers at school were not welcomed back.

For me, the upheaval at school and home meant that suddenly I was no longer popular. I didn't get along with my black classmates—they resented me for tutoring them, they said I acted white. By the fourth grade, there were enough black families in Wickliffe that separate societies emerged, and blacks and whites hardly interacted or talked. At the end of that year, my best friend, another black boy who had started Wickliffe kindergarten with me, was held back. So going into fifth grade, my only black classmates were newcomers. They seemed always to isolate and tease me. They lived on neighboring streets, but we were not allowed to play with them. That year, serious fights broke out all over town when a black teenager who was the high school star football running back, began dating a white cheerleader. I fought my fellow fifth-graders, and Pizarro fought his fellow eighth-graders over this relationship. By the sixth grade, the influx of black families slowed. No more white families moved, no black families left, and no new black families arrived. Our classes became stable.

However, our problems at school paled against what now began at home. When we were small, our mother was chiefly responsible for discipline, for ensuring that we practiced good manners and did our homework. But when Pizarro was twelve, and on the cusp of adolescence, my father awoke, determined to guide us and to ward off temptation with the whistling end of his belt.

POPS EXPERIMENTED WITH child rearing. He and Mops held long discussions about what to do with the three of us. When it came to discipline, my parents formed a united front. My mother cared most about manners and behavior. My father had strident philosophies about instilling work ethics in his children.

When I was nine, and Pizarro was in the sixth grade, my father announced that at age twelve, he was expected to contribute financially to his family. My father had always made pronouncements, and at some point, when pronouncing to us children as a group, he had begun referring to us as "Pizarro you all." So this is what he said now: "When I was twelve, I was working, and Pizarro you all will do the same." As the little brother, I wanted to do whatever my big brother did; so it happened that by the third grade I had a job. Pops collected "rent" from us. Pizarro, who was also called P.Z., got a paper route, and I helped. We had to deliver 120 papers from bikes towing wagons every morning, starting at 4:00 A.M. This is when we discovered that Pops could see in the pitch dark. He kept an egg timer beside his bed. When he heard our alarm clock ring, he'd turn the egg timer over. We had three minutes to get dressed and get out of the house, three minutes exactly because Pops could see every grain of sand pour through the timer. We couldn't fake him out because the floorboards creaked, and he could hear any noise made beyond the three-minute limit. He drilled us in dressing quickly. In military fashion we learned to lay our clothes out the night before, and soon we could leap out of bed, throw water on our faces, get into our pants, socks, shirts, shoes and coats, and race out the front door before three minutes were up.

If we tarried, Pops would appear over us, his belt, laced with a cat-o'-nine-tails, whistling through the air. Every morning brought a headlong rush of adrenaline and terror. The worst turn of events came if one of us forgot something critical, like gloves in winter. We'd have to dart in and out of the house again, praying not to be caught. If we did get caught, there would be days of lectures and weeks of references. Any failure was unacceptable. If we did something wrong, we got the belt. But often what we did wrong was impossible to predict—we'd get the belt for watching TV when Pops thought we should be working or doing homework. We lived by the "wait till your father gets home" rule. But he never just lit into us. First he'd line us up in the living room and march up and down, railing against the sins of his children. He'd pick up the belt, only to put it back down. Then he'd pick it up again, and drop it once more. Sometimes the tension got so thick I'd pray for the belt, just to get it over with. Often we tried to convince our mother to punish us before he got home.

He didn't always reach for the belt right away. We'd spend the afternoons in our rooms studying, then come down for dinner. Sometimes we made it through most of the meal before he'd start mumbling into his plate: "My sons and daughter are not responsible. They do not obey." We'd freeze as the diatribe began. Once, when one of us received poor grades, a week passed. Just as we thought the grades might escape his notice, one night at dinner he began talking to himself: "I have a feeling in the pit of my stomach. I'm so depressed." He hadn't missed it, and the diatribe was no less severe with the passage of time.

It wasn't so much his childhood he was inflicting on us, but his experiences in the army. He drew disciplinary policy from what he'd undergone in the military. It was barracks treatment: If one of us made a mistake, all of us were punished. Pizarro, at twelve, was old enough to handle the disciplinary demands, Pops said. Yvette and I were the rest of the troop. Pops would stare down at us over the dinner table, or call us into the living room—"Pizarro you all, come in here!"—where we would line up according to age. Then he'd launch into lectures that lasted for hours.

"Black men in particular, because of their long heritage of slavery, performed rigors for whites without question, now you sure as hell are going to perform such rigors for yourselves.

"Blacks worked when they were forced to work as slaves and sharecroppers, but now that we are responsible for ourselves, we have become lazy, trifling and no-good.

"Blacks feel work is bad because we were always working for the white man, all our labors were for someone else, we were never rewarded for our labors and work was something we wanted to get out of. That is the attitude of modern blacks. Pizarro you all have to understand that your efforts are beneficial for you. That's the problem with blacks and the capitalist system. Black society has not bought into the capitalist system because for centuries we had not been rewarded for our labors. So it grew to be that the slackers, the ones who didn't work, were admired, while the field hands and laborers were disdained. This is especially true of the black church, where religious leaders did not work, they were just given money by parishioners. Somehow they became the community leaders, while the people who worked nine to five and gave their wages to the church had no power or influence at all."

We stood at attention, or sat motionless at the dinner table unable to eat while our food grew cold, listening for the umpteenth time to harangues that would last late into the night. When it began, I was nine years old.

IN 1965, MY father wrote a pamphlet called "Free Enterprise and the American Negro," which expanded on his theory of how blacks needed to understand that working for themselves was the true path to equality and freedom. Integration, he wrote, wouldn't take us there. He believed that most blacks wanted integration because they wanted to share in the white man's vices, like leisure time. He began then to repeat a line around the house that would echo throughout my childhood: "We must take the white man's virtues and not his vices."

Black people, Pops believed, owed nothing to whites and everything to themselves. But the black family had disintegrated, beset by welfare, drugs, powerlessness and hopelessness, because it accepted that this was the way things were supposed to be. It was easier, my father said, to give up before we started and blame the white man for keeping us down. To my father, any complaint about white racism was only an admission that the white man had power over us. He rejected that idea. Only blacks were responsible for our success, only blacks to blame for our failures. Black people would succeed only when they understood that with economic independence they could force society to look at them through their grades, business profits, property holdings, tax revenue, voting power. Through the numbers that were color-blind.

Work was a virtue, and welfare was a vice. Welfare was slavery in new robes. We were now chattel of the federal government. In opposition to the sloth welfare created, my father threw himself into one business project after another in a personal crusade to prove his theory about blacks and free enterprise. Blacks would find economic viability only through black-owned businesses, where they could serve the black community, hire blacks, draw black customers. For several years he owned a successful barber shop. Pizarro, Yvette and I had to sweep and clean the shop at night. It failed after it was burglarized during the Hough riots. Pops invested in an auto parts store. It failed after the surrounding neighborhood deteriorated into a slum. Then my father invested in a project to turn a group of single-family homes into apartments. It floundered after several years because poor people couldn't pay their rent, or apartments stood empty for lack of tenants.

Lured by a white politician who admired Pops's emphasis on responsibility, my father took a job as head of one of the nation's first workfare programs. But the project frustrated him. Often he'd come home, sit down at dinner and angrily denounce the black participants in the program who refused to listen to his harangues on free enterprise as the great racial equalizer. These talks always ended with the same declaration: "I will speak and they will tremble." He'd look down the table at us and shout, "Tremble! Tremble!" We'd helplessly comply.

In spite of his obvious weaknesses, throughout my childhood I believed my father was God. As an adult, I realized that he had stamped us with his character. I never made any choice, looked at any opportunity or took any action without feeling my father's presence and sensing whether he would approve or disapprove. Pizarro, Yvette and I inherited his system of values, his commitment to hard work and self-discipline. We did not simply oppose but actively warred against welfare, affirmative action or any other system of dependence that weakened the will or lessened the ability of black men and women.

POPS WASN'T LIKE any of my schoolmates' fathers. He never let up. Every day ended with a training session. He was as relentless in his expectations of my mother, who returned from her teaching job in Cleveland around four o'clock. He would sit at the head of the dinner table, saying nothing, supervising her as she quizzed us about what happened in school, how we'd done on tests. Mops didn't show much leniency, either. If we got a grade she disapproved of, she would spend countless hours tutoring us.

My father's mother, Willie Mae, lived with us at the time. Aunt Elizabeth—Big Mama—had called to say Willie Mae wasn't well and couldn't care for herself, so my father drove to Alabama to collect her. He did this even though she hadn't raised him, and he had always disapproved of her drinking and her three marriages. When she moved in, he let her know in no uncertain terms what we were allowed to watch on TV and read. We called her "Dear," and she took care of us, lightening the load for Mops, who taught high school in a tough Cleveland ghetto. Dear was our only reminder of the Deep South. Mops and Pops had become "Connecticut Yankees" in speech and manner. Pops demanded that Dear aid in disciplining us, too, but she was soft. When Pops gave us a licking, we ran to her to cry.

No matter which one of us displeased him, Pops would lecture all of us: "Pizarro you all did not do your work the way you should. And the reason you didn't do your work is because you're more concerned with what little Joey Blow down the street thinks about you than what I think about you. You don't understand that little Joey Blow doesn't give a damn about you, and you'd better learn to give a damn about yourself. You're failing in your duties to your family, to your race, and the white man loves to see little Joey Blow down the street not to do his homework because that's what the white man expects to see. They want to see you fail because you're MY son."

Pops decreed that many of the children in our school were unworthy of association. We were not allowed to play with them. He didn't blacklist individual children so much as take away our play time. Indeed, some children were not allowed in the house (those who got in trouble at school), but generally if Pops thought we were idle, he just gave us lists of chores— particularly in the summer. The most common was ditch digging. Adjacent to our house was vacant farmland, and at some point tractors had created deep trenches in the earth. After it rained, water collected in the trenches and mosquitoes bred. My father assigned Pizarro and me to dig and maintain a series of drainage ditches to divert the water that collected and often overflowed into our backyard. In the early 1970s, my father got the idea that Pizarro should use money saved from his paper route to buy the vacant land. Pizarro was about fifteen, and the land cost him $2,500. He was proud of his property. Since the family now owned the lot, Pops decided to bring the grade up to the same level as our yard. He ordered several dump trucks of dirt unloaded on a corner of the lot, far from the trenches. Then he bought new shovels and announced that our project for the summer was to level that land.

"For three hundred years we dug ditches for the white man," he'd repeat, pacing the front hall of our brick rambler house as we stood in a line in the shadows. "PLEASE don't tell me that you're not prepared to do the work for yourself."

I was twelve, and already knew that manual labor was the closest thing to godliness in my father's opinion. Our lot became the most landscaped in the neighborhood. No other kids labored through junior and senior high the way we did. They couldn't have, since they always seemed to be walking by our house and teasing us as we worked. The black kids shouted out, "Field niggers!" At fourteen, I developed a crush on a neighborhood girl named Effie. One day I snuck away from home on my bike and ended up on her front porch with a group of other admiring adolescent boys. I was pleased to be singled out when Effie asked me to rub her shoulders. But I was deflated when she cried "ouch!" at the huge calluses on my palms. "Get those field-nigger hands off me!" The other guys doubled over in laughter, pantomimed shoveling and mocked: "I can't help it, Effie, I just gotta dig!"

I'd been clashing with these same kids since fifth or sixth grade. I'd run into groups of kids hanging out on each other's porches and yards while I collected subscription money for my newspaper route. They teased me, and after a while, I responded by mimicking my father: "What are all you guys doing? Why are you just sitting there? You should be working, like I am. That's the problem with Negroes, you don't work." Needless to say, they liked me even less. A favorite means of teasing me was to attack my dark skin. When they saw me coming, they'd start contests over who had the best skin color, holding their arms out and taunting me to compare. Dark always lost. I accepted that. Television, radio and black magazine advertisements all taught that light skin was good, that the closer to white someone was, the better. My hair was too kinky, my lips too thick, my nose too broad to find acceptance among my own race. We all accepted that, somehow, someone like me was less human than a lighter black. Soon we hurled the same slurs at each other; I called them lazy blacks, they shouted, "Shut up, you nigger!" We argued over facial characteristics, hair texture, dialect, black cultural figures. We took sides between Muhammad Ali and Floyd Patterson (some kids and their families didn't approve of Ali becoming a Muslim); we taunted each other about someday dating white girls or black girls. Those who were deemed less manly and desirable were stuck with black girls. Cool guys got white girls, with their long, loose and flowing hair. One day a group of kids on a porch included the twin Salter sisters, and I asked one if she liked me. Laughing, she said, "I wouldn't date you, you black nigger," and the others chimed in with a chant I'd hear for years on porches, at school, at the library: "I's Orlando! Boy am I black! I'm pitch black! I'm blacker than black! I'm blacker than blue!" Another afternoon, I came home to find a gang of classmates taunting my dark-skinned grandmother in our backyard. They were ten or eleven years old. My grandmother had berated the kids for littering as they cut through the vacant lot next to our house. Now they were shouting at her: "Shut up, you black nigger monkey!" "Where's your tail, you black ape?"

For the most part, these spats and slurs were part of the age-old tradition of adolescent competition, bickering and cruelty. I usually gave as good as I got. The divisions were also rooted in our search for who we were as blacks, for identity, for pride in being black. As teenagers, we didn't think about it, but real questions arose: Could we only feel pride in being light-skinned? In small features and soft hair? In other words, as close as physically possible to whites?

One day, after fighting with kids encountered on my collection route, I went home so angry that tears welled in my eyes. For once, my father was speechless. Utterly confounded, my parents had no idea what to make of black-on-black taunting. They had never told us, "Be proud to be black." They'd just said: "You *are* black, so you have an obligation to do something important." To comfort me, my brother bought a record of James Brown's hit song "I'm Black and I'm Proud" and played it over and over. My parents very carefully controlled the music we listened to (they favored Dean Martin and Frank Sinatra), the records we bought, the radio stations we heard. This time they let us play the song without comment. Soon I was spouting an ideology of militant black pride. I declared myself a Black Panther. The Panthers had recently exploded onto the national scene, and they preached about self-responsibility and dignity, ideas that my father advocated. But the Panthers gave me a way to set myself apart from my father. A staunch believer in the military and an advocate of the idea that every black man should do a stint in the army to learn discipline, my father thought the Panthers were an antiwar movement. I liked the Panthers because they taught that if your rights were threatened, fight back, throw punches.

When sixth grade started, I wrote "Property of the Black Panthers" on all my schoolbook covers. I taped my desk closed and scrawled "Property of the Black Panthers, Do Not Touch" across the tape. I drew Mrs. Skaggs, the same teacher who had kept my brother from holding hands with white girls. When she tried to place me, alone, at the end of the class line, I exploded with rage and screamed at her: "I don't want to hold hands with any damn white girl anyway! But you're going to treat me like a man!"

Mrs. Skaggs ordered me to remove the tape from my desk, and I refused. She called the Panthers "evil" and said she wouldn't have their influence in her classroom. We marched to the principal's office, my father was called, and I was expelled for a day. Mrs. Skaggs told my father that she was not prejudiced, that she really meant to give my brother and me greater responsibility as proctors at the back of the student line. But now I had defaced school property, even if it was only with tape.

My "I'm Black and I'm Proud" conversion didn't endear me to my black peers, either. The other black students weren't interested in the Black Panthers. Most of them sided with the Southern Christian Leadership Conference nonviolence movement. But mostly they were too busy just being suburban kids, riding bikes and hanging out. Once again, Pops didn't help. The street behind ours had a corner market, and kids would stop there for candy, pop and ice cream after school. Then they'd cut through the empty lot adjacent to our house, dropping their wrappers and cans or bottles as they went. They'd laugh and argue and horse around. When he heard them, Pops went outside and stood at our tree line, glaring. Spotting him, the kids dropped their voices and stepped gingerly and quickly through the lot. Only when they were safely on the street would their chatter and laughter burst forth again.

After Pizarro bought the lot, our father erected a chain-link fence. Still, neighborhood kids would jump the fence to cut across the property. So Pops informed us that if we didn't prevent this, he would beat us. "You fight those kids, or you fight me." We challenged the trespassers, challenges that ended in fights. Often it was just the two of us against a group of kids rambling through the lot. If they were our age, our father left us to it. If they were older, he would stand outside and watch. One day the football star who had dated the white cheerleader jumped the fence with a gang of his friends. They were older than us, huge and intimidating. Pops insisted that we chase them off the lot. Pizarro and I set out to fight them with tears in our eyes. Pops watched from the property line. When the football players caught his relentless stare, they jumped back over the fence and disappeared.

IN SEVENTH GRADE, I looked for acceptance in other places. Pizarro and I had played on the school football team, but that year Pops launched a crusade against black student athletes. He insisted that teachers, coaches and the school district just wanted to herd black kids into athletics instead of studies, even though they knew that none of the kids were good enough to get scholarships or become paid professional athletes. He railed about how short the basketball players were and how small and slow the football players were, and how ridiculous it was that scores of black kids spent all their time shooting hoops and throwing passes.

My friend Terry Steplight—nicknamed "Pumpkin"—was five feet six and lived for basketball. He spent the majority of his time practicing his shots. Wherever he went, a basketball rested between his arm and hip. Pops believed Pumpkin was ridiculous, and never let him forget it. "Boy, what are you going to do? You're five foot six. What are you going to do?" he'd scold, until Terry was near tears. Terry's pain only encouraged Pops. "You're in my home, so I will treat you like my child. I'm going to tell you what your parents may not be telling you. Since you're coming over here, I'm taking an opportunity to teach you something." Terry learned what other kids knew—if you went to the Jett house, don't step off the sidewalk because the father will say, "As long as you're in my yard, come on in here." A lecture was bound to follow. "Sports build character and teach team skills? Well, they may say that. But I think there should be a straight-A requirement. You get straight A's, you can play basketball."

In junior high, Pops announced that Pizarro and I would not play any more organized sports.

My family attended a predominantly white United Presbyterian Church, and one weekend a guest preacher appeared. The Reverend Victor Frederking was a controversial firebrand. He was divorced, and he came to church with a stunning second wife, dressed in a miniskirt, and a cute twelve-year-old stepdaughter named Robin. His Sunday-morning sermon was quiet, but at the end he invited the congregation back for a night service. The miniskirt attracted most of the adolescent boys, and the girls came because of the guys. This time, Reverend Frederking's sermon was fiery, and he lunged around waving his arms. He shouted a Bible story about lamps that never run out of oil, and hollered that the oil of God was in all of us. Suddenly his beautiful young wife began shouting that the oil of God was in her at that very moment. Reverend Frederking responded, "Let me taste the oil of God!" and right in front of everyone they grabbed each other and began a deep, passionate French kiss. Then the Reverend Frederking turned to a woman in the congregation and told her to taste the oil of God. Within minutes, everyone was French-kissing. I grabbed Robin, the minister's stepdaughter, and joined the wave. She was the first girl I'd ever kissed like that, and I was overwhelmed with a love of God.

Soon I was attending Holy Roller services three times a week. Reverend Frederking decided to remain in Wickliffe, and more young people started coming to his services. Most of them were white; Pizarro, Yvette and I were the only blacks. It wasn't long before I believed I had the power to heal. I'd chant, "The devil is in you, and the power of God can heal you, accept God and be healed," smack my patients on the forehead, and they'd fall over and stand up "healed." Colds were cured, back spasms were healed, arthritis pain cleared up. I spoke in tongues. I started reading the Bible voraciously, and the Reverend Frederking's services became the center of my social life. I took to wearing starched white dress shirts and dark pants to school, and carried a briefcase emblazoned with a GOD LOVES YOU sticker. I proselytized at every opportunity. I decided to adopt a philosophy of turning the other cheek, one that was hard to uphold when my father ordered Pizarro and me to beat up kids crossing the vacant lot. The more conservative members of the church didn't like the French kissing–dominated services. Mops forbade my sister to attend. Reverend Frederking was ordered to tone down the sharing of God's oil. I began to think twice about my spirituality one day when Reverend Frederking riled the congregation into a fit of "Holy Rolling." The idea was that the spirit of God hit so hard that believers collapsed with seizures. Robin and I managed to knock into each other and roll around on the floor together. Suddenly I was so utterly filled with lust that it was obvious even to me that God had little to do with what was happening. After that, doubts gnawed at me. I looked for books about Christianity other than the Bible. But I was so dependent on the church group for my social life that I didn't want to look too closely at my real motivations.

I might have continued ignoring my doubts if not for the suicide of a popular football player. The high school student shot himself in the head with a rifle, stunning his classmates and friends. Sobbing and upset, football players, their girlfriends and most of the kids from school came to a memorial service conducted by our regular Presbyterian minister, Reverend Gowman. These were the popular students, the ones who didn't socialize with us Christian kids. Reverend Gowman explained to this distraught group that their friend's suicide was a sign intended to bring them all to Christ. He'd killed himself as a sacrifice for them, the minister said. I could not follow that line of reasoning because Christ had supposedly already made that sacrifice. Why did the football player have to die? I began a serious search for answers. I turned to the books I'd dallied with before, and the more I read, the more I understood that Christianity was actually a compilation of pagan and religious rituals conjoined to unite many different cultures. However, at its core, it was based on a primitive practice of sacrifice. Modern man had simply elevated this sacrifice from a calf or a lamb to the son of God. At about the same time, I began reading *The Story of Civilization* by Will and Ariel Durant. I opened Book 1 and read through Book 9, *The Age of Voltaire*. When I read about Voltaire's rejection of Christ, I put down *The Story of Civilization* and took up Voltaire's writings about the Catholic Church and its treatment of the Huguenots, and the barbarism of the Inquisition. My faith didn't stand a chance after that.

I threw away my briefcase and my turn-the-other-cheek philosophy, and at the end of eighth grade got into a bloody fistfight with an eighteen-year-old white kid nicknamed "Fishlips." Even now, I can't remember his real name. Despite his age, and the fact that he was a giant oaf, he was in eighth grade, too. Other white kids called him Niggerlips. One day, as I was peeling the JESUS SAVES and ONE WAY stickers off my briefcase in study hall, I heard him shout, "Don't call me Fishlips, look at those nigger lips over there!" A week before, my Christian persona would have mouthed, "God loves you." This time I demanded, "Are you talking to me?" When Fishlips said, "Yeah, nigger," I jumped up and kicked his legs from under him. This was foolhardy, for he beat me senseless until a teacher intervened. Fishlips whirled and decked the teacher, who turned out to be the football coach. Fishlips went down shortly after that.

The fight marked the end of my Christianity and my submissiveness.

Ironically, it earned me my first best friend. Don Ingram, a black student I first met when I tutored him in fourth-grade reading, witnessed my outburst. Fishlips had terrorized him and several other black kids, calling them Niggerlips, too, but they feared his size. Ingram was impressed at my heedless assault on the bully. We discovered a lot in common—Ingram had been beaten up by other black kids for "acting white." The same gangs chased and beat us both up after school. While I'd become a born-again Christian and then a nerdy junior version of my father, Ingram had fallen in with the acid rock crowd. His family lived on Ridge Road, a street that was considered closed to blacks, and he was isolated geographically from the other black kids. He befriended his white neighbors instead, kids into heavy-metal bands and marijuana. By seventh grade, while I was barely speaking to my classmates except to say, "God loves you," the cool black kids were calling Ingram Uncle Tim Tom, because his best friend was a white kid named Tim. Essentially, the black kids didn't like either of us because we were at opposite ends of the black spectrum.

About this time I decided to invest in some style. After dressing in white shirts and dark trousers, I was keen to be fashionable. This was due mostly to a newfound interest in girls. When I took a neighborhood girl, Vanessa, on a date (the Wickliffe pastime, a drive-in movie) she teased me about necking, saying, "I'm not doing anything with you, you're L7. I want a fine man, a man who dresses like a man. You dress like a white boy." L7, I knew, was slang sign language for "square."

I persuaded Pops to take me into Cleveland, to a "fly shop," so named for the 1970s genre of movies like *Super Fly* and *Shaft*. I used my paper-route money to buy clothes. I had a 4.2 grade point average—thanks to some Advanced Placement courses that were worth extra credit—and my father let me blow my money as a reward. I bought red and black platform shoes that must have been four inches high. To go with them, I chose black houndstooth bell-bottoms with enormous legs like sails. Complementing them was a skintight, red turtleneck and, over it, a black mesh troubadour shirt with puffy sleeves. That shirt was my favorite. The second outfit consisted of bright green bell-bottoms with a very high waist and huge flaring legs, and a bright yellow satin shirt. I bought a calf (or "midi")-length brown tweed winter coat with leather strips on the sleeves and a big fur collar. Finally, I wanted a large felt hat with a wide brim and a feather. Pops drew the line. He refused to let me have the hat. I begged, thinking about a kid in my school who wore a kelly green suit with a bright green derby. Still he said no, stating flatly that I had reached my limit. I spent $300 on these two ensembles and the coat.

Ingram, meanwhile, still wore only blue jeans and T-shirts emblazoned with logos of heavy-metal bands. When I struck out as Shaft, he started dressing like the lead guitarist of Thin Lizzy, tying a red bandanna around his upper arm and through his belt loops, and adopting an earring. I countered by practicing walking the "pimp roll," but I could never get it right. My limited wardrobe meant that I could only dress cool some of the time. Otherwise, I still wore jeans suitable for digging in the vacant lot. A lot of my clothes were rugged hand-me-downs from Pizarro—by this time he was at Ohio State University and Yvette was enrolled at John Carroll College, a Catholic school. In spite of my occasional Super Fly outfit, for the most part the local black girls still didn't want anything to do with me.

Part of the reason couldn't be helped—I was too dark to be popular with the black girls. But I didn't think it was right to date white girls. Other black guys seemed to think that white girls were somehow better, with their fair skin and long hair. Such ideas were contrary to my political and cultural sentiments. I don't believe I was racist about girls; most of my friends at school were white because the black kids disdained me. At the same time, the white kids who shared my college preparatory classes never invited me to their parties because black and white kids did not mix outside school.

After lunging at Fishlips, I got into more and more fights, probably in an effort to make up for all the cheek-turning I'd done as a Christian. I always lost, but I didn't learn from defeat. I fought blindly, out of anger. Suddenly I had a very short fuse, and reacted violently to any provocation, real or imagined. Pops had to meet with school officials to stave off an expulsion for fighting. He encouraged me to take up judo and weight lifting, disciplines he'd suggested before and I had piously rejected because they violated my religious ethics. This time, Ingram and I developed a keen interest in weight lifting. We didn't take it up for exercise, or sport, or discipline. We intended to bulk up and beat up our enemies. I had a detailed plan to get revenge, one by one, on the black kids who picked on us. As teenagers, our verbal sparring had evolved from name-calling to merciless derision. I'd encounter groups of kids while collecting for my paper route, and they'd mockingly imitate me by shouting "Gee whiz!" or demand to know something like "Joe, did you get you some mack?" They threw street terms at me that I didn't understand. I couldn't admit that I didn't know the cool slang, so I'd bluff, but they'd tease me further until it was obvious I had no idea what they were talking about. If I tried to leave for the next house, the kids would follow and push me down the street, letting loose a chorus of slang-laced talk that went over my head. In defense, I began reading the dictionary so I could hurl $20 words at them. I'd bellow, "An antipugnacious attitude on your part would prove inexplicably salubrious!" That stopped them in their tracks, and my stiff vocabulary became a buffer that prevented the pushing from becoming uglier.

The kids always hung out in groups. I coaxed Ingram, who by nature was more easygoing, into helping me hunt down the ones who picked on us. I had the idea that with the resumption of school in the fall, we would hang around the halls as the kids left for home alone, and then confront each one separately. I planned to emulate my brother, Pizarro, who had taken up weight lifting and had developed into a heavily muscled young man. No one messed with him. During the spring and summer of tenth grade, Ingram and I followed his example, pumping iron and bulking up, determined to stop the bullying.

Before I could put my plan into action, I learned, finally, how monumentally different I was from the black mainstream. At sixteen, I signed up for a summer engineering program in Dayton. I was pretty sure I wanted a career as an engineer. I was keen to experience engineering courses and eager to meet the students I'd share my studies with. I expected that everyone in the program would be smart. They'd be nerdy black kids like me. Dayton was a disappointment, but not over the engineering classes. I learned just how far ostracism can go, just how much of a price I'd have to pay for contradicting my fellow blacks.

The seminar began with two days of preparation for standardized college entrance examinations. But that year our group was special. The leaders of the seminar were experimenting with entrance exams that had been written especially to remove racial biases. Educators had maintained for several years that standard tests were written for the white, middle-class mainstream. Blacks and other minorities were at a disadvantage with those tests, they maintained, and the unfair results had often been used to cast doubt on the intelligence of young blacks like us. So that summer, we were to take two entrance exams—the traditional, standard test, and a prototype of the new, racially unbiased tests. Our results were to be reviewed by a psychologist.

The lecturers passed out two exams. The first was a typical SAT exam that I completed quickly; I turned to the racially unbiased exam, expecting to breeze through it, too. The first question stopped me in my tracks. "Who is buried in Grant's tomb?"

It was a multiple-choice question. I chose Ulysses S. Grant. But on second thought the answer seemed too obvious. Two other choices were both of historic figures surnamed Grant. The last choice was: "Your momma!" I looked again at this absurd option. I decided that "Your momma!" was intended to put minority students at ease, and thus render the exam less biased. The rest of the questions featured the same sorts of answer choices. So the idea, I realized, was to lessen the stress level of minorities. I finished the exam quickly and then read lecture handouts.

Two days later, the psychologist talked to the class after lunch. I remember she explained that "the test results went far to support our theory with regard to standardized intelligence exams. Nearly all of you saw dramatic improvement when the cultural bias was removed from the test. In fact, there was only one exception. The cultural bias in standardized testing is something that we have fought against for several years. We are only now gaining the attention of educators in this struggle. The use of a standardized test to exclude qualified minority men and women is similar to the Jim Crow laws of the Old South. We use the results of testing by volunteers such as yourselves to fight the racial bias that is inherent in the standardized intelligence exams."

The class only wanted to know one thing. "Who got the highest score on the regular exam?" It was me, but the psychologist tempered that achievement by saying I'd had "great difficulty with the unbiased exam." She reassured me and the others that this was because I'd grown up in suburbs with few blacks around me and little background in my own culture. "We're all members of the same culture, the same family, so we share a common body of cultural knowledge," she said. "If you are not a member of the family, you are simply unaware of these things."

"That is not true!" I jumped up in anger. "My parents teach me black history every night. Who is Benjamin Banneker? Who is John Morgan? Who is Crispus Attucks? That wasn't on that exam and you don't know. You don't even want to know. That test was not about black culture, that was just stupid ghetto slang."

On the bus back to the dormitory, I sat by myself. The other kids laughed about the exams and loudly called themselves The Family after the language of the psychologist. I laughed, too, but at their laughter and their pride. They were actually proud to have underperformed white people on a standardized exam. Without that psychologist's explanations, these kids would have tried to improve their performance. Now they believed that substandard performance was evidence of a sinister racial bias that only their failure had exposed, that as blacks, they should not expect to or attempt to compete intellectually with whites because the competition itself was biased. Now they believed that a black who studied, worked and scored highly was betraying his black culture by not failing.

For the next couple of days, I wandered through the seminar alone. My dorm roommate moved into a room down the hall. Lonely and miserable, I called my parents and told them that the other kids wouldn't talk to me. Mops sounded very sad when she heard this. The first day of the next week, I heard a commotion. A gang of kids were beating up on another nerdy student in a dorm room down the hall. For reasons of his own, he'd stayed aloof from the group that now called itself The Family, and they wanted to break him. I ran to his room. They'd pinned him to his bed and were trying to light the effluent of an aerosol-spray can with a cigarette lighter. Three guys dragged a fire extinguisher into his room. The kids taunted him with the improvised flamethrower and the fire extinguisher until he agreed to join their ranks. Two days later the same kids broke down my dorm door while I was reading in bed. From the light in the hallway, I could make out a cluster of ten to twelve people; three carried a fire extinguisher aloft, two others had ropes. I grabbed a chair and swung it violently, pursuing the kids into the hall. They escaped into an open elevator. Someone threw the fire extinguishers and it hit me above the eye. Tired, cold and bleeding, I sank down against a wall and cried myself to sleep. I awoke to the voice of the dorm counselor: "We better get you an ambulance. You just be cool." It took twelve stitches to close the cut over my right eye, but other scars from that seminar never healed. I went home from Dayton convinced that I'd never fit in with black students.

Back home, I showed shades of my father's penchant for melodrama. And hyperbole. By the eleventh grade, I could give his lectures for him. I would lie in bed at night conjuring up maxims, only to hear Pops pronounce them the next day. I began looking for confrontation. I marched up to Colby Park, where a large group was playing basketball. I stole the ball, leaped onto a park bench and shouted, "Hear me, it is time that we as a people stop making baskets and start making A's. We must throw down the basketballs and start picking up our textbooks. Now, during the summer, it is not too late to compete in the game of life." Understandably, the crowd looked at me in shocked bewilderment. Someone shouted, "Get the ball from that damn nigger and let's play!" and they bum-rushed me out of the park. But I was relentless. I preached to any gathering of black kids, just as my father preached to us. I knew his tone, his pauses, his speech patterns, just where to raise my voice. If four or five black kids were sitting around, I harangued them about responsibility. They were only doing what high school kids everywhere do, but I was on a mission. I believed my father's philosophies about hard work. And besides, the other black kids excluded me. Haranguing them got their attention.

Now when they derided me for my lack of knowledge about black slang, I would pound my fists on my chest and shout, "Here I am! Here I am! I am the essence of the Black Man! We are not meant to be petty Negroes mouthing ghetto slang. I could be a nigger too dancing the jigaboo. But this is not a game. Pick up a book! Read! Learn to enunciate! You are failures to yourselves. You are failures to your families. You are failures to your race. I am the Black Man. Here I am! Here I am!"

In the middle of the year, our school sent a three-student team to participate on a television show called *Academic Challenge*, an annual scholastic tournament. The popular northeast Ohio competition had been sponsored by local television stations for years, but no black students ever appeared on any of the teams. That year I was part of the Wickliffe High team. Tryouts were held in October, and the competition show was taped in November. We lost, but we performed well and were on television. After that, my black classmates seemed to warm up to me. The academic accomplishments that previously branded me as "white" now suddenly meant I'd done something to boost black people. Slowly, I began to feel a grudging respect from the black kids. They stopped teasing me and Ingram. Had I toughened up and scared them? Or were we all simply growing up?

IN MY SENIOR year, I devoted my attention to college entrance exams. I took the SAT at a distant high school, one that flew a Confederate flag and called its sport mascot and teams The Rebels. I got off the bus in the wrong spot and was chased toward the school by a group of guys shouting, "What's that nigger doing here?" Still, I managed to earn high marks on the SAT.

I wanted to be an engineer. I did well in the sciences (after all, Mops was a science teacher) and had a more natural affinity for those subjects than for liberal arts. I applied to Carnegie Mellon University and Ohio State University, two local schools with excellent engineering programs. Then I filled out a form for Harvard University, for no reason other than it was famous and prestigious and it sounded good to me to say I was applying there, too.

I was accepted at all three.

Suddenly Harvard had new appeal, even though I had no idea how we would pay for it. I daydreamed about a leafy campus, and long afternoons studying and arguing philosophy. I changed my plans, deciding philosophy would be my major, until one Sunday when my father shoved the classified section of the paper under my nose and barked: "Fine, here are the want ads. Show me the ad that says Help Wanted, Philosopher."

I was excited about the prospect of college, until a classmate, Doug Vanek, scorned my acceptance letters: "The only reason you got in is because you're black, and they're letting you in." Doug was in all my Advanced Placement classes, and he knew I had a 4.2 grade point average, that I'd qualified for the *Academic Challenge* team in eleventh and twelfth grade. His comment hurt, and made me angry. I believed I was very bright. At the time, affirmative action was a relatively new concept, and Doug's dismissive comment sparked a nagging question: Was I truly qualified or had I been let in unfairly?

Then Doug said, "I bet you can't get into the school of my choice without putting your race on your application." Fine, I replied immediately, name the school. A bunch of us went to the library and looked up the schools with highest average SAT acceptance scores. Doug chose the Massachusetts Institute of Technology, MIT. I'd never heard of it. I read up on it, and was pleased to discover that it had a strong engineering program. I could major in philosophy and physics. While on the surface those subjects seem vastly different, to me they were part of the same deterministic universe. Scientific knowledge frees man to think. So philosophy and physics were complementary.

The more I read about Harvard and MIT, the more I realized I wanted to go to one. There had to be more blacks like me somewhere, and I wanted to find them. My parents assured me that this would be easy at college—school would be full of superachieving blacks. Mops was ecstatic about the Ivy League, saying, "The black kids there will be more like you, it's going to be different." The only problem would be figuring out how to pay for such a school. The cost was daunting, and I never thought I would actually attend either one. I just wanted to win the bet with Doug.

I did. MIT accepted me immediately. More important, I learned that the Ivy League offers needs-based financial-aid packages. Essentially, this meant anyone who was qualified to enroll could afford to enroll—or at least, could afford the debt to enroll. MIT's financial-aid package wasn't as good as Carnegie Mellon's—and Ohio State's was even better, with a monthly living stipend of $1,000. The MIT deal would leave me with debt after graduation. But the phrase "Ivy League" was already ringing in my ears, and I had gone quickly from never having heard of MIT to being enthralled with its status as a world-famous institution. At school even my teachers treated me differently, knowing I was fielding offers from MIT, Harvard and Carnegie Mellon.

MIT, HOWEVER, WAS a shock. Right away, I discovered that most of the freshmen had already been to college. They'd taken their Advanced Placement courses at local colleges. Many had graduated early, in eleventh grade, and spent their senior year at a local college. The overall quality of their education was daunting. While Wickliffe High offered one crude, introductory calculus class, these kids had taken advanced calculus with differential equations at their private schools. Such a thing wasn't even offered in Ohio! Neither was physics, which many of them had already studied. In the first week, professors assumed that the students had a degree of background knowledge that I simply lacked. MIT offered classes of three difficulty levels—calculus for poets, calculus for normal people and calculus for masochists. My nature compelled me to take the masochists' class. Whenever there was a masochists' course, I signed up. But it meant that my classmates were better trained than me. I couldn't admit I was in the wrong place, or let myself withdraw from the class. Instead, I spent every waking hour studying. Fortunately, at MIT, studying was the social scene. I fit right in. The campus was Nerdsville. People had fun with school-related projects. Groups of students, a dozen or more, sat in study hall all night and into the early morning, arguing over concepts like how to build an atomic bomb. No one dressed well, no one spoke slang, no one worried about the hit music of the day, no one gossiped about girls or dating. We talked relentlessly and endlessly about physics, engineering, calculus, study programs, projects or research. Everyone had a one-track mind.

The black students at MIT were nerds just like me. But the school had a cluster of fraternities, and they threw freshmen recruiting parties every year. The fraternities courted me, partly because I looked athletic, a rare feature at MIT. Each fraternity had a reputation—there was one for jocks, another for heavy beer drinkers. I wore a muscle T-shirt to a recruiting party, so guys from the jock fraternities crowded around me. When I visited Sigma Alpha Epsilon, the brothers took me directly to their weight-lifting bench and said, show us how much you can press. At the beer frats, I saw rows of kegs in the basements and heard promises that the brew never stopped flowing. I thought I liked SAE, but when I talked to my father, he discouraged me from pledging a fraternity. "You'll end up in a group-think situation and won't be independent."

During rush week I passed a group of black freshmen who asked, "Aren't you going to the housing meeting?" The Black Student Union was sponsoring it. I'd seen a few blacks around campus, but none in the fraternities. It turned out that the black students at MIT were all familiar with one another. They had told the school their race when they first applied, and the admissions office had passed their names to the black student groups. So all spring and summer they'd been receiving literature and information. There were summer orientation programs, and many had signed up and met that way. They'd come to school three weeks early for seminars on housing and tutorials organized by the Black Student Union. I missed all this because I hadn't identified myself as black on my application. I began to think of myself as the "Negro who walked in from the cold." I'd gotten on only one mailing list—from the Hispanic student association, and I think that must have been because my first name was Orlando.

I joined the guys headed to the housing meeting. The auditorium was packed—if MIT had four thousand undergraduates and four thousand graduate students, perhaps two hundred of us were black. It looked as if everyone was in this auditorium. An extraordinarily well-spoken black woman talked about why the Black Student Union tutorial program was important, where students should go for help, and so on. "Now, on to housing," she said, and her voice and manner changed diametrically. Her neck began pumping with her words, and she hollered: "If you hate honkeys like I hate honkeys, if you don't want honkeys in your business, you'll live on the fifth floor of McCormick! Can I hear it for McCormick!!!" Whooping, cheering and yelling followed. Forced busing was tearing Boston apart at the time as whites and blacks fought in the streets over public school integration, and the racial climate was very bad. But I was shocked at the racial virulence in that auditorium. I'd never heard such open race-baiting. A black man stood up and announced: "We've got two places for you: It's Chocolate City in the house!" Cheers erupted again. "We've got good news, we've taken over the twelfth floor of McGregor, and we've added a new house to Chocolate Cittttttttttt-taaaaaaaaaayyyyyyyy!!" Everyone started chanting, "Chocolate City, Chocolate City, Chocolate City." "Whitey ain't gonna tell us how to live. The brothers is gonna be brothers! The brothers is gonna be loud! The brothers is gonna partay!!!"

The bantering about honkey and whitey surprised me. The open antipathy surprised me. It was as if Boston's racial conflicts were being mirrored right there on campus. What I'd seen of the school, the fraternities, the study halls, the classes—the kids at MIT were all nerds. It looked to me as if the nerdiest kids from my high school had multiplied a thousandfold and were set loose in Cambridge, free from worrying that they had no social graces because no one was teasing them anymore. The black students were the same. They wore horn-rimmed glasses and talked "white" until they got up to the podium and adopted a black slang that, frankly, they didn't do very well. Yet the speakers were carrying on as if the Irish thug-cops of

Boston were their fellow students. Some white threat must exist on campus, I thought, but I couldn't pinpoint it.

I left the meeting before it was over. These black students were just like the white guys who rushed fraternities—both looking for a club to belong to. I wasn't interested in a fraternity or the Black Student Union. I never joined either. I did tutor at the union for four years. But the tutoring program was not a social organization, it was designed to help students make it through a tough school. I taught math, chemical engineering and chemistry, sometimes to Asian students, occasionally to Hispanics, but mostly to blacks.

I moved into a dormitory with little rooms we called "coffins," and in order to make more space, I took the bed out and dragged in a padded bench from the common area. I wedged the bench next to the huge standard-issue armoire that all the residents called "the elephant," leaving just enough room to squeeze through to a sink. A desk and a long, narrow shelf made up my study space. I decorated the room with fishnets hanging from the ceiling, and weight-lifting and martial-arts paraphernalia. Later, when a girlfriend and I got our first apartment, we bought a used hotel bed. For the next six years, I lived in Cambridge and studied at MIT, finishing my undergraduate and graduate degrees. At MIT, my overriding identification was for achievement, merit and academics. I ignored everything else, and I thrived. I felt more at home at MIT than I'd felt anywhere else. I never did join any clubs or groups; I never formed a social clique, but MIT certainly opened a broader world for me. I had friends of all races, sizes, sexes and colors. We were a most wonderful collection of misfits.

There were black role models in abundance. They did not hesitate to stop black undergrads in the hall to say, "I haven't seen you at the Black Student Union tutorial programs recently. Can you get over there tonight?" Once, one of them stopped the members of the MIT basketball team on their way to practice. "I hate to tell you, fellas, but you guys suck. No amount of practice is going to stop you from losing. So you may as well throw down that basketball and start studying for the physics exam you have next week." The black graduate students at MIT approached the world just like my father.

In my second year of graduate school, I worked on a research project that attempted to transform coal into crude oil. Success might have meant that another oil crisis like the one in the 1970s would never be repeated. At the end of that year, in 1981, I took a summer job with Corning Glass in Ithaca, New York. Corning had an enormous program that drew summer interns from predominantly black colleges, and I found myself working in Corning's corporate headquarters with a large number of blacks from schools in the South. One day as I rode a glass elevator, I looked out toward a commotion in the atrium below. A group of young black men had trooped into the lobby, shouting a slogan. Men and women in suits stopped to watch. The guys were summer engineering interns like me, only now they wore bright green shorts, orange tops and green suspenders. They formed a line and started a dance routine. I got off the escalator just as people—white people—streamed out of their offices. I stood with the gawkers on a balcony overlooking the atrium and watched as these young black men began break-dancing while chanting a song. Everyone laughed; I was aghast. I couldn't hear the song, but it sounded something like "We be dancing . . . ," and at the end they chanted, "We be Q!" I ran down the "up" escalators in a rage, determined to stop them before they started another number, before they made further fools of themselves and me. But they were done, smiling and high-fiving each other, telling everyone who asked that it was all part of an initiation rite for their fraternity in Georgia. The purpose was to prove that although they worked in the white world, they were still united as Brothers.

Breathing hard at the bottom of the escalator, I felt betrayed. Betrayed by these budding black engineers who felt they needed to show they weren't selling out and "acting white," betrayed by the white managers and workers who stood around clapping like there was nothing the least unusual about a black minstrel show in the very headquarters of corporate America. Clearly this wasn't MIT. I was back in the real world, one in which I didn't belong—and didn't want to belong—to either side.

GE, ROUND ONE

GRADUATED FROM MIT in 1982 with a master's degree in chemical engineering and a job. I bought a BMW and pigskin driving gloves, packed my few belongings in the car and drove to the General Electric plastics factory built by Chairman Jack Welch in Albany, New York. GE was the largest corporation in America, a huge conglomerate that made everything from lightbulbs to supercomputers. To a chemical engineer, a job with GE was a plum. I wore pin-striped suits to the laboratory and was assigned to tackle problems the plant was having using crystallization as a separation process. At the end of the project, I presented a paper, and the company's vice president, Phil Gross, offered me a new position that paid the salary of a Ph.D. engineer.

When I first moved to Albany, I rented an apartment in the back of a house only a few blocks from the factory. I decided to plant a garden. As I dug in the yard, the same purple liquid that we used to eliminate toxins at the plant seeped from the soil. I gave up digging and stopped buying local produce. When I came home at night, I reeked of chemicals. My clothes and hair stank, and the smell was impossible to get out. After a few months, I had to escape that neighborhood. I moved then to an old apple-cider barn near the Massachusetts state line. It had been the summer home of the Albany Light Opera. I liked it for its rural ruggedness. But the barn had no heat, so I had to start a fire in one of two wood-burning stoves as soon as I got home. I signed up for classes in opera appreciation, jazz dance, ballet and adult gymnastics. I joined a horseback riding club. Soon I had a large group of friends, and we'd throw potluck dinners for a dozen people in my barn.

At GE, my title was Research Engineer, a more junior position than the Ph.D. salary level I was paid. After I moved into that job, my progress seemed to slow. I soon realized that there was nothing unusual about this. To my dismay, I discovered that progress at GE was based on seniority and a hierarchy carved in stone. It took five years—no more, no less—to become a senior engineer, then another five years to earn a more advanced title. Promotions did not seem to hinge on merit, but simply on logging time. I chafed under these restrictions. My manager was nicknamed The Big Cheese by plant workers. It was an open joke—he kept a large plastic model of Swiss cheese on his desk, and all his notepads said THE BIG CHEESE across the top. Each time I went to him with an idea or suggestion, he'd nod and smile wanly and send me back to my desk. The kind of passion my classmates and I felt about our projects at MIT wasn't welcome at GE. Most people were proud of doing as little as possible and were content to fit a mold. Ambition meant work. Ambition meant standing out. GE didn't like misfits.

I, however, expected to be plant manager in four years.

Thus, The Big Cheese told me constantly: "Wait, wait, you have to pay your dues. You have to understand—everyone here has paid their dues! I have twenty years' experience. You can't walk in here thinking you're going to shake up the world. This world doesn't shake. It's well established."

Believing he was mentoring me, he'd tell me what to expect from my career. There were three tracks at GE—Research, Plant and Technology. Entering the Research track required a Ph.D., so that was closed to me. (I'd forgone the advance degree because funding for my doctoral thesis had dried up just as GE offered me a job at a Ph.D. salary level.) The Plant track, which was faster than the others, meant controlling vast amounts of infrastructure and line workers. The Technology track meant working for The Big Cheese for five years, then on another project for five more years to prove I could handle variety, then five years in management, and then five years in a job just like his. At the time, I was earning $36,000 and The Big Cheese made about $70,000. I looked at him and thought: You mean, in twenty years, I get to be you? I was twenty-four.

Part of my dissatisfaction stemmed from habits learned at MIT, where students routinely critiqued one another's projects. We gave our opinions freely, especially at the graduate level. Students criticized one another's procedures and pointed out flaws. I brought that practice to GE, unaware that it wasn't appreciated. I did my own work and then, out of curiosity, studied other people's projects as well, oblivious to the fact that no one liked me looking over their shoulders. When I offered a suggestion or criticism, people would frequently ask how I knew what I was asserting. My answer was always the same: "You do understand, don't you, that I don't make technical errors?" I meant it. Soon I rubbed people the wrong way; my ambition and cockiness irritated them and threatened their comfortable structure. As a reward for my impatience, I was sent to GE's famed Croton-on-Hudson Professional Development Center, to undergo sensitivity training. Many of the students were managers with grating or abrasive personalities, and I had to admit I fit the bill. The center's goal was to bring assertive people together and turn them into touchy-feely types. To me, it amounted to a full frontal lobotomy sans surgery. We sat in a classroom with an instructor who asked us to describe the unhappy or disappointing aspects of our lives. While others understood that they should talk about their families, relationships and compulsions, I described my job at GE. I returned to work unchanged.

In the winter of 1983, frustrated with The Big Cheese, I requested a transfer to the Plant track. I went from a pristine lab environment to a plant floor dominated by huge furnaces, chemicals and fumes. Our section of the factory made the plastic for car dashboards. I sold my BMW and built a jeep by hand with the help of some guys from the factory. I started wearing jeans and work shirts, and carried a pipe wrench in my back pocket. I got along with the blue-collar technicians better than I had with the white-collar crowd. I loved the physical labor. If a flange needed to be changed, I did it myself. We weren't a unionized shop, so there was nothing to prohibit me. I didn't have a major project of my own to supervise, so I spent a lot of time with the technicians on monitoring assignments, making sure the plant ran smoothly. I saw how they worked—or didn't—and saw the plant frailties. Other engineers seldom left the offices because in the plant, noxious fumes clung to clothes and hair, and the smell was impossible to wash out later.

I didn't gain much by switching managers, however. My new one, Olaf Tant, was a white South African in his mid-forties who made it clear that he hadn't hired me, I'd just been assigned to him. On the first day he told me he'd heard my presentations and knew that I'd helped develop a chemical catalyst that increased production from 80 to 96 percent. The Afrikaner wanted me to know that in being bright, I was very different from the savages back home. I guess he imagined we were bonding. He told me that the only blacks he'd ever seen still carried spears. Then he warned me about a group of blacks among the technicians who manufactured the catalyst. They were on a semistrike over charges of racism in hiring and firing practices. The recession of 1982 had forced GE to let many workers go, and many minorities hadn't had the seniority to escape the layoffs. Their fellow black workers thought they'd been let go in disproportionate numbers. Tant believed these blue-collar shift workers would listen to me, an MIT-educated manager, just because we were all black.

That winter, in 1983 and early 1984, I started my own project. The plastics we worked with are called monomers, and when grouped together, form a polymer. To create monomers, we poured oil over a catalyst, which converted the oil into monomers and waste material. Distillation purified the monomer—separating it from the waste material. We then processed the monomers to create plastic for products. I used software written by a cutting-edge company called Aspen to create a computer model of our entire plant. The Aspen software had only just become commercially available, but I'd worked on its development at MIT, so I knew what it could do. I had often turned to computers at MIT for just these kinds of projects. I believed the Aspen model showed that GE was running its purification systems backward. I was methodical and slow in my work, checking, rechecking and triple-checking everything. I couldn't bear to make technical mistakes. When my research was ready, I presented it to a managers meeting, urging them to consider what I called "reverse distillation." They smirked. Tant reminded me that I was just a research engineer, and they all questioned the veracity of a computer model. Computers were not yet commonly used to model chemical reactions and the physical characteristics of complex chemicals. At least not outside academia. Trial-and-error was the preferred method. Engineers experimented with new systems and waited to observe the results, adopting the ones that worked and eliminating those that did not. The managers didn't believe the computer was reliable. But I had depended on computer modeling all through MIT.

When my research and recommendation were dismissed, I was despondent. Every plant engineer's ambition is to be awarded a huge project with a big budget and staff. I knew my idea was sound, and I didn't want to see someone else take it on. I wanted to revolutionize the procedures at the monomer plant. But my presentation had fallen flat. What was the incentive to stay at GE? I refused to give up, and hounded Tant, and then his superiors, about my project. I tried to go over Tant's head. I confronted Tant and told him I thought he was blinded by his homeland perceptions of black people. I told his supervisor, the man who had encouraged me to leave the Technology track for the Plant track, that "this is science, pure science. I don't care if we don't like each other. That should have nothing to do with it. If he's standing in the way of this project, it's because he's lost his technical objectivity. Every decision we make must be based on the numbers. It has to be technically objective." The supervisor merely said, "Look, Olaf has years of experience. He started up plants in Holland. I'm not going to overrule him. I have to go with my manager." My complaints only earned me another tour at the GE sensitivity-training course.

By 1984, however, change reached GE, this time initiated by CEO Jack Welch. An evolving worldwide economy dictated that companies like GE could no longer be technology driven. Now they had to be market driven. In the past, GE engineers labored over a technology, perfected it, and then the marketers looked for a way to turn it into a saleable product. Now Welch wanted GE marketers first to determine what consumers wanted to buy, then instruct the engineers in the plants what they should be working on. Suddenly a wave of GE marketing account executives and managers washed through the plant. They came for tours and exploratory meetings and information-gathering sessions. They came to check on the engineers' progress. I began to meet a lot of people with MBAs from Harvard and Stanford. One day I recognized a classmate from my MIT undergraduate days. He'd gone on to Stanford for an MBA when I went on to my chemical engineering master's. He was earning $54,000.

Another of the MBAs was a young black woman. She arrived driving a beat-up old car, and rented an apartment. Soon, however, she traded her beater for a Porsche and bought a house. She moved around the plant with an air of confidence and authority, and grousing followed. There was a good deal more resentment and suspicion directed at her than at any of the other MBAs, and always the gossip centered on how she had managed to win a well-paid spot at GE only because of affirmative action. Her success unnerved just about everyone, and they used affirmative action to denigrate it. It didn't matter whether what they said about this black woman was true—not to them, and not to me. I knew that they warded off a black person's success by raising the specter of affirmative action just the same.

About six months later, I learned that GE had hired a consulting firm to help design a replica of our plant in Osaka, Japan. The consulting firm had recommended that GE reverse the distilling process it used to create monomers. We were running ours backward in Albany, they said. They knew this, it turned out, because they had created a computer model of the process with Aspen software. Within two weeks, GE appropriated $3 million to reverse the distillation process in Albany. I was vindicated, but any victory I felt was hollow. I'd already decided that I had no future at the plant. The future lay with an MBA.

By the summer of 1985, reverse distillation was under way, I was running the huge project, and had been accepted to Harvard Business School. I strutted around the plant, proud of my accomplishments. I knew that few people liked me, but I was determined to force them to acknowledge that I'd been right all along. I stood up at a meeting to present a progress report on the distillation work, stared hard at Olaf Tant and then greeted everyone with a favorite quote from the German philosopher Nietzsche: "The poisons of which weaker natures perish, do but strengthen the strong, nor do we call it poison."

I heard a friend mutter, "Uh-oh, burning bridges." I reminded everyone at the meeting that they'd rejected reverse distillation, but it had been installed quickly and worked like a charm.

"We as engineers must stick to technical objectivity, whether you like it or not. I have swallowed the poisons of GE and they have made me stronger. Thank you." My friends cheered, a vice president shook my hand and complimented my presentation, but Tant stalked out. The next day the plant manager took me to lunch and told me that the vice president wanted to ensure that I returned to GE after business school. GE would pay for

Harvard, he said. In return, I had to commit to work at least five years. I couldn't picture myself tied to GE for that long. I didn't know what my future held, but I was pretty sure it wasn't at GE.

The only thing I knew for certain was that engineers were no longer in the ascendancy. MBAs were taking over. Jack Welch was an engineer, but already it seemed clear that the next leader of GE would not be a technology geek like him, but rather someone from a marketing background. My communication and social skills were poor, and I had begun to think of business school like a finishing school—the opposite of MIT. Most of all, I needed to learn to disagree without antagonizing people. I chose to apply only to Harvard after a marketing specialist who visited our plant told a story that he said illustrated the difference between Harvard and a business school like Stanford's. "Two MBAs are having an argument—one from Stanford, with a more technical education, and one from Harvard, which emphasizes case studies. The guy from Stanford is right, but the guy from Harvard wins." That decided it for me. On technical issues I was always right, I just needed to learn how to win the arguments.

THE HARVARD MBA SHOW

N THE SPRING of 1985 I was invited to an interview at Harvard. The admissions officer took one look at me and confessed that she'd wanted to be sure I wasn't some sort of skinhead. As part of my application, I'd written an essay praising self-responsibility, self-reliance, small government and free enterprise. I'd cited affirmative action as a violation of all of the above and an egregious example of bad government. She'd been afraid I was a militant separatist.

At the same time, she realized I was not a likely candidate for black student groups. "You may have some trouble here. The Afro-American Student Union is very strong. They really keep a tight rein on all their members." I knew from experience that black college students face pressure to conform to the idea that blacks on campus speak with only one voice. Without saying so explicitly, she seemed to be trying to warn me that I might run into obstacles. I knew that I would, but I was less worried about it than her. By now, I reveled in being different. I didn't perceive myself as an outsider, I viewed myself as independent. Before I left Boston, I bought Harvard Business School T-shirts and took them back to Albany to distribute at work.

I hooked a trailer to the back of my jeep, tossed in my few pieces of furniture from the apple-cider barn and drove to Cambridge. The jeep wasn't legal for street driving—it had huge "mudder" tires with knobs designed for off-road racing, and they tore up asphalt. In Albany my friends and I spent weekends taking our trucks and jeeps to muddy fields and plowing through the muck until it was three or four feet deep on the tires. The jeep also howled terribly at anything above fifteen miles per hour. To top it off, the guys at the plant had attached an empty machine-gun rack to the back. It looked quite out of place in Boston. Once in Cambridge, I discovered that Harvard's dorm rooms were no bigger than those at MIT. I drove my stuff back to Albany and left it with a friend.

When classes opened, it was immediately evident that Harvard was very different from MIT. At MIT, race was paid lip service. There were more strident tests of whether you belonged at MIT—chief among them, your grasp of chemistry, physics, engineering and other scientific principles and concepts. At Harvard, race played a much larger role in defining who belonged and who did not. My class of roughly nine hundred people was fairly evenly divided between men and women. The majority of students were Jewish. There was a significant number of Asians. Blacks, as usual, were few. It quickly became clear that the white and Asian students believed that any black at Harvard Business School had been admitted via an affirmative action program. While they boasted openly about where they'd gone to private school and done undergraduate studies, their questions to blacks were tentative and tinged with lower expectations. Sometimes they were downright condescending. Among the whites and Asians, the de rigueur answer to the question "Why are you here?" was an explanation of future ambitions and plans. For blacks, the answer was expected to focus on the past: because of a scholarship, because of a diversity program, because of affirmative action. It made us instinctively defensive and even secretly ashamed.

Within the first month, my classmates formed into like-minded groups, and I could see that there was a clique with engineering backgrounds like mine and a clique with business and finance backgrounds. The engineering students struck me as dull and not engaged in the world around them. I'd known engineers like them at GE, people who had little interest in politics or culture but instead worked all day in a factory and then went home to watch TV. I was determined to break away from that culture. I felt more comfortable among the Wall Street types. They were aware of the world around them, and they were outgoing. They were interested in politics and the economy. I had dabbled a bit in the stock market, buying a few stocks and bonds, and I thought I had a good sense of how Wall Street worked.

At first I found myself making friends with people simply because we shared common interests. But the more I heard about investment banking and the financial industries, the more I realized those professions might offer me the level playing field I was seeking. I'd entered Harvard believing I wanted a career in marketing. Now I realized it was more important to find a career where I would be rewarded for initiative, productivity and dedication.

During our first year, companies sent representatives and speakers to address the students. Because it was Harvard, the speakers were often CEOs and presidents of major corporations. GM sent its CEO; so did Quaker Oats. All the major manufacturing players came, and I glimpsed the GE culture in all of them. Their speakers were dry and methodical. Each talked about change. "We intend to make changes, and change is under way," went the spiel. "If you work with us, we'll train you for five years, then you'll spend five years assistant-training someone else, and then another five years. . . ." I often shuddered, emotionally as well as physically, as I listened to these talks.

The Wall Street representatives, on the other hand, put on shows. They were outrageous. The women who represented investment banks and trading houses came wearing the latest dark stylish suits with impossibly short skirts and high heels. Their hair was beautifully cut and their makeup classic and subtle. None of the little silk floppy bow scarves around the neck of a high white blouse for them. The men were confident in expensive suits, hand-sewn shoes and gold cuff links. Their arrogance made us all want to be just like them. One day, a young woman in a tight miniskirt and sheer black stockings came to Harvard to tell us about Drexel Burnham Lambert. She'd been a secretary at Pillsbury five years before, she said. She'd been determined to change her life, and Drexel had sent her to a training course.

"Are you prepared to walk over hot coals for your future? they asked, and I said, I am!!" she thundered at us like a Holy Roller, and then pranced from behind her podium in an imitation of coal-walking, her long legs swishing from under the miniskirt. "And I did! I walked over hot coals. I made $25,000 as a secretary and I make $800,000 at Drexel. What do you want? Do you want to work for Drexel Burnham or for the Pillsbury Doughboy?!"

Another afternoon, Shearson Lehman CEO Peter Cohen was scheduled to speak, but he didn't show up at the appointed hour. An auditorium full of students became restless. Half an hour later, a deafening thudding noise drew everyone out of their seats. A sleek helicopter clattered to the ground just outside, and Cohen leaped nimbly onto the lawn. His elegant suit hardly creased, he took a seat near the podium and pulled a long cigar out of his breast pocket. It seemed to take him twenty minutes to cut and light the cigar. Then he got up and started to speak. He never apologized for being late or offered any explanation.

The pièce de résistance was Michael Milken's speech for Drexel Burnham Lambert. It was 1986, a year before the collapse of Wall Street, and Milken was the junk bond king, with a personal fortune of $500 million. He didn't simply take the stage. First, the standing-room-only graduate-student audience was treated to a pounding, earsplitting concert by a Madonna lookalike and a raft of Boy Toy backup dancers and singers. The Madonna lookalike belted out her own version of "Material Girl": "Well, I'm livin' in a high-yield world, and I am a high-yield girl. . . ." At the end of the song, the stage exploded in flashing lights and white smoke, and when it cleared,

Milken stepped out of the clouds and up to the microphone. The auditorium erupted in wild screaming, whistling and cheering that went on for many long minutes.

For many of us, the gauntlet was thrown down that day: We had a choice—Quaker Oats, or Madonna.

WHEN RECRUITING FOR summer jobs began in earnest, a representative from Salomon Brothers posted a chart with the names of his company's department heads, and I recognized one of my old dormmates from MIT. By the time I saw the list, I'd already signed up for job interviews with engineering firms. It was too late to join the interview schedules for Wall Street companies. Nevertheless, I called Larry Hillenbrand, now the managing director of fixed income futures trading at Salomon. He had the same engineering background as me, and when he'd started on Wall Street four years before, had discovered that few people there were comfortable with computers. They let him run his department because no one else was interested in it. Then suddenly technical analysis of fixed income products took off, and Hillenbrand found himself in the right place at the right time, one of the few people who understood computer-intensive trading. That also meant there was no one to contradict or oppose him. Salomon gave him money to invest and let him run his own show.

After that I looked more closely at Wall Street careers, and I discovered that there was still a shortage of people with technical skills. I noticed something else—there seemed to be more objectivity on Wall Street than I'd found in any other profession. All I lacked was some experience.

I took a summer job at the Ford Motor Company, in its Dearborn, Michigan, treasury department. I was there to study investment techniques. In reality, I spent virtually all of my day on the phone with traders, brokers and salespeople. Soon I found myself with a number of "phone friends," other interns, assistants and junior traders who also spent endless hours on the phone. Eventually, we'd start talking about subjects other than the market or investment statistics. Most people were friendly and easygoing, but I hit it off particularly well with two people. One was a young woman named Val, a sales assistant in the New York office of Drexel Burnham Lambert. We talked a couple of times a day, and from our first conversation we had a comfortable rapport. That first talk was strikingly appealing and pleasant. It was more than work; there was a chemistry between us, even over the phone, that is rare between two people but immediately recognizable when it happens. I looked forward to talking to her, and we both began to find any excuse to call. Whatever small bit of business might prompt the call was soon dispensed with, and we carried on long, interesting and entertaining conversations. During one of the earliest, we both wanted to know what the other looked like. She described herself as a petite blonde, and I told her I was of average height, athletic build and was once mistaken for the comedian Eddie Murphy. She laughed at that, and I thought she sounded impressed.

Val and I talked every day, and soon she asked for my home number. We continued our conversations late into the night. I learned about her family and her interests. We read favorite poems to each other, and talked about our hopes and fears. By midsummer I was convinced I'd fallen in love with her over the phone. She felt something similar, because she began a campaign to get her managers to fly me at Drexel's expense to New York for a weekend. When they approved, I nervously and a bit disingenuously asked her what hotel I should use; when she said not to worry about a hotel, I knew I'd guessed right about our feelings for each other. I didn't have to do a thing, she said, her voice happy and excited. She made restaurant reservations and bought tickets for two Broadway musicals. We agreed to meet on the afternoon of my arrival at the Water Club.

Val said she would be wearing a blue dress and had bobbed her blond hair short. I told her to look for me in a gray suit and pink "bull and bear" suspenders. I arrived a few minutes early and took my jacket off, hooking it in a finger over my shoulder so my braces would be visible. I watched for a blonde in a royal blue dress. I stood off to one side and soon saw an athletic young woman rush in, a few minutes late. I hesitated, waiting for some sign that it was her. She was lovely. I was disappointed when the girl looked around momentarily, then raced up a staircase. I waited. Then, several minutes later, the young woman reappeared. She paused briefly, then walked outside. Five minutes later she was back, a puzzled look etched on her face. She questioned the maître' d and then went to a phone. Her face was crestfallen. I stepped forward.

"Val?"

She looked up and instantly reeled backward. Her jaw dropped. Her eyes widened just as my lungs constricted. I stopped breathing. I'd never seen such shock, confusion or dismay in a face. She simply gaped at me.

"It's me, Val. It's me."

Her knees actually buckled. I helped her to a chair and asked a waiter to bring us drinks. Val said nothing. I said nothing. I don't know what went through her mind, but mine filled with fury. When the water arrived, she drank the whole glass. Her hand shook, and she started to cry. I struggled for something to say.

"Obviously," I began slowly, "my darkness has caught you by surprise. But I told you that people in Detroit were all mistaking me for Eddie Murphy."

"I forgot!" she bleated. Tears rolled down her face.

"But Valerie, it's still me. I am the same person, the same person that you spoke to last night, that you laughed with all summer; that, I believe, I truly believe, you loved just this morning."

"I know this makes me a terrible person. And I feel like a monster. But it does matter. It changes everything. Oh my God, I wish I were dead!" She let herself sob hysterically. The maître' d looked as if he were about to intervene. Val excused herself to go to the ladies' room. I sat alone, thinking about the things she'd said to me on the phone that morning— that she'd told all her friends she was finally meeting me, and they were all waiting to hear her report. She'd told them about my two degrees from MIT, my Harvard MBA, the poetry and opera I liked. So now what—Prince Charming was a black man, and therefore not a man at all?

Val came back, and we sat in silence for several minutes. Finally, I spoke up.

"Has this whole thing been a charade? It's just that I feel that you knew all along. I am certain that I told you. I told you about when that boxer Thomas Hearns mistook me for Eddie Murphy. I know I told you about that."

She didn't look at me.

"Yes, yes, you did. Somehow, I just honestly forgot. I forgot. My mother even asked, 'What if he's black?' And we decided I could tell by your voice that you weren't black. She even listened in on the phone once. It's just that I would never date a black person. It's never come up because I can see if someone's black and I just don't get involved with them."

"So you're just racist."

"No! I'm not a racist! I mean, if you were Asian, it'd be okay."

"What if I were an Indian? There are Indians as dark as I am."

"Indians are okay. It's not just color. It's that black people are . . . are . . ."

"Are what?"

"My parents just told me not to . . . I mean I was brought up . . ." Her voice trailed off. "I don't know what to do. I don't know what to do!"

Probably we should have gotten up and walked out of the restaurant. I was simply too stunned to believe her reaction was really happening. A feeble hope tinged my anger. I had really looked forward to meeting this girl, and I just couldn't let go of my fantasies about her and our relationship in a split second. I still hoped she'd turn to me and say she'd made a mistake, that we could somehow restore the easy friendship we'd had over the phone, and go on as if this horrible episode had never happened. Neither one of us had the fortitude to walk away. We were both in such shock we simply pantomimed our way through the evening's plans. We forced down a few bites of our dinner in silence, and then walked without speaking to the theater. I have no memory of the play we saw. We left after the final curtain and walked across town and up Fifth Avenue without exchanging a word. I had no idea where we were going. Finally, she stopped in the middle of the sidewalk.

"I know, I know I'm a horrid person. But it matters to me. I can't do this."

I stood still for a moment, then turned and walked away. She said my name once more. When I looked back, she was already walking away, too, her shoulders hunched, her head down.

SADLY, VAL WAS not the only disappointment at Ford. Another sales assistant called every morning to report daily investment figures, and soon he and I were chatting about things other than how much money would be invested that day. We laughed and talked about sports, mostly, for ten or fifteen minutes every morning. There was also a heavyset guy who came into our office every afternoon to deliver accounting reports. He routinely said hello to and chatted briefly with everyone in the office except me. He seemed uncomfortable, looking my way occasionally with the uncertain expression I recognized in many white people.

One afternoon our entire department was called together for a meeting, and I was shocked to discover that my sports buddy from the morning phone calls and the heavyset guy who delivered the afternoon reports were one and the same. He appeared just as shocked. After that, he lost interest in sports talk and had little time for pleasantries on the phone.

BACK AT HARVARD for my second year, I had a chance to think about my summer, and the thoughts were painful. People I believed I'd known had turned out to be racists, uninterested in me as a person, able to look right through me or walk away from me as if I weren't there. I'm black, so therefore I am not fully human. I realized I'd prefer to have someone say to my face that they didn't like me, or couldn't love me, than have them say they accept me as human. I learned to presume that people are racist. That's just the way the world is.

So what did that mean for me? In my career, I realized, I couldn't expect a fair shake. My performance must be measured as it was in school, with grades or some similar objective standard. The more I thought about this, the stronger my feelings became. The effects of race are so pronounced in American society that the only way to overcome them is to enforce a color-blind culture with brutally objective standards. I knew I could achieve this as a Wall Street trader or salesman because both do most of their work over the phone. My customers and clients wouldn't know what color I was; their evaluation of my service or performance would be, by default, based only on how successfully I invested their money. Only then would we be able to let the chips fall where they may.

My personal philosophies evolved around my professional plans. I decided I didn't want help—not affirmative action, not an equal opportunity policy, not a diversity guarantee. I didn't need a leg up or a handout. Blacks like me are perfectly capable of taking care of themselves. American blacks are just as capable of climbing the social ladder as black immigrants from the West Indies or Africa. Equality programs do nothing to eliminate inherent, low-grade racism in nonblacks. I'd seen that at Corning, at GE, at Ford, at Harvard. Those programs just force people together, and once they're together, the old animosities surface, and the programs themselves give racists an excuse for their racism. I wanted to participate in something else. Instead of setting minimum standards and then telling blacks there is an affirmative action program to help them cover the last mile, society should set objective, color-blind standards for achievement. This would not only defang white racism, but would remove the argument of many blacks that there's no point in even trying to achieve because white people won't let them succeed.

THE RÉSUMÉ I prepared was color-blind. Though it didn't mention my race, a pattern developed anyway. At some stage in every job interview process, often at the last minute, someone would say, "Hey, this guy's black, get him over to the affirmative action office." I wanted nothing to do with those programs. They implied that I couldn't win a job on my own. They didn't just ensure fairness and entry into jobs from which blacks were excluded. They created an assumption that a black was gaining access with fewer skills than a white. Thus, no matter how the black performed, he was suspect. He was assumed to be incompetent. The first time I confronted this was after three campus interviews for a full-time job at Shearson Lehman. I'd finally been invited to New York to meet Vincente Poppa, the head of the Fixed Income desk. When I walked into his office his face showed shock.

"Have you seen our affirmative action manager?" That office was catty-corner to Poppa's, and a mid-forties, balding black man with glasses and a paunch greeted me enthusiastically. He wore a lot of bracelets, and a medallion.

"Pleased to see you, Mr. Jett. I don't know how this happened. Somehow you slipped by us." He scanned my résumé. "There's nothing on here that says you're black, nothing on here that says you're a brother."

Like what, I wondered? "Well, weren't you a member of the Afro-American Student Union at Harvard?"

I explained that I never joined groups. His face fell as I said, "I think those groups contribute to weakness more than strength. When you're out in the real world, you don't have a group of minorities to bolster you and lick your wounds, and creating that environment is detrimental. Especially in school. School is where you are supposed to learn how to stand on your own."

He stared at me. "Brother, let me tell you who I am. I started this affirmative action department because of racism. There's racism on the trading floor every day, and the only way we survive is if we stick together. I see to it that everyone knows each other, supports each other, sticks together. It's very embarrassing to me that you went through three rounds of interviews without ever having been flagged for the AA program.

"You've never worked on Wall Street, so you obviously don't know what it's like. Let me tell you. If we don't hang together, we'll hang separately. They don't like us, they don't want us here, and the only reason we are here is because the law says they've got to let us in."

I disagreed. "If that's the case, then how do you explain me? As you've just noted, you can't tell my race from my résumé. Yet based on my résumé and on how I've handled myself in all of these interviews, I've reached the final round."

I felt my father's oratory stirring in me.

"The entire AA process is white men letting black people in and saying to them that they don't have the ability and credentials to get in on their own. Once you accept that status, you no longer have the right to challenge your white benefactors in the race up the corporate ladder. We're always running around trying to find some white person to like us. It doesn't matter. Let them hate. If I have the ability, I'll still overcome."

He stood up on the other side of his desk. "I've worked my entire life to get us represented on Wall Street, so that blacks could have opportunities." We were practically shouting at each other.

"But affirmative action is not an opportunity," I thundered. His secretary could probably hear me. "It is nothing more than an admission of your intellectual inferiority. It's an agreement that says hire me and I will never challenge you. It's an agreement that says the only reason I am here is that the great white father has let me in here. There used to be a saying that it's better to die on your feet than to live on your knees. Affirmative action is living on your knees. And the worst part is, it's taking the best of us, the smartest of us, and placing us down on our knees in subjugation."

He looked at me for a second. "We all have to pull together," he said finally.

I snorted. "I am not about to let you pull me down to your level."

He looked stunned. "I don't have anything more to say to you. I'll go talk to Mr. Poppa. If he wants to hire you, he can hire you."

After fifteen minutes, I was escorted into Poppa's office.

"Well, listen, I've spoken to . . ." Poppa sputtered. "I just want to tell you, I'm Italian, and I'm proud to be Italian, and I think you ought to be proud to be a member of your race. Our affirmative action manager has tremendous influence over our hiring decisions with minority applicants."

I sighed. "I don't want to be a minority applicant."

We shook hands, and I left the office. No job offer was forthcoming from Shearson Lehman.

*　　*　　*

IN MY SECOND year of business school, I'd taken a class on technology and new financial instruments. My research paper topic was collateralized mortgage obligations, and to prepare it, I called several people on Wall Street who worked with those kinds of derivative instruments. One of them was Charles Johnston at Morgan Stanley, and I phoned him again, hoping he would remember my project. That year, I'd signed up for early job interviews with Wall Street recruiters, and I told Johnston that I had an appointment with Morgan Stanley at Harvard in February. Morgan Stanley was Wall Street's blue-chip investment firm, and although it was not the most profitable, it was certainly the most august and prestigious. Its legacy could be traced to J. P. Morgan, the powerful financier and industrialist of the early twentieth century. After the stock market crash of 1929, Congress enacted laws to ensure that never again would a handful of individuals control the U.S. economy so tightly. In 1933, Congress passed the Glass Stea-gall Act to break up privately owned banks into separate divisions, creating the commercial and investment banks that we know today. The investment area of the Morgan Bank ultimately became Morgan Stanley.

Johnston remembered me, but it didn't seem to help much when I faced two blond, handsome recruiters in a hot little cubicle at Harvard weeks later. Their demeanor made it immediately clear they had little interest in me. They asked a few perfunctory questions, and then one of them said: "Do you have any questions for us?"

I knew this signaled the end of the brief, fruitless interview. So I answered: "Yeah, why does Morgan Stanley only hire Face Men?"

They both looked at me. "What's a Face Man?" one asked.

I laughed. "You know, guys like you. Who are always doing this." And I ran my fingers through imaginary locks of blond hair and threw my head back as if I were flipping the hair out of my eyes. I'd seen the gesture from guys like them a million times.

"The women swoon!" I said with another laugh. "All my life I've been picking up your leftovers at bars. But it's guys like me who do all the work. You Face Men just get all the credit. All I've seen from Morgan Stanley is Face Men. Who actually does the work?"

They both broke into laughter. The mood relaxed instantly.

"Hey, listen! We work. We work hard! It's not our fault the women love us!" they protested. When I left the interview, we were fast friends. When I got home that afternoon, I found a message inviting me to a follow-up interview at Morgan Stanley in New York. While I was there, Charles Johnston dropped by the meeting room and casually told my interviewer: "Hey, he's pretty good. Already knows his product."

A few weeks later, I was packing again, tucking my Harvard books into a box and moving from Boston to New York City.

FROM MORGAN STANLEY

TO KIDDER SPY

N MID-1897, I was twenty-nine, and Manhattan enthralled me. Morgan Stanley's office was on the Avenue of the Americas in Midtown. I moved first to the Upper West Side, to an apartment on Seventy-fourth and West End Avenue that belonged to a classmate from Harvard. He and I had traveled for five months in China after graduation. For a while I looked at apartments in the city, but they were expensive. Twelve hundred a month for a small one-bedroom! Even though technically I could afford it, I just couldn't justify spending that amount of money on rent when I knew I'd hardly be home. After four months of bunking with my friend, I moved to the Fort Greene neighborhood of Brooklyn.

Fort Greene was essentially a huge slum. Some streets had been slightly gentrified, and I rented a one-bedroom apartment on one. Still, a few doors down was a rooming house. Farther down the block was the Brooklyn Academy of Music, and across the street from it a huge welfare hotel that was also a drug den. Gunfire erupted there frequently. I got used to the contrasts of New York: middle-class people dressed in finery on their way to a classical music concert stepping around drug dealers mumbling promotions of their wares, pimps pushing young girls forward, and prostitutes working the doorways and corners. It was a fairly dangerous neighborhood in 1987. On the subway, punk kids always carried giant ghetto blasters, the trains and stations were marred with graffiti, a line of telephone booths right outside the station never worked because someone had just crowbarred the coin boxes, and shouts and scuffles from muggings were often heard.

I lived in a newly renovated apartment complex in an old building right above the Fulton Street subway station. Gangs hung out in the station entrance, and often pounced on commuters. In a way it was like passing through groups of trolls demanding a toll. I wasn't a likely target, and was never threatened. I think the sight of a respectable black man in a suit defused the gang kids. If they played a ghetto blaster loud and I asked them to turn it down, they complied. For the most part the gang kids mugged other kids, and were themselves mugged by older guys who lived and did drugs at the SRO. The gang kids were half Latino and half black in number. I took to thinking of the black kids as vampires because they only came out at night. Daytime, the streets were Puerto Rican territory. Meanwhile, the gentrified shops and businesses were run mainly by gay white men. The owners of the gift store where I had my packages delivered both died of AIDS. Up the street, a Jamaican woman opened a little place that featured jazz music. When the gang kids with their ghetto blasters came in, she'd chide them in her Jamaican accent. It was the first time I became aware of the tension between American blacks and West Indian blacks. It was sometimes funny to hear the Jamaican owners of local coffee shops yelling at the people who worked for them, calling them lazy American blacks. The workers and customers then cursed the "damn Jamaicans."

My fourth-floor apartment was a railroad flat—no part of it was wider than ten feet across. A window in the front rendered the living room nearly unusable because of the noise from the street and the subway. The room rocked and the windows rattled so loudly with each passing train that I couldn't hear myself talk. I have no idea how anyone lived on lower floors.

Right after I moved to Fort Greene, I bought a small kitchen table in Manhattan. I flagged taxi after taxi, but none would take me home. I rode the subway with the table. As I left the station, I passed a girl talking on a pay phone. A round-faced black kid of about twelve or thirteen ran at her and grabbed her purse. The girl screamed, and without thinking, I dropped the table and ran after the boy. The purse snatcher threw the bag over the turnstiles to a cohort. I knocked the boy down and chased the second guy, who then threw the purse to a third person. The third guy jumped onto the tracks and scrambled away on the opposite platform. I jumped after him and immediately saw a sign reading THIRD RAIL LIVE. I had no idea what that meant. I landed where the thug had landed, petrified to move. Gingerly, I retraced my moves to the platform. The second mugger had disappeared, but other bystanders had grabbed the boy. Some of them thought I was his accomplice and grabbed me, too. We all went upstairs. My table was still there, along with the victim, who cleared up my identity to the police. It never occurred to me that a simple mugging could be so orchestrated and involve so many people, including a child. Already, New York had taught me something.

* * *

FROM SEPTEMBER TO December, I sat in a classroom at Morgan Stanley for eight hours a day being drilled in the inner workings of Wall Street. The company ran a remedial training program for MBAs who hadn't learned the nuts and bolts of investment banking in graduate school. I was in seventh heaven because instead of case studies and touchy-feely discussions about whether workers communicated well, we crunched numbers. Fifty of us filled the class: twenty-six MBAs and twenty-four Japanese exchange students. Many of the students were tall, handsome Protestant white men with blue eyes and a shock of sandy or blond hair that they frequently flipped back with a twist of the neck—the Face Men.

Living in Brooklyn made it hard to socialize after work. The subway barely ran late at night, and I could never hire a taxi in Manhattan to take me to Fort Greene. But partying after hours with my fellow trainees soon became as important to the job as the classes we took during the day. Wall Street was flush with money, and young brokers and traders and analysts flooded out of offices every evening to the bars and restaurants at the South Street Seaport. When the weather was warm, the historic pier complex would grow so packed with people that it was impossible to walk. Someone always got arrested for drunk and disorderly mayhem. Hundreds of women vied fiercely to attract attention from traders. Most every night, sooner or later, a girl would climb up on a bar and start dancing. Stripteases were not uncommon. It was a virtual Roman orgy. It was exciting then, but today I don't even remember the names of the bars.

Life was uncomplicated, boisterous, easy. Every day someone in the trading program called a livery car service and ordered a couple of limousines. The sleek black vehicles idled outside Morgan Stanley at 5:00 P.M., and groups of us rode to Chinatown, where we'd tuck into Peking duck. We'd move on to a nightclub or bar, wading through the crowds until all hours— or until we got lucky. That was the sum total of our evenings—men and women chasing each other. We hit different places, depending on the day of the week. Some nights we changed direction and went to Moran's, a huge meat market down by the World Trade Center; if it was balmy, and we were bored with the seaport, we'd head for an outdoor place in Tribeca.

One of my fellow trainees, a macho, gung-ho army veteran, coined the phrase we used to describe our technique with women in the bars—"Drop the H-bomb!" We'd all been to Harvard, and we exploited that credential ruthlessly. To the women, it was a sign on our foreheads that read MARRIAGE MATERIAL. For us, it was a guaranteed entrée. "Like a neutron bomb which wipes out humans but leaves buildings standing, the H-bomb leaves brunettes standing but puts blondes on their backsides," we'd shout in the limo. It worked very simply. We'd wade into a crowd with a beer in each hand, start talking to a girl, and casually mention we'd gone to business graduate school. If the girl asked, "Which one?" we paused, looked at her with slight curiosity and then said quietly, "Harvard." Someone scored with the H-bomb every night. For the Morgan Stanley Face Men, there was never any question. They'd be out of the bars with a new girl within half an hour. For me, it was different. The cultural gap was real—there were few minorities and fewer black women in the Wall Street world. Later, when we started frequenting New York's velvet-rope nightclubs, being black became a ticket. It was cool to be black, the clubs wanted blacks to keep the dance floor hopping, but they didn't want hip-hop kids. The clientele had to look good, respectable and intellectual, so that the atmosphere seemed elite. I was the perfect combination—a mature black man in an expensive suit. It meant automatic entrée to the clubs. Looking back, I can't remember a time I waited to get into a club. Some nights I was shooed in while groups of hipper blacks cooled their heels. As a result, people wanted to hang with me and girls wanted to be on my arm. The women in our training program asked to go out with me after work because they knew they couldn't get into the hot clubs on their own.

I got caught up in the game. I'd walk up to a velvet rope and tell the bouncer I was on his list. When he asked my name, I'd say, "The Wolf." Pretty soon they knew the nickname or pretended they did. I owed it to the bartender at a club called Nell's. I hated to dance, so I'd sit at the bar and ply women with pickup lines. The bartender called me a lone wolf in waiting. I perfected an act that worked amazingly well. I'd wait until I saw an interesting woman, then I'd send her a drink. Usually she came over to talk or thank me, and I'd stare at her and say: "When I walk alone on high mountains, for whom do I seek, if not you?" And then I'd kiss her. It worked because I knew that if you wanted something, you had to press your case immediately, not allow room for thought or alternatives.

It was the last gasp of the 1980s, and people were still flush with money and excess was everywhere. People thought it was all going to last forever, and so they had no worries. Drugs were rampant on Wall Street and in the clubs. I'd gotten drunk twice at MIT and hated the loss of control. It made me agitated, angry, uncertain. I need to be in charge of my faculties at all times. I was an admitted control freak. Drugs were worse than alcohol, and I never had the desire to surrender like that again. In the clubs, I was the picture of military bearing. Women were my only vice. Yet everywhere, people handled cocaine, passing it around, laying it out, snorting it. Bathrooms became drug dens. Even at the more refined clubs, the drug trade oozed into the bar and onto the dance floor. When you sat down at a new table, the cocktail waitress often had to brush away the grit of cocaine from previous occupants.

Nell's was a long, narrow club with couches near the front door, a bandstand to one side, tables for food toward the back and a kitchen at the end. Often when I arrived, I'd walk past couples groping each other on the couches. Someone's pants or blouse was always open, skirts were hiked, limbs were asprawl, and there were no qualms about openly fondling breasts and between legs. Downstairs there was another room with couches, and it seemed like someone was always having outright sex down there.

Stories about the Studio 54 era and movies had dulled the shock of the New York club scene for me, and this drug-and-orgies wildness struck me as clichéd. The downtown cocaine and sex scene didn't differ a great deal from Fort Greene's mean streets of drugs, subway filth and muggers. Both just meant that everything I'd seen in gritty movies about New York was real.

I concentrated instead on the training program at Morgan Stanley. A woman named Janet Dousma ran the program. One day, cops appeared at the office, asking to talk to the Japanese students. One of them had apparently accused a prostitute of stealing his wallet. They all lived in a hotel at Thirty-third and Lexington, an area that was hooker haven. The police learned that the prostitute had a standing date with the man, and he'd forgotten his wallet the last time. She was just holding it for him. The cops brought the guy's intact wallet to him at work. Since I'd been tutoring some Japanese students, Janet Dousma asked me to talk to them. I went to their hotel and warned them about prostitutes and AIDS. Ten guys quickly pulled out condoms and said, "Oh no, we use these!" They weren't worried, and not about to stop. Their hotel rooms and meals were paid for, the yen was very strong, and they could afford three or four streetwalkers a night. One fellow faced the ultimate embarrassment. His fiancée and soon-to-be in-laws visited from Tokyo. As he ushered them to his hotel, a tall, black prostitute wearing fishnet stockings and a red leather miniskirt began hailing him by name. His explanation of mistaken identity fell flat when the prostitute followed the family to his room. She sized up the fiancée and declared herself available for a threesome, if he would pay extra.

Our daytime activities paled in comparison. During class we learned how to determine the value of different bonds, how to compare corporate and Treasury bonds, how to measure risk, how to determine the price of a security. We were taught how to use concepts like the present value of a bond or the duration of a bond as indicators of value and risk. None of these areas were covered well in business school. Morgan Stanley also trained us in cold-calling customers—how to persuade someone to spend time on the phone listening to us pitch securities. Word spread like wildfire that only a limited number of trading positions were available. Soon everyone in the class talked about nothing else. There were three kinds of positions on the trading floor—a trader (you were given a certain amount of the firm's capital to invest for profit), a salesman (you sold securities to customers), or in marketing or research (supporting roles). Traders earned a percentage of their profits. Salesmen earned commissions based on the volume of securities they sold.

Toward the middle of the training program we were supposed to declare our preference—trading, sales, marketing or research. I wanted to trade; it would be the best place to show off my technical skills. We discussed openly what everyone wanted to do after the training course. When I said I wanted to be a trader, my fellow students quickly informed me that the six open trading slots had already been filled—with six of them. "Sorry, Joe, but I've already been promised this position and he's been given that position. . . ." By October I was frustrated because it seemed clear that I'd be relegated to marketing or research, or sales. Sales concerned me because I'd heard that white money managers did not like black salesmen. Since Morgan Stanley was the ultimate Face Man firm, it put Face Men in sales jobs. You could literally walk through the office and identify the traders and salesmen by their degree of Face. So it was beginning to look like I'd be stuck in research and marketing.

Then, in mid-October of 1987, the whole world changed.

ON A MONDAY, six weeks into the training program, classes were suddenly canceled because all the "teachers" were urgently needed at their desks. The market was imploding. On the trading floor, people ran amok, screaming and shrieking; traders cried and wailed at their desks. They bawled, literally. Grown men stormed around shouting, "What the fuck is going on?" Every other word out of everyone's mouth was "fuck." Hearing all the excitement, we students wandered onto the Fixed Income trading floor, bright-eyed, bushy-tailed and stupid. It was my first time on a trading floor. One of our classmates ventured: "It's going to crash! Let's try to sell short some securities!" We traipsed across the street like a group of teenagers at the state fair and rushed up to the Equity trading floor. We wanted someone to take our order to sell securities. We'd worked it out in the elevator—we were going to pool our money and sell a huge block of IBM. None of us owned any IBM, but that didn't matter. Such a trade is called "selling short," or selling something that you don't actually own. You promise to deliver the item in the hopes that in the meantime, it will drop in price. If we had committed to sell IBM at $10, and then the price dropped to $8, we would buy at $8, deliver to the customer for $10, and pocket the $2 difference as profit.

But we couldn't just sell short IBM. Any time you initiate a trade, you have to balance your move with an opposite action. That is called "hedging." If you buy a bond, for example, you must sell something else to balance the cost of that bond. Buying the bond creates a debt; you hedge that debt by raising cash through the sale of something else. On that Monday, as we plotted to sell short IBM, we decided to hedge our position by buying options. The added advantage of this was that if IBM's price went up instead of down, we could buy IBM at a lower price guaranteed by the options. It seemed like a great idea, just like they'd taught us in class.

Except that no one would take our order to sell short. The idea violated rules against selling a stock on a down-tick. It was exploitative. Brokers screamed at us, blisteringly mad at our interference. We shifted gears, deciding excitedly to conduct the whole transaction in the options market by buying the right to sell IBM—something called "puts" on Wall Street—at a price just below where the stock was currently trading. Then we'd buy what are known as "calls" at a lower price. Such a move was called a straddle. Our ideas were a perfect illustration of the myriad complicated ways money is made on Wall Street by layering trade upon countertrade, by interweaving strategies to bounce figures across balance sheets, by juggling stocks, bonds, commodities, or parts or all of the above, until they either cancel each other out or combine to reproduce. Either way, until profit results. If we'd been standing there with textbooks, we couldn't have done better.

But no one paid any attention to us. No one would take our order, and a shouting match erupted with a freaked-out trader who was getting reamed by the market. We were just a bunch of MBAs trying to make some money. The head of the Equity area descended on us in a rage, demanding our names, threatening to have us all fired. We fled in all directions, scurrying like cockroaches for the elevators. We dashed back across the street to Fixed Income. One of the students grabbed a free phone and called his broker to place our order for options puts and calls. We did okay—after splitting the profit we each earned about $1,700. I felt the bloodrush of Wall Street excitement, and learned a valuable lesson—the best time to make money is when everything is falling apart.

What we missed in the adrenaline high of that afternoon was that the crash spelled the end for most of us. Within two years, nearly everyone in my training class would lose their job as Wall Street retrenched. For me, however, the crash was a godsend. Morgan Stanley's head honchos saw the handwriting on the wall, and decided to winnow the wheat from the chaff in the training program. They laid off trainees before any of us actually made it to the trading floor. The golden boys who thought their jobs were secure enough that they hadn't worried about attendance and grades suddenly found themselves in trouble. Test results became vital. The Face Men didn't understand that, until we all had to take standardized exams like Series 3, Series 7 and Series 63. These are the licensing exams for Wall Street.

Anyone interested in the ugly underbelly of American society should take a look at the candidates for the Series 7 exam. The brokerage industry is filled with ugliness, with flimflam artists and get-rich-quick cons, with people who two days before were auto mechanics or janitors. Most fail the test repeatedly. But anyone can take the Series 7 exam four times, then wait a year and start all over again. We took our Series 7 and Series 3 tests in a classroom that looked like it belonged in the Rikers Island prison. The proctors administered the tests in two, three-hour sessions. I scored well on both tests. After these standardized exams, my Morgan Stanley classmates feared that I might take one of their earmarked jobs. When the time came to declare our job preferences, my friends said things like "Hey, buddy, you know I wanted that position. Why put that down as your first choice? You don't want to do that to me." I wasn't supposed to vie for my first choice of job. Soon we weren't hanging out together, and I found myself no longer invited to the after-work soirees.

At about the same time, a trader was fired for losing a bundle of money. Rumor had it that he "hid tickets," one of the worst crimes on Wall Street. For each trade, a transaction ticket has to be filled out. A trader could try to escape a bad deal by pretending that he'd never gotten into it in the first place; all he had to do was not turn in his ticket. If there was no record of the trade, there was no trade. This is called "hiding the ticket," and it's fraud.

The head of mortgage-backed trading asked Janet Dousma which of her students could leave the training program early to fill the slot. She sent me to meet him. I told him that I wanted to work in mortgages because of my math background, and that I wanted trading and not sales because I preferred a job with an objective standard of measure. I was assigned as an assistant to a mortgage trader named Jim Galgano. Being an assistant was like being a grunt in the army. Assistants were called dogs, and treated as such. Galgano explained it to me.

"Any idea of equal rights as a human being are thrown out the window. You are no longer human. You are a dog. In fact, you no longer have a last name other than dog." He picked up a ruler from his desk and tapped me on the shoulder. "I now anoint you Joe-dog. Your first job—don't take any offense!—is to find a shoeshine guy and get him over here. Look at these shoes! I'm the best trader on Wall Street, I can't walk around like this!"

For the first time, I wanted to fit in. I wanted to be liked and accepted. But my first day on the floor, I discovered that I didn't even have a desk. Though the company had recently moved into new offices, the market crash had put the skids on the purchase of new equipment. In Fixed Income, there were rows of new desks with no phones. No one could move down to make room for me next to Galgano, but I couldn't sit at an empty desk, either.

Nevertheless, I dove into my job. I went to the gym every morning before work and was still in the office for opening bell at 8:00 A.M. I simply restructured my day. I'd leave work at 5:00 in the afternoon and go home to sleep until midnight. Then I'd get up and meet friends at the clubs, partying until 4:30 or 5:00 in the morning. If it was Thursday, when I didn't go to the gym before work, I'd continue to an after-hours club like Save the Robots; which opened at 3:00 or 4:00 A.M. Then I'd go home, change into workout clothes if it was a gym day, then head to the office. I slept only four hours a day. That was all I'd needed ever since I'd had my paper route.

I felt on top of the world, even though being a dog wasn't much fun. But I'd come from a discouraging summer job the year before at the Ford Motor Company to a position on Morgan Stanley's trading floor. I'd gotten the job ahead of anyone else in my training class, all because of merit.

I spent my days fetching coffee, hailing the shoeshine boy, ordering takeout lunches, taking phone messages. In between, I tried to learn a bit here

and there about bond trading. Galgano wasn't much help. I had been assigned to him without his input, and he protested by not teaching me. He
had little to say. He was fascinated with the weather, however. He sat at
his desk talking about The Weather Channel all day and chatting endlessly
about the forecasts. Adjacent to us on the desk was a trader named Tom
Jutebok. He was a braggart and a prima donna who had earned Wall Street's
top accolade—Big Swinging Dick. Superstar traders were anointed with this
most macho of titles. Jutebok was a superstar, always locked in dramatic
deals, always earning obscene amounts of money. Watching him, my ambition doubled. If I could trade, I knew there would be no stopping me. It
was obvious that everyone despised traders because they were arrogant assholes. But because they made so much money, their behavior was usually
overlooked.

Before the month was out, I was dying to work with Jutebok, but a guy
named Lundy Wright was his assistant. Wright had heavy jowls and thick
curls, and his claim to fame was having spent time crisscrossing the country,
counting cards in casinos until he got caught, thrown out of one, and then
hired at Morgan Stanley. We worked side by side, a computer nerd with
no computer and a cardshark. Wright had a desk, though. Frustrated with
Galgano, I stood in my assigned spot at his shoulder and strained to eavesdrop on Jutebok's conversations with Wright. That's how I learned to trade.

News events affected the bond market. Different indicators—unemployment, the consumer price index, the commodity research bureau index, the
gross national product, interest rates, and so on—all had impact. Government has huge influence on the bond market, specifically through the person of the Federal Reserve chairman. Jutebok began his career in research
at Bank of America, where his job was Fed watcher. That meant keeping
an eye on what the Federal Reserve's Board of Governors did with interest
rates. He analyzed and estimated how the Fed would react to inflation, and
when he explained it to Wright, I soaked up his words, too. Jutebok knew
I was listening, and soon took mercy on me. He had a habit of quizzing
Wright, and after a while, started declaring, "Hey, I bet Joe-dog knows!"
Assistants were always the butt of criticism. Jutebok would tell Lundy
Wright: "Lundy-dog, I'm supposed to be training you, but I could better
train Joe-dog." As punishment for failing a question, Lundy-dog would
scurry to find the shoeshine guy. Soon Lundy Wright and I were competing—whoever got an answer wrong would be sent on some mindless chore.
Jutebok waited for us to scurry off, and then he'd get on the public address
system and call out, "Joe-dog, here boy! Here boy!" Wherever I was, I had
to turn and run back to his desk, through the trading floor, past everyone
who knew I was just a dog.

My trainee classmates all got jobs in less prestigious areas of the firm.
But that didn't stop them from joining the chorus. Soon they were all calling
us Joe-dog and Lundy-dog, too.

Working on my feet made it virtually impossible for me to complete one of my tasks, "maintaining the trader's position." This was before computers, and we recorded every transaction, what was purchased, when it was purchased and for how much on a large blotter. With a glance a trader could see whether he was long or short the bond market: Long meant he owned more bonds than he'd sold, and if their price went up, he'd make money. Short meant he'd sold more than he'd bought, and if the price went down, he'd make money.

Normally, a trader's assistant sat next to the trader and recorded his transactions on the blotter as they occurred. The assistant and trader shared a joint phone, so the assistant could listen to the trader's conversations and record transactions. But there was no desk for me next to Galgano, and no phone that was convenient to use. Anyway, I wasn't allowed to sit. I had to stand to the left of Galgano all day, balancing the big floppy blotter in my hands. If I tried to listen in on his calls from a phone extension, I had to guess which line he was using. Sometimes I cut off his calls. Immediately, he'd smack at my hand. I tried to eavesdrop but often couldn't hear what he was saying. He refused to repeat his business dealings to me, complaining that it took too much time. So I struggled to keep up with the blotter, growing increasingly angry and frustrated. I'd so wanted to get off to a flying start, and so far the job was a disaster.

Finally, in March, Jutebok interceded. Two desks appeared for me and Wright. We called them "turrets" because the flat desk with a wall of computer monitors on all sides resembled a castle tower. At last, Wright and I could sit down. With my own chair, phone and monitors, I decided it was time to have my own trading position, too. I was now too far from Jutebok to eavesdrop on his pearls of wisdom. I couldn't talk to Galgano after four months of hearing nothing from him. With my own turret, I had the technical capacity to trade. Mostly, I was keenly aware of our desk's profit and loss, and we were faring badly in the aftermath of the market crash. People had been laid off. I wanted to show my worth before I became a casualty, too. I asked for a trading "position," or a budget to use to conduct trades. I was surprised when the head of Fixed Income agreed. It usually took two years for a trader to earn his own position; now I'd gotten one in six months. Our department head was an absentee manager, one of the very young multimillionaires who'd come to Wall Street in the late 1970s and early 1980s, when the Fed moved to end inflation by raising short-term interest rates. Making money was easy then because the government was so predictable. Everyone just rode the crest of the wave. Many traders made a bundle between 1982 and 1987. Promoted to manager superstars, most succumbed to the life of excess. They partied hard and constantly for years. When I saw them at Morgan Stanley, they looked older than their ages. Our head manager seemed to work two or three days a week, and showed his face on the trading floor even less. But even though it displeased Jim Galgano, he gave me part of Galgano's position to trade.

From the beginning and throughout the summer, I outearned Galgano. I traded mortgages in the Federal National Mortgage Association, known as Fannie Mae mortgages. My fellow trainees congratulated me, hoping that my success would show that they deserved their own trading positions, too. Soon everyone was clapping me on the back and calling me "Money-dog!" I swelled with pride. So naturally I started making mistakes. Not trading mistakes. Social mistakes.

Right after I joined the trading desk, I met a guy named Tony Chung. Tony came from a wealthy Hong Kong family, and worked as a bond trader at Salomon Brothers. But his real calling was as a playboy, and it wasn't long before he quit. Soon after he rang to tell me he'd rebounded and hit the jackpot—family money meant he didn't really need a job, so he'd taken work as a chauffeur for the Elite Modeling Agency. He was surrounded all day by aspiring models and actresses, and he was eager to show off the town to them. But he didn't think he was cool enough, and he wanted my help getting into clubs. Soon Tony and I were riding around all night in Elite limos with Elite girls, hanging around in nightclubs, bars and restaurants with beautiful women. We went to Nell's, Save the Robots, and another place in SoHo called Hole in the Wall, where the entrance was exactly that, and patrons had to crawl through into darkness and wait for someone to pull them out the other side and into a cavernous nightclub. I met Eddie Murphy and Arsenio Hall, and regaled my colleagues the next day with tales of chatting with them. If I left my house, it was to climb into a limousine. My Morgan Stanley superiors wanted a part of this endless supply of luxury and women. Even though I was just Joe-dog, they invited me out for drinks, dinner and partying. It was a real eye-opener. I assumed that the young bloodlust of twenty-four- and twenty-five-year-old trainees explained all the late-night running around. To discover that the older, married traders wanted to do the same was a surprise. After a day of work, they still had the energy to invite me to dinner at a steak and lobster restaurant, complete with limo and expensive wines. Then we'd head for a club, with most of them pulling off their wedding rings and stuffing them into their pockets before wading into the crowd with reckless abandon. They had some discipline—because they had to be at work early, they usually refrained from copious drug use.

Once I won my own position, I curtailed my evenings. Tony and I had been clubbing since December, and he was blowing big money on jewelry and nights out for a bevy of girls and models. But I'd started dating a French woman whom I'd met at Nell's. Now I just went to office and Wall Street parties. I meant to get serious about my career, and decided it was time to put an end to my dog status. My first mistake occurred when I decided that no one at Morgan Stanley other than Jutebok and Galgano could any longer call me Joe-dog. When a trader on the Mortgage desk who worked with Charlie Johnston ordered me to find the shoeshine guy, I stood up and said,

"Who are YOU calling dog?" Everyone stopped to listen. I pointed at Jutebok. "This guy is making $3 million a month and he trained me. If he wants to call me dog, he can call me dog." I pointed at Galgano. "This guy trains me, if he wants to call me dog he can call me dog. But I don't owe you shit. My name is Joseph Jett."

I overstepped. Dogs are not allowed to break their own bonds of dogdom. After that, even Jutebok and Galgano were uncomfortable calling me dog. They'd say it, but without heart. Slowly, I became an outsider. People still shouted heartily to Lundy-dog. He was nonthreatening. But I had upset the social order, and suddenly found myself left out of desk banter.

I learned the hard way that being an assistant is closer to an apprenticeship. I'd studied shaolin kung fu in Boston for years, and knew that if someone had joined the order prior to you, they had seniority. Your skills at the martial arts may be greater, but they remain your big brother and you must obey them. The same is true of bond trading. You may learn from your teacher, you may surpass your teacher, but you still owe him respect and deference. The bond trader wasn't my teacher, but he was my senior. I'd failed to understand that. Instead, I thought it time someone challenged the social order. At first, I was smug. Anyway, I believed I was more comfortable outside the social stratum than adhering to it. But as I asserted myself, resentment grew. People commented on how often I looked at the profit and loss, or P&L, sheet. It was clear I wasn't just looking at my own P&L, but at everyone's. That's when I made my second mistake. P&Ls were known but not openly discussed. Above all, no one ever said, "I outearned . . ." Ostensibly, you weren't supposed to look at anyone else's P&L. Occasionally, Jutebok mentioned someone's P&L, but he was exempt because he was a superstar. I wanted to be like him, to imitate his swagger and boldness. I talked, acted and felt like no one could better me. I bragged. I let people in the office goad me. Jutebok would allow that he was tied down—that his wife watched him—and then he'd say, "Tell us about your social life, Joe." Thus, my third mistake. I bragged about the models, the beautiful girls in the back of limos, the nightclubs. Everyone loved the stories, so I grew indiscreet in the telling. One night at Nell's I met a girl who was fighting with her boyfriend. We retired to her hotel, but in the morning the estranged boyfriend showed up, banging on the door. I couldn't get out of her room until he went away. Lying low with her made me late for work, and when I called the office, I heedlessly explained why I was going to be tardy. When I did get to work at about ten, everyone wanted to know how the adventure had ended. I was too happy to oblige.

I was a braggart, and loved the camaraderie I thought I shared with the guys on the desk. I wasn't the only one. The trading floor was like a junior high locker room. We spent a good part of our day telling raunchy stories and talking trash about sex and women. We'd go around the table, taking turns trying to top each other. The Big Swinging Dicks encouraged the idea that their potency wasn't limited to simply making money. The name pretty much covered the attitude in the office. One salesman took all his clients to strip joints, and paid the strippers to go home with the customers. If the clients were in other cities, he sometimes took such a shining to the strippers that he'd fly them to New York for parties. Whenever someone in the office celebrated a birthday, he arranged for a stripper. Two of Charlie Johnston's traders lived downtown near a joint on Sixth Avenue called Billy's Topless, and they stopped in every night. They never did anything else. One day they'd be urging people at work to join them—"There's this beautiful girl, really beautiful, and she's only going to be there for a week, you guys gotta come see her!"—and the next day one of them would bring his newborn baby into the office. Another trader snorted so much cocaine three or four times a week that his attention deficit became an office joke. He'd order the purchase of a hundred bonds, then wander away from the desk. As a dog, I was often sent to track him down. Usually, I found him having a conversation with someone about girls, sometimes in the back office. The staff there were young women from Brooklyn and the Bronx with tall, teased hair, layers of heavy makeup and long, daggerlike fingernails painted vampire colors. Their job was to collect all the trading chits and blotter notations at the end of the day and enter them into the computers.

All around us, Wall Street was disintegrating. The head of our Fixed Income department complained that our overhead was too high for our revenues—there were too many people in research, too many people trading, too many people employed. In order to build revenue, in the fall of 1988 he decided to boost trading of what are called "loss-leader products." It happened that I traded in that area—the Fannie Mae mortgages. They were pretty generic mortgages, with a slender potential for profit. However, they could be used to create something known by the cumbersome name of Collateralized Mortgage Obligations (CMOs)—another complex spiral of trading strategies, designed for no reason other than to make money. I found myself ordered to conduct trades that didn't look good on my P&L, but would create revenue for the department. All I cared about was my own P&L, though. I wanted to change the strategy so I'd get a better price for my trades. I suggested such to the department head.

"Look, we're all one desk here. Why do we want to do all this paper shuffling?"

The CMOs were labor-intensive, and I decided that the department was conducting them just to give everyone something to do. It was a last-ditch effort. But I didn't appreciate being the point man, the one who had to sacrifice to keep everyone else employed. My critical mistake was in failing to understand how highly Morgan Stanley culture valued team-playing. I'd learned about Wall Street from fast talkers at Drexel, and had assumed that trading was a meritocracy. I expected it to be the land of milk and honey for a black man from my background. I could work on Wall Street and receive a fair shake. But Morgan Stanley's Fixed Income department really existed only to support its Investment Banking department. Over there, it was relationships with customers that counted. Bottom-line numbers were not important—Fixed Income was there to provide a service to customers, whether it made money or not. Cooperation and loyalty were prized. My ego blinded me to that—I just wanted to outperform everyone else. And I couldn't grasp why that was a bad attitude.

IN SEPTEMBER 1988, I met a girl at a nightclub who turned out to be an ex-girlfriend of Charlie Johnston. She wasn't very happy with Johnston, and spent the better part of our evening together telling me unflattering stories about him—that he was a wimp, that he lived at home with his mother, that when she wanted to sleep with him, he refused. This image didn't reconcile with the Charlie Johnston I knew, who acted the tough guy at work.

A few days later, when Johnston shouted, "Hey, Joe-dog, get me some coffee!" I stood up at my desk and hollered: "Get it yourself!" Around me people stopped working and looked up in astonishment, Johnston included. I was tired of being a dog; Joe Jett was a hot bond trader now, a big success who handled huge amounts of money by day and rode in limousines with beautiful models by night. I had decided it was time to end my dogdom. Having gotten everyone's attention, I said carefully, "Hey, Charlie. I met a friend of yours the other night." I then regaled the desk with a vivid description of the girl's affections.

It was a stupid, brash comment, but I was too full of myself to know it. I never stopped to think about the implications of what I was saying. I was going for the laugh, for the shock and then the macho approval I'd always gotten from my co-workers. We spent so much time at work and in social conversation talking trash about sex and women that I'd come to believe there were no lines left to cross. I crossed several that day. I went too far by including my boss in the crude banter. Moreover, I really entered into forbidden territory by stirring up racial demons. I'd forgotten that race and sex are a powerful combination, more dangerous than any other aspect of racism in our society. Clearly, Johnston's ex-girlfriend was a white woman. Not only had I admitted a relationship with her, but I had put myself in direct competition with Johnston, a white man. And I was saying I'd won, that I'd made his ex-girlfriend happy in a way he could not. Johnston probably wouldn't have liked anyone publicly trashing his masculinity. Having a black man do so had repercussions that neither of us expected.

Within days I was informed that my trading position was being eliminated and I would be back to working as an assistant, only this time directly for Johnston. I was on probation and facing a job performance review. Johnston placed me at the end of his desk, with no phone and no chair. Wall

Street was running with rivers of blood at the time. There had already been two rounds of layoffs at Morgan Stanley; people were being cut loose all over the Street. Nobody was hiring, so desperate, disbelieving brokers and traders and analysts scrambled and clawed for phantom jobs. Ivan Boesky, Michael Milken, Drexel Burnham Lambert—the names appeared in news reports everyday, along with tales of shady deals and trading. I was lucky to have a job, so I ate humble pie. I had to clean out my old desk, throwing away an array of books on trading, kung fu journals, weight-lifting and bodybuilding magazines. It was stupid to keep them at work—later they would just be grist for gossip about me. I was scared, anxious, deflated. I'd made money, but it didn't matter. Because of a crude comment, I was stripped of my desk, my phone, my position to trade. It had nothing to do with my performance; it had nothing to do with merit.

I tried to quietly encourage Johnston to give me responsibilities, but he didn't have any to share. So I sat, every day, trying to gin up a job. One computer was available, so I stayed late to borrow it to analyze bonds. It seemed that a lot of the bonds rotting in our inventory and considered unsellable were actually valuable under certain conditions. I tried putting a research project together, but failed. Then I tried taking portions of the CMOs and slicing them into further pieces and then rejoining them into synthetic bonds. That didn't work either, but the basic principle stuck with me. My efforts seemed increasingly hopeless. I was humiliated, my empty desktop seeming to glow like a neon sign at everyone who walked by. I tried to approach the head of our department, but he just waved me away. "Look, you belong to Charlie. I'm not going to interfere."

I quit running around all night and quit telling wild stories in the office. Another round of layoffs hit. A few weeks later, at the end of April 1989, Charlie Johnston called me into his office. The problem, he said, was my social habits. "If you want to have a social life like that, it's appropriate if you work at a place like PaineWebber, but it's not appropriate at Morgan Stanley."

I knew that my social life was just a pretense for letting me go. There was no point in protesting. I went to my meager desk. Unfinished particle board covered the spot where the phone should have been installed. Jutebok, who rarely spoke to me, came over to shake my hand. "Hey, Joe-dog, I tried to put in a good word for you, but you've got to have someone willing to back you up, and I've already got Lundy-dog. But hey, you'll do okay." As I left the office, I looked at my P&L once more. It was still higher than anyone else's. But I understood now that making money counted less than fitting in.

THE JOB MARKET was terrifying. I wasn't a golden boy, but I'd had a year of good profits. Traders are fairly marketable as long as they make money.

I immediately sent out résumés, and landed three or four interviews that I thought went very well. But each time, when I called to follow up, the interviewer had had a brutal change of attitude. I survived four rounds of interviews at Donaldson, Lufkin & Jenrette. Some of the people there remembered me from graduate school. When the interviewer finally told me over the phone that he wasn't interested in me any longer, I pleaded with him. "I thought I was a very good fit. I thought I had a very good interview and everyone seemed positive. I know you guys have rejected me, but if I'm making some sort of mistake, can you help me out? Did I rub someone the wrong way?"

He paused. "I'll be honest, Charlie Johnston is really bad-mouthing you. We called for a reference and they really ripped into you. Charlie Johnston says that as far as he's concerned, you're never gonna work on Wall Street again. They said you claim you got out of the training program early and that it's not true. They said you claim you got the highest score in the training program, and that's it's not true. They said your résumé is full of lies. They said you sit around all day reading muscle magazines and kung fu books. I really liked you, but if people are saying things like that about you, then there's nothing that I can do."

Angry at the jobs I'd lost already, I felt powerless to stop Johnston from blackballing me. In my foul mood, I was just looking for a way to strike back. I'd just moved from Fort Greene to an even tougher neighborhood on the Lower East Side of Manhattan. Directly across the street was a crack house. People sold drugs on stoops, in vestibules, and in the well beneath the front stairs. I'd lived there less than a month when a female friend had her purse snatched as she rang my doorbell. Another day my buzzer went off, and I heard a panting, throaty voice pleading for help. Someone was getting beat up in the building vestibule. Some neighbors and I got together to patrol our block. I argued with a drug dealer one night, and the next day the woman who ran the crack house warned me to leave her boys alone. We worked out an arrangement—if they didn't sell drugs on my stoop, I'd stop hassling them and their customers. As we talked, I worried that this heavyset Dominican woman in her sixties was packing a gun.

The week I learned about Johnston's nasty references, I walked past a guy on my stoop at about four o'clock, just as it started to rain. "Yo, got some reds, got some greens, got some Ecstasy. Brother man, why don't you help a brother out? I've got all types of goods." Angry already, I exploded: "Who are you calling brother? If I'm your brother, then you're committing genocide against your own race and someone should stop you. Get off my damn doorstep." He waved a beer bottle defiantly. Stupidly, I pushed him off the stoop. He dashed the bottle on the steps. I jumped down and we scuffled near a parked car. He must have been on drugs because he was moving in slow motion, hardly able to fight. I hit him four or five times before he retreated down the street, shouting, "You stay right there. I'm coming back with my nine, and I'll blow your fucking ass off the face of the earth. You stay right there, nobody fucks with me." Defiant, I shouted, "Yeah, you bring your nine," knowing he meant a Glock-9 pistol, and turned to go inside. Suddenly I realized the guy knew where I lived and that he probably would come back. "You want to kill me, you kill me now!" and I ran after him. I must have looked absurd in my Brooks Brothers suit, chasing a street urchin. He repeated the taunt about his gun, but I followed him around the corner anyway, past the cop who stood all day watching the drug dealers, and caught the guy. He ducked under my punch and my arm glanced off him. My dress loafers skidded on the wet pavement, and I landed on my back. He tried to run again; I jumped up and caught him. I pounded on him in fury. Crying, "Wait, wait . . . wait brotherman," he pulled a wad of dollars out of his pocket. "Here, take it all. Take it all." But it was too late. The guy represented everyone—Charlie Johnston, Jim Galgano, Jutebok, Morgan Stanley. Never mind that he was a drug dealer with a Glock-9 who wanted to kill me on my own doorstep. I stooped, crouched, and put all my energy into what I hoped was a final blow aimed at his throat. But I missed and my fist went into his mouth. My knuckles and fingers bled profusely. The drug dealer pitched forward. A homeless woman on the corner scuffled up, staring at the wad of money on the pavement. "Do you want that? Do you need that? You don't look like you need it." She picked up the money, mumbling, "I didn't see anything" as she disappeared.

I HAD TO cancel a job interview. My hand swelled like a balloon. When I first examined it, I saw white bone poking out of the scraped skin. The swelling covered the wound, which became infected. When I finally went to the doctor, he told me I had a telescoping fracture. Then he dug a white tooth out of my hand. The nurse suggested I get tested for AIDS.

Years later, in the aftermath of the Kidder scandal, the story of my broken hand would end up in the tabloids as a tale of how I punched someone at Morgan Stanley while on a steroid-induced rage over being fired.

CHARLIE JOHNSTON REFUSED to talk to me when I called. I phoned another trader, who protested that he was just repeating Charlie's evaluation of me. He vowed not to stop, even when I told him to check my training records with Janet Dousma. Finally, at the end of June, I called Morgan Stanley's Human Resources department. The managers there apologized profusely and scrambled to cover Morgan Stanley. I wasn't supposed to have been laid off, they explained. I'd only been a last-minute nomination to the latest layoff list. They promised to put an end to the slander, and urged me to come back to Morgan Stanley and interview for jobs in other parts of the company.

After the Fourth of July, Morgan Stanley offered me a job in Portfolio

Management. But I preferred trading. I'd asked Jim Galgano to replace Charlie Johnston as my reference. He told interviewers that I'd worked diligently and earned money during a period when most traders were losing. Soon I found myself with two other job offers, at Smith Barney and First Boston. I had sent out other résumés, and I wanted to see what interviews or offers they might turn up before I chose between the two jobs on the table.

First Boston was falling apart. It had been through three different CEOs. The economy was part of the problem, but mostly it was due to First Boston's own conservative culture. While Mortgage departments at other firms were trading high-risk, high-profit mortgages, First Boston insisted on sticking to the old methods. Kidder Peabody and Bear Stearns were cleaning up with mortgages so risky and profitable that they were called "Nuclear Waste" on the Street. The name referred to the fact that nobody wanted them on their desk for long. They allowed Kidder and Bear Stearns to go from last place to first in mortgage trading profits.

Before I broke my hand, I'd developed the habit of drowning my sorrows at a score of weekly unemployment parties at the Harvard Club in Manhattan. The parties replaced the South Street Seaport frenzies. So many alumni had lost their jobs that they flocked to the club looking to network, pick up tips and run through mock interviews. People scoured the bulletin boards and the newsletter. By the end of nearly every day, thirty or so unhappy, unemployed graduates loitered around. Someone would suggest a local bar or restaurant, and off we went to commiserate. That summer was really the last time I had a lot of contact with my ex-classmates. It seemed that 20 or 30 percent of my class were jobless. I remembered that the class bulletin in 1987 said a record 40 percent of graduates had gone to work on Wall Street. By 1991, about 6 percent of them were left.

We sat in the bars, commiserating about unemployment, until drink and the late hour pushed the talk toward heartfelt conversations about why it was time to get married. For many of my classmates, it seemed to amount to one reason: "I'm losing my hair!" As soon as these macho guys noticed their hair getting thinner, they decided they'd better land a cute girl. Many had convoluted explanations for why they wanted to marry a ditsy blonde. Several had dated our female classmates at Harvard, and didn't want to marry anyone like that. Too stubborn, too argumentative, too headstrong. I pined for an ex-Harvard classmate who herself always pined for someone else.

I'D SENT MY résumé to the Fixed Income department at Martin Fridson, an established mutual fund company, and was cheered to hear from a manager named Hugh Lamle. He had a proposition: Fridson was prohibited from doing business with a large number of pension funds because the assets in those funds were set aside for management by minority-owned firms. Lamle ran down a list. They wanted not to hire me, but to set me up as a minority corporation. Martin Fridson's firm would provide the back-office operations, the research staff, and run the entire operation. I would be the Face Man. A black face.

I must have shown how upset I was because he began rattling off the names of several minority-owned firms that he said were, in truth, just fronts. Black faceplates either jointly or wholly owned by a major white firm that in reality did all the work and controlled the purse strings. But I had only two years of experience. Lamle quickly pointed out that most of the titular managers of black-owned firms lacked experience. He gestured at his list. "This guy was a lawyer, for God's sake. He doesn't know anything about investment. The women-owned firms are worse. Look, she was an interior designer a year ago. Her husband runs that fund. He's a portfolio manager at Fidelity. I'd let her pick my pillows but not my stock. He's making the investment decisions."

I didn't want to be a black faceplate, and I told Lamle that I was capable of handling investments myself. I left his office in deep doubt, and for a month agonized over the proposal. My gut reaction was an image of myself opening doors for white people while shuffling my feet and crying, "Mammy, I'm from Alabamy, gimme your money!" On the other hand, if I could structure the deal to give me real power and independence, was it truly immoral? I liked the notion of working for myself.

I went back and forth over it in my mind. I knew perfectly well that I had a two-year track record on the Street. If I were white and went to a pension fund and said, hey, I have two years of experience in the investment business, let me handle all your money, they'd laugh me out the door. Yet this proposition meant I was tempted by affirmative action, minority set-asides, all the things I had warred against. There's no question that the plan would have made me wealthy. Fridson was prepared to set me up, and all I had to do was take my 5 percent off the top. It was money for the taking. Why should I turn it down? Lots of people have doors opened for them, paths smoothed, the way paved by some social status. In my case it's color. At Harvard I had countless classmates whose fathers and grandfathers guaranteed that their offspring had enviable advantages and connections. Why should I turn down an offer simply because my grandfather's legacy was race and not country club ties?

A few weeks later, in August, I went to a get-together of ex-Harvard classmates. I had the Martin Fridson proposition, and the First Boston, Smith Barney and Morgan Stanley offers on the table, but I didn't know what to do. None was particularly stellar. I wanted advice. At these gatherings, we always discussed job prospects, offers and career trajectories. I explained my moral quandary over setting up a shop to take advantage of minority set-asides, hoping as I talked to justify the proposal to myself. My classmates had been in courses with me where we'd analyzed case studies involving affirmative action. They knew my views. A dozen of my section-mates sat around me, and I could see the disappointment in their faces. My integrity was at stake. "Joseph. I have to tell you. I can't believe you'd do that." It was a classmate who often had asked for my opinion on affirmative action case studies in class discussions. "I think you should do it," a woman countered, but I caught a flash of her dismay. She averted her eyes.

I couldn't take the Martin Fridson offer. I called the guy back and gave him a list of other business school classmates who might be interested.

I CHOSE FIRST Boston over Smith Barney because I would be number four in a three-man operation. I'd be working on the Mortgage desk, and my job was to develop new ways to structure bond deals to compete with Nu-clear Waste. The job was highly technical and required mathematical and analytical expertise. My new manager warned me that it was also a fractious group of three people who didn't like each other very much. He wanted us to compete, he said, and at year's end would choose one to run the oper-ation. The winner would have the right to form his own team—meaning, to get rid of the others. The scheme appealed to me because it carried a one-year deadline for promotion.

First Boston had let go of a great many of its talented workers—they were simply too expensive to employ. My competition was what was left; people who ordinarily would never work in the highly technical arena of Fixed Income. Gina Hubbell was a lawyer, a fact which made me smirk when I heard it. Gordon Ritter was the son of a corporate bigwig who'd gotten his first job on Wall Street as a salesman covering his father's com-pany. Now he was in charge of marketing mortgages. At Morgan Stanley, marketing was traditionally an area where women worked, and traditionally an area that meant your career was going nowhere. Gary Reback managed the computer system, writing programs to create derivative securities. He had only a bachelor's degree.

A lawyer, a marketing guy, a computer geek. I thought I had an obvious advantage over each of them.

WHEN I STARTED at First Boston, I knew only one thing for certain: don't socialize. Don't reveal anything personal. Don't talk about what you do after-hours, don't hang out with co-workers. Work was all work. It hap-pened that my new policies went unnoticed because the other three hated each other anyway. There was no banter and no bonding. We all knew that at the end of the year, someone was going to win and fire everyone else. The decision would be completely bottom-line oriented—who had made the most money. When it came time to dump this deadwood, I wouldn't be firing friends. It was going to be a meritocracy.

On my first day in September 1989, the manager walked me toward my new desk to introduce me to Gina, Gordon and Gary. Seeing us coming, all three got up and walked off the floor. On my desk was a letter, dated the previous April. In it, my three co-workers complained about the hiring of someone named Alan Galishoff. "Given our desire to remain lean and mean, we feel that it is unnecessary to hire an additional CMO structurer, at least for the remainder of 1989," the letter said. They didn't need a fourth colleague, hiring Galishoff would disrupt group cohesiveness; the three were prepared to settle their petty squabbling and work together. Galishoff was supposed to get the job I'd just taken, but he'd never been hired. I tossed the letter in the garbage. For the next two years, each morning, a copy of that letter was waiting for me on my desk.

A meeting that afternoon demonstrated that the three hadn't resolved their petty squabbling. They blamed each other for everything. Gina Hubbell assembled the prospectus—called a "red herring"—that informs investors of how the bonds are expected to behave. It was a horrible, boring task. Each prospectus took hours to prepare. The job kept her in the office until late at night (which made me believe she was responsible for replacing the daily Galishoff letter), mostly waiting around to proofread the final copy. It was really a clerical task, so Hubbell wrote children's books at night. She obviously coveted Gordon Ritter's job. If he disappeared to the men's room, she'd announce the marketing program over the PA system. Ritter, a tall, Nordic blond, would hear and come rushing back, clutching his pants. Gary Reback, the computer guy, reminded me of Woody Allen—whining and demoralized. But he had a crude sense of humor, and to myself, I began calling him El Sabat, for saboteur, because I soon suspected him of sabotaging other people's efforts—erasing computer files, changing deal parameters. Ritter accused Reback of failing to structure bonds according to customer parameters. Soon Ritter was again demanding that Reback be fired. Then Reback sided with Hubbell in her effort to oust Ritter. Meanwhile, I kept to myself, working on new ways to structure bonds to compete with the Nuclear Waste so successful at Kidder and Bear Stearns. First, however, I had to learn to operate the computer system and to structure securities, so I was dependent on Reback. But he refused to teach me a skill that I could use to take his job. I appealed to the Research department for help. Ritter concluded that with my allies in Research, we could oust Hubbell and Reback both. But I wanted to take no sides. Let them destroy themselves. My intention was merely to understand what they were doing, overwhelm them and fire them.

The opportunity for anyone who was prepared to work hard was obvious. Wall Street operated like an ultimate pyramid scheme. The middle managers were partners who had started on the Street in the early 1980s and risen to where they were no longer producers but took home the lion's share of the pay. Now they came to work only twice a week. There was no need for more, because they didn't actually do anything—they didn't interact with customers, didn't make investment decisions. It would be two years before these absentee middle managers started getting fired.

When I'd been at First Boston for three months, an intact team of traders was hired from Salomon Brothers. They'd left Salomon en masse to form a boutique investment firm, and that firm had been bought by First Boston. The Salomon guys built a glass-walled compound in the middle of the trading floor. First Boston employees were banned from their fortress. The Salomon vets never came out. They conducted their own business, and they were keen on high-risk leveraged transactions. First Boston had lost its leadership in this area because it was so conservative. But the market had gone from being relationship driven to value driven. First Boston was still only interested in customer-oriented deals, the ones based on a salesman selling securities to his child's godfather. The Salomon Brothers team had no interest in customers at all. They wanted to do trades that ignored customers and used First Boston's own capital to invest in high-risk futures and options. They didn't need to talk to anyone. They just needed access to First Boston's capital.

I had interviewed with the Salomon Brothers group before they came to First Boston. I understood we were ineffective in the market, and that our manager wasn't around to run the show. So I put together a number of lucrative structures, believing I was just doing my job as directed by our manager. For months I worked on a classic "Harvard B-School" competitive strategy analysis—examining what our competitors were doing. I reverse-engineered Kidder and Bear Stearns deals, taking them apart to see how they had been built. Then I put together the same deals myself. They appeared very lucrative. But our Research department decided that these derivative securities were too risky for our customers. Our clients counted on us for plain vanilla investments. But Research didn't like Nuclear Waste. They agreed the product had a big margin for profit, and that we could sell them to our customers. But they'll turn around and bite our customers in the future, they said. And the customers will remember that. We're a long-term relationship–oriented company, they decided, and we'll pay for this in future.

Investors Daily magazine ranked the research analysts at investment houses, and First Boston was always ranked high, so the department had a lot of power. When it said no, that was it. I had to watch as our customers flocked to our competitors to buy. So I redoubled my effort. I was determined to figure out how Kidder and Bear Stearns were making so much money with Nuclear Waste. I wasn't interested in long-term customer coddling. My horizon extended one year. I pored over every mortgage structure produced on Wall Street for the last two years. There were about 260, and I hoped my analysis would show what kinds of securities were selling. At the time, a trader normally structured a bond deal by choosing from four different bonds with four different maturation dates—maturity in four years, in seven years, in ten and in thirty years. It just depended on what he thought he could sell, or what a specific customer wanted. Each maturation bracket is called a "tranche," French for a cut of the pie. Soon I uncovered that Kidder and Bear Stearns had expanded the number of tranches from four to as many as twelve. Thus they could carefully structure a security for a particular customer. It also allowed them to put all of the security's risk in one tranche—the Nuclear Waste portion. If only four tranches existed, all four investors shared equal risk. A more complex structure meant all the risk could be placed in one tranche, leaving the other investors with a more attractive portion. First Boston didn't know this, and so it didn't know why our plain vanilla securities were no longer attractive. It wasn't brain surgery; if someone is making a huge profit, find out how and copy him. Yet infighting and laziness meant no one else had thought of this first. I compiled a seventy-page analysis, and took it to the Salomon Brothers glass fortress. I told the Salomon Brothers vets what I knew—that with our one-a-week bond deals, First Boston was earning about $200,000. Our rivals were cutting four deals a week at $3 million each. They instructed us to set up the same deals, but Research stepped in again. This time, they pulled no punches, telling our customers not to buy any of our bonds. I couldn't give up on the idea that we might have gone from $200,000 a week to $12 million. I was sure that just having discovered and suggested the possibility would win me the promotion to head our operation. However, I ran afoul of First Boston's determination to protect its franchise, even if we were protecting it from ourselves.

My manager was willing to let me try to sell Nuclear Waste to someone other than First Boston's bread-and-butter customers. I learned that insurance companies are required to report their portfolios to state government, so I wrote to the state, hoping to identify insurance firms that owned Nuclear Waste. Some of them turned out to be our long-term customers, the very ones Research said we had to protect. It didn't matter. My managers insisted that once the waste blew up, those customers would abandon Kidder and Bear Stearns and rush back to First Boston with even higher expectations. I knew I was sitting on a golden egg; I just needed a Jack to carry it down the beanstalk.

I tried a form of corporate espionage. Although I had completely stopped socializing, I began to strike up acquaintanceships with structurers and marketers from other firms, looking for information about their customers. I went to gatherings of the Bond Structurers' Association. I looked closely at my reverse-engineering reports and called up rivals, pretending I was about to do a "slot," or a bond deal, with a customer who already owned one of theirs. We'd chat about the bonds, and I'd ask who else they sold to. Strangely enough, Morgan Stanley traders often came through. I went out for drinks at Billy's Topless with their lead structurer. He was frustrated, he allowed, because he knew all sorts of potential customers, but his sales team was in a shambles because of all the layoffs at Morgan Stanley. He knew that one firm, MMR, was buying all kinds of Nuclear Waste bonds from Kidder, but he'd been unsuccessful in selling any because they didn't like his structures. He couldn't find out why because Morgan Stanley's antiquated computer systems left him unable to reverse-engineer the Kidder bonds. But I could.

MY ANALYSIS REVEALED that one of Kidder's deals did not agree with its prospectus. It didn't behave like it was supposed to. I called Kidder to ask how they managed to get it to work, since the specs in the prospectus didn't add up. It turned out they couldn't get it to work either. Kidder was forced to pull the deal. I immediately informed MMR that their Kidder bonds would not behave as promised. But I could deliver a bond that would.

I made $3 million with MMR in August 1990. A lot of money, and a triumph for me. But it was still only $3 million after a whole year of work. And it happened largely because Research didn't stand in my way—MMR was a dealer, not one of our regular customers. MMR just passed the securities on to widows and orphans, small investors who had little understanding of the risks.

Quickly, we pulled together four deals for MMR. They all sold well, until the fourth one. Reback had to double-check each deal, but since he was out of the office, two fellows from Research approved the structures. When Reback returned, he told a trading manager: "I was just looking at the deal that Joe here put together and I've noticed a little problem. It doesn't work." When we reran the computer program used to structure the fourth deal, there was no backup file for the original work. The fourth structure no longer worked the way it was supposed to, and we couldn't re-create it. I had to kill the deal. It was acutely embarrassing. Hubbell and Reback gloated; the mortgage traders fumed. But no one was more frustrated than me, because I was convinced that my structure had been tampered with. Still, my deals were earning $3 million while Reback's pulled in a paltry $200,000. It was time, I decided, to agitate for my promotion. I knew my manager didn't admire Reback. I learned only then that he and Hubbell had become friendly. In November 1990, he told me he'd decided to honor Hubbell's desire to switch to marketing. After all, she'd been at First Boston for six years and I'd only worked one. It was clear I'd lost. To my mind, I had been beaten by someone who made no money, whose job was to look for smudges on freshly printed prospectuses, who couldn't cope with highly technical calculations.

I decided to look for another job.

* * *

THE RESEARCH MANAGERS at First Boston had often said, "Look, if you want to structure these kinds of deals, why don't you go work at Kidder or Bear Stearns?" So I called Kidder, Peabody & Co.

Michael Vranos ran Kidder's Mortgage operation. He invited me for an interview during the second week of November, told me he could match what I was earning at First Boston but not pay more, and we shook hands on the deal. Greedy, I decided to seek competing bids. I should have known better. I went to Shearson Lehman, and while waiting in an anteroom, heard my interviewer on the phone next door. "No, I'm telling you, I have his résumé right here. Joe Jett! He's going to be here any minute. Joe Jett!" I said, "I trust you weren't talking to anyone at First Boston." The interview consisted of him stuttering and me, furious, staring at him. I rode the subway back to the First Boston building, and when I arrived, my card key didn't work. I couldn't get in the office. When someone else came out, I slipped through the door. Reback smirked and asked if I'd ever met anyone named Lee at Shearson Lehman. Lee had been Reback's college roommate. Fifteen minutes later, my manager called me into his office.

"Look, we've had a lot of layoffs here, and morale is very, very low. If someone is intending to leave, I don't think it's right or fair to everyone else to keep them here. Since it's apparent that you intend to leave, we prefer that you just leave now." A guard waited outside his door for me. I wasn't allowed to clean out my desk; everything would be sent. As I was escorted out, Reback and Hubbell waved at me through the glass doors.

I DIDN'T TELL my parents that I'd been fired, and I didn't go home for Thanksgiving. My sister called First Boston the next day and found out.

Since I had a handshake agreement with Mike Vranos at Kidder, I called and accepted the offer. I went to Kidder Peabody on the Monday after Thanksgiving, expecting to report to an orientation. Instead, Vranos pulled me aside and said he'd heard I'd been fired. Kidder had its own money crisis, too, he allowed. Things were tight, they hadn't made their targets, there was actually a hiring freeze on. He'd still like to have me on board, but now $180,000 was out of the question. He'd only been able to squeeze in an assistant's salary. Could I be flexible? I smiled. Of course I could be flexible. But what did he mean, an assistant's salary? He replied, well, you know, thirty, thirty-three thousand.

Quickly I decided it didn't matter as long as it was a bonus-eligible position. I agreed. Then he told me to give him a call the following Monday. With that, my hopes faded. Clearly, Vranos was backing away from his job offer. We'd shaken hands, but I had no pledge in writing. I thought, what the hell just happened? It had to be more than getting caught looking for a job. Maybe Charlie Johnston had resurfaced. The next morning I called a more senior manager at First Boston, demanding six months' severance pay that had been promised with a handshake when I was hired. He agreed that I had not been fired for cause. He also wanted me to sign a ninety-day noncompete agreement. With that, he paid me the six months' wages. I took an extended vacation to Brazil.

When I came back to the job market in April, the Persian Gulf war was in full swing, Drexel was about to go down, and another raft of people was being dumped on the pavement in more Wall Street bloodletting. I called Kidder, only to hear Vranos ask again how little money I'd accept. I contacted headhunters. The elite work only with people who still have jobs; they wouldn't see me. So I went to the second tier. They all told me to forget it, nobody was hiring on Wall Street.

One headhunter, a guy named Peter James, seemed to be an exception. After receiving my résumé, he called me, his voice excited. "Where have you been?" I remember him saying, "I've been looking for someone like you. I'll have twelve job offers for you by tomorrow." He described listings he held for openings in trading and structuring. We made an appointment to meet the next day. When I arrived, James stared at me as if he'd seen a ghost. "You're Joseph Jett? You like skiing?"

My résumé listed my interests and hobbies as the poetry of Lord Byron, the symphonies of Gustav Mahler, the writings of Nietzsche, skiing, tennis. That's who I am. It also says: Don't assume. I didn't want to be railroaded into an affirmative action category. James asked some perfunctory questions, but he was obviously uncomfortable. Finally, he concluded: "You have a very strong résumé, I'm sure that something will turn up for you."

"I hope so. Each of the opportunities you described last night sounded very interesting."

He sputtered. "I described?" He seemed surprised, and then told me that none of those jobs were quite the right fit. He made motions to look at a list, then said I was overqualified for a couple of the openings. I asked about a trading job he'd described to me the night before as the perfect fit for my talents.

"Trading, trading . . . we don't have anything available in trading. But listen, I'll give you a call, jobs turn up, don't lose faith."

MINORITIES TRADITIONALLY WORK in certain positions on Wall Street, and trading is not one of them. Municipal bond brokerage is, however. Since many big cities are now run by black mayors and black officials, Wall Street likes to send black municipal bond brokers to meet them. Headhunters have to be savvy about these things, and to offer clients the candidates they want. For traders, social commonalties are very important. At Salomon, the traders were rolypoly guys, and the myth said thin people couldn't get jobs on Salomon's trading desk. Morgan Stanley had its Face Men. And why are all trading assistants gorgeous young women? Does it just happen?

At higher salary levels, companies hire people with management potential. They take upward mobility seriously. They want movers and shakers, but they want to be comfortable with who moves and shakes them. Bosses plan to take golden boys under their wings, to mentor, nurture and grow them into future leaders. In the old days, such a worker might eventually marry the boss's daughter.

I was not that guy.

I'D SEEN THIS philosophy work in reverse, too. Once when I was hiring traders, every candidate sent to me from one headhunter was black.

Now, Peter James wasn't willing even to try me with his client list. My résumé made him believe he could send me out for interviews and I'd be snapped up by grateful clients; my face made him realize his clients would call him and wonder, Hey, what are you doing sending us this nigger?

I didn't confront him. I never do with racists. Sure, it's possible to demand that someone in that situation tell you what is going on. I could have told James that I knew his decision was based on racism. But that's not how I handle things. I am confrontational when there is a logic to the confrontation. When there is no proof, only a look, a hesitation and a feeling that I know is rampant across society, then objecting, yelling or otherwise railing against the system will accomplish nothing. I never believe that by confrontation I can make it better for the next black person to come along. I choose to seek another way. If I shout or yell at someone for discriminating against me because I am black, I put that person in a position of power. Instead, I view that person as nothing more than another hurdle that I must overcome. I'm the one with the degrees and the credentials. James was nothing more than a headhunter. If I couldn't get by him, I shouldn't have those credentials.

It's just like all the times I've stood on a New York City street, a black man at night trying to hail a taxi. One evening in the Village, taxi after taxi passed a friend and me. My friend got so angry that he grabbed a garbage can and hurled it into the street, where it slammed into the pavement and rolled around. Traffic screeched to a halt and everyone stared at us. All they saw was a well-dressed black man throwing a garbage can. So who won? Another night a date and I flagged a taxi in the rain. The driver stopped, but when he got a good look at me, he waved us off and sped away, his spinning tires spitting water all over us. Drenched, embarrassed and angry, I ran after the taxi to the next red light. The driver jumped out of the car and fled. I felt like an idiot, standing there in the rain. What was I going to do, beat the guy up?

It doesn't matter if I wear an expensive suit, carry a briefcase and stand outside a Wall Street office building hailing taxis. Empty cabs will whiz by. I long ago realized it does no good to yell, gesticulate at or chase the drivers.

That's not the battlefront. It's elsewhere, where the game is bigger and the stakes are higher. I have to ride the bus, drive my own car or work my way to such affluence that I can order a limousine.

Black people worry too much about the everyday slights that should roll like water off our backs so we can concentrate instead on the higher goals. I didn't come to Wall Street to teach a headhunter how to be politically correct. Who the hell is he to me? Why the hell should he be in a position to judge me? His personal prejudices are an impediment, so I should just remove him from the equation. I began sending my résumé directly to employers.

When I was fired from First Boston, I wondered if race had anything to do with it. Was race preventing me from succeeding? Had my race inhibited me? I thought long and hard about what I'd done, the obstacles I'd over-come, the choices I'd made, the opportunities I'd been given or denied. Was race a factor? I had to answer no. Instead, I was a complex person in a complex environment. I chose to avoid socializing with colleagues, because of my experience at Morgan Stanley. I'd gone from being a hail-fellow-well-met to not socializing at all. In fact, a great deal of the appeal of the First Boston job was because the team so disliked one another. That meant no socializing, which I believed meant there would be pure objectivity. But I'd overcorrected. Socializing was important, as I'd learned when I realized that Hubbell and our manager had become friendly enough for her to win the promotion over me. I was fired because First Boston found out I was looking for another job, because I stumbled into an interview with Reback's college roommate. Was that an act of racism? I didn't think so.

FINDING A JOB as a trader was virtually impossible in the economy at the time. I started replying to ads for financial engineering and computer tech-nicians. I knew I could fall back on my technical skills, doing financial engineering of mortgage securities and interest rate swaps—jobs that were essentially computer programming jobs. I'd write software that would math-ematically describe what a given security was going to do, how it was going to behave. The software would be used to determine whether or not a bond would be profitable, and to analyze that profitability. Though the jobs paid about $60,000, far below what I expected to earn, I would be writing soft-ware that traders used, and that, I felt, would keep me close to the trading desk. But it wasn't my field—and my MBA was worthless since the job didn't require one. I was desperate, however. In April 1991, I landed an interview with John Sun at Kidder, Peabody & Co. Before I went, I called Mike Vranos again, hoping that by telling him someone else at Kidder wanted to hire me, he might extend his offer once more. Vranos said his department was still under a hiring freeze.

John Sun was the head of Kidder's Derivatives area, an esoteric, complex kind of security. It was a highly technical area. John was fascinated when I described how I had reverse-engineered one of Kidder's mortgage deals. "The company may have a stronger need for your knowledge in another department. There's someone who wants to talk to you."

ON MAY 20, 1991, a security guard handed me a pass to enter the Kidder Peabody building where Richard O'Donnell had his office. I tucked the pass into a pocket to keep as a memento. Kidder's corporate headquarters was actually in six buildings in Manhattan, and I was on my way to meet the chief financial officer.

I guessed that O'Donnell was in his mid-forties, an accountant with an MBA and two law school degrees who had spent his entire life working on Wall Street. We sat down to lunch in Kidder's executive dining suite; the table was laid with fine china, and a personal waiter hovered behind each of us. We chatted for a few minutes, both of us a little surprised to discover we had a good deal in common. Though he'd come from a large Irish family, O'Donnell had also grown up in small-town America with a severely strict father.

O'Donnell told me he was deeply suspicious of a man named Edward Cerullo. I'd met Cerullo in passing during my interviews with Vranos, but knew little about him. Cerullo headed the Fixed Income department at Kidder, the area responsible for buying and selling bonds and mortgages. The name of the department, Fixed Income, refers to any security that generates fixed income from set interest rates. Every investment house on Wall Street had a Fixed Income desk, but it was not generally the most lucrative financial arena. For about a year, Cerullo's department had been the only one making any money at Kidder; in fact, since the end of 1990, Cerullo had been earning 110 percent of Kidder's profits. Because the other departments at Kidder all lost money, Cerullo kept Kidder afloat. No matter how intensely his enemies despised and mistrusted him, they couldn't topple him. Kidder's CEO, Michael Carpenter, was one of those who distrusted Cerullo, and at the end of 1989, had ordered the paperwork prepared to fire him. Carpenter even had someone waiting in the wings to replace Cerullo. But before he could act, Cerullo's Mortgage desk, a part of the Fixed Income department, started making money. By the time I met with O'Donnell, Cerullo was earning so much that he had become untouchable.

But O'Donnell wondered about Cerullo's success. The CFO was sure that Cerullo was hiding huge losses in a $1.3 billion backlog of what is called "aged inventory"—securities that have been on the books for a long time and cannot be sold either because they are overpriced or because they are composed of unattractive parts. O'Donnell believed that Cerullo's department was deliberately creating securities that it couldn't get rid of, and was also putting too high a price on them. He'd feel a lot more comfortable if Cerullo simply sold the inventory and proved it was worth $1.3 billion, instead of keeping it on the books and claiming that as its value, he said. But even though he was the CFO, O'Donnell was powerless against Cerullo. When he sent auditors to investigate operations at the Fixed Income department, Cerullo and his staff refused to talk to them. Instead, they blustered, threatened, spewed crude and raw epitaphs, and threw the auditors out. When O'Donnell hired an accountant from General Electric to go over Cerullo's books, Cerullo co-opted the man. In the space of a year, the accountant, David Bernstein, was refusing to talk to O'Donnell, much less cooperate with any internal investigation. So O'Donnell fired Bernstein, only to see Cerullo hire him directly and name him the head of New Business Development, even though Bernstein had never worked on Wall Street. After that, anyone checking up on Cerullo or the Fixed Income department had to go through Bernstein. Though I didn't know Ed Cerullo, I felt a begrudging admiration for him. Clearly, he knew how to protect his turf.

I later learned O'Donnell didn't share my regard. He kept a diary, and wrote of Cerullo: "I think he's going to put us all in jail."

Now O'Donnell was ready to try again. His diary entries described how concerned he was that Cerullo reported to no one and that no one had oversight or control over the Fixed Income department. He wrote that as the CFO with responsibility for reporting to Jack Welch at GE, he worried about being ultimately responsible for activities of Cerullo's that he knew nothing about. As I sat in his expansive office, he told me that when he saw my résumé, he thought he'd found the perfect foil. Since his staff didn't understand the securities market, they couldn't evaluate whether the aged inventory was truly unmarketable or mispriced. His mild-mannered accountants were blown out of the office by Cerullo's crude traders. I'd worked as a trader and was at home in the macho culture; I understood securities and had the technical expertise to analyze the aged inventory. O'Donnell needed someone who could stand up to Cerullo's traders, demand to see their books, and then make sense out of the line they'd been feeding him about the inventory. I showed him the forty-page analysis of mortgages that I'd done at First Boston.

"I'm hearing from you that you can actually reverse-engineer this inventory and can tell me, bottom line, what they're worth?" O'Donnell asked me. I answered that I could determine at least a range of values. Then he told me his plan.

"What I have in mind would be a real political minefield. Ed Cerullo doesn't take kindly to my people questioning his traders. In fact, I'm certain that you'll make fast, lifelong enemies. I need someone who can determine the market price for the aged inventory and attempt to convince the traders to sell those securities at the market price."

He looked at me. "If they prove unable or unwilling to move the securities, you would make a bid for the securities and they would be forced to sell the securities to you. You would be expected to flip those securities out to the Street that same day. We need that type of discipline enforced here. Does that sound like something you could do?"

If I sold the securities on the open market, Kidder would allow me to keep the profit for myself, O'Donnell added. How much I made would depend on how savvy I was as a trader.

First, I'd have to warn Cerullo that I was coming. O'Donnell didn't want me simply to show up one day as his employee and take over Cerullo's aged inventory. He was after Cerullo, but he didn't want to spark an all-out war. So I made an appointment to see Cerullo. I didn't mince words. I wanted to meet him because I'd been hired, I told him, to take away his aged inventory.

MY APPOINTMENT WITH Cerullo was set for the same day as a massive ticker tape parade through downtown Manhattan celebrating the return of troops from the Persian Gulf war. Clad in a suit that I had obviously outgrown, I walked through a throng of cheering tourists and gawkers, soldiers and tanks, at Bowling Green. A palpable *joie de vivre* filled the air. Tiny bits of paper drifted onto my shoulders and hair. As I walked I thought about the Edward Cerullo I'd met once or twice months before, when negotiating with Mike Vranos. He'd struck me as frazzled, even unkempt, man distracted and at the end of his tether in a tiny office crammed with books and papers strewn on the desk and stacked on the floor. It was hard to imagine him rebuffing O'Donnell's accountants with bravado. It was even harder to imagine him rebuffing me.

At Kidder, I followed a secretary down a long hall to a corner office that was twice the size of my tiny apartment. Cerullo, executive managing director, chief, Fixed Income department, had new digs. This office was spacious and neat, framed by an expansive city view through a large picture window. Nothing sat on the floor, and when Cerullo stood up from behind his wide desk, I noticed the surface was virtually empty of paper. Obviously, success, power and a huge staff of people working for him had changed Cerullo's management style. He stuck out a firm hand, his gaze confident.

"Have a seat. Do you go by Joe or Joseph?"

He stared steadily, his brilliant blue eyes very direct from behind small, yuppie-style tortoiseshell glasses. The man opposite me had short-cropped, straight, dark blond hair and a plain face. A dead ringer for the conservative television commentator George Will, I thought. He looked only a few years older than me, a lot taller but just as athletic. He leaned back comfortably in his chair. Did I work out? he wanted to know. He swam laps twice a day at a downtown athletic club, just a few blocks from the office. In my mind's eye, I see Cerullo as always wet—he swam so often that he seemed perpetually to have just gotten out of the pool. In the office, his hair was usually damp, combed back until it was plastered against his head.

I sat stiffly in one of the odd Art Deco–style chairs opposite Cerullo's desk. Other than those chairs and the view, the office was austere, barely filled with a few pieces of standard-issue furniture. The arms of the green-and-beige-striped chairs were high and rounded, and came together so closely in front that I had to turn sideways to slip into the seat. I sat primly, my arms behind me and leaning forward, almost in supplication. The chairs seemed guaranteed to make visitors uncomfortable. Pictures of Cerullo's two children sat on his desk and on a filing credenza that ran the length of the wall behind him. For a few minutes he busied himself with something on his desk. Then he asked offhandedly what had become of my talks with Mike Vranos. Finally, he looked up at me.

"Tell me, what exactly is Dicky O'Donnell asking you to do?"

I explained that O'Donnell wanted me to move the aged inventory. Cerullo's eyebrows shot up.

"You're going to sell the securities out of the traders' position?" he asked, genuine surprise in his voice. He stared intently at me for several seconds. "My traders are pretty tough. They've done an excellent job of self-oversight, and you probably won't make much headway trying to take over the trading of their positions. And my traders are not answering any questions from O'Donnell's office."

He paused, and I thought I saw a slight smile flicker on his face. "They'll answer to me. I'll get the job done. If I have a job to get done."

We talked for a minute more about O'Donnell's plan, and abruptly Cerullo asked me to step outside his office. I stood in the hall for a few minutes until I saw Mike Vranos appear. He clapped me on the shoulder as he passed.

"Hey, dude, I've been trying to reach you. Where've you been?" Vranos disappeared into Cerullo's office. A few minutes later, he passed me again with "Hey, dude, we're going to work something out."

Cerullo called me back into his office. He looked at me closely. "So what do you really want to be doing in five years?"

I hesitated. Clearly, Cerullo was about to make an end-run around O'Donnell. Trading, I said, but trading from a position with an objective standard of measure, one where merit was based on performance and nothing else. As I talked, he reached for his phone. A few minutes later, two more managers, Peter Klein and Mel Mullin, appeared in his doorway. Cerullo explained that I wanted to be a trader; the three of us should adjourn to Mullin's office and see if I fit into any of the openings they had.

Klein looked uncomfortable; it was clear that if he hired me, it would be under duress. Mullin seemed genuinely interested in my résumé. His head government Strips trader had left three months before. He couldn't pay much—only $75,000—but he could guarantee that I'd have six months to learn the market. Was I interested?

* * *

WALKING FROM CERULLO'S huge corner office to Mullin's smaller one, I knew two things for certain: I wanted to be a winner, and Cerullo was offering me a second chance at the brass ring. I still believed that a black man like me can succeed only when measured against an objective standard. I still believed that Wall Street operated that way—the only thing that mattered at the end of the day was how much money you made. Not color, or gender, not who you knew. I'd had an opportunity to be a winner at Morgan Stanley, but I'd screwed it up. It had been the perfect job at a venerable firm, with a lavish salary that allowed me to send more money home to my parents than I spent myself, and guaranteed a ticket to an even more prestigious, lucrative career—and I'd lost it all because of my ego and stupidity. I'd become incredibly skilled at all of the white man's vices that my father had warned me about. I'd betrayed my parents' values, their trust and their expectations—and they had paid the price along with me.

Now I was about to betray O'Donnell, and I didn't like that, but there was no sense in accepting his offer over Cerullo's. If I managed to force Cerullo to sell me his aged inventory, eventually that backlog would be depleted. I'd sell them myself on the open market, maybe even at a huge profit. But once they were gone, what would my job be? Cerullo would hate me by then, so he certainly wouldn't hire me, and O'Donnell would have no further use for me. The only real attraction about O'Donnell's job offer was that until the moment I met with Cerullo, it was the only game in town.

Cerullo knew that. He didn't want an emissary of O'Donnell's—particularly not a smart one with attitude—in his midst. So he removed me as a threat by offering me the job I coveted. I could be a trader again. His offer was more than work, however. He offered me the objectivity I longed for, a leadership position I knew I was ready for and deserved, an entrée to Kidder that had a future, and redemption. The salary was mediocre, but the real money was in year-end bonuses anyway.

Cerullo had sized me up as the latest weapon in his war with O'Donnell, and from what I could see that afternoon in his office, made a battlefield decision to hire me before O'Donnell could put me to work. Joining Cerullo made sense to me. I accepted the job, hardly considering what I'd tell O'Donnell. Like Cerullo, I rarely thought about consequences before acting.

PART
TWO

KIDDER, PEABODY & CO.

N MONDAY, JUNE 24, I got out of bed at 4:30 in the morning to watch the Tokyo business reports on TV while I read *The Wall Street Journal*. I jogged to my health club on Fifty-sixth Street and worked out until six. Then I went home, dressed and headed for my first day at Kidder, Peabody & Co.

I was to start work as head Strips trader on the Fixed Income Government Bond desk without having met anyone else on the desk. At least this time, I was joining the group as a leader, not a peer. But I was to be head trader on a desk that for several months had made no money. Kidder Peabody was a one-trick pony in severe trouble. None of its other departments—Investment Banking, Mergers and Acquisitions, Retail—lived up to expectations; only Fixed Income made any money. On the Street, the company was known as Kidding Nobody. Kidder had played a central role in the insider trading scandals of the late 1980s, when its chairman had been forced to resign and two of its traders had been led from the trading floor in handcuffs. Kidder's leading light in the high-profile mergers and acquisitions market, Martin Siegel, had testified against the famed arbitrager, Ivan Boesky, and the junk bond king, Michael Milken. Kidder had become a black eye for Jack Welch, the dynamic, blowhard CEO of General Electric, who boasted that no company of his would rate lower than first or second place in its industry. He'd paid $650 million for an 80 percent share in Kidder in 1986, and then in 1987 had had to pay a $25 million fine for

Siegel's crimes. Rather than being number one or two, Kidder was nineteenth on Wall Street.

I wasn't joining a financial powerhouse, that was certain. As I entered the office on my first day and headed for Mel Mullin's area, I cared only that Kidder had potential that could be translated into potential for me. The calm on my face as I crossed the trading floor belied my nervousness. The Strips trading desks occupied the last four along a length of fourteen desks that comprised half the Government Bond trading area. Each desk I passed was loaded with a phalanx of computers. Traders stare all day at between four and eight screens displaying bids and offers—the selling and buying prices—of bonds. A trader's desk also has an intercom with a microphone and speaker, and a multiline phone or several phones. With those computers and phones, a trader can do the job of matching the bids and offers extended by other firms and brokers without leaving his swiveling desk chair.

Mullin waited for me in his office. He wanted to go over the strengths and weaknesses of the current Strips desk traders before I met anyone. Three people would work for me, he said. Monica Flanagan was "very new to trading but has picked it up quickly and has been continually profitable. She is the person most interested in learning on the desk. She is trading Refco securities, Strips from the savings and loan bailout funding bonds. These bonds are no longer being issued, so she is eager to start trading generic Strips and has been fighting with Kevin for an opportunity. I don't know if she is ready just yet.

"Kevin McLaughlin means well. He's been filling the role as head trader without much success. He has an accounting background and is very good with the technical details of the profit and loss accounting systems. He really has shown no willingness to do customer business and I will move him back to concentrating on short and intermediate maturities. Or maybe let him do intermediates and bring Hugh Bush in to handle the shorter term maturities.

"Now Hugh is the sharpest in the group. He helped develop the computer program, the Government trading system, that tracks traders' positions and P&Ls on a real-time basis. He's a little high-strung, but very earnest. He's been with me for nearly seven years now. I hired him after he dropped out of college, practically after high school. He moved recently from programming to trading private-label zeros. He's very young and not very disciplined, so I have to keep an eye on him; but when he's focused he is a very hard worker."

Mullin hesitated a moment, then explained that my predecessor had left because he was more interested in proprietary trading than customer trading. Proprietary trading, essentially, means putting the firm's capital at risk while buying low, selling high and trying to make money from the difference. It's also known as arbitrage. Mullin didn't like arbitrage because it required too much market savvy and depended on too many variables. Instead, he preferred that his people concentrate on trading bonds with customers with big investment portfolios, like insurance companies, mutual funds or pension funds. Those customers would buy large quantities of bonds intending to hang on to them for several years. They were solid clients from whom a thin profit could be taken on every trade. Arbitrage, while often potentially more lucrative, was much riskier.

"This is a young desk with a relatively small allocation of the firm's capital. I like to play things close to the vest without taking major risk. Okay, let's get you out to the desk to meet the traders."

As we walked back to the trading floor, I felt acutely aware that Flanagan, McLaughlin and Bush had never laid eyes on me. Like the traders at First Boston, they'd had no say at all in my hiring. The last thing I wanted was a repeat performance of the conflict at First Boston. Mullin veered toward a fellow with Pat Riley–style hair slicked back into a neat, tight line that stopped just above his collar. He lounged comfortably in a double-breasted suit I immediately recognized as custom tailored, at a desk with considerable legroom. Colorful socks peeked above shoes polished to a high gleam and matched the vivid shades in his silk tie.

"Kevin, this desk belongs to Joseph as head trader for this group and you should move over to your normal seat." Mullin sounded abrupt.

I stuck out my hand, aiming for a light mood. "Hi, I'm Joseph, and I take it that you're Kevin McLaughlin, the renowned chair thief." He grinned and welcomed me while shifting chairs. Mullin turned to Flanagan, who greeted me with a slight Queens accent, and then introduced me to Bush. I looked at a barrel-shaped fellow with an unruly mass of curls covering the first signs of male-pattern baldness. He looked back through owlish glasses and said a wary hello. I thought he smelled of beer. After the introductions, Mullin reminded all of us that we were invited to a Fourth of July party at his beach house that weekend. It would be a good chance for me to meet more people in the department, he said.

LIKE THE REST of Wall Street, Kidder Peabody was in trouble in the summer of 1991, but it was impossible to detect from the extravagant world of many of its managers. What better way to meet my new colleagues than in the country? As any New Yorker of class knew, that meant the Hamptons, which in turn meant a weekend of parties at someone's expansive country house. Those who had truly arrived owned a summer house; the rest rented for exorbitant amounts from local people who knew an opportunity when they saw one. New York City's entire upper class—and the entire population with upper-class aspirations—decamped to the Hamptons for the summer. I hired a nondescript Chevy sedan for the drive out of Manhattan, and smiled to myself as I parked it alongside several Mercedes-Benzes and BMWs in front of Mullin's house that weekend. His place turned out to be a large, split-level ranch house with an enormous pool, hot tub, tennis court and elaborately landscaped gardens. It was a far cry from my tenement apartment with the drug dealers on the stoop. I'd dressed in my customary weekend outfit—trousers with a razor-sharp crease and a crisp business shirt—and when a tuxedoed waiter pointed me toward the backyard patio, I saw that everyone else wore shorts, T-shirts and bathing suits. For several minutes I stood alone, not recognizing anyone, until I spotted McLaughlin. As I loosened up and started chatting, I realized that the partygoers were not just Kidder employees; there were people here from Mullin's entire career—colleagues from his previous jobs, people he'd known in his days as a college professor.

Mullin had a Ph.D. in mathematics from New York University and had come to Wall Street in 1977 after a short stint as a professor. He didn't look professorial, any more than he looked like a financier. He reminded me more of a truck driver. A big man in his early forties, with a full head of thick, curly dark hair sprinkled with gray, Mullin stood six feet tall and carried a large beer belly that made him appear pregnant. But his most striking feature was an ugly goiter on his neck, a benign growth protruding from just beneath his ear. Terrified of doctors, hospitals and surgery, Mullin let the goiter jut undisturbed from beneath his skin. At least, it didn't seem to bother him. For others, the sight was definitely disturbing—it was a constant struggle not to stare at this unnatural growth.

Mullin began his career as an assistant in the Equity arbitrage department at A. G. Becker. By the time he left, he was manager of a group of stock option traders. In 1980, he took a job managing option trading at a company called ComCorp Securities. After that, he became a consultant to the McConnor Group, eventually managing derivative trading in metals, currencies and mortgages. In 1987, he went to work at Irving Trust to start up its mortgage trading business. Eventually, he also managed Irving's securities area, which included its Government Bond department. In June 1988, a business acquaintance, Ed Cerullo, offered him a job as manager of Kidder's Government desk. Now he headed the desk that conducted proprietary (that is, trader initiated) and customer (institutional and retail) trades in Treasury bills, notes, bonds, Strips, government agency securities and an assortment of money market instruments.

Mullin had used his expertise in applied mathematical theory to specialize in options trading. In their simplest incarnation, buying a call option gives the purchaser the right but not the obligation to buy a stock once it has risen to an agreed-upon price. Options are a highly technical security, and among the most risky to trade. But since that also means they have the greatest potential for reward, it's a popular area. Trading options is also very computer intensive. In his previous jobs, Mullin had assembled a team of computer programmers and traders, and those people had followed him to each new job. Mullin was renowned for his loyalty, his patience, his even temper. A people person, he didn't like firing anyone. If he was unsure about someone, he'd err on the side of compassion. The bottom line didn't matter as much to Mullin as the chemistry among the members of his team. He could have hired traders with more savvy, who could have made more money, but at the cost of his team cohesiveness. Mullin didn't want that. He wanted to work with friends.

I wandered among the guests, headed for the punch bowl, when a young woman asked my name and where I was from. Her accent sounded slightly Latin.

"Well, I guess I've spent most of my adult life in Boston. How about you?"

"Puerto Rico," she said. "I have to tell you that you're the first black person I've ever seen at a Kidder function."

"Oh yeah!" I laughed. "Well, how long have you been with Kidder?"

"Oh, this is probably the umpteenth of these little gatherings I've attended. So I can tell you that we're rare in the Kidder book. Just look at this crowd. Doesn't it get lonely when you're the only minority?"

"Lonely? To tell you the truth, at this point, I almost expect to be the only black person. In the real world, from nine to five, you go solo, and you have to be prepared for it."

"I'm always thankful to meet other minorities because I feel more comfortable having someone more like myself to talk to." She smiled as she talked. Behind her, a heavyset, balding man in his fifties approached us. I'd seen him floating in the pool earlier. He ignored me.

"Are you ready to go?" He asked the girl angrily.

"We just got here!" she exclaimed in surprise. The man scowled at me, and stomped angrily back to the pool. The young woman looked at me again. "That was J.J., my husband."

She meant J. J. McKoan, Kidder's national sales manager. Sales were Kidder's lifeblood, and McKoan ran the show. He'd graduated from Yale in 1980, worked Dillon Read and U.S. Trust, and then moved on to Drexel Burnham Lambert. He'd left before Michael Milken's heyday, but not before he'd acquired a reputation as a take-no-prisoners manager. On the strength of that, he'd joined Kidder in 1986 as a salesperson, was promoted shortly thereafter to eastern regional sales manager, and then to national sales manager. I was surprised that this young woman was married to a guy McKoan's age.

"He's not as old as he looks," she explained. In fact, McKoan was just thirty-three, his girth just made him look older. "He's a really good man. He has adopted my three-year-old kid, and her father was black. So he's an *exceptional* man, a rare man. Can you understand that?" She stood and followed her husband. As I watched her join McKoan, my opinion of him softened.

I went into the house and ran into a petite blonde named Denise. We'd already met; she headed the Government desk's marketing area. She offered me a tour of the house, and I followed her from room to room, muttering admiration for the decor. It was her work, she admitted—she was married to Mel Mullin. That surprised me. If she marketed options for Mullin's desk, that meant her husband was responsible for deciding how much her bonus would be at the end of every year. As Denise Mullin prattled on about her courtship with Mullin, I realized how little I knew about my colleagues. I was in over my head already, I thought. It would be better to learn a little more about these people before becoming buddy-buddy with them and their wives. When she finished, I looked at my watch and exclaimed at the time. I'd better get back to the city, I said.

MULLIN HAD ASSURED me that I'd have six months to learn my new job, and in July I concentrated on my first priority: mastering the buying and selling of U.S. Treasury Strips.

The U.S. government sells bonds to raise money to finance the national debt. Essentially, the government borrows that money from the public, offering the bonds as collateral. When the Treasury sells a thirty-year bond—also known as a "long" bond—for $1,000, it is really just borrowing that $1,000 for thirty years. Each bond has a coupon, or the portion that represents the interest it will pay. If a bond has a 10 percent coupon, the government agrees to pay $100 a year in interest, and then in the thirtieth year, to return the $1,000 when the mature bond is cashed in. The $100 interest payment is called a "coupon payment," and most government bonds make two coupon payments of $50 semiannually.

A U.S. government bond is like a home mortgage—part of it is principal, part of it is interest. Every bond can be stripped into its component pieces—the semiannual interest payments and the payback of the bond's principal—just like a car can be stripped into parts. Similarly, just as automobiles are sometimes stripped because the car parts are worth more than the whole car, so too can bonds be legally stripped into component pieces that are more valuable than an intact bond. Every bond can be dismantled into individual Strips that can be bought and sold separately. The Strips can also be reconstituted into a bond—thus the Wall Street phrase "Strips and recons."

The term "Strips" stands for Separately Traded Registered Interest and Principal Securities. This concept was set up in 1985 by the U.S. Treasury to allow holders of bonds with ten-year maturity or more to separate the interest and principal components from a security to create discounted securities. Reconstituting is another service of the Federal Reserve that makes the reverse possible: The components are sent into the Federal Reserve and the bond is put back together. The Fed takes orders for such reconstitutions from customers like banks, investment firms or depository institutions. The major players in the Strips arena are banks—like the Bank of New York or Chemical Bank (now Chase Manhattan Bank).

The procedure is very simple. A customer, like a bank or Kidder, wires a bond into an account at the Federal Reserve Bank of New York via the FedWire. A computer separates the interest components from the principal component, gives each separated component its own unique identification number, and then sends the individual components back to the customer. The original bond is "retired." About thirty people work in the Fed department that handles Strips, and it takes them about an hour to strip or recon a bond. The customer gets a computer-generated acknowledgment that his order was received on the FedWire and is being processed. His final notice comes when the bond pieces are returned to him. The Fed workers don't actually talk to a trader or salesman at a bank or investment firm. Processing is immediate, and no processing is done for future dates. No money changes hands, and the Fed has nothing to do with the price or quantities of Strips involved.

The principal component of a bond is its final, maturing payment. When a bond is stripped, the principal component is turned into a thirty-year "zero coupon." It's called a zero coupon because it pays no interest; it represents the maturity principal payment as opposed to the interest payments. The value of zero coupons is that they can be exchanged together with the interest components for the bond in either direction.

My job as the Strips trader was to buy and sell only Strips. However, because Strips can be reconstituted into a bond, the price of bonds mattered to me a great deal. A difference in the price of Strips and the price of a whole bond creates room for profit. It can be cheaper to get a bond by reassembling underpriced Strips rather than buying a whole bond. Then the newly reconstituted bond can be sold for the going price of whole bonds. Making money from the difference is called "arbitrage," and requires up-to-the-second monitoring of bond and Strips prices. A trader—any trader—always wants to buy anything that is underpriced and sell it at a higher price. From my first day on the job, one of my goals was to take advantage of any arbitrage opportunities that came my way—in spite of Mullin's admonition that arbitrage was a bit too risky for his taste.

But Mullin was preoccupied introducing me to the tool of my trade. On my desk sat an old battle-ax of a computer, a wildly outdated Intel 286 PC that was my entry port to our database. Every trade had to be inputted into this terminal. The machine was networked to computers all over the office, each of them so old, so slow and so limited in processing power that trades were agony to conduct. The computer ran proprietary trading software written by Mullin and a programmer named Moishe Benatar, but that had been six years before. In the meantime, it had become so temperamental and cumbersome that Mullin spent half the morning explaining its idiosyncrasies to me. He sat alongside my desk, legs crossed, leaning on one hip so his belly rested to the side, and warned me that every trade entered into the database caused the system to freeze for nearly a minute while the processor churned and struggled to compute the information. That wasn't its most limiting factor. The program also restricted the variety of bonds that could be entered into the database, Mullin explained. Every bond has a settlement date—that is, the day on which payment for the bond was actually made. Though bonds could have a variety of settlement dates, our computer limited our choices to only four. They were: cash settlement, meaning that the trade settled on the same day; next-day settlement, meaning the trades settled tomorrow (the norm for Treasury bonds); skip-day settlement, meaning the day after tomorrow (another fairly common choice when trades were done late in the day); and corporate settlement, meaning five business days in the future (the manner in which all equity trades and corporate bonds normally settled). If we conducted trades that settled on any other day, we couldn't input the information correctly into the computer. Anything that didn't fit neatly into one of the four categories was input by default under corporate settlement, which was as far forward as the system allowed. This caused the computer to generate price mismatches, which in turn created tremendous reconciliation problems each night. Mullin warned me that it took about two hours every evening to correct the data and ferret out the price problems.

Mullin had helped write the software used in Kidder's system, called the Government Trader. Essentially, it had been developed to help traders manage risk. It identified and kept track of relative values among similar securities, monitored the risk in a trader's overall position and highlighted moneymaking opportunities like changes in the spread relationships between bonds. Mullin explained that records of transactions from the Government Trader were handled two ways each day. Every evening, end-of-day price data were downloaded from the Government Trader to the Kidder mainframe computer system, where they were automatically integrated into the central accounting system. All the day's transactions were also recorded on trade tickets, which included the trade date and settlement date. Traders wrote most tickets by hand, but the Government Trader also printed out some tickets. Either way, the tickets were then handed to data entry clerks, who inputted them into Kidder's books and records.

My first days were filled with Mullin teaching me how to trade in the Strips market. First, he explained the mechanics of my job, beginning with the broker screens above my desk that filled my line of sight. He pointed out how the screens displayed the bids and offers of other dealers; he showed me the difference between those and the screens for interdealer or blind broker trades. He demonstrated the Government Trader's touch-screen system. He pointed out options for offsetting customer trades in zero coupons, and explained Kidder's philosophy about hedging. All trades should be hedged, he said. Kidder liked to think of trades in groups or pairs of trades that offset market risk. Mullin gave me a number of choices for hedging. Each had a different degree of profitability, and a different degree of risk.

In addition to the Kidder computer system and the array of trading screens, I bought an IBM laptop computer for my own use at work. I installed a personal organizer program, Lotus Agenda, to keep track of appointments and personnel matters. Sporadically, I typed in comments or impressions of people and of meetings I'd had. It became a sort of electronic diary. If I entered comments during the trading day, in the evening, or even the next day, the program's agenda system would assign it to the correct day of the week.

I could deal with the problems inherent in Kidder's archaic computer hardware. In fairly short order, however, it became clear that the computer system was only part of the reason the Government Bond desk did not make money. Its people were an even more important factor. Since accepting Cerullo's offer, I'd spent the better part of each day planning to build my trading desk in my image. It was an unmatched opportunity. I wanted a cohesive group of traders who would specialize in complementary areas. The four of us should fit like a glove. I imagined us working hard from the early morning hours to stay abreast of market trends and prices. I assumed the three traders working for me would be galvanized by the possibility of turning the desk around, too.

I wanted a good working relationship with McLaughlin, Bush and Flanagan, so I tried chatting with each one separately every morning. I told Mullin that I thought I could best learn if I sat alongside McLaughlin and Flanagan and just watched them work. I also wanted to check out their work style, so that I could comfortably direct them and eventually increase the intensity of our workday. Immediately, underlying tension and competition between Flanagan and McLaughlin became apparent. When I sat next to McLaughlin and asked questions about trading strategy, Flanagan often second-guessed his decisions. Neither was comfortable trading directly with customers, and I soon figured out why. Kidder's customers were some of the worst pick-off artists on Wall Street. Mostly they were second-class firms and a motley collection of bond brokers and middlemen who sought to buy low and then turned around and sold to investment funds themselves. Kidder's institutional sales force actually focused on these ragtag customers, and that in itself was highly irregular. Where were all the powerhouse customers, like insurance companies and pension funds? A trading desk must develop strong relationships with the quality investors if it hopes to profit. Mullin's desk cultivated a customer base that virtually guaranteed money-losing trades.

But when I asked about the quality of our customers, Mullin insisted they were the cream of the crop. In my first days at work, I sometimes watched Mullin react to a missed trade by demanding that we take another shot at it, this time at a money-losing price. His goal seemed to be to avoid conflict with the sales managers, even at the cost of running a second-class operation.

TRADING DESKS ARE close knit, and my presence cast uncertainty over our detached island. I looked for signs that, though young and largely untested, McLaughlin, Flanagan and Bush shared my eagerness. To fill the gaps, I chatted about the day's events; I hoped it didn't sound lame, but it was better than talking about the weather. I always started each day by reading two or three newspapers, so I knew that the news that summer was full of speculation about an upcoming London summit between the president of the Soviet Union, Mikhail Gorbachev, and President George Bush. At issue was whether the West should offer massive economic aid to the collapsing Soviet Union. International aid piqued my interest because bailouts were often financed with bonds. I knew that, and I assumed my traders did, too.

The news barely registered on their faces. None of them had read the morning papers, it turned out. The TV news seemed to suit them well enough. But the newspapers had also reported a new World Bank study on economic reforms in the Third World, and the seizure in seven countries of the operations of BCCI, the Bank of Credit and Commerce International. A huge, far-reaching scandal appeared to be brewing in the financial industry. In our own backyard, the papers were filled with speculation about whether the Federal Reserve Bank was going to increase interest rates to prevent inflation, now that most people believed the recession was over. Several important economic indicators were due soon—wholesale trade figures, housing completion statistics, the product price index and retail sales figures. Most important, the Treasury was auctioning $9 billion in seven-year bonds in my first weeks on the job, and the papers carried analyses of what that might mean for the near-term outlook. Would there be a bond market third-quarter rally? Why did economists believe the recession was over but business owners did not? What did new statistics on the length of the average workweek have to do with inflation anyway?

My traders wouldn't engage. The Wimbledon final had been played that week, too, and that match was just about the only sort of news that got anybody's interest. Worse, Bush, McLaughlin and Flanagan didn't understand why I was so worked up about the news. They didn't get the connection between political events and the market. I could almost see them writing me off as a nerd.

I liked the three, but by Friday my spirits had sunk with the realization that they didn't share my ambitions. I expected a higher educational level, first of all. My own personal bias lent more credence to Ivy League degrees, but I would have been happy had any one of the three gone to a good business school. Instead, they'd attended schools not known for their finance departments. After MIT, Harvard and the Wall Street boot camp I'd endured at Morgan Stanley, I'd hoped for people with similar education and training. In addition, they had very little practical experience in trading, but did almost nothing to compensate for that. None of them appeared to believe education or experience mattered much. Theirs was a passive approach to their jobs, overall. McLaughlin and Flanagan didn't know how to use the bond trading software in our computers; Bush was familiar with the software because he helped write it, but he didn't know enough about trading to make his familiarity useful.

Thus, the only person who could answer all my questions about our computer system was Mullin. McLaughlin, Flanagan and Bush bided their time in the office, treating their jobs like something of an extension of their social lives. Bush was the class clown. He was part of what Mullin and our chief, Ed Cerullo, jokingly referred to as Mullin's "Jewish Mafia." This was a group of about eight traders and analysts, including Bush, Moishe Benatar and others, who had followed Mullin from job to job. They'd worked together for nearly a decade, and were more friends than colleagues. As a result, they spent a good part of each day talking trash about women, dating and sex. Flanagan, who wasn't part of the original group, hated their banter, which often made them deliberately try to antagonize her with sexist remarks.

Few barriers divided the various trading departments arrayed across the huge trading floor of Kidder's building at 60 Broad Street. Hundreds of men and women scurried back and forth between the islands of desks that formed the trading areas, sales sections and data and secretarial areas. Only Cerullo and a handful of managers had private offices. By the end of the first week, I learned how to tell when a young woman approached our desk.

"Periscopes up!" a male voice barked. Whoever noticed her first would shout so the others could stop what they were doing and watch. McLaughlin's job was lure the passing woman over to his desk for banter so other traders could turn their chairs toward her, ogle and gossip. McLaughlin displayed an array of tricks for enhancing the entertainment value of these encounters. If a woman was wearing a short skirt, he'd remain seated but try to show her a document that required her to bend over. The women, mostly sales assistants in their mid-to-late twenties, went along with these games and often gave as good as they got. For many of them, a significant part of their job seemed to revolve around which trader they were dating. Bush and McLaughlin kept track of individual women with a litany of crude observations and locker-room nicknames. One well-endowed blond sales assistant was called Hooters by everyone in Fixed Income. This enraged some of the women sales and trading assistants, data clerks and secretaries, but they were powerless. Complaint only egged on the traders. Others, like a statuesque saleswoman named Anita Day, seemed to exploit the sexist atmosphere. Day was responsible for the Prudential Insurance account, a company with a huge investment portfolio. She was one of the best salespeople at Kidder. She was elegant, beautiful and always dressed in expensive clothes. She favored miniskirts, or if they were long, skirts with high slits. She never conducted trades from her desk. She always walked over to our section, and liked to do business with traders while leaning so close and so far over our desks that her long hair grazed the surface, and if you turned to look at her, you'd find your face against her neck. Often you'd find yourself staring at her cleavage as well.

Late one afternoon in my first week, McLaughlin's desk chair creaked as he leaned back and put his feet on his desk. His shoes were gone, revealing a pair of the most vividly decorated socks I'd seen in a long time. My own feet were clad every day in black socks. I owned two dozen identical pairs. It made life easier. They always matched my shoes and the gray or navy blue pin-striped suits I wore on alternate days, and I never had to worry about lost socks or mismatched pairs. I also owned ten white shirts that I had laundered at the end of the week, and a limited array of striped school ties. After a few days, it was clear that my clothes were conservative in comparison to McLaughlin's constantly changing array of stylish suits and designer ties. I was about to find out that he was particularly creative with his socks.

"Whaddaya think?" he asked anyone passing our desk, wiggling his toes and pulling his pant leg back a bit. It came to be a familiar sight. Anytime our work pace slowed, or McLaughlin was bored, he removed his shoes, put his feet on his desk and asked passersby for commentary on his sock-tie combination. He was proud of his daily coordination. If he wore a suit with a blue stripe in it, his tie would bear a blue pattern and his socks shared the same hue. His clothes cost a small fortune, but he could afford it: For all that he was a dapper Master of the Universe, McLaughlin, at thirty, lived at home with his parents.

McLaughlin filled one important role for me—he had once been a profit and loss accountant for Kidder, so he understood the company's accounting procedures. He reconciled the profit and loss accounts each night, ensuring that the profits as determined by our office computers agreed with the numbers in Kidder's mainframe. McLaughlin, however, believed he was at work to pick up women. He and Hugh Bush had a chant: "First you get the job, then you get the money, then you get the women. . . . But first you need the big, the big big, muuunnnneeeehhh. . . . Ha! Ha! Ha! Ha! Ha!" If someone asked them what they were doing, they'd shout: "What do you mean, what am I doing? I'm making the big, the big big muneh!"

The sexual banter unnerved Monica Flanagan. She complained all the time, not only about the crude atmosphere in the office, but also about the fact that when McLaughlin and Bush went out with salesmen or brokers, they usually chose strip clubs and topless bars. They'd invite her, and then say something like, "You can even strip!" Flanagan refused to join business dinners in these places. Her discomfort and complaints only encouraged McLaughlin and Bush. At times they seemed to go out of their way to be as crude as possible, just to upset her.

After a few days, I realized this behavior was going to mean a lot of wasted time for me. I didn't join the banter; my philosophy at Kidder would be the same as at First Boston. Joking, teasing and gossiping weren't going to get me anywhere, and could only harm me—as I'd seen at Morgan Stanley. The road to success was paved with money, nothing else. I had to improve my bottom line, and the hurdles were not going to be removed by our current leadership. In my first weeks on the Strips desk, Cerullo rarely made an appearance on the trading floor. Worse, I gradually realized that Mel Mullin was afraid of his own shadow. He spent the day in retreat, tucked away in his office. It wasn't as large as Cerullo's, but it was bigger than anyone else's, and messier, too. Mullin's desk was a blizzard of paper, while files and reams of computer printouts covered every other surface. The chaos seemed to illustrate his confused state of mind. His lack of initiative meant that we fared badly at the Federal Reserve Board's quarterly auction of bonds. Four times a year, the Federal Reserve Board sold bonds to the highest bids from qualified buyers. The auctions were blind, so we needed to be well prepared, to know in advance what bonds and what prices were of interest to our customers. My traders needed an aggressive understanding of their markets. They had none. Instead, they allowed other firms, like Salomon Brothers, to control the initial distribution of bonds by carrying the day at auctions. Then we bought from middlemen, which cut into our profits.

Our performance at federal treasury auctions was so poor, in fact, that we were often at risk of losing our credentials. The government requires that investment firms conduct a minimum of about 2.5 percent of customer trades with bonds bought directly from the Treasury. Because we didn't participate in the auctions, we barely met the minimum required to maintain this "primary dealership status," and were often in danger of having it revoked.

Once again, I saw that our poor relationship with quality customers hurt us. We didn't know our customers well because our sales staff had not cultivated strong ties with any of them. Salespeople are responsible for finding such customers, those end-users who buy a bond as an investment for several years. Kidder's Fixed Income area dominated Wall Street in one market, the most profitable—mortgages. But we were far from number one in government securities. Our sales force was controlled by J. J. McKoan. When McKoan came to Kidder from Drexel in 1986, he insisted that all Kidder salespeople report to him, stripping Mullin of control over the sales force. He made Kidder's sales force a generalist team, in which a sales manager oversees the sales force. It was also a commissioned sales force, meaning the salespeople earned a commission for every bond that they sold.

For a mortgage bond, this commission could be upward of $5,000 per million dollars of bonds sold. For government bonds, the commission was far less lucrative—a measly $32 per million. Of course, this meant that salesmen spent their time trying to sell mortgages rather than government bonds.

I preferred a specialist sales force. Under that system, traders oversee the salespeople, since they are in the best position to judge whether a salesperson is doing a good job of selling and buying bonds. Specialist salespeople earn a commission based on the quality of the sale, an aspect determined by the trader. Therefore, the specialist salesman had a strong incentive to help the trader make money.

Our generalist sales force was a detriment rather than an asset. They sold almost exclusively to intermediaries, customers like brokers and regional traders who turned around and immediately sold the bond to someone else. Their goal was to make money on the "spread," the gap between the buying and selling price. I knew that there were end-user customers out there. Our competitors managed to find them; so should we. Since finding end-user buyers took more work, the salespeople opted for the easy way out and sold to brokers. Also, the salespeople assigned to help us seemed to be the least talented at the firm. Anyone who failed at a more important job was dumped on the broker and regional trader accounts. Since neither was very profitable, the incentive to work hard was nil. And those accounts were much more price sensitive, since brokers and regional traders looked for the cheapest bonds. They'd call ten Wall Street traders who were each offering a bond at $100. The brokers wanted to pay $99, but the only way to get that was to find a trader who made a mistake on his price. My traders ended up making dozens of small, highly competitive transactions. If a trader makes a pricing mistake with a large investment customer like an insurance company, he or she can call the manager with whom they have a relationship and explain. The manager will probably scold, but he'll return the deal. Mistakes made with a regional broker will only earn a terse comment: "That's life."

THE THIRD WEEK of July, Ed Cerullo ordered the Strips traders to his office for a meeting. I hadn't seen much of him in my first month on the job, so I was surprised at the summons. Cerullo's office looked the same—his secretary kept his files in order and his work space neat. When Cerullo wanted information, he'd ask for a document, and woe unto his secretary if she couldn't find it immediately. As soon as he was finished, he gave it back to her for filing. Cerullo wasn't obsessed with neatness as much as with efficiency. Order was essential. He expected the same of the people who worked for him. He kept no desk on the trading floor. Instead, he spent most of his time looking down, both literally and figuratively, on the traders on the floor. His attitude was simple: Everyone is here to make money.

Come in, do your job, make money. Otherwise, you're fired. I grew to think of him as Napoleon, observing his empire, immune to the muttering and complaints of his foot soldiers.

Cerullo had started out as a trader, moving up rapidly in the four years he'd been at Kidder. He'd done his share of running around with other traders, late nights on the town, a familiar face at popular bars and night-clubs, drinking, partying, picking up women. His management technique stemmed from his experience as a trader. If he erred, it was on the side of action. He'd shoot first, ask questions later. Unlike Carpenter and O'Donnell, Cerullo acted without considering the consequences, a trait I recognized from the trading desk. Traders who hesitate, who are indecisive, are lost. They've got to be prepared to act at any moment. If anyone asked Cerullo to stop and consider consequences, he'd respond: "It doesn't mat-ter." He had nerves of steel. All he cared was that a decision was the correct decision for the moment.

He believed wholeheartedly in the concept of Big Swinging Dicks, of Superstar Traders. There was always someone smart enough and with balls enough to make huge profits in a trading position. Just because most traders couldn't do it, didn't mean it wasn't possible. Cerullo knew that a manager just had to find the Superstar, then nurture and promote him, and turn him loose on the market. The money would roll in.

As we shuffled into Cerullo's office, I noted the scowl on his face. He didn't look at anyone directly, just immediately demanded an explanation for the poor performance of the Strips desk over the past six months. I began to speak.

"Ed, our customer base is . . ."

"Shut up! I'm not talking to you! You don't even know where the desk is!" He glowered into the room. "Now, I expected this operation to gen-erate $1 million each month. You have done nothing but break even since March. What's the problem?"

No one spoke. He turned to Flanagan, who blamed McLaughlin for not following her instructions. McLaughlin then explained why he couldn't du-plicate Flanagan's trades in his market sector. Cerullo rolled his eyes.

"I need improvement in these Strips ledgers and I need it now, or there will be changes."

As we slunk back to the trading desk, the bickering began. McLaughlin and Bush hung back and blasted Flanagan for what she'd told Cerullo about McLaughlin. Flanagan told me she was afraid; this was the first time Cerullo had called such a meeting, she said. I told all three that I thought the meeting had been to send a message to me.

News of the meeting upset Mullin. He hadn't known anything about it. Right away, Mullin, who had been a disinterested manager for most of my first month, became a daily fixture in my life. Cerullo's criticism galvanized him. He was still not physically present—most of our communication was over the phone. From his office, he could hear the public address system, and he listened to all the "inquiry," as it's called when salesmen contact the trading desk to inquire about a price of a bond. A salesman could be in Chicago, Los Angeles or just across the room, but still talked to us over the PA system. For the rest of the summer and into the fall, Mullin hovered over us, listening to our trades, reviewing the bonds we put together, keeping an eye on our profit and loss sheets. He became intimately involved in our trading, he knew what the traders were doing, and showed real interest in our positions. But he wasn't intrusive. Mullin allowed us to trade as we saw fit, as long as we explained what we were doing and why. Our biggest handicap remained our sales strategy, and our redoubled efforts had little effect without a revitalized sales force to market our bonds.

The first week of August, I took over trading the high-risk sector of the Strips market. I had watched Kevin McLaughlin for an entire month and now knew that he rarely took any initiative. He reacted only to inquiry from the sales force, and since our customer base was so poor, that inquiry was extremely light. In my conversations with McLaughlin, I realized that he never analyzed the interest rate environment for himself. He had no personal opinion of the market. In fact, none of my traders did. They just waited for the salespeople to call them. As a result, all three spent several idle hours each day, waiting for the phone to ring. Often when it did, the call ended badly. Unless a trader takes an active role, it's hard for him or her to know the correct price of a bond from moment to moment.

At the end of the first week in August, Cerullo wanted to see us again. This time he waited with a profit and loss form in his hand. He dropped the P&L report onto his desk. He spoke in a very quiet voice, his eyes settling on each of us in turn, "There has been no progress since I spoke to you three weeks ago. That's all I'm saying. That's all I should have to say. Now get this straightened out. Okay?"

The next Monday, the Soviet Union collapsed and an attempt to overthrow Mikhail Gorbachev destroyed my market analysis. We lost $90,000 before we walked in the door that morning. The next day, I found myself in Cerullo's office again. This time, Mullin joined us. For the first time, Cerullo wanted to talk to me. I explained that the Soviet coup attempt had caught us badly prepared. In addition, I said, our customer base was the worst I'd ever seen.

Cerullo snorted. "Trading Strips has nothing to do with accounts. It is an arbitrage market, and it's fairly simple. Does the sum of the parts equal more than the whole? That is the only thing you need to be aware of. Concentrate on the Strip and reconstitution arbitrage."

Mullin didn't like that, and reminded Cerullo that customer business was more important. Cerullo glared at him. "I want profits from this desk, not buddying-up to customers. And I want profits in short order. If your account base is not a source of profits, you simply concentrate on the arbitrage opportunities. Is that so hard to understand? Is that clear to you? Is it?"

Cerullo turned to me. "Joseph, have you done a Strip or reconstitution since you started here three months ago?" I had not. Cerullo looked back at Mullin. "Mel, I expect you to work with Joseph in looking at the market and understanding how to take advantage of the arbitrage opportunities. All right. I'll talk to you again in a couple of weeks, and I hope to see some progress."

Each day for the next three weeks, Mullin pulled a chair over to my desk and, leaning his large frame over my shoulder, painstakingly taught me how to do Strip and recon arbitrage trades. With his hip cocked and one hand on his knee, he explained the steps to this computer-intensive form of trading. Whenever Mel turned his back, McLaughlin tapped me on the arm. He crossed his legs crossed in the same effeminate manner as Mullin, and raised his left hand to his neck and pretended it was Mullin's goiter. Behind him, other traders snickered at his imitation. I'd refocus on Mullin's descriptions of how arbitrage applies mathematical analyses to determine whether a security is valued correctly. If the Strips were underpriced, buy them, reconstitute them into a bond, then sell the bond. If the Strips were overpriced, sell them, then buy and strip the bond.

Until then, I didn't know how to spot a profitable arbitrage. McLaughlin and I had never looked at the computer screen that showed stripping and reconstitutions. So the first thing Mullin did was to activate the touch-screen computer trading system to bring up the stripping and reconstitution screen. He explained stripping and reconstituting bonds, and how I could use the Government Trader because it showed theoretical values for a bond's principal components by calculating the prices of the bond and all its coupon pieces. Mullin pointed out that stripping or reconstituting a bond would change my inventory. He then explained that Strip arbitrage depended on judging the price stability of Strips and their underlying bonds. We talked again about always hedging; one way to offset risk was to reconstitute a bond after buying Strips, he instructed.

Mullin explained the stringent rules governing the trading of Strips with the Federal Reserve Bank. The Fed must be notified at the time of a trade, and delivery of the Strips must be made between 9:00 and 11:30 A.M. on the date of settlement imprinted on the trade ticket. Failure to deliver meant onerous penalties.

Finally, when Mullin thought I was ready, he set up a trade for me. The transaction went into my computer terminal and onto my books, but Mullin walked me through the process, punching all the keys on my computer himself.

The last Monday in August, Cerullo stood at my desk when I arrived from the gym at 7:30 A.M. "I'm expecting improvement this month. Just a reminder." He glanced at the row of empty desks. "Are you the only one here? Tell your friends, 'Let's get to work.'"

Flanagan had made money trading savings and loan–related bonds, and Mullin wanted to give her greater responsibilities. Then one of the salesmen accused her of mismarking her bonds. When Flanagan complained about the salesman to Mullin, I found myself caught in the middle of their dispute. I estimated that Flanagan had a $130,000 discrepancy in her pricing. I informed Mullin, who asked Bush to take over Flanagan's ledger. Flanagan balked at turning her trading position over to Bush. They got into loud arguments over whether Flanagan should adjust her prices before relinquishing her ledger to him. In September she had to admit to a $130,000 loss from mispricing. One evening, when we both worked late, I gave her a lecture that I'd find myself using with other traders throughout my career at Kidder.

"Monica, you are in a war. And you have to act from here on as if you know that. The first rule of war is to know your enemies, what motivates them, what are their strengths and how their strength compares to your own. Hugh is like a son to Mel. You don't want to be in his crosshairs." From then on Bush had it in for her.

Finally, Bush took over Flanagan's ledger. Within an hour he was shrieking that the loss I'd estimated at $130,000 had actually been $400,000. Later that day, he raised the estimate to $700,000. Soon Bush and McLaughlin insisted that Mullin fire Flanagan. Two days later, Bush figured her trading losses at $1 million. At the end of that week, Mullin fired Flanagan. She responded with a threat to file a discrimination claim, so Mullin ordered the rest of us not to talk to her.

Flanagan's firing cast a dark shadow over the desk. The distrust and competition among my three traders had cost us $1 million. Mullin spent an entire day hovering over my shoulder, supervising my trades. I grew angry and impatient, and took my frustration out on Bush and McLaughlin. Suddenly I was sick of the childish repartee between them and other traders, the constant banter about sports, girls and bodily functions. McLaughlin often got so carried away with this ribbing that he ignored his trading position. I started barking at them abruptly, commanding Bush or McLaughlin to cut out the chatter and concentrate on the market. I often felt like a junior high school teacher in a class of unruly adolescents.

I decided the best way to clean house was in one fell swoop. I'd stamp the desk with my character, demanding intense teamwork. I insisted that all Strips traders remain at work until we finished reconciling our trading ledgers each night. Bush railed against staying late. Many evenings he declared he was "leaving anyway," even though McLaughlin and I were still at work. I replied that if he left, I'd see him fired. We began to exchange words over my imposition of discipline.

As I moved to change the atmosphere on my own desk, I went after a more profitable relationship with the sales force as well. I believed traders and salesmen should have a symbiotic relationship, with the trader providing market intelligence and pricing, and the salesman providing the distribution network. Ultimately, the trader must choose his accounts. At Kidder, I lacked that control. Through the end of 1991, I watched helplessly as the sales staff continued to rely heavily on the middlemen they could count on to trade bonds. The consequence of that easy availability was lower prices. After all, the middlemen just turned around and resold the bonds. I began to harp on one theme: Cut out these middlemen and sell directly to the investors. The best salesmen were already wealthy and no longer cared. The less successful ones were responsible for poorer or cautious clients, and regional brokers. They never seemed to try to find better customers. I became loud and vocal about my disdain for our customers and the quality of our sales force. But I didn't have Mullin's support.

All these new ambitions meant I worked long days and into the nights. I was rarely home, though that didn't bother me because home wasn't particularly inviting. I still lived on the Lower East Side, where the crack dealers had settled into a routine of ignoring the mainstream residents on our block. The crack-house trade was still openly active, and the dealers brazenly went about their business at the corner market that I called the Deli Drug Den. My home embodied all the urban ills that afflicted city residents, black men most of all, and yet twenty minutes after I left it each day, I was at work in a haven of power and riches. I stayed on the Lower East Side because my cost of living there was practically nil, and there were better things to do with my salary than spend it on housing. I helped my brother and his wife, who was in medical school, with money for college, and I regularly sent money to my parents. Nevertheless, my girlfriend didn't think much of the neighborhood, or my crummy apartment. I was dating an Australian woman who'd come to New York after winning a modeling contest back home. Lisa was a tall, athletic brunette with blue eyes full of stars. She'd modeled in Brazil, Argentina, Greece and Japan, and was eager to break into modeling's top tier. But New York is a tough town and her agency was unable to find her steady work. Finally, she went back to Japan. Before that, I took her to several Kidder Peabody office dinners and parties. It didn't surprise me that several people looked at us for a few seconds too long. Lisa always drew appreciative curious stares. But the interest was a little too intense. The day after one party, a female sales assistant shouted at me across the trading floor: "Hey, Joe, we heard you were playing tonsil-hockey with a white woman at Steve's party last night! I didn't know you liked white women." Her comment mystified me. I raised my eyebrows in her direction and sat down without reply. Later, in a hallway, she asked the same question as a group of her friends giggled in the background.

"I hope color doesn't matter to any of us," I replied, and kept walking past her. I decided not to think about the conversation.

Cerullo's displeasure with me continued, often for violations of some arcane ritual at Kidder. In the fall, when my desk completed its maiden forward reconstitution of a bond, I announced our deal over the public address system. The PA was known as the "hoot and holler," and was reserved for important traders with huge deals—the Big Swinging Dicks. The hoot was linked to all of Kidder's U.S. offices as well as those in London and Tokyo. It got worldwide attention. Announcing your trades on the PA was a signal that everyone should listen to you because you are a force to be reckoned with, a guy with big balls who is willing to throw around large amounts of money. Only traders with that kind of bravado, power and success were allowed to use the hoot and holler. Announcements of big trades cue other traders to call their customers. No one wanted to hear over the hoot that your dry cleaning was late. As much as I wanted to be important, my little forward recon didn't rate an announcement on the hoot, and Cerullo let me know it. "What are you doing making announcements over the PA when your area hasn't made a dime?" he railed at me that day.

In mid-December, Mullin called me into his office. I expected a year-end performance review. Instead, he immediately told me, "Your 1991 bonus will be $5,000. This will make your total 1991 compensation $33,000."

I barked a laugh, thinking he meant to tease me. His face was blank. "You're kidding, aren't you?"

Now Mel looked surprised. "No, I'm not kidding. You have to understand that the Strips desk operated at a deficit this year. I'm not saying that it's your fault. But there's just no profit out of which to pay you a bonus."

For a speechless moment, I thought that I'd never heard of anyone on Wall Street earning so little. Then I found my voice. "How can you say that we've made no profit? Our profits are over $5 million for the year."

"You're not taking into account the costs. You have to subtract from your profits the sales credits that you paid out to the sales force. That money for the salesmen's commission doesn't just fall like manna from the heavens. When the costs are subtracted from the revenues, the desk operated at a net loss for the year. Since you're the senior trader, you suffer the brunt of the desk's nonperformance."

This news flew in the face of the salary agreement I'd made with Mullin and Cerullo. Mullin pointed out that I had no written contract. I protested that I didn't even have an offer letter. But we had shaken hands in a gentleman's agreement. I was to be paid $160,000, prorated over the six months. Mullin told me to take it up with Cerullo.

I stared at him. I had shaken hands with the man, and I believed a trader's word is his bond. If that's the way they wanted it, so be it. I'd worked hard to learn the Strips market for six months, I'd worked hard to transform a flabby, inefficient desk into a productive team. Profits had improved. And now they wanted to pay me less than a back-office clerk. My respect for him diminished greatly.

"So be it," I said to Mullin. "I will become harder, colder and more driven than I have ever been."

The astonished look on Mullin's face only dimly registered as I left his office. I walked directly to Cerullo's door. He was inside, his hair still damp from his afternoon swim. I knocked and stepped in. Cerullo looked up warily.

"Just briefly, Ed. Are you aware that Mel intends to only pay me $5,000 for bonus?"

"I am aware of the bonus figures, but I leave it in the manager's hands as to the amount." He raised his hand, cutting off my response. "A bit of advice for you, Joseph. Last year is over. Let's get the new year off to a strong start. Okay? And if you need to speak to me I am always here."

I stood silently for a second, feeling nothing but rage. Turning, I marched out of his office.

Bush met with Mullin that afternoon and came back to the desk spewing venom, too. McLaughlin and another trader teased him for the rest of the day about his anger. I hid mine behind stoicism. But when Bush began blaming his low bonus on price mismarkings that he attributed to me and McLaughlin, he finally got my attention. It was the same accusation that had gotten Flanagan fired. Bush managed to convince Mullin to double-check prices in the trading ledger that McLaughlin and I used. Since the Strips prices we traded were also printed each morning in *The Wall Street Journal*, mismarking was well nigh impossible. Mullin found no errors. I made a mental note never to turn my back on Bush. As the holidays passed and the year ended, it became more apparent than ever that if I was going to prove that Wall Street was a meritocracy, I had to get control of my desk. That meant wresting it away from Mel Mullin. I decided to stake my claim by asserting responsibility for hiring and firing. My first exercise of that control would be firing Hugh Bush.

The office Christmas party was riotous that year. A bond trader threw a beer bottle at a saleswoman. The two had to be restrained. Several of us ended the evening at the swank nightclub Nell's. I danced a couple of times with a saleswoman named Linda Mead. I wasn't surprised when, the next morning, several people made jokes about us; office gossip always zeroed in on relationships. Then the jokes began to center on white women and black men. One day, Hugh Bush said: "You know why white women are dating you? Because of the myth. But what they don't know is that Hugh Bush is hung like a baby's arm holding a small peach!" Jumping up from his desk, he grabbed his right elbow with his left hand and holding his right forearm aloft, wrist bent, hand grasping an imaginary peach, strutted up and down the aisle. Everyone burst into laughter, shouting, "Huge Bush! Huge Bush!" It was funny, but strange, too. For all the office gossip and joking I'd heard in my life, I'd never heard anyone mention the sex stereotype about black men. I didn't like it. It was the wrong kind of ribbing. Later, I pulled Linda aside. If we were going to be friends outside the office, we should be discreet about it. "There's something strange here, something really weird," I said. Surprisingly, Mead was upset not by the gossip but by my demand for discretion. After that we barely spoke at all.

On January 3, Mullin pulled me aside and offered me a New Year's gift: Cerullo wanted me fired by the end of the month.

"Joseph, I can't protect you from Ed. You've got to have a good month. Ed has asked me to review your progress at the end of the month and make a recommendation on your continued employment. I'll help you, but you've got to come through."

"So much for my six months of learning the job."

"You've had six months. The training period is over. It's time to produce."

I sighed. I'd been over this with him before.

"I have produced. Revenues have increased every month from August to December. December was a down month only because we held off taking our December profits until the new year. I appreciate the warning about Cerullo, but I am certain that I am one of the better traders you have. I am your most serious student of the markets. I am the first one here every morning and I am the last to leave. But there is very little that I can do with position limits as severe as they are now. I have to have a larger balance sheet to protect my trading position."

"How large a position are you talking about?"

I wanted to quadruple the amount of money I traded with. Since the only way to earn money is to spend money, I decided to take the plunge. I explained to Mullin that Japanese investors were dumping their long-dated Strips, and no one was buying them. I believed the Japanese selling would continue, and that the only way to survive it was to have a short trading position in long-dated Strips. I also believed that if we had stronger customers, we could buy Strips from the Japanese and sell them to our own clients. But we didn't have the customer base.

"I can't move the bonds to the Street since every trader knows that the Japanese sold these bonds and that they are going to sell more. I have only one option and that is to take full advantage of our proven ability to reconstitute a long-dated bond using borrowed Strips for cash delivery to the Fed."

Mullin looked puzzled.

"The Japanese sell us $500 million in principals. Our financing desk borrows the required Strips. I submit to the Fed the purchased principal and borrowed Strips for reconstitution. The Fed returns a bond to me which is subsequently sold.

"It is a beautiful strategy because it is a double blind. I can buy billions of dollars of the principal Strips from the Japanese without ever showing up as a seller of principal Strips in the domestic market. Given larger trading limits, I would use the reconstitution mechanism to establish and maintain a short position in long-dated principals. I will continue to hold a portion of the resultant bonds and also purchase the short maturity end of the Strip curve that is not being devastated by the Japanese selling pressure."

Mullin thought it over. "That appears to be a sound strategy, but I don't want your position growing out of control. I'll allocate a modest increase in your position limits. Keep me up to date on the Japanese activity."

WITH FLANAGAN GONE, it took us until nearly 8:00 to reconcile our trades each night. Eventually, Mullin agreed to hire another trading assistant. He chose a thirty-year-old MBA from Columbia University named Jeff Unger. Unger took an instant dislike to Bush, irritated by the fact that Bush, with no formal education and a crude personality, had a trading position, and he, with his Ivy League background, was just an associate. I quickly informed him that he was not an associate at all. He was a dog—Unger-dog—and that it was my duty to train him in the tradition of Wall Street.

One day several months later, I walked up to the Strips trading desk to find Unger lying on the floor in paroxysms of laughter. McLaughlin had told a joke. I stood over Unger and yelled: "What are you laughing about, Unger-dog. This isn't a game. You can either be like him, or you can be serious about trading. Trading isn't a game. It is a war. It is a protracted conflict. Every morning when you walk in here you had better be prepared for another pitched battle.

"Don't sit here giggling, hoping that someone will notice that you laughed at their joke. You're not here to be liked. You're here to get the job done. So you've been here six months. What do you know?"

"Well, I've traded . . ."

"Six months of wasted time, that is all you know," I yelled. "You have been coddled, you have been misled, you have been betrayed by this system. This system, this environment is poisoned, poisoned by sloth, poisoned by levity, poisoned by gamesmanship. Every day I've watched you running for the exits at five o'clock. No more. Every day I've watched you socializing and playing games from eleven-thirty on. No more. No one works here, no one. There is no work ethic here. It boggles the mind that people earning six-digit incomes whine and complain about staying at work after five o'clock. Well, here on my desk you're going to work. If you want to change your mind about working here you better do so now."

I lowered my voice and leaned closer to Unger. From his ridiculous position on the floor, he looked ready to cry. "Let me make it clear to you. You are not going to be like they are. Hugh and Kevin are too far gone, and there is seemingly little that I can do to change them. But you are mine, and I am at war."

McLaughlin's voice broke the silence between us. "Hey, it's Carpenter!" He turned up the volume on the hoot and holler for the Kidder CEO's New Year address. Carpenter praised the Mortgage desk and the year in Fixed Income that had propelled the firm to record earnings. Then he moved on to Kidder's responsibilities to society. He spoke about charity, about living and working in New York City, and about Kidder's obligation to have a work force that mirrored the racial makeup of the community. Kidder, he said, had to set affirmative action goals to attract more blacks and Hispanics. His words reflected concern over recent press reports depicting Kidder as one of the most racially and sexually discriminatory on Wall Street. Certainly I'd noticed the amazing homogeneity at Kidder. Virtually no Jews worked there, and I thought I could throw a stone across the trading floor without hitting a single Asian. Other than myself, there was perhaps only one professional black male on the trading floor.

McLaughlin turned to me. "So, Joseph, what do you think about that? You know, affirmative action. Carpenter said we're going to have a racial makeup that mirrors that of the city. That's why they hired those four new black mailboys and fired poor Sparky."

Everyone burst out laughing at the thought of the white octogenarian mailboy, Sparky, losing his job due to affirmative action.

"Yeah, right, Kevin, I guess they're well on their way to filling their quota. By next week they'll promote those mailboys to salesmen. And at the end of the year, when they fire them, they'll once again proclaim that despite their best efforts to promote blacks, the minorities that they hired were simply not up to the task. That's how affirmative action works. White men selectively find these, these Negroes who are willing to be beholden to whites."

Around me, people stopped to listen to my response. "I'd support an affirmative attempt to recruit minorities from Ivy League schools. As long as they recruit from Ivy League schools so that they are hiring competitive members of the minority community rather than trying to hire people that they know and intend to fail, I would have no problem with that. But in my experience, when white men speak of affirmative action, Kevin, they intend to hire simply to fill a quota and they on no condition want to hire black men who will challenge them for leadership or have a chance to be successful. But, hell, this firm is so sorry it doesn't even hire whites from Ivy League schools. I don't think any of you jamocks on this desk have a combined SAT score over a thousand, so maybe the mailboys would be an improvement."

TWO WEEKS LATER, Carpenter shocked me. He announced that Kidder had lured its first black managing director away from Goldman Sachs, the premier Wall Street investment bank. Mustafa Chike-Obi would join Kidder's Mortgage desk, bringing more strength to the firm's dominance in that area and demonstrating its commitment to recruiting the best minority candidates on the Street.

I was disappointed. Kidder had hired one of the best managers on Wall

Street. Why not simply leave it at that? Why did the announcement have to include mention of "minority recruitment"? I'd heard of Chike-Obi for years, and had even met him briefly at a Goldman Sachs recruiting soiree at Harvard. He had a reputation as an aggressive trader. When I saw him in a Kidder hallway the next week, I relaxed my trademark scowl and nodded. It was our only communication.

BLACK MALE SEXUALITY

T HE FIRST WEEK of February rolled around, and I hadn't been fired yet. Trading had picked up, and profits, too, so neither Mullin nor Cerullo had said anything more about letting me go. At the end of February, Kidder held its worldwide Fixed Income meeting at the Waldorf-Astoria Hotel in New York. At the opening presentations, Dennis Dammerman, a vice president from our parent, General Electric, asked for better communication between Kidder Peabody and GE. GE shareholders were surprised to read in *Barron's* that Kidder held over $11 billion in high-risk mortgage bonds, he said. They thought they were investing in lightbulbs and refrigerators, not derivative mortgage bonds that they can't even understand, Dammerman joked.

Though I'd been at Kidder less than a year, by that time I'd become so proficient at Strips trading that I led a symposium on the strategy, explaining how we'd grown more aggressive by using forward reconstitutions. After the symposiums, little business got done; instead, many of the traders and salespeople paired off. We were all young and single, and many of us were far from home. Back in the office, there was much talk and kidding about symposium romances. The two-year bond trader helped a saleswoman from London miss her plane. Cerullo called the trader into his office, and when the young guy came out, he muttered, "He gave me shit for it."

Then Cerullo said he wanted to talk to me.

"I'm a little concerned that you were seen with Jean from London," Cerullo said, his eyes downcast as he fingered some papers on his desk. Was he interested in the saleswoman? I wondered. Cerullo was married, but I knew that hadn't stopped many philanderers on Wall Street. Had I inadvertently stepped in his way? He seemed ready to lecture me like he'd lectured the two-year bond trader.

"What's going on between you?"

I assured him that Jean and I had no relationship. He changed the subject then, and started talking about the market.

Unger proved himself a helpful assistant, but his irritation with Hugh Bush generated more petty rivalry on my desk. Unger tattled on Bush relentlessly, one day urging me in frantic whispers to pick up an extension and eavesdrop on a phone call. I heard Bush talking to a trader at First Boston. Monica Flanagan used this trader as a reference in her job search. The trader admitted that whenever prospective employers called him about Flanagan, he trashed her skills and experience. He'd just told an employer that Flanagan was really only a secretary; then he suggested that Bush apply for the opening that Flanagan had found.

I warned Flanagan that her reference was undoing her chances of finding a job, and I agreed to act as a reference for her. But there wasn't much I could do about Bush. On the contrary, if he found a job elsewhere, then he'd leave my desk of his own accord and I wouldn't have to quarrel anymore with Mullin about firing him.

A week later I walked into the mailroom to retrieve a price sheet from a pile of the end-of-the-day pricing documents. These lists were faxed each day to our offices in London and Tokyo, usually by a secretary. Hard at work at the fax machine, Bush didn't notice my approach. Since I knew that Bush rarely took on any extra work, his industriousness intrigued me. I glanced at the fax machine—and immediately noticed he was faxing the price sheets to a 909 prefix. I was sure I recognized a First Boston telephone number.

I went back to my desk, the puzzle pieces falling in place in my mind. For the last couple of weeks, someone on the market had been jumping into my sales, making offers on precisely the bonds I was trying to sell, at precisely my price. It had seemed like they had inside information. Now I realized they did.

I pushed back from my desk and walked to Cerullo's office. He listened to my suspicions. If Bush was looking for another job, he shouldn't be working here. Cerullo asked for the phone tape of Bush's job-hunting calls. We stored stacks of audiotapes in a back office, and I settled at a desk there for several hours to scan each one. The traders noticed my absence, and the fact that I was last seen in Cerullo's office. After that I'd disappeared, which could only mean, they concluded, that I'd finally been fired. Euphoria flashed briefly around the desk, several traders high-fived one another and came to shake hands with Bush at his good fortune.

I found the incriminating tapes and Cerullo came to the tape room to listen. Bush had to be fired, he shouted. Furious, Cerullo summoned Bush.

"If you want to look for another job, that's fine, but giving my trading position away is not part of the deal."

Bush decided to lie; he hadn't been looking for a job, he insisted. But the phone tapes were indisputable, and the lie only angered Cerullo further. He didn't wait for Mullin, but fired Bush on the spot. It was a euphoric moment for me. Finally, Bush was gone. Though I hadn't fired him myself or convinced Mullin to, Bush's dismissal without any input from Mullin was a great coup for me. I had to follow up by controlling who was hired to replace him. But first his departure meant that I had to hang on to McLaughlin. Mullin was eager to jettison him as well, but now I already had one hole on my desk. McLaughlin's accounting skills remained useful. I wanted to hold off firing him until I lined up a replacement who knew the back-office operation as well as he did. I barely noticed that with Bush's firing, I truly became persona non grata on the trading desk. Many of the traders stopped speaking to me at all.

IN MID-MAY, THE trading floor was consumed with rumors of Kidder's impending sale to Smith Barney. Word leaked that Ed Cerullo was meeting with his managers about what to do in the event of a merger. Mullin told us that he understood that the Fixed Income division was not included in the Smith Barney sale. Rather, Fixed Income would become a subsidiary of the General Electric Capital Corporation. This was Cerullo's brainchild. This way, he could jettison the money-losing Investment Banking division and get rid of his archenemy, Kidder CEO Michael Carpenter.

Then Carpenter intervened with a public announcement that negotiations had ended; Kidder was not for sale. When we came back to work after Memorial Day, the rumors resurfaced. We were going to be sold to Smith Barney. That day, Carpenter admitted he'd reopened sale talks. But at the eleventh hour, negotiations again broke down. The sale was not to be. After that, Carpenter's position seemed untenable to me. He looked like a professional dilettante and a man without direction. Expectations of his resignation ran high throughout the firm.

Cerullo, on the other hand, reacted like a man fully in command. He called meetings to discuss the aborted sale. He explained that Fixed Income had generated 115 percent of Kidder's net income in the last year. The entire Smith Barney negotiation was GE's attempt to rid itself of the Investment Banking division while hanging on to Fixed Income as the cornerstone of GE Financial Services. His own desire, he said, was to take Fixed Income private or find a suitable European partner, like Deutsche Bank.

Later, Mullin dragged a chair over to my trading desk and, crossing his legs and shifting his belly to the side, elaborated on Cerullo's position.

"Cerullo has Carpenter by the balls, you see. Many years ago, when Carpenter took over as CEO, he placed Tom Ryan in charge of Fixed Income instead of Ed Cerullo. Later, Ryan was moved to head the Equity trading department, but Cerullo never forgave Carpenter for the slight. Carpenter has simply backed the wrong horse. Kidder Peabody had briefly had its day in the sun as an investment banking powerhouse when Martin Siegel and Ivan Boesky were in their glory. Carpenter has invested all his energies in restoring Kidder's Investment Banking operation, meanwhile ignoring the Fixed Income division. Now Fixed Income dominates the firm, and the man he insulted brings in over a hundred percent of the revenues.

"And Carpenter seems too proud to ever own up to Ed that he made a mistake. So Ed treats him with complete disdain in all the executive meetings. This is just going to make things worse."

THE NEXT MORNING, I stood at my desk studying my computer screens. The office was quiet until peals of laughter captured my attention. Near the Mortgage trading desk, Linda Mead held court with a group of people, telling an animated story that I couldn't hear to a group of people. The lights flashed on my phone console. I grabbed the receiver and was surprised to hear Cerullo's secretary so early in the morning. I walked back to Cerullo's office. He ignored me for a moment, clasping his fingers behind his head and yawning. I sat in one of the uncomfortable Art Deco chairs. Finally, he spoke.

"I've asked you in because I made a decision this morning that affects you. It affects you in a sensitive manner and about a very sensitive subject. I wanted to be certain that you heard about it directly from me rather than through the rumor mill."

He paused. "This morning, I was forced to fire Mustafa Chike-Obi and I wanted to tell you before the rest of the firm becomes aware of this. You are the only other black professional in Fixed Income, and I feel an obligation to make you aware of this."

He paused again. "This is a very sensitive subject and I want no part of our conversation to go beyond this room. Okay?"

"Of course, Ed." I felt a growing uneasiness that my color had earned me this tête-à-tête.

"Mustafa was fired for sexual harassment of a Kidder employee. The allegation has been substantiated by a second Kidder employee. I did not want to fire Mustafa. I do not like firing anyone. I am taking this step only after a second employee confirmed that Mustafa had sexually harassed her as well. I have to tell you that Mustafa had similar problems at Goldman Sachs. When I first hired him I took Mustafa aside and warned him several times about this and I am now giving the same warning to you."

The last words were completely unexpected. I sat back in surprise, but the chair arms poked at me. "Warning me? Warning me?"

Cerullo stopped and busied himself adjusting the things on his desk. He didn't look at me. His voice, when he continued, was soft and low. I'd never heard him use it before. I imagined it might be the voice he reserved for conversations with his small children, or his wife. He was almost gentle.

"There is something that you must understand about the Kidder culture. Kidder is a very homogenous firm. Not many minorities work here. In fact, very few Jews work here." He chuckled to himself. "Brian Finkelstein is forever complaining about being the lone Jewish trader. You must understand that this is an old-line firm that was led by people from the South with very southern attitudes towards race. I will tell you that in my experience the people at Kidder are very sensitive to what, for lack of a better term, I will call black male sexuality. And by that I mean the whole idea of feeling threatened by the virility and sexual aggressiveness of black men."

He waited for me to respond, but I just stared. I wanted to say that the "culture" of Kidder was more like a locker room or fraternity house, but I couldn't speak. I felt the stiff antique chair, the unnatural arch in my own back, I saw the wide, gleaming desk, and Cerullo, leaning casually back in his executive recliner. The room shifted out of kilter. I reminded myself that this was my boss, that we were in the office. This conversation wasn't just inappropriate, it was surreal. It wasn't about me, and I wouldn't let it be. I sputtered.

"What . . . what precisely is it that Mustafa is supposed to have done? Are we talking about, what, about rape, or what, here?"

"I don't think that it is appropriate to get into that. I can only assure you that it was a difficult decision, but one in which I had no other choice. Again, the sexual harassment involves two distinct incidents and they were flagrant. There is no doubt and I had no choice. I think that there is cultural pressure on black men to be and to demonstrate sexual aggression and perhaps Mustafa was caught up in that. I warned him on several occasions and I feel that it is my responsibility to warn you."

I breathed hard. Cerullo had brought it back around to me. I couldn't help being defensive.

"I did not know Mustafa. I find it puzzling that a managing director would risk his career in such a pedestrian manner. What concerns me more is your feeling that I need to be warned. My race hopefully does not make me a rape threat. That is a very dangerous, dehumanizing stereotype."

Cerullo's expression was mild, without a trace of anger or outrage. His familiar, soft tone revealed that we were having a heart-to-heart talk.

"I'm not talking about stereotypes. I am talking about facts, you know, black men always being great athletes, having greater physical and sexual prowess. You're someone who obviously takes good care of yourself and there are more black men statistically with physiques like yours than there are white men. That's a statistical fact, Joseph, not a stereotype. It's because of these facts that people will react strongly to you and will view it as a threat if they see you becoming familiar with women at this firm."

My right triceps twitched suddenly and violently; an impending charley horse propelled me out of the cramped chair. I had to get out of there or explode. I jumped up and stood at parade rest, my arms behind my back. I struggled to calm myself, chanting "discipline must be maintained" in my head. Then I tried to smile. I probably looked sick.

"First, I am not here trying to get laid. I am here to get the job done. Second, what do you mean by this warning? If I talk to a woman here, I'll be fired?"

Cerullo sighed. "Look, I'm not telling you not to talk to people. I'm just saying that workplace relationships are inappropriate given the culture here, that's all. Again the Kidder culture is particularly sensitive to issues involving black male sexuality and black male sexual aggressiveness."

He paused, and then went on in a tone that suggested he was mentoring me.

"We've just had the example of Anita Hill who showed that no matter what your educational level, the cultural pressure applied to anyone can make them behave in a more sexually aggressive manner. I won't tolerate it here. I've made you aware of this as I made Mustafa aware, and I hope *you* behave accordingly. No doubt, you're going to hear all kinds of ugly rumors. I wanted you to know the truth so that you don't react with hysteria or paranoia to what has occurred. Okay?" He stood up to indicate the chat was over. But I was too upset to leave gracefully. The mention of Anita Hill made me furious.

"Look! I want the names of Mustafa's accusers so that I can protect myself from them. You're saying that they are particularly sensitive to black men. It's only fair that I know who the hell they are."

"Joseph, I don't want to argue with you. This is not helping the situation here, and it's not helping you. Now I've told you that there is no reason for you to be paranoid. I made the decision to fire Mustafa, no one else made it. I used my judgment and, again, I had no choice. *I had no choice*. It was that flagrant. Now let's put this behind us. Mustafa is fired and that's the end of that. Let's move beyond this. I asked you back here so that you would not be surprised by the news."

I left his office in a daze, his warning echoing in my head. Ricocheting alongside it were some plain facts: Chike-Obi had been fired, Cerullo hadn't wanted to hire me, I was unpopular with Mullin and the other traders for my role in the firing of Hugh Bush. Even though Bush had been caught red-handed, he was still "like a son" to Mullin, and his transgressions would have gone unnoticed if I hadn't brought them to Cerullo's attention. So my position was not one of strength. Cerullo and Mullin wouldn't hesitate a minute before axing me. All they needed was a reason. A trumped-up sexual harassment charge would do just as well as any. Perhaps someone was already out to get me by exploiting the general discomfort with the idea of black men and white women. The Rodney King verdict and the riots in Los Angeles had already proven us a nation divided.

I almost whirled around and marched back to Cerullo's office to quit. But was it sane to quit a lucrative job because I'd been warned not to date white women? If I resigned, wouldn't I be saying that black men were so crazy over white women, they'd do anything? Should I file a complaint? I wondered. I almost laughed at the idea of marching up to Human Resources and reporting that "my manager told me not to date white women. . . ." I couldn't do it with a straight face. Instead, I decided Cerullo's concerns reflected his own inadequacy. I'd already noticed his fixation on sports competitions, weight lifting, bodybuilding and other men's physiques. Obviously, his constant comments pointed to feelings of inferiority. Was he telling me to stay away from the women in the office because I threatened his masculinity? Because he worried that I was trying to take away anything that belonged to him? A score of pop-psychology explanations skittered through my mind. Any of them could be true. They all meant one thing—Cerullo was weak. When I returned to my desk, everyone was discussing Chike-Obi's firing. Linda Mead circled the trading floor, telling everyone about a black bond trader who had dated her sister four years before at Goldman Sachs. Was that Chike-Obi's crime, I wondered?

Over the next few days, as news of Chike-Obi's firing spread, rumors flared that his victim was Anita Day, the tall, elegant blond saleswoman. No one knew the true story—in fact, no one would ever know what really happened—but that didn't stop the gossip. Thus, my concerns about my own position increased when Day seemed suddenly to reach out to me. We didn't know each other, she had never approached our desk to do a trade, so I figured she was concerned that the Chike-Obi rumors made her look racist. She said hello in the office and tried to chat in hallways. One morning soon after Chike-Obi's firing, while we waited for an elevator, she talked to me as I paced up and down the lobby. I didn't know how to treat this woman. I believed the gossip mill, that she had been the one to complain about Chike-Obi, and part of me was convinced that her charges were exaggerated or even bogus. When the car came, it was empty. I was not about to get in an elevator alone with her. For the first time, I realized the depth of my discomfort and mistrust of Cerullo. This might be a setup, I thought.

"I have to get a newspaper," I said as she offered to hold the elevator door. I walked away and went across the street to have my shoes shined. It was the end of June 1992. The very next day, Cerullo called me into his office again. Hadn't I heard him before? Black male sexuality, he said, might cause me problems in the office.

"I warned you about this just the other day." He was angry now. "This firm is not comfortable with relations between black men and white women. What does it take to get through to you?"

"What are you talking about, Ed?" His words enraged me, but I seethed at the suggestion that he would fabricate some aggressive behavior on my part.

"Just be careful." People don't understand what they see, he warned. His anger subsided; now he didn't want to talk about it anymore. I was furious. Was someone watching me? I demanded to know. Was someone actually exaggerating and reporting my movements to Cerullo?

"No, no, nothing like that. No one is watching you. Just be careful."

I left his office, angry and ready to lash out. The saleswoman nicknamed Hooters was in her usual spot next to Kevin McLaughlin's desk. It occurred to me that I hadn't ever seen this young woman do a lick of work. She seemed to spend entire days gossiping and flirting at the trading desk. Since I often worked standing up, I could count on turning around and finding her standing next to me, chatting away as if it were part of her job description. Suddenly I was convinced that Cerullo's lecture came after someone reported seeing this girl hanging around me.

As I walked toward the desk, a trader looked up and gestured with two cupped hands, grinning toward the girl. That was it. I decided: This area will be a "cordon sanitaire," a demilitarized zone. Obviously, if a white woman was in proximity to me, it could lead to a bizarre lecture about "black male sexuality." Someday those lectures were going to show up in a report about harassment that could cost me my job. So I would establish a woman-free zone. I looked at the sales assistant, whose real name was Joanna.

"Are you here for a bid or an offer?" She glanced at me, not noticing the tone in my voice. "Are you here for a bid or an offer?" I repeated it once more, and then a third time. I glared at her, fierce and belligerent, and shouted angrily: "Are you here to work, or are you here wasting my traders' time? My traders aren't here to play games. They're here to work. Do you have a job to do? Then go do it. If you don't have a job to do, then I don't understand what you're doing here."

Startled, Joanna started to cry and fled to her desk as everyone stood up from theirs, some with phones in hand, to see what was happening. A lot of them were still angry with me for the firing of Bush. Now they broke up into small groups, muttering, upset. McLaughlin and a few traders huddled in a hallway. Then he marched over to me. "I don't think you should have done that. She wasn't doing anything, she was just here talking to me, and I can talk to my friends if I want to."

I locked my eyes on his and spat words at him.

"No, no, you can't. You're here to work, not to socialize. If you want to date, wait until after work. Any woman who comes to this desk better be here for a bid or an offer. If she's not here for a bid or an offer, she is to leave immediately."

* * *

THE QUALITY OF life on the Bond desk diminished considerably after that. Several more traders refused to speak to me at all. The banter, the ogling of women, the shouts of "periscopes up!" all stopped. Joanna avoided me, clearly genuinely afraid. I stuck to my guns, refusing to talk socially and glaring pointedly at anyone who did. People gossiped openly and muttered sotto voce about my maniacal, paranoid and scary personality. But there was no question it put an end to the confrontations with Cerullo over black men and white women.

I told myself I didn't care. I wasn't at Kidder to make friends. If there was an informant, he was simply an obstacle I couldn't remove. I'd go around him instead. When the air of antipathy on the desk got so thick I felt I could cut it, I just reminded myself of why I was there. All that mattered was how well I did my job, how much money I made. This was war, and my score at the end was all that counted. But the truth is, I couldn't understand why my insistence on hard work made everyone hate me. Especially because I didn't think I was that tough. Occasionally, I made people stay late, but basically I just demanded that they work. What was so hard about that? I told myself I didn't need friends, but in reality, I wanted my traders to like me. I wanted their respect.

What I failed to see was that other people didn't perceive of discipline the same way I did. Their perceptions were universal; mine were adopted from my father. I should have understood that the same merciless demands that sometimes made Pizarro, Yvette and me resent our father would make my colleagues resent me. I didn't realize that I was employing the same barracks philosophy—I was angry at one person, Cerullo, so I punished everyone. No one liked that, and their dislike was not tempered by the fact that I also punished myself. I never stopped to think about it, any more than my father ever did. I probably would have decided that I was right and they were wrong. Anyway, the end result was the same. I expected discipline and was merciless in pursuit of it.

When Kevin McLaughlin had left his accounting job to become a trader, the person who took his old position was Joe Ossman. Ossman had worked in the business unit controller's office, policing traders to ensure they were not doing anything illegal or unethical. He was tall, ramrod straight and wore his hair in a buzz cut. I thought he looked like he'd just stepped out of a 1950s Norman Rockwell painting. Everyone called him Joey-o. While working in the Accounting area, he finished his MBA at night. He was quiet and efficient; whenever he came to the desk he stood silently behind us like a butler, waiting for attention. He brought me the profit and loss figures each night, and he always had the numbers right. He'd stand quietly beside me while I worked on them, and then say "How are the markets doing?" It was refreshing. McLaughlin never cared what the markets were doing. Ossman let his interest be known. After Cerullo fired Bush, I convinced Mullin that Ossman should take Bush's place on the trading desk. In July 1992, Joey-o became a trader.

The "cordon sanitaire" meant that McLaughlin now had to wander the office in search of women to dally with. I'd look up and see him across the trading floor. One afternoon I hit the switch on my intercom and dialed the number of the young woman's desk where McLaughlin lingered. "Kevin, are you doing a trade? What trade? Do you know what we're trying to do over here? Do you know how much risk we have on this desk over here? Are you going to do your fucking job or waste my time trying to get laid?" A female voice gasped and said, "He can't say that!" and I shouted: "I can say whatever the fuck I want! I'm trying to work! I'm trying to make money! I'm taking the fucking risk! Get your ass back over here!" Pretty soon I was chasing McLaughlin by intercom several times a week. He always came scurrying back. Our strategy of buying securities with short maturity periods (McLaughlin's area) and selling securities with longer maturity times (mine) meant that if I sold, McLaughlin needed to buy. We were linked. Whenever one of us traded, the other needed to hedge his position.

Soon I was constantly lecturing my traders. I was making money, but the salespeople were angry, my traders weren't talking to me and I wasn't talking to them. When a woman said hello in passing, I responded with a zombielike expression and a mantra: "Discipline must be maintained!" and walked away. I'd chat with men if we were in an elevator or hallway. But I allowed no socializing at the desk. I refused to deal with the female sales staff. If a saleswoman called an inquiry over the PA, I ignored her. If I did business with her, she'd end up near my desk. If a saleswoman called me on the phone, for the same reason, I'd pretend that her account was too small for me and hand her over to someone else. It was bad business, but not of my making. I refused any interaction with the white women in the office.

I devoted my attention instead to creating my own business. I concentrated on arbitrage transactions, making it important to know the constantly changing price of bonds to within a hairsbreadth. I calculated the price of a bond, applying mathematical formulas to figure the value of Strips and the interrelationship of Strips to bonds to determine what a bond price should be. Very often my calculations told me that a bond was priced too high. Thus, I could buy all the Strips, put the bond back together and have a reconstituted bond at a lower total price. I'd then sell that bond for the higher market price. It didn't matter how many people thought the higher price was the correct bond price that day. They were wrong as long as I could buy Strips at the lower price and build a cheaper bond from them. As a result, I was always on the lookout for the cheapest Strips. I wasn't supposed to buy and sell myself; rather, I depended on my bond trader, Billy Glaser. He was like an in-house broker, and his job was to create a market for me. At least that was how it was supposed to work. But trading desks are very hierarchical, and Strips and bond traders often don't communicate. They are usually rivals in an antagonistic quest for the same market. The dominant trader is traditionally the bond trader because of the glamour and influence of the position. Bonds represent the U.S. national debt, and the financing of America's multitrillion-dollar deficit derives from the ability of Wall Street traders to purchase and distribute federal bonds. This work keeps the nation afloat. Among bond traders, the person who deals in thirty-year bonds is the most powerful member of a Fixed Income trading desk. Strips traders trail as the least among equals.

I didn't want Glaser to control my arbitrage strategy because he didn't follow prices as closely as I did. There was no incentive for him to pay closer attention, either, because the profit of my trades was booked to my desk, not his. Supporting my business meant he had to take on more risk. Asking him to pay closer attention to prices just made me a pain in his neck. He didn't want to do it, so by June 1992, we had a problem.

Glaser sometimes solved this dilemma by telling me to buy the bonds myself, either directly from the Street or through another broker. Those purchases went on my books, not his, alleviating his risk. It also meant that he gave up turf. And once he let me into his turf, I plowed through. Soon I no longer asked him to buy bonds for me or informed him of what I was doing, even if my purchases ran counter to his. A few times I bought a security on the Street, which was called "lifting an offer." The purchase raised the price of the bond because it reflected demand. It was the opposite of what happened when a buyer was looking for a bond at a certain price. If you met, or "hit" his bid, and sold him the bond, then the bond's price would go down. That's because it became known that there was a willing seller at that price. For example, if there are buyers looking for bonds at $50 and $51, how do you know which price is right? You know as soon as someone "hits" the $50 bid—that proves that the price is not $51.

Soon my turnover was much higher than Billy's, leading to angry exchanges and a tug-of-war for control of bond buying. Truthfully, however, I was the one who violated the hierarchy. I owed Glaser an apology. But when he complained about the number of my trades, I realized I did more volume than he did. I was the bigger trader.

One day I needed bonds to cover Strips I had shorted. I asked Glaser to buy them for me. His screen showed someone offering bonds at a price I thought was too low. It should be higher, I said, based on what the Strips are trading for. Glaser agreed, but he wasn't very interested in making a purchase for me. He might be able to sell me ten at the offered price, he said. I fidgeted while I waited for his answer. It's not every day that someone underprices bonds, and my gut told me to leap on them. When Glaser didn't respond, I impulsively picked up my phone, called a broker and ordered $100 million. That was a huge trade for me at the time. Suddenly all of Glaser's telephone lines went off at once, their lights flashing. Picking up the first line, he listened and then shouted to everyone on the desk: "Wait a minute, wait a minute, I'm out! I'm being lifted!" To the phone he said, "He wants to buy a hundred? Yeah, sell it to him!" Then his excitement turned to anger. The broker had told him, "But it's your own guy!"

Trading houses are never supposed to sell to themselves—it's a sign that the right hand doesn't know what the left hand is doing. It's humiliating. Glaser was embarrassed, and furious. He ordered the broker on the phone to break the offer, but was told "there are four guys behind him!" So I wasn't the only one who'd seen that those bonds were too cheap.

Glaser marched over to Mullin and demanded that he order me to stick to Strips trading. Conciliatory as always, Mullin promised to rein me in. It's unprecedented for a Strips trader to muscle in on bond trading, Mullin told me patiently. But the Mortgage desk had always bought bonds directly, so I believed I should be able to do the same. I refused to back down. I ignored Mullin and Glaser and continued to conduct my own bond trades. A week after the $100 million offer, Glaser quit and took a job at Morgan Stanley.

Stress mounted on our desk throughout the summer as it became clear that Mullin had balance sheet problems. I wasn't sure why, but I suspected that it was because Kidder was spending more of GE's money than GE wanted. Already unhappy with me because I continually urged him to confront J. J. McKoan, the head of sales, about our sales force, and because I might have driven Glaser and Bush out of Kidder, Mullin targeted my area to bring his budget into line. Suddenly he demanded that I reduce my trading position from $8 billion to $6 billion. Do it or you're fired, he said. His ultimatum left me no good way out. If I reduced my position, I'd earn less, and that would bring Cerullo crashing down on me, demanding to know why I was making so little money. I was the dominant trader in Mullin's area, too. Did it make sense to curtail the most profitable trader? I sniffed around and discovered that Mullin hadn't asked the Options desk to reduce its position. His wife worked there. Instantly, I was furious. If our area was a meritocracy, then Denise Mullin and her colleagues should have been among the first to reduce their position, because they made the least money. I wasn't going to let Mullin's warped priorities destroy my business. My success was due to discipline and the forcefulness of my personality. Mullin was an appeaser. I wasn't about to follow his advice.

I refused to reduce my position; in fact, I increased it a bit, sending Mullin in a rage into Cerullo's office. As he walked away, he muttered, "You've gotten both of us in trouble." But to his surprise—and mine—Cerullo decided to gamble. Since I'd consistently made money, he ordered Mullin to increase my position. I fairly strutted around the trading floor. I'd defied Mullin, and won.

It was a victory only I appreciated. I looked down the aisle of desks at a row of empty chairs. Not only was no one talking to me, but there seemed to be a mass exodus under way. At the end of June, Glaser had quit. A week later, in early July, the head options trader, Bobby Friedlander, resigned, saying he was disgusted with the way Hugh Bush had been treated. Mullin's inability to protect Bush had shattered the confidence of his work family. I didn't regret that. On the contrary, I wanted the right to fire the deadwood and hire people who were more like me and less like Mullin. But to do that, I'd have to take Mullin's job. I still wanted to replace Kevin McLaughlin, but I couldn't fire him without a candidate ready to step into his job.

For a couple of weeks, I worked undistracted. Then, at the end of July, Cerullo informed me that the two black salesmen in the Los Angeles office had suddenly quit. After Chike-Obi's firing, that left only me and one other black professional in the 2,500-man workforce. We met in Cerullo's office. It was the first time I'd been there since the black sex lectures, and the irony of the topic didn't escape me.

"I'm putting together a group to look into cultural diversity at the firm." He handed me a list detailing how many of the blacks, women, and other minorities at Kidder were associates, vice presidents or senior vice presidents. There were no blacks in the VP ranks. Thus the new Affirmative Action College Recruiting Team comprised a salesman named Michael Ricciardi, a senior vice president named Kathy Dalton and me. Cerullo also wanted me to serve as mentor for a high school summer intern who was starting shortly.

I was the obvious choice—the only choice—for a black teenager. Everyone else seemed to lose interest in the boy after he arrived wearing baggy overalls and a huge pacifier around his neck. Looking up from their desks, people saw a street kid. He dressed like one, walked with a slow, defiant swagger like one, and talked in slang like one. He fulfilled the image of what a black teenage boy should be. Everyone knew he'd landed the internship because he was one of the brightest kids in his school, but they probably questioned the caliber of the school. And the kid probably knew they did, too. It was obvious that the boy didn't know what to expect from the white working world. The first week, I advised him to dress professionally. Even on casual Friday, I wear a suit, I told him, because if I don't someone will mistake me for the mailboy. He continued to wear street clothes, and a week later someone in the trade support area started yelling at him for misplacing a mail delivery. The kid nearly burst into tears. I took him back to his cubicle, and let him have my father with both barrels: "The same thing has happened to me. You must dress professionally. You can try yuppie casual, like polo shirts, but frankly I tried that and was still confused as a mailboy." He wouldn't look at me. "Look at yourself, you look like you just crawled out of the ghetto. Those are harsh words. But my father used to always say to me, 'Take the white man's virtue's, and not his vices.' The first step is to rid yourself of the black man's vices. We have enough obstacles without carrying street baggage into this working world. This is a different culture, a different manner of man. If you're going to compete in this world, you have to defend yourself against the prejudices against your clothes, your manner and how you walk."

After that, whenever I saw him shuffling through the office, I commanded: "Soldier, stick your chest out and your shoulders back." I insisted he stand up straight if he was near my desk. But he'd forget and slouch across the office. Still, the kid understood my message. Unfortunately, he also saw the traders sitting around talking about girls and reading porno magazines, the salespeople idle and complaining, and he picked up the Kidder credo—nobody worked hard. Jett was a freak. Why should he listen to me? There were no better examples to follow.

Reluctantly, I had agreed to participate in Cerullo's effort to recruit more women and minorities. A glance around the trading floor on any day proved that Kidder was woefully behind the times in hiring both women and minorities. But I joined the affirmative action team only because I understood that we'd be recruiting based on merit, first and foremost. We met to schedule recruiting trips to Ivy League and top business schools. None of us had done this before, and no one had given us any rules. We had to work out differences of approach. We debated whether we should determine a figure for how many women and minorities we wanted to recruit, or just go out and find as many as we could. We decided that naming a number in advance sounded too much like a quota. We wondered how to identify black candidates from résumés, Asians and women being easy to spot from their names. My partners assumed blacks would list affiliations with Black Student Union groups. I worried that we'd end up interviewing a lot of unqualified people who used those affiliations to exploit affirmative action programs. When Cerullo heard of our schedule, he erupted. "This is nonsense! Absolute nonsense! Our goal is to reach out to those who are unfortunate and hire them on Wall Street. You can't tell me that Joe Jett here is unfortunate. I want to see us hiring from City University of New York, or Manhattan City College. We want to hire real minorities!"

I was surprised. Of course, we would recruit from Harvard, Yale, the Wharton School of Business. It never occurred to us to consider other schools. Now Cerullo wanted us to target city and community colleges. Those weren't competitive schools. Cerullo wanted to bring in the disadvantaged poor rather than accomplished minorities. I'd seen the results of that kind of minority recruiting before, at Corning. The minorities who got hired were set up to fail.

"I'm sorry, I can't participate in that. There seems to be an effort to hire mailboys, or people who you know don't have the skills or the capacity to compete with you or to ever challenge you. The people who are brought in are not of a common culture, they lack the mental firepower, and they lack the discipline to compete. The skills it takes to succeed here are a lifelong endeavor—you can't bring someone in here from a community college and say voilà, you're now Wall Street material. And I'm not going to participate in that charade." I resigned from the team and left the meeting. The next day, Kathy Dalton told me "that was a pretty bold move. I told them I see your point. But Cerullo has his point, and he's the boss."

*   *   *

MY DAYS SOON took on a familiar routine. I spent a great deal of time pressuring Mullin to stand up to J. J. McKoan, the national sales manager, and demand that customer accounts be reassigned among the salespeople. The sales assignments were a thorn in my side. Soon I took my complaints directly to McKoan, and quickly we found ourselves haggling continually about them. One day when I needed to talk to him, I pushed into his office without knocking. I was surprised to find McKoan, Cerullo, Ricciardi, the Finance desk head Brian Finkelstein, and Mike Vranos sitting around in a cloud of smoke. They had their feet up on chairs and the desktop, and were puffing away on expensive cigars. This was the managing directors' cigar club.

Since I couldn't get any response out of this cabal, I decided simply to take charge. I'd circumvent the regional brokers. I didn't want to conduct business with them, so I wouldn't. Instead, I'd go straight to the Street. It didn't take the brokers long to figure this out, and soon our salespeople were complaining to Mullin that I'd cut them and their clients out of my business. I wouldn't take their calls, or return messages, they complained, and Mullin came to me with their grievances. They were right, I told him. I'd cut them off. This angered Mullin because in early 1992 we'd made a cross-country trek to visit regional brokers. We'd promised them our business.

THAT SUMMER WE plunged into trading municipal defeasance bonds. Those deals made traders happiest—profit is virtually guaranteed in municipal defeasance trades because municipalities agree to a forward purchase of bond Strips at a set price. No matter what happens in the market in the intervening period, the customer is committed. A trader can then purchase Strips at a price lower than what the municipality has agreed to pay.

Municipalities borrow money to pay for schools, roads, police forces. They have to make interest payments on these loans, so they raise money by issuing bonds. When they sell the Strips from those bonds for exactly the amount of the interest payments they must make, that's called "defeasance." When the municipality buys Strips, it doesn't pay with cash, it pays with a bond. It's a swap. Often the swap is for future delivery of the bond. The trader will own the bond at some future date, so he must find a way to hedge that bond—to protect his profit margin from the sale of the Strips. If a trader knows he's going to own a municipal bond on a date certain, he has to protect his investment. Because once he owns that bond, he's exposed to market risk—to price fluctuations. You hedge your position by selling a security similar to the municipal bond you will soon own, one that you believe will behave in the same fashion as that municipal bond. That way the acquisition of one bond and the sale of another balance each other. You've hedged your position.

IN MID-JULY 1992, Kidder decided that what the company had lacked all along was a cultural diversity workshop. The country was reeling from the aftermath of the Rodney King verdict and the riots in Los Angeles. Race polarized people everywhere, and Wall Street was no exception. From friends in other professions and businesses, I knew that these mandatory workshops were sweeping the country. I was assigned to a session with McKoan; Brian Finkelstein, the managing director of Finance; Michael Ricciardi, who had been on the affirmative action recruiting team with me; and several nonmanagement staff. We trooped into an upstairs conference room and sat down at a table headed by a young black consultant. He drew pyramids on a board and described how black people were trying to work their way up. He lead word-association games, asking us to link ethnic groups with words like "lazy," "intelligent" and "hardworking." "Be honest, be honest," he kept saying. All the negative words conjured up images of blacks. "That's not prejudice, that's experience," someone said. The conversation then turned to acceptance—the acceptance of blacks in everyday life, in the workplace, in neighborhoods.

"Hey, let's be frank," Brian Finkelstein said. "If I brought a black woman home, my mother probably wouldn't like it but would think I was just having fun, but if my sister came home with a black guy, it'd kill my mother. I'd probably have to shoot her, because it would just kill my mother if she found out."

McKoan was completely silent throughout the session. He looked uncomfortable, and said nothing in answer to Finkelstein. I cracked, "Brian, looking at you, I have difficulty envisioning anyone wanting to date your sister." The facilitator offered, "These sorts of attitudes are throwbacks to when there were lynchings. If that strong a barrier exists in something that has nothing to do with earning money, well, people get really concerned when it comes to earning money. If minorities are viewed as a threat to job security, the reaction can be even stronger than what Brian expressed. It's important for white men in managerial positions to be confident enough to open their doors to black candidates."

"Well," Finkelstein said, "we've got J. J. McKoan, and J.J. only hires minorities."

Everyone laughed at his reference to McKoan's sales assistants. In firms across Wall Street, sales assistants were frequently pretty young females. McKoan particularly liked to hire women of color, and his staff was usually made up of exotic-looking Filipinas, Indians or Latinas. It was one of the few places in the office where any ethnicity was visible.

To my mind, the workshop only served to expose Finkelstein's ignorance and racist perceptions. But it wasn't until that workshop that I understood Cerullo's lectures about the "Kidder culture." Now I knew it was the managerial mind-set. Cerullo, Finkelstein, Ricciardi, McKoan and Vranos were close friends. They vacationed together, socialized on weekends, shut themselves up in an office for their cigar club. Mullin was the only managing director excluded from the group. They seemed thick as thieves, and like-minded as well.

A week later, on a Monday morning, I rode up in the elevator with Cerullo and a handful of co-workers. "So, Joe, what did you do over the weekend?" Cerullo asked mildly.

"Blondes."

Everyone burst out laughing. Except Cerullo.

BY AUGUST 1992, Cerullo hadn't mentioned black male sexuality in weeks, and had stopped talking to me about the affirmative action effort. Whenever he called me into his office, it was to discuss business. He wanted continuous reports on my progress, especially since Mullin had tried to cut my trading position and Cerullo had responded by ordering Mullin to increase it. He'd asked Mullin to explain my trading strategy. My desk was doing well. I'd retreated from my fight over the sales force, backing away from trying to convince Mullin to go head-to-head with McKoan. Instead, I'd concentrated on the arbitrage trades we could do ourselves.

One afternoon Cerullo appeared on the trading floor. A buzz arose; Cerullo rarely mingled with the working classes, and when he did, he spoke only to the Big Swinging Dicks. He wandered the floor, and I felt dozens of pairs of eyes doing exactly as mine, following his every move. Cerullo made a beeline for me. As he approached, people at desks nearby fell silent. He was Napoleon—albeit with damp hair—visiting the troops in the field.

"I've been taking a look at your profit numbers. How are you doing this?" he demanded. I told him about the arbitrage strategy that was responsible for my huge trading volume. He wanted specific information: What advantage did I think I had that would continue? How long would it go on? Why did I think it would keep up? The only thing limiting me, I said, was my budget. I could use more capital.

"All right, is this sustainable? I'm being asked to put together a budget for this year and next. Can I count on this flow of profit? For how long?"

I believed it would last until November because my trading was driven by the Federal Reserve's lowering of interest rates. It looked like the Fed would continue to lower rates at least until the presidential election. Recession had hit the country hard in the period after the Persian Gulf war and the presidential contest between George Bush and Bill Clinton. The Federal Reserve Board had eased interest rates on the short end, meaning the yield curve was going to continue to steepen, I told Cerullo.

"So all of your profit is being driven by arbitrage and risk-related trading? What about customer business? You remember that, don't you, where you buy or sell securities and try to take a little money out of the spread?" Cerullo said. The arbitrage market could dry up, he believed, and now he wanted me to focus again on customer trading. He forgot that he was the one who had insisted that I concentrate on arbitrage. Now he had another problem. "I mean the salesmen are complaining to me that I ought to sit you in a corner somewhere and let you do this arbitrage because you're not responding to their customer needs."

His eyes were flat and his voice menacing. The visit turned icy. I became combative. "There's a reason for that. The salesmen are lazy, trifling and no good."

"Not all of them. We have some good salesmen out there. Look at our mortgage operation. They're number one in market share. Those are my salespeople who have gotten us there."

"Your salespeople aren't interested in the penny-ante commissions that government securities pay, and why should they be? They can sell a mortgage and earn $400 per million. If they sell a government, they make $30. It's a joke. If I were a salesman, I wouldn't pay any attention to me, either."

Now Cerullo became angry. "I'm telling you, build up your customer base." He wanted me to go after money management firms, insurance companies, pension funds. He knew they all bought bonds, they just didn't buy them from us. "This year you made $18 million. You've only paid out $300,000 in sales credit. Profits and commissions should be equal. If you don't get it there at the end of the year, I'm going to bill you for it anyway."

Cerullo was taking the salespeople's side. But he wasn't going to fire me. I was making money. The only thing Cerullo could do was force me to pay the salespeople—whether I did business with them or not. It was up to me to turn this ultimatum to my advantage. I'd already thrown down a gauntlet, defying Mullin at several key junctures. I got Bush fired, I refused to deal with the regional brokers, I circumvented Glaser, I balked at reducing my trading position from $8 billion to $6 billion. Now I was determined that this appeal of Mullin's to Cerullo would fail. I decided it meant that I was now taking orders from Cerullo, not Mullin. I would use that as an opportunity to win over the salespeople. If Cerullo was going to charge me anyway, I might as well use the money to bribe the sales force. The timing, from a trading perspective, was perfect. All spring and summer I had been selling short long-dated Strips. These were Strips that didn't mature for thirty years. I'd accumulated a short position of approximately $6 billion— meaning I'd sold Strips I didn't actually own. Now the time had come to begin buying them. I'd let the sales force do that for me, if I could get them to pay attention to government sales over mortgages. I told Cerullo and McKoan that beginning after Labor Day, I was going to make a big push to increase government bond sales. I planned to offer an incentive. Normally, salespeople earned a commission of $32 per million dollars in government bonds sold. My idea was to quadruple that to $128 per million.

I planned to announce my offer right after Labor Day. But the first day following the long holiday weekend, a friend surprised me at work. Robin was a tall blonde, standing six feet four, and I hadn't seen her in a long while. She bounded into the office to ask me to lunch. I stood up, alarmed. I had no choice but to greet her. People stared. Her height made her miniskirt all too mini. I grabbed my coat and steered Robin off the trading floor as quickly as possible, but a few traders cheered and hooted anyway. It was noon when we left, and I didn't return to the office until 2:30. I always had lunch at my desk, working while I ate my deli sandwich, so I told myself one long lunch wasn't out of line. However, when I got back to the office, Cerullo's secretary was on the phone. "You'd better get back here. Mr. Cerullo's been calling you for two hours."

Cerullo stood with his back to me. "Close the door." He didn't move, and didn't say another word. I shut the door and stood still. He hadn't told me to sit. Finally, he turned, his face red with rage, and put his fists on his desktop. Leaning forward, he bit off his words.

"We had a talk. Just in June. And I recall that we spoke again, just a few weeks later. How many times do I have to tell you? That I will not tolerate any type of relationship with any women at this firm? How many times do I have to tell you that this firm will not tolerate the type of sexual aggressiveness that you seem intent on displaying? How many times? How many times do I have to go over this before it sinks in?"

He'd been calling me since 12:30, he said. He'd heard that I'd gone to lunch with a woman who had been on the trading floor. "What did I tell you about having relationships with people at this firm?"

I was defensive; I had long-lunch guilt. If one of my guys had disappeared for two hours, I'd have given him hell. I wouldn't tolerate it myself. Robin didn't work at Kidder, I explained. The guard had let her come up to the office, and we'd gone to a lunch, a long one for sure, but it was practically the first time I'd left my desk during the day since I started my job.

Cerullo raged on. "If you need a vacation day to visit your friends, then take a vacation day. But if you're here at work then I expect you to be here at work." His tone softened. "Listen, I'm just telling you that you have to be careful. I've told you this before. I've told you about the firm's culture and how people here are very sensitive to interracial relationships. I think it's to your advantage not to have her come up here. Why cause trouble unnecessarily?"

His comments ended as they always did, with a lilt that said he was just giving me friendly, fatherly advice.

"Look, this firm is very sensitive about black male sexuality. I get reports about what you do. And if people are offended by your relationships with other members of this firm, I think it would be best for you not to do it."

This was the first time I'd heard that he "got reports." I knew that people watched each other and gossiped incessantly, and I had believed that Cerullo kept tabs on me that way.

"Now wait a minute. Who's giving you reports? This is what I asked you back in June. If there is someone at this firm who is offended by my behavior, just tell me who they are. Let me talk to them. Or at least let me know who it is."

Cerullo paused. "This is not a person. It's the culture. Again, you have to understand that Kidder is an old-line firm with old-line people who are very set in their ways."

We looked at each other. I was still standing by the door. "I'll admit that no one should take two-hour lunches. But I'm not here trying to date anyone. And if someone from outside the firm meets me here, and for some reason I'm going to find it thrown back in my face, then you've crossed the line. I think you've crossed the line anyway. I'm not here trying to date anyone. I think this is going too far."

He shook his head. "No one is trying to tell you who to date. All I said to you, and all I've ever said to you, is that this firm has a concern. It has a concern because of what has happened in the past. If people cannot control their sexual aggressiveness, then I have to do something about it. I'm not going to tolerate the kind of aggressiveness that Mustafa brought into this firm, and I'm not going to tolerate it from you."

Abruptly, he changed the subject, wanting to know about my plan to quadruple the sales commission for anyone bringing in $20 million in sales. I walked out angry, feeling that I was being watched. Everyone would love to see me fired, but who had the access to Cerullo to make it happen? It had to be Mullin, I thought. We clashed constantly about the sales force and half his staff was gone due to me. He'd had to ask Cerullo to force my hand. I was making money, however, so getting rid of me wouldn't be easy. What would be the best way? Obviously, Chike-Obi's legacy lingered. And Cerullo was paranoid about black men. So, if I had anything to do with women at work, I'd be fired without notice.

My conflict with Mullin had never been open warfare. I tried not to be defensive, but after the last confrontation with Cerullo, everything seemed suspect. Why was Denise Mullin, all of a sudden, so interested in being friends? Denise—very blond, very married Denise—suddenly began commenting on my clothes. True, the repetitive quality of my wardrobe was an office joke. But Denise had never offered clothes tips before. Now I'd often look up to see her traipsing down the aisle toward my desk, where she'd stop and make a comment about my gray suit, or on alternate days, the dark blue one. Or one of my striped ties. True, Denise didn't have a lot of friends in the office—there was a constant low-grade resentment over the perception that as Mullin's wife she enjoyed preferential treatment. And this at a firm where the culture allegedly frowned on interoffice relationships. Mullin had hired her at Kidder. She wasn't part of his original Jewish Mafia. Had his marrying her contributed to the breakup of his little work family? In trying to befriend me, she may have simply been hoping to find a soulmate in a fellow outcast. No one talks to me, no one talks to you, so why don't we talk to each other? But I was wary.

Uncertainty turned to downright concern when Denise began hinting that we should see each other outside the office. Mullin was often out of town, so many days when she causally suggested, "Hey, let's get together," it was clear that she meant just the two of us. Probably there was nothing untoward about these invitations. Denise was a nice woman. I worried anyway that she was part of a trap laid by Mullin. I evaded the invitations.

Some banter returned to the desk. But since I refused to have anything to do with Kidder women—near the desk, over the PA or on the phone— there was no chatter about women, dating or sex. "Periscopes up" resumed to some extent, because all ogling of women now had to be done at a distance. For the most part, sports, athletes and game scores filled the gossip void. Bathroom humor took on an egregious life. McLaughlin and the Canadian bond trader often bought chili dogs for lunch from a street cart, just so they could make fart jokes all afternoon. Soon they developed a flatulence rating system, and would look all over the neighborhood for fast food with the greatest potential. For a time, they occupied themselves for hours making jokes and comments about farting. They talked as loud as they could, in increasingly gross detail, all to attract the attention of the women on the Repo staff at the next desk. Most of these young women were working-class Brooklyn and Staten Island girls who favored heavy makeup, tall, starched hair and long, brightly lacquered fingernails. They were just as ribald as the traders, and took the bait every time. It was exactly like being in junior high. Finally, I told Mullin that we had to separate McLaughlin and the Canadian bond trader.

THIS IS WAR

FTER CERULLO'S LECTURE about my friend Robin, I actually sat down to consider how to accumulate more power. I'd need it as leverage the next time someone came after me with taunts about black male sexuality. I was making money, but not as much as the Mortgage desk. Everyone found me troublesome, and that rendered me expendable. For the time being, Cerullo's greed protected me from his racism. But I suspected he intended to fire me once he felt he'd gotten what he wanted from me. It would be easy to get rid of me, especially if the groundwork was already laid.

With power, I could conduct my business any way I pleased, just as Cerullo did. He wasn't creative or imaginative, but he was an effective leader, and he was a better leader than Mullin. I didn't intend to be everyone's friend, like Mullin. I wanted to lead, like Cerullo. And I thought I knew what it took. It's a mistake to confuse leadership with good feelings. Too often people apply charitable, Godlike concepts to leadership: care, compassion, understanding. But the best leaders lack compassion, or at least are prepared to overcome it to control, improve or dominate their territory. Indeed, very often leadership means causing pain or injury. Few people want to hurt others, but leaders must be willing and able. Work is like war. A leader must throw assets at the enemy. People and employees are an asset, like any other investment, tool or part of the capital. Leaders cannot be emotionally attached. If someone has to be fired, leaders cannot be handicapped by the anguish that firing might cause. A leader—or manager—has to be prepared to give the order. Cerullo and Mullin were perfect examples of two approaches to leadership. Mullin cared deeply for the people who worked for him; they were like his children. He knew all about their lives, he counseled and mentored them, he overlooked their foibles. The world thought of him as a great leader, but he wasn't an effective one. Cerullo was.

My accumulation of power began with a plan to pay four times the going commission to any salesperson who sold my Strips securities. This applied to five hundred salespeople, firm-wide. Anyone—from the hotshots to the dregs—was eligible. Normally, the Big Swinging Dick salesmen ignored me when I came on the hoot and holler. I didn't do sizable enough trades and the commission was too small. On each desk, hoot-and-holler speakers could be set to receive announcements from the Government, Mortgage and Corporate areas. The night before I launched my plan, I walked down the sales force desk line and saw that every Government speaker switch was turned off. People routinely ignored the entire Government desk.

The next morning, I picked up the hoot and holler and hit the Mortgage area button instead of my own. Then I recited a statement I'd planned and rehearsed.

"This is Joe Jett on the Government Bond desk. I realize that most of you in the sales force have your Government hoot and holler permanently switched off. In fact I walked the floor last night and saw that ninety percent were off here in New York. You're not even listening to what I have to say. You think this is a game. This isn't a game, this is a fucking war. We're offering four times the commission on your trades. And listen. You'll earn four times on any trade over $20 million. We don't want any of your little panty-ass trades. If you don't have a $20 million trade, don't bother. You can go back to playing games with the little Mortgage boys and girls. We want trades of size and substance."

I left my number for anyone who wanted to call back.

Pandemonium broke out. Instantly, the Mortgage desk called. "You're trying to fuck me in the ass!" a trader screamed. Several top salesmen called immediately: "Hey, Jett, we'll take your money."

Every inquiry call from a salesman required followup to make the trade happen. A trader has to be ready with a price at which he will buy a security and a price at which he will sell. The object is to make money from the difference. But this time I threw in a wrinkle—the price at which I was prepared to buy and sell a bond were exactly the same. It's called "locking the market." That shows that as a trader, I am not trying to make any money, I am just trying to facilitate business. When the salespeople called to ask, "What's your level on Fed-09s?" and I responded, "723," they'd counter: "Is that your bid or your offer?"

"That's my bid *and* my offer." My message was clear: If you can't do a trade in a locked market, well, you're not much of a salesman. It's not the trader's fault.

For a week, our trading was off the charts. Suddenly there was more activity on my desk than I'd ever seen at Kidder. Before Labor Day, I had paid out about $300,000 in sales commissions for the year. A week later, it was close to $2 million. But I wasn't worried about payouts—I wasn't even trying to earn money. I wanted to prove that the Government Bond desk had tremendous potential that was habitually overlooked. I wanted to identify the salespeople with the clients to make the trades happen. I wanted to show that the business was out there, only the salespeople were not willing to go after it. I wanted to consolidate power for myself.

The following week, I called off the quadrupled sales commissions. But I was back on the hoot and holler on Monday, offering to trade in a locked market. Nothing happened. Clearly, without a bribe, my trades were not worth the time of day to the heavy hitters. They only wanted to do business that would pay them $128 per million. At the end of the day, I launched into a diatribe over the hoot and holler.

"We are trying to build business for Kidder Peabody. Our efforts are being hampered because of the salesmen's greed. Last week we paid four times sales credit on these accounts. We are in the Government sector and we can't afford to pay four times sales credit. But you showed the trades are out there. This firm needs those accounts. Are you telling us we can't have this business because you don't get paid enough so you can't be bothered to call your accounts? Maybe you're getting paid too much. Maybe we should take those accounts away from you and give them to someone who is lean and hungry and will work for them."

I ran to Cerullo's office. I had to have my own sales force! I'd proven that the accounts were out there. The only way to reach them was to control the salespeople. Cerullo called in McKoan, who looked at my numbers. "Well, I don't think that a large enough effort has been made to show that you're committed to this market. You can't offer four times sales credit one week and then take it away. It takes time for it to sink in. I think it is premature to corrupt what has been working successfully for us for years. We have a generalist sales force and we're number one in fixed income in the world."

I looked at McKoan, shocked. I never expected to have a proven plan for making millions of dollars in the palm of my hand, and have McKoan oppose it. For a moment, I was quiet. Giving me a sales force would do two things: increase my power, and decrease his. Okay, maybe as McKoan said, I hadn't offered the quadrupled commission for long enough. So there was nothing to do but offer it again. The next week, the end of September, we resumed. I held up for two weeks more, and then dropped it to a doubled commission for trades greater than $20 million. Even so, business declined precipitously. This time I couldn't lock the market just to get trades moving. The 1992 presidential election was just around the corner, and George Bush was falling behind in the polls. It was too late for the Fed to ease interest rates anymore, and Bill Clinton was already talking about lowering mortgage interest rates when he took office. I needed to cover my short in long-dated securities, and I needed to do it quick. I needed to reverse my position and buy long-dated Strips. I'd been short these securities all year, and they had gone down in price. Throughout the spring, I'd also shed long-dated Strip securities. It was rumored that one of the biggest buyers was a large insurance and asset management firm, Kemper Securities in Chicago. Just as eagerly as I'd sold long-dated Strips, Kemper had been buying them. Their strategy was to take the opposite side of my position, and go long in long-dated securities. But the market hadn't been kind, and they'd taken a beating.

I took my Angry Young Man act back on the hoot and holler. I was aggressively seeking long-dated Strips, I said. The salesman responsible for Kemper Securities had never contacted me during our first round of quadrupled commission. Even four times the usual sales credit was apparently peanuts to him. He made so much money as Kidder's number three salesman that any effort spent on government bonds was effort wasted. During our second-week offering, a Mortgage desk trader strolled over to tell me the Kemper salesman was looking for me. Apparently, the guy didn't even know which of his PA switches connected to the Government desk. So he'd raised the Mortgage desk on the hoot and holler. Then I heard him over the firm-wide PA.

"Joe Jett, Joe Jett? You still paying quadruple, still looking for size on long-dated Strips? Kemper wants you to make a bid on $2 billion May 18 principals."

A $2 billion sale would earn the salesman a $250,000 commission that afternoon.

Mullin's voice came over the hoot. He and Cerullo could hear the firm-wide inquiry in their offices. "If you're looking for size, looks like you've got it." I needed Mullin's permission, because my position limits were still $8 billion. I checked my calculations, and asked whether I was in competition with other trading houses. Pick up a private line, the salesman said.

"They don't want the Street to know, but they may have more paper to go." As soon as the Street heard about the sale, the price would drop. I got the message. I should be in a position to buy the long-dated bonds and hang on to them, not alert the market by turning around immediately and selling them. Obviously, Kemper had been sitting on a massive backlog of these bonds, just waiting to get rid of them. Just about everyone on the Street had done the same all year, so there were few buyers.

The difference between long-term and short-term interest rates was large—at least, it had historically been large. Since March 1992, the gap had been getting bigger and bigger. That alone signals a potential to make money—but also cues buyers to be cautious. Any time a security shows a dramatic, breakthrough value, there's bound to be a correction. Most of the Street had continued to buy long-dated securities, expecting the price to correct. But I'd been contrarian, and taken the opposite view. My strategy was much riskier. This time, it turned out to be right.

Now I discovered that I had the room to bail Kemper out of their position. No one else seemed willing. They all wanted short-dated securities. The timing couldn't have been better. I could buy Kemper's long-dated securities; in fact, I needed to buy them because I'd been short those securities all year. And the beauty of it was—I could hedge my investment by selling the short-dated securities I had accumulated. It was perfect.

I entered the trade into the computer. Our clunky 286 seized up, as usual, taking minutes to perform the transaction. I wrote the ticket.

The next day, the salesman came back to me with another $2 billion in securities that Kemper wanted to sell. In two days, he made a half a million dollars in commission. Trades of that size are impossible to keep quiet. The Street knew almost immediately that Kemper had done a massive transaction. But my role didn't show up anywhere in the market—I wasn't selling the thirty-year securities, I was hedging them with my two-year notes. No one made the connection.

By the following Monday, I was sure the salesman must be planning to take the rest of the year off. Then Kemper called again. They wanted to sell another $2 billion. I knew I had the room. My position limit was $8 billion, but with all my obligations, I could still manage $6 billion. I took the third trade, but that was enough for me. "I've covered my short," I told the salesman. "The next one is going to be harder."

"That's okay, Joe, because they're through. We fit like a glove."

THE EFFECT OF money on people is striking. Immediately, I became popular at work. A few dramatic trades virtually wiped my slate clean. McKoan was ecstatic—to him, the Kemper trades proved that his generalist sales force could make money from government bonds. I knew my battle for a sales force of my own would be more difficult now.

At the same time, I was suddenly one of the gang again. The week after the Kemper trades, I walked past the sales desks. A saleswoman reached out and pinched my rear. "I've always wanted to do that," she giggled. Unprepared for this, I stopped and stared at her.

"You know, we voted you best butt on the trading floor," one of the other saleswomen said, with her colleagues chiming in.

I turned around to go back the way I'd come. "Discipline must be maintained." The saleswomen were unimpressed.

Laughing, the pincher shouted: "He's blushing, I think he's blushing!"

From then on, women on the floor were no longer bothered by my attitude toward them. Teasing and needling me challenged them, and getting a reaction from me was their new sport. They seemed determined to drag me into banter, since I'd made a point of banning such talk. Anytime

I walked across the trading floor I'd hear a titillating comment: "Hey, Joseph, did you see Joan's new miniskirt?" or "Hey, Joe, you know what they call these? Hooters!" I kept walking as they laughed.

I couldn't end the comments, but I could ensure they always occurred in passing. I refused to stop long enough in one place to be considered lingering with women. The teasing hadn't attracted Cerullo's attention, and I was determined that it wouldn't. As for its effect on me—I actually felt better. Obnoxious banter is the norm on a trading floor, and it was evidence that people had relaxed around me. No one feared me anymore. I felt looser and friendlier toward my co-workers. Maybe not everyone was part of the Kidder culture, I thought. Some of the saleswomen who teased me eventually started bringing their tickets to my desk in person. The first few visits made my stomach knot with tension, but when the phone didn't ring with Cerullo's voice at the other end, I began to relax.

One afternoon in October, Anita Day interrupted me as I filled out a ticket for a couple of saleswomen. Her voice carried an edge. I still sent all of her business to Joey-o. This time she insisted on talking to me in person.

"I keep trying to call you on your hoot and you switch me to Joey-o. I have accounts and my accounts can do business. You treat me like shit, like you don't want to talk to me, but you're talking to them." Her face was steely, but I could see she was shaking and upset. "You're talking to them, why won't you talk to me?" I turned to Joe Ossman. He'd done three trades already with Anita that day. "Joey-o, what the hell happened? Did you answer her inquiry?"

"I'm not talking about Joe Ossman," Day screamed. Motion stopped around the desk, and the saleswomen gaped. "You won't talk to me! I haven't done anything! I haven't done anything! And you won't talk to me!! You're friendly to them, why won't you be friendly to me?"

"I'm not here to be friendly to you or to anyone. If you want a friend, buy a dog." Just running into Day in the lobby had gotten me in trouble once already. And I hadn't forgotten that she was involved in Chike-Obi's firing, the event that sparked all the nonsense about black male sexuality. I wanted nothing directly to do with her. "We answer all inquiries. If you have an inquiry, we answer. Joe Ossman, what happened?"

Day walked away, but was back five minutes later. Now she wanted to speak to me privately, off the floor. I didn't have a single piece of business on my desk. "I'm sorry, I have a major position I'm trying to get rid of and I don't have time. If I get done, I'll let you know."

FIRST THING THE next day Cerullo wanted to see me. He congratulated me on the big Kemper trades; I explained how they'd fit perfectly with my need to cover securities in which I'd been short all summer.

"That's good, that's good." He paused. "I've got some complaints recently. I know you're driven. I have to tell you, when I was a trader I was just like you, a real hard ass. Sometimes you have to be a hard-ass just to get things done. You have to be . . ." His voice trailed off. "However. A trader needs to be approachable. It's important that the sales force feels you're someone that they can approach to ask about trading strategies, to ask about what a major customer should be doing, or maybe just to say hello."

I stared at him. I can't win, I thought. If I talk to women, I'll get fired. Now the same woman who had gotten Chike-Obi dismissed for aggressiveness has complained that I'm not approachable. I had no doubt that this chat was about Anita Day.

"We both know that every time I talk to anyone out there, someone accuses me of trying to have sex on the trading floor. We've argued about Mustafa Chike-Obi before, and I'm not interested in getting into another argument. But I don't feel comfortable with the situation. I really don't think that I have to be buddy-buddy with people at this firm in order to do my job."

Cerullo's expression remained mild. "No one's asking you to be buddy-buddy with anyone. I just told you, I was just like you. But if people have inquiry, you can answer the phone. And you can't refuse to answer the phone when people do have inquiry. You have to answer everyone's inquiry. You can't not talk to certain people."

"Fine, I don't talk to anyone. To tell you the truth, I haven't said a word to anyone in four months. I don't say hello to anyone at this damn firm."

Exasperation flashed across Cerullo's face, warning me I was being unreasonable. "That's not conducive to getting business done. I find it hard to believe that you can effectively communicate with the sales force if you're not prepared to say hello to somebody."

"I'm not prepared to say hello to somebody if it means you're going to call me in here and give me some lecture about black male sexuality."

He looked annoyed. "That hasn't happened. No one at this firm cares about you saying hello to anyone. That just isn't true."

"It has happened. Ed, I've had discussions with you after I've just been standing in proximity to someone, when I haven't said a word to them."

Cerullo's scowl deepened. "I'm not trying to have an argument with you. I'm just trying to say if someone calls your desk with inquiry, that you respond to that inquiry."

BY THE FALL of 1992, I'd been at Kidder for just over a year, and had booked $28 million in profit. My strategy of trading huge volumes of Strips had paid off. A great deal of my success had come from the Kemper deal, a risky call that played perfectly into market conditions. Being in the right place at the right time. I'd done such massive trades in the last few months that I'd earned a reputation—whenever I said buy, salespeople, brokers and traders assumed I meant $100 million or more. Completing the trades was a struggle, however. Our computer system was so outdated that I sometimes felt I might as well calculate prices and interest rates with a quill pen. The computers rumbled and clunked along like old jalopies. The small screens blinked dull green and black, the plastic monitor casing scratched, stained and covered with indelible smudges and fingerprints. We waited at least a minute—a painful eternity in a crazy trading market—for the processor to unfreeze after every data entry, and Mullin's software still restricted us to four settlement dates only: same-day settlement, next-day settlement, skip day or corporate settlement. If we had a trade that settled on any other day, we were out of luck. Lots of our trades settled farther in advance, like the high volume of municipal defeasance bonds. Everything like that was simply input under corporate settlement, because it was as far-reaching as the system allowed. We were still spending hours at the end of each day correcting the data to avoid price mismatches between our computer's calculations and the actual price of securities.

So it was cause for rejoicing in October when Cerullo decided that we had earned enough money to overhaul the computer system. A chunk of my $28 million profit paid for Intel Pentium processors with ten times the speed and power of our old system. Moishe Benatar had been hard at work writing a third generation of Kidder software, and now we owned new PCs powerful enough to accommodate his programs. The new software eliminated our reconciliation problems overnight. With it, we could input actual settlement dates. Our lucrative municipal defeasance, for example, could now be correctly accounted for from the moment of data entry.

IN THE WEEKS the programmers and technicians readied our new computers and software, I attended a regular meeting of the Federal Reserve Board of New York. Traditionally, every three weeks, the Federal Reserve Board met with Wall Street traders and chief economists. Usually the only people who came to the meetings were economists; bond traders couldn't be bothered with federal bureaucrats. The Fed representatives wanted to hear from traders who could discuss customer flow and strategies for selling securities. The Fed decides which securities to offer—whether they'll be bonds with a two-year maturity, a five-year maturity, a ten- or thirty-year maturity. If traders or economists can tell the Fed that there is a need for bonds in a particular maturity sector, the Fed may pass that information on to the U.S. Treasury, and the Treasury may issue bonds they think will bring the best price. So the Fed needed traders more than traders needed the Fed. Since the meetings were also dull, most traders didn't go. Thus, the Fed representatives ended up talking to ten or so economists. I was one of the few traders who regularly attended the Tuesday meetings. I liked the dry, clinical talk about numbers. And sometimes things got interesting. After Bill Clinton defeated George Bush, one of his first orders of business was to reduce interest rates so homes would be more affordable to the American public. The credibility of his administration, he proclaimed, could be measured by the affordability of American homes. He chose radical measures to reduce interest rates. Normally, each year, the Treasury issues approximately $45 billion in new thirty-year bonds. Clinton decided to reduce that to $20 billion, cutting the supply of new bonds by about 60 percent. As a rule, thirty-year bonds were auctioned four times a year—in February, May, August and November. The Fed's idea was to simply cancel two of the auctions. Bonds would issue in February and August only. The resulting scarcity would increase the price of the long bonds, and that, in turn, would reduce interest rates. Since most home mortgages are thirty-year mortgages tied to long-bond yields, it looked like Clinton's move would result in more affordable homes.

In its winter meetings in 1992, the Federal Reserve Board of New York began floating this plan. It wanted to see how traders, economists and investment bankers would react. I thought reducing the number of Treasury bonds was an insane idea. By omitting two auctions, the Fed would greatly hamper the liquidity of Treasury bonds overall.

"You should not do this!" I said at one meeting. "If you do, it's going to greatly disrupt the Treasury markets." I doubted the Fed would carry out this plan. Back at work, a Kidder economist teased me about arguing with the Fed.

"You had good reasons, but quite frankly, they were rather self-centered," he laughed. "If they're thinking about the greater good of Joseph Jett and Joseph Jett's trading position, then maybe there won't be a reduction. But if they're thinking about home buyers and home builders and how a reduction of interest rates will help them, then they're going to do it."

I didn't think much more about the Fed for the next few weeks. I was more concerned with jump-starting my campaign for my own specialized sales force. I took my plea directly to Cerullo. I now met—or rather had an audience—with Cerullo every other day. My progress in working with McKoan's sales force interested him acutely. Since I didn't report directly to Cerullo, these conferences were unusual and they unnerved Mullin. Often when I left Cerullo's office, Mullin would be waiting for me, anxious to hear the details of my talk with Cerullo. Abruptly, he decided to adopt my idea of a government sales force, and began lobbying for it.

After the presidential election, Cerullo chimed in, pushing McKoan to give me a sales staff. McKoan countered by offering a few unremarkable salespeople. "You want 'em, you can have 'em," he told me. This wasn't what I'd had in mind. Three of the five salespeople he offered had never covered an account on their own. Three of the five were women, so I rejected them immediately for no reason other than their gender. All three were young, one was a former assistant of McKoan's that he wanted to promote, and two had just finished the Kidder MBA training program. One of the three was Linda Mead, who had just spent a year as apprentice to a top salesman. They all had potential. But it was too risky for me to work closely with any of them. I couldn't just scuttle their candidacies; I had to have a reason, so I blamed it on their inexperience. There was some truth to that—I wanted McKoan to turn over some of his big hitters. I gave him a list of the salespeople I wanted—and they rejected me. None of them wanted to become government bond specialists. McKoan countered with another list, four men and two women. I interviewed each of them personally. When I talked to Harry Haigood, he surprised me with a bit of gossip I hadn't heard.

"Listen, you've garnered a lot of attention at the Government desk, and I have to tell you there's a grassroots movement afoot to have you replace Mel Mullin. If your name was put up to replace Mel, would you oppose that?"

The only thing I'd ever heard about the sales force was that they all disliked me intensely, so this news was unexpected. "Sure," I said carefully. "I'd entertain that, definitely."

Linda Mead's name was particularly unwelcome on McKoan's list because of the lecture I'd gotten from Cerullo in 1991 after she and I danced at an office party. That dance was my first brush with race paranoia at Kidder. We'd barely spoken since then. Mead knew I wasn't likely to accept her candidacy now. But she wanted the job. She drew me aside; she knew she could do the work, she said. She'd watched the other salespeople sitting around, talking, wasting time. She could do better. But not in her current job. The only accounts she was allowed to cover were useless. Frustration drove her to think about quitting. I was her last chance. She was eager to work for me, to prove she was capable and had a future at Kidder.

"Please don't destroy my career."

I looked at the floor. At the wall. Over her shoulder, never at her. Then I glanced at her desk, a few feet away from where we stood. I couldn't trash her life. But I had to ensure that she didn't inadvertently trash mine. I pointed at the hoot and holler on her desk. "You see that box? That's how you communicate with me." With that, I hired her, and walked away.

Cerullo hovered in the background during my negotiations with McKoan over sales staff. He never insisted that if a government sales force was going to be set up, it should be composed of the sharpest salespeople possible. Instead, he left the choice to McKoan and me. But his support of the idea in general was the only thing that allowed it to finally happen. I remained acutely aware that any discussions with women candidates were being watched. Cerullo didn't call me into his office. It was as close as we would ever come to openly agreeing with and supporting one another.

* * *

I GRAPPLED WITH learning our new software and Pentium computer system. Even with ramped-up speed and processing power, it was still impossible to pinpoint the profitability of a single trade. Our investment position was so huge, and the volume of trades we did so massive, that individual trades couldn't be singled out. Sure, selling a bond for a higher price than we paid for it generated a profit. But the complexity of our trading made it impossible to break down each day's activity. Until the day after Christmas.

I walked through the heavy glass doors and onto a subdued trading floor. The office was almost unrecognizable without the frenzy that usually swirled through the place. The quiet around my desk was soothing. A handful of people worked silently at their desks, reassuring me that it wasn't too odd to be in the office over the holidays. Very few trades were conducted, but one of the day's deals was mine. In late afternoon, I entered the trade into the computer. It was a forward settling reconstitution of a bond. Because of Federal Reserve regulations, the transaction would only really take place when the bond was delivered to the Fed. That's because the Fed doesn't process Strips or recons for future dates. All processing is same-day, and only starts when the Fed has the bond in hand. When a bond is physically delivered to the Federal Reserve bank via the FedWire, only then does the stripping or reconning begin. Until then, the transaction is merely on paper and cannot be fulfilled.

The Pentium processor churned through the data quickly. The quietness of the Street meant there were no concurrent price changes or trade inputs between the time I entered the data and the end of the day. When I checked on the profit and loss before going home, I was surprised to see the computer tally a profit far in excess of what I'd anticipated. The reconstitution should have earned $30,000, according to the software's profit calculations for Strips and recons. Instead, the screen showed that I had made $300,000, ten times the profit.

I looked at the data again. Then I examined the calculations. The Strip-recon trade I'd entered was done in virtual isolation, so I could identify the profits and trace them directly back to the reconstitution. The office was quiet around me, only a few people still milling around. Hardly any phones rang. I stared at the numbers in front of me. They were a bit confusing at first, but gradually I began to understand why the computer had come up with $300,000.

The software's Strip-recon calculator determined profits based on the price of bonds on the day of the trade. We didn't expect it to take into account any additional profit earned over time from trades that were booked to settle in the future. We had a lot of trades that were booked to settle thirty days in the future, bonds that should have accumulated greater value over a month's time. But we had no way of calculating or tracking the value of a bond for those thirty days.

Under the old system, we could only tell the computer that a bond was settling five days into the future. That was as far forward as our four settlement categories offered. About half of all bonds had a healthy arbitrage potential—meaning, if a trader sold the bond in fairly short order, he could make a profit from the difference between the price of the bond and the price of its Strips. On the other hand, a trader usually had to hang on to a bond for a week or more before the value of hanging on to it outpaced the value of getting rid of it quickly for its arbitrage potential.

The old software system couldn't give us any idea of what the value of hanging on to a bond might be, because it could only calculate five days forward. So the passage of time—and the value accumulated over thirty days—were never factors. The passage of time was never calculated by the computer when the software projected profitability from trades. And we'd never noticed because it was impossible to isolate a single trade and examine its performance. We'd never been able to examine the "time value" effect on the money invested in our Strip-recon trades.

On this quiet winter day after Christmas, with our new, swift, powerful hardware, with our updated, sophisticated software, and with the system processing a fraction of the trades it chewed through on any other day, I saw for the first time how the value of time could be factored into the profitability of forward trades.

As complicated as the calculations appeared, what had happened was actually fairly simple. When someone buys a government bond, they are essentially loaning the government money in return for interest payments. They get their money back when the bond matures. So, for example, if someone buys a one-year, $1,000 government bond with interest of $1 dollar a day, at the end of twelve months he will cash out and get his $1,000 back. In the meantime, however, he's earned about $30 a month in interest.

When bonds like this are traded for a forward settlement date, the purchase price might be agreed upon on a Monday, but the settlement may not be scheduled to occur until Friday. Because the government pays $1 a day in interest, by the time the deal settles, the buyer will owe the seller the Monday price of the bond, plus $1 for each additional day until Friday. That's $5, which the seller could count as profit to him.

That $5 represented the effect of "time value" on the profitability of a trade. Suddenly our new software was taking that potential profit into account.

Moishe Benatar was in the office that day, too, so I called him over and asked him about the computer's calculation. He wasn't surprised by the $300,000 profit. Yes, he said, that's how the new system is supposed to work. The profits, Benatar explained, were due to the fact that the Strips increased in value over time, whereas the whole bond maintained a constant value over time. He'd written the new software to perform this way explicitly to bring it into line with Kidder's accounting regulations.

"You can tell that our local computer network is correct because it agrees exactly with the profits as measured by Kidder Peabody's gigantic mainframe computer." In other words, it was just the way things worked.

BUT WERE THE profits real? Wasn't $300,000 instead of $30,000 too good to be true?

No, Benatar said. The profits were not automatic. They were "unrealized profits," a common enough term on Wall Street. That meant there was no profit until sale of the inventory. In our case, the profit could only be real if I actually owned the Strips that comprised the reconstitution. I had no trouble understanding that. It was precisely the same with municipal defeasance trades. Those profits were as large, and as proportional. The difference: In municipal defeasance we sold Strips to a municipality and got back a bond. With recons, we sold stripped securities to the federal government and got back a bond. As Benatar explained, I began to lose interest. It was the same old thing, so familiar, it wasn't really even engaging anymore. It represented another source of profit, so we'd go after it just as we'd hired specialists to nail down customers for our municipal defeasance trades. With our new software, forward reconstitutions behaved the same way as defeasance trades. The profit wouldn't be real until I went into the open market and completed the trade by purchasing the underlying Strips securities. I had to own those Strips.

The next time I saw Mullin, I mentioned the software's capacity. "Mel, did you know the Fed acts just like a giant muni defeasance customer?"

"What do you mean?" I described booking a forward recon the night before, only to discover that the Strips had a "time value" that generated profits. The profits were just like those calculated for a sale of Strips for forward settling of a muni defeasance, I said. Mullin thought for a moment.

"Yeah, but . . . how can you hedge the bond?" We both puzzled over that. A trader had to find some way to hedge a bond—to sell one item every time he bought another—or he would expose himself to the vagaries of the market. If a trader didn't hedge, a normal market would wipe out his profit. There didn't seem to be an obvious way to hedge the "time value" of the bond as calculated with the new software. After a few minutes, Mullin and I talked about something else. The software's performance seemed an idle curiosity, at best.

BY MID-DECEMBER, CERULLO had made his support for my sales force clear. The hiring process was a nightmare of clashes with him over women, but without his backing McKoan would never have offered me lists of potential salespeople for my staff. Finally, we agreed on five names, and only a few details remained to hammer out. It was critical that my traders work with the salespeople, to guarantee that there were trades to make. I stood up at the desk and asked all the government traders to gather around.

"We may be getting our own sales force, and if we get them, we have to support them. Not just on Strips, but with Treasury notes and bills, too. If we don't support them, if we get them and they starve, we'll never have this opportunity again."

As the traders dispersed, Mullin appeared. He rushed over to them. What had we been talking about? He didn't ask me.

Mullin was out of the office for the next two weeks. The goiter on his neck had finally grown so huge that he could no longer avoid having it removed—and the sales team was finalized in his absence. I called another meeting of the trading desk, and we used Mullin's office.

"It's official, we have five salesmen starting next week. We have to support them, and every effort to do business will be appreciated. Their current accounts suck, but I intend to get them access to the big accounts so they can do business and make big profit."

Cerullo opened the door and stuck his head in. "What's going on here? Is this a rebellion? You guys staging a coup?"

"No, no, we're just Joe Jett's private army," one of the traders quipped, and everyone laughed. As we trudged back to the desk, the same trader said to another man, "Joe Jett's private army, get out of my way!" He started marching like a soldier, and the other traders fell in line behind him.

That night, Mullin called several traders from his hospital bed to ask about our meeting. Someone told him we'd been talking about where the new salespeople were going to sit. He didn't believe it. He'd heard the meeting was a coup plot against him, and that I'd taken over his office. The conversation was repeated to me the next day. I didn't like the way it sounded. Mullin was the one who would determine my year-end bonus, after all. And Harry Haigood had already told me there were rumors about my unseating Mullin.

Traders typically earn 10 to 12 percent of gross revenue in bonus. I'd earned $28 million that year, so I had a reasonable expectation of a bonus of $2.8 million. The October figure is usually annualized, and with that my twelve-month revenue would be $34 million. So I could even expect a $3.4 million bonus. The year before I'd gotten $5,000.

Mullin was known to shaft traders, and I was sure he'd try to shaft me again. I'd also heard another Kidder story. In 1991, the head of Human Resources, a man named Granville Bowie, told a black trader named Buddy Fletcher that he was not going to be paid the standard 10 percent because he was already earning more money than almost any black man alive. By this reckoning, Fletcher should be content with a smaller bonus. Fletcher quit. Fortunately, he had the presence of mind to tape-record his conversation with Bowie. Fletcher sued Kidder charging racial discrimination and won, saw his verdict reversed, appealed and won again.

So when, at the end of the year, my bonus was revealed to be less than half of what I'd expected—$1.6 million—I was livid. Everyone else received 10 percent, more or less. My percentage trailed the others', in spite of my accomplishments. I'd worked to build a business beyond arbitrage, I'd gotten the sales force's attention, I'd created my own sales team. It hadn't mattered. My anger flared when I saw my performance review. Mullin had given me a number-one rating, which ranked above "excellent," for virtually every category: "Job, technical knowledge" one; "organization of work and time," one; "quality of work," one; "work relationships," one; "motivation and initiative," one. He'd also cited my overall performance as "outstanding," and written that I'd developed an efficient team, worked with the Repossession desk, used the new systems, nearly quadrupled the customer business, and increased profits significantly from previous years. He praised me for putting the new Government Trader system to work, exploiting its transformation from a stand-alone to a network system so that several people could maintain price information in different bond sectors and give my desk a faster look at moneymaking opportunities. It was all there in black and white in my performance review, and still, Mullin had shafted me on my bonus for the second year running. I went to his office in a rage. Again, he pleaded powerlessness. He had nothing to do with setting bonuses. That was Cerullo's purview, he said.

Cerullo's office was next.

"You've had a good year, but you're not an established trader. You just got here. You have to prove yourself. We're not going to pay you for a fluke year."

"Have you ever heard of Buddy Fletcher?"

"What? What?" He picked up a stack of papers from his desk and slammed them down. "I gave you the opportunity to work as a trader, and now you're going to throw racism at me?" His eyes practically bulged from behind his tortoiseshell glasses. "I can't believe this. I can't believe this. You show me that you can sustain your performance, and you'll be paid like a proven trader. You've made a lot of progress. But you want to have everything now, and it doesn't work that way."

I stood perfectly still. "I don't see how you can say that. I've been on Wall Street five years. I'm not some rookie who just walked in the front door, who's never worked before. And even if I were, is the dollar I make somehow different than the dollar someone else makes?"

He stopped me. "This conversation is not profiting you. I'll tell you right now, this conversation is not helping you at all."

MULLIN WENT TO London, and while he was gone, Denise suddenly needed to talk with me. I'd avoided meeting her outside the office, but this time she was adamant. We went to dinner at an Italian restaurant in Greenwich Village. The food was terrible, I believe, but I can't be sure because the mood of the meal was so unpleasant that it colored the whole evening. Nervous and agitated, Denise talked nonstop about her husband's admiration for me, his pleasure that I was a part of his team, his preference for working with the same people over a period of years and establishing loyalty to them. They were his family, she said. If I wanted to talk, either to her or Mel, I should call them at home. She gave me the number. I doubted that Mullin knew of this direct appeal. I knew that Mullin had been reporting on me to Cerullo, so he could be sure that I was unlikely to turn to him. I tried to remain neutral with Denise, telling her that I had no conflict with her husband other than the blowup over my bonus. Now I knew he had nothing to do with that; it was Cerullo's decision.

Clearly the Mullins were worried about insurrection. Denise practically pleaded with me not to take her husband's job. "I love my husband very much," she said. She repeated it twice more before we finished eating. But ultimately, Mullin's fall had little to do with me. His Options desk had booked a 1992 profit of $26 million. Then, in the first week of January 1993, the desk lost about $13 million. Had he reported the loss a month earlier, everyone's bonuses would have been significantly lower—including his wife's. Rumors arose that Mullin had exploited the system so his wife could pocket more money. The office rumbled with disgruntled talk of dirty dealing. The idea that Denise Mullin got a healthy bonus while losing money was more than I could stomach along with my paltry bonus. I put out feelers to other companies. I discovered right away that Cerullo had played me correctly. When I talked to traders I knew in other shops, I learned that they shared his opinion. I wasn't established. I couldn't expect to be treated like a golden boy. I needed another year. I could get another job, certainly, but I'd have to start from scratch and rebuild my asset base, the amount of money I was given to trade with. I had $8 billion at Kidder already. I also had too much in the works at Kidder to leave now. I'd earned my own sales force. I spoke openly. I'd won the battle to cow my manager, Mullin. I'd spent a great deal of time and effort maneuvering with McKoan. I couldn't give up all that now. There was more to life than bonuses. There was power.

The best I could do was devote my attention and energy to my new sales force. On the hoot and holler, I announced that my sales force had begun work, and encouraged those Mortgage salespeople who did not want to be bothered with selling government securities to please turn them over to us. I had no power to enforce this suggestion, but that didn't stop me from implying that I did. It was a wild overstep, and earned me another reprimand in Cerullo's office.

"Watch what you say over the PA system."

I stood at attention and spoke in a deliberate monotone. "I have a list of accounts who did business when there was four times the sales credit, and they've disappeared from the face of the earth. Those salesmen have the ability to do business but are making so much money doing mortgage accounts that they aren't making the government calls. Those accounts should be pulled from those salespeople and given to my government specialists." I handed him a list. He set it aside on his desk without looking at me.

The salespeople were unperturbed when they heard about this threat. They didn't think I could take their accounts away from them. For me, the maneuver was intended to do more than improve our business. I needed to build a defensible position. McKoan was a threat to that.

Anita Day decided that I was not going to expropriate her best account, Prudential. Furthermore, she was determined to force me to handle her trades. She tried calling the desk, but I still handed her inquiry off to Joey-o. So she tore a page from my book. She marched over to my desk with a pad and pencil. She'd written down the bids and offers she wanted for Prudential.

"Here's my list." What were my prices for each one? Her pad rested on my desk. I couldn't ignore it, and I couldn't hand it to someone else. I hesitated, then gave her numbers that were deliberately too high. Any halfway decent competitor could beat those numbers, I knew, and she'd miss the trades. I'd done it on purpose, to discourage her. She picked up the pad and walked away, ecstatic. And she was even better at her job than I'd thought. She made the deals even with noncompetitive bids. She had a good relationship with her account. Her counterparts at Prudential didn't "check away," or check to see what competitors were offering. They had faith in her as a trader.

My No-Women zone was crumbling.

At the end of January 1993, I joined Cerullo at Walt Disney World for a conference of Kidder's top earners. People came from Fixed Income, Retail Sales and Investment Banking. On the first afternoon, as I checked into the hotel and meandered around the complex, I couldn't walk two feet without someone shaking my hand and saying, "You must be here for the affirmative action program." Eventually, my response became angry. "No. I'm the Strips bond trader." I wanted to add—presumably you know that I made $34 million last year, placing me around the seventh top money-earner for the firm. I was the Strips trader, I was the Government trading representative, I was at the conference because of merit, I wanted to shout. In my room, I found a package of conference activities and a list of attendees. There it was. My name, Joseph Jett, and after it, "Affirmative Action Program." I almost cried angry tears. I immediately looked up Michael Ricciardi's and Kathy Dalton's names. They were also listed as part of the affirmative action program. Apparently, someone had prepared the directory from information given them the previous summer when I had briefly participated in the affirmative action program.

I sat on the bed, desultory. The conference was a meeting of Kidder's top money-earners. I was one of them. But now my effort and achievement were spoiled. I knew I'd carry this affirmative action label around all weekend like a brand that revealed I owed my presence to the munificence of management—of my white masters. I thought back over the looks on people's faces as they walked up to me. As I approached them, I'd seen that familiar look of uncertainty and concern in their eye, the one that all black men get from white people. It was replaced with a look of relief as they settled on an explanation for my presence. The black man was the affirmative action representative. They could properly, and safely, categorize me. I was not a threat.

I had to get out of that room. I threw on athletic clothes and went to the gym. It was a childish attempt to work out anger and aggression. I needed to demonstrate prowess, that I could compete, and that I was worthy of respect. I was pretty bulked up at the time, twenty pounds heavier than my usual weight, and all of it muscle from weight lifting. I didn't feel powerful, however. I felt small, servile, slavelike. I discovered that I hadn't packed my sneakers, so I went to the gym barefoot. On the way I passed the swimming pool. A Kidder crowd stood at the edge, shouting at someone in the water. It was Cerullo, racing through his usual hundred laps. He'd encouraged the Kidder employees to count for him. Every so often he stopped for a tally and the group would shout a number. "Sixty-three!" rang out as I passed. In the gym, I attacked the weight machines. McKoan arrived after me, his round belly out of place. Soon Cerullo joined us, full of praise for my physique and questions about exercises for various muscle groups. The little crowd following him gathered to watch us lift weights. When we finished, Cerullo announced that the hundred laps in the pool and the lifting regimen had whetted his appetite for a ten-mile run. I should join him, he suggested. I didn't really want to go, but couldn't say no. I borrowed shoes and stuffed socks in the toes so they'd fit tighter. Even so, after half a mile my feet were raw. It was a sweleringly hot day and no one else passed us. The grounds of the Disney complex were huge and covered with manicured paths. Apparently, Cerullo knew which course covered ten miles. In the distance, I could see the giant swan sculptures that adorned the top of the hotel. After we had run a short way, Cerullo distracted me from the pain in my feet. He was grateful, he said, to Mike Vranos for hiring me. I reminded him that Vranos hadn't hired me, that he had, to lure me away from O'Donnell.

"Oh, I thought I hired you directly after you interviewed with Mike. Oh well. Listen, Mike has a great place in Sweden. We should all get together there sometime."

He stopped running.

"Hypothetically, if you were in charge of the Government desk, and there was a need to bring in almost completely new blood across the board and you had to fire a lot of people, could you do it?"

He was talking about Mullin's job. Everyone was still angry about the Options desk loss and the huge bonus paid to Denise right before.

"Yes, I could."

We started moving again, and as we ran, talked about weak spots on the Government desk and traders who should be replaced. About 90 percent of the people on the Government desk needed to be fired. Cerullo agreed.

"Except for the long-bond trader," he said. "I think he's in the same position you were in two years ago when you were hired—he's bright, eager, and we should give him a shot at handling the job. I know you think the long-bond trader should be a senior person, but look at what you've done."

By then I was trying to hide the limp I'd developed. I looked at Cerullo.

"I am a Scotsman."

"What do you mean by that?"

"The English writer Samuel Johnson said it takes an Englishman to build and design a rifle, but it takes a Scotsman to pull the trigger. I'm the Scotsman. If you want it dead, I'll kill it."

Cerullo laughed. I did too, with relief, because I could suddenly see the hotel over the ridge. "I have to stop here."

"I knew you couldn't keep up with me!" Cerullo declared before disappearing down the path.

THE DISNEY RETREAT included an affirmative action seminar, and as the affirmative action representative, I quashed any notion that the program was intended to make life easier at Kidder. Kidder shouldn't recruit from among disadvantaged students at city and community colleges, I told the gathering. Instead, I repeated what I'd told Cerullo before: We should look for people at Ivy League schools, where minority students excelled through hard work and talent.

"Those of you in the majority need not try to hire people who don't threaten you. Hire people who can work here. They may be smarter than you are, but do it even if it threatens your job, because it's good for the firm."

BACK IN NEW York, I developed another strategy to wrangle accounts away from McKoan. I'd lure the successful salesmen back to my desk by offering them quadruple sales credit once again. As soon as they showed the ability to trade a dormant account, I'd earmark that account and demand that it be reassigned to my sales force. The plan was even more successful than I expected—it resulted in twenty accounts being brought to my attention. I argued to Cerullo that the customers apparently wanted to do business, but the salespeople wouldn't make the effort unless they were paid outsized commissions. It was in Kidder's interest to switch those accounts to my salespeople, I said.

That wasn't the end of it. I wanted to dictate which salesperson handled which account. I wanted salespeople to split up the business with large customers, so that one salesman could pitch mortgages to the customer, and a second salesperson could pitch government bonds. By the middle of the year, three of my salesmen ranked among the top ten earners in our department. Even people who didn't work for me started making more money. Some of them were women, so it was inevitable that Cerullo put two and two together in his own unique way. At the end of January, he asked me about the assignment of sales accounts. Anita Day's business has been picking up in the Government area, he mused. Anita had been thinking about quitting the business, but seemed to be having a good time now, Cerullo added.

"She's had close relationships with people at Kidder before. In fact, I thought she was going to marry Billy Cohen, the managing director of the L.A. office. So I want you to be careful with your relationship."

I wasn't surprised. "What relationship?" I asked wearily.

"I'm not saying you're having a relationship with Anita. I'm just saying, look but don't touch."

I didn't react to Cerullo. My goal was not to earn the right to date white women. My ambition was to take Cerullo's job.

BY JANUARY 1993, it had become clear that the Fed was going to go ahead with its scheme to reduce bond auctions. In his inauguration speech, Bill Clinton vowed to make homes more affordable. Then he named Robert Rubin as secretary of the Treasury. Rubin, I thought, was likely to initiate significant change.

Suddenly there was a new opportunity for arbitrage, and it hinged on the "time value" of forward Strip and recon trades. If we could take advantage of historically low financing rates, we could make money from recons booked with the Federal Reserve Bank. Basically, the engine that drives the profitability of forward recons is the fact that Strips yielded between 4 and 8 percent interest. But in the open market, we could finance those Strips for about 2.5 percent. Sometimes the financing was flat—we didn't have to pay a dime for the Strips. In any event, the difference between the Strips' yield and the cost of financing them made profit possible. But that profit would exist only as long as the Fed didn't increase short-term interest rates. If those went up, the cost of financing versus the yield we'd get from the Strips would diminish until the profit was lost. Our job was to figure out what the Fed was likely to do with short-term interest rates and whether or not the yield on Strips was going to be higher than our financing costs. It looked like it was, making forward recons a profitable trade.

In addition, the "time value" profit calculations that had been a mere curiosity inherent in our new software suddenly became potentially useful. We could generate profit with forward trades. If the Fed was about to create a huge shortage of bonds, then there was money to be made by having an inventory of those very securities. The shortage would drive up the price of those bonds, and I'd be able to sell my inventory at a profit. But it wasn't as simple as going out on a Monday and snapping up as many of the specific bonds involved as I could. Any time I acquired bonds, I had to hedge my position. In order to stock up on bonds, I'd have to sell something of equal value. The "cash" bonds the Fed was planning to restrict were very specific in nature—they could only be exchanged for another bond with the exact same date of issuance. There was, however, a derivative of Treasury bonds that was looser—Treasury bond futures contracts. They could be exchanged for any bond with a matched maturity period. Issue dates didn't have to match, just the maturity period. So they offered a good way to balance the books. The greater looseness of the futures contract allowed a trader to hedge a wider variety of cash bonds.

A futures contract is simply another name for any commodity. As soon as something is labeled a commodity, it loses its identity. In the futures trading pits, for example, oil belonging to Mobil Oil or Shell Oil or Pennzoil may be available. But in the pits, that oil trades as a nameless commodity, one contract no different from any other. It's just a contract for oil. Treasury bond futures contracts represent the commodity that is a derivative of a cash bond. Normally, thirty-year cash bonds and futures contracts for thirty-year bonds track each other closely in price. I decided that would change when the federal government sharply reduced the number of thirty-year cash bonds. There would be a scarcity of cash thirty-year bonds. But there would be no shortage of Treasury bond futures contracts. Under normal circumstances, a futures contract would be exchanged for the most easily available bond—that is, the one most recently issued. If a trader wanted to do a deal in March, he'd probably get bonds that had been issued in February. Now the issuing of bonds was about to be halved. Cash bonds would be in short supply. Instead, people would dig into their portfolios and sell bonds that did not have the scarcity that thirty-year bonds were now going to have.

I decided to buy cash bonds and hedge their purchase by selling short futures contracts. The relationship between bonds and bond futures is called "the basis." To own cash bonds and be short futures contracts is known as being "long the basis." To be long the basis meant that I hoped to profit from an increase in the price of a cash bond relative to the price of a futures contract. I gambled that Treasury bond futures contracts would drop in price.

Instead of laying out cash for them while I waited for that to happen, I'd borrow them from someone else for a fee. I didn't want to actually buy those futures contracts first, since that would just create another debt I'd have to hedge. Instead, I opted to sell short futures contracts. Selling short means selling something you don't actually own. You promise to deliver it at a future date—and then you have the interim period to actually acquire the bond. During that time, you hope the price will drop. It's all a carefully calibrated juggling act. But when millions of dollars of profit are at stake, the risk of keeping all those balls in the air becomes worth taking. The potential profit was even greater than I'd thought if these transactions worked the same way as municipal defeasance—and our computer calculations demonstrated that they did. Massive profit could be made by putting off settlement of the trade until thirty days in the future.

I was excited. The government was about to intervene in the securities market, preparing to reduce its bond auctions to manipulate interest rates. I could take advantage of that. An action of this magnitude by the government was almost without precedent. It was, in my opinion, going to be just as disruptive as Paul Volker's decision to increase interest rates to combat inflation in 1979. And I wanted to be ready to ride the wave, rather than be drowned by it.

PERFECT TIMING: FORWARD
RECONS AND THE FED

T HERE'S AN OLD Wall Street adage that says: "He who sells what isn't his'n, buys it back or goes to prison."

By summer, I'd accumulated a $7 billion short position in Treasury bond futures contracts, larger than anyone else on Wall Street at the time. I'd promised to deliver futures contracts to buyers in the open market, meaning I didn't know who they were. Eventually, I'd have to buy those futures contracts to fulfill those sales. I was gambling that the price would drop so I could pocket the difference. The risk, of course, was that the price would rise, and I'd owe a fortune to cover the discrepancy. I couldn't let myself think about how much I might lose.

Very soon—by February 1993—it became difficult to find and buy cash bonds. I was reluctant to go after them too aggressively because the Fed had not formally announced its scheme. I didn't want to tip off the market. Traders in the Chicago futures pit knew what I was doing; since they worked on commission, they vied to get a piece of my action. But they only knew that I was accumulating a huge short in futures contracts, they didn't know how I was counteracting it. They didn't know what I was long. I covered my tracks to some extent because I was not formally a bond trader. I was a Strips trader. Buying Strips and reconstituting them into bonds camouflaged my activity. Strips and bond traders normally don't communicate anyway, and that helped, too. I moved quickly because I had to accumulate futures contracts before the cash bonds began to rise in price. Timing was crucial. I needed to act before everyone became convinced at the same moment that cash bonds were scarce; my profits would come when the rest of the market bid up the value of cash bonds. This wouldn't happen until the Fed announced its intention to halve issuance of thirty-year bonds. But I knew that in order to profit on Wall Street, you must buy on the rumor, and sell on the fact. My objective was to reconstitute Strips into bonds but put off settlement of the sale of those bonds into the future, to coincide with the Fed's announcement.

My aim was twofold. One was to maintain my precarious position until the very moment that the market flipped. At that point I'd abruptly sell my massive inventory. Two, our new software enabled us to calculate in advance the profits of that massive sale, and to figure them into our accounts right away. We wouldn't have to wait until the trade was complete to take our profit. The software allowed us to book it up front.

I DISCUSSED MY plan with my traders and Moishe Benatar, the software expert. On paper, it looked sound. I began in earnest, but for the first two months, it looked like my idea was wrong. Nothing panned out. In March and April, the computer showed no great profits. Prices were not yet moving; the rumor about the Fed auctions hadn't picked up momentum. It wasn't until May, when the rumors became too strong to ignore, that the bond market reacted just as I'd hoped.

IN FEBRUARY MCKOAN asked me to step into his office.

"I know you're frustrated, but I want you to know that your government specialist sales force is off to a good start. I don't want you to think that your efforts are unappreciated. The sales force appreciates you. In fact, I've been approached by a number of people who think you should be running the Government desk instead of Mel."

This was not a total surprise, not since my jog with Cerullo at Disney World. But the irony of hearing it from McKoan did not escape me. I doubted he could ignore it, either.

"I have to do what's best for my salespeople. I'm in charge of international sales. But before I go to Ed with any proposed changes, I want to make sure that you'd be comfortable with that situation."

So he wanted my gratitude to him as kingmaker. Cerullo had already spoken to me about this job; now he was probably searching for a consensus from the other managing directors. I needed McKoan's approval. His might even be the controlling vote. In return, I would owe him some measure of fealty.

"Yes, I'd be very comfortable with that situation," I said, and watched McKoan's face open in surprise. I think he expected me to demur out of consideration for Mullin.

*   *   *

FOR A WEEK, Mullin didn't speak to me, and then he called me into his office to discuss our "derivatives presence." The man running it was too academic, Mullin said. We could get that area moving in the right direction, he explained, but it would take a lot of time. He'd told Cerullo that he wanted to take over the Derivatives area, but he couldn't do that and his present job. So he'd suggested that Cerullo promote me to "chief trader" with responsibility for overseeing the Government Bond desk.

Damn, I thought, I'm not going to replace him, I'm being tucked in underneath him. There wasn't any such thing as a chief trader. Mullin would remain titular head of the desk. I would oversee day-to-day operations and report to him still.

He sighed. "Well, that's what I've proposed. But Ed seems to have different ideas. He wants to bring you in as head of the Government desk, with the Government desk being a separate entity from the Derivatives desk. I think that's a mistake, because of the synergy that exists between the Derivatives area and the Government desk. So, effective the day of my taking over the Derivatives area, you're going to take over as head of the Government Bond desk."

I swallowed the words that had been on my tongue. For once, I didn't want to gloat. "Congratulations. . . . That's great, Mel. Glad to hear that you're taking over all of Derivatives."

MULLIN HAD SEIZED some of Cerullo's thunder. The next day, when Cerullo asked if I recalled our run in Florida, he didn't realize I'd already heard of his plans.

"I've made a decision. Mel is going to move laterally, into a new position called Derivative Products. You're going to be taking over as head of the Government Bond desk. You're going to have to give him the Options area, the options traders, and the government agency securities."

The Options area was generally good for about $1 million a month. But it was operating at a loss because of the write-down Mullin had taken at the end of the year after bonuses had been paid. I wasn't that interested in the Mortgage area. We had never focused on the Fannie Mae and Sallie Mae bond markets, so we weren't competitive. Still, Cerullo was removing traditional parts of the Government desk. They weren't critical by any means, but I would still have preferred to keep the traditional desk intact.

"You only have two traders out there worth salvaging, only two. I expect you to make changes and to have implemented those changes in under one-half year."

Recruiting wouldn't be easy, especially since I wasn't completely certain of where all the deadwood lay in Mullin's troops. I'd have to sit down with someone from Human Resources and pore over every personnel file. In the meantime, Cerullo wanted me to tell the traders exactly what my plans were. "You have a no-nonsense reputation, and some people are afraid that you're just going to start firing."

Cerullo was planning to announce my promotion the next day. As I left his office, however, I wasn't thinking about my new position. Instead, I mulled over the new information from Cerullo. Mullin had not been promoted, he'd been moved aside. What, then, should I do for an encore? I daydreamed about reunifying the Government desk with Mullin's newly spun-off derivatives operation.

THE NEXT MORNING I announced over the PA: "There are traders and there are managers. I'm a trader first, a trader second and a trader third. On the Government desk, we will not have managers, we will have leaders. On the Government desk, we are engaged in a war. On the Strips desk, we were engaged in a war and we won. Now there is going to be a war fought on all fronts. The battle will be joined in Treasury bills. Two-year notes. The five-year sector. The ten-year sector. The Mortgage desk will no longer be the place you call to sell or buy ten-year securities. We will handle the major flows from the ten-year desk."

This last was a slap at Mullin because he had always allowed our ten-year securities to be handled by the Mortgage desk, which used them as a hedge against mortgages. I wanted to take that business back.

THE AFTERNOON OF the day I took Mullin's job, the office door opposite Cerullo's opened, and David Bernstein stepped into the hall. His face, with a sharp nose and thin, wide lips covering large teeth, wore a pinched look. He appeared nervous, unsure of himself. I knew of Bernstein only by name. He'd been an accountant at GE and had been assigned to audit Kidder's Fixed Income department. Instead, Cerullo hired him, just as he hired me years later. Cerullo named him new business manager, but in the nearly two years I'd worked at Kidder, I had seen no evidence of his job. I thought he was still just an accountant. That morning he corrected me.

Bernstein walked up to my desk on the trading floor, introduced himself and asked me to join him in his office. The room was orderly but festooned with paperwork. A large, white erasable board was covered with scribbles. Bernstein spoke in fits, his long pauses filled with "ums" and then punctuated by rapid-fire bursts of speech. He got to the point, however.

"Often during the course of the day there might be a meeting that has to do with larger operations of the corporation that might require you to reduce your position. Chances are, I'll be the one that tells you that. There will be a meeting, we'll have a discussion, Ed will make a decision, and I'll be the one who tells you what he wants and makes sure you get it done."

I was so taken aback by this new link in the chain of command that I didn't believe him at first. I went to Mullin's office to verify that I was to take orders from Bernstein. It was true. Bernstein was Cerullo's right-hand man. He'd come to Kidder from GE, where he'd gone to work at age twenty-two directly after graduating from Brown University in 1976. Bernstein had never worked anywhere but GE and Kidder. For several years, he took night classes to earn an MBA. One of his bosses at GE had been Richard O'Donnell, and when O'Donnell became Kidder's CFO, he told Bernstein to apply for the job of business unit controller for Fixed Income. At thirty-four, Bernstein had no experience in the securities industries, but he got the job anyway. He was put in charge of a group of analysts who watched over Fixed Income's financial positions, and became friendly with Ed Cerullo. In 1991, Cerullo offered him the job of manager of business development; Bernstein quit O'Donnell's staff and went to work for Cerullo. His task was to envision where Fixed Income's future lay, forecast budgets, predict which products and customers to focus on, and allocate resources.

Bernstein didn't have a staff, he didn't have a budget, he didn't earn profit. He monitored everyone else's budgets and profits, and he spoke for Cerullo, except that his high-pitched voice was often nervous, which made me think of him as sniveling. I came to picture him as the mongoose that follows the Lion King around. He carried the weight of the Lion King, but he was tentative and ingratiating. He snuck around carefully, because although his connection to the Lion King meant no one could challenge him, he knew that everyone wanted to.

I FIRED ONE of Mullin's longtime traders almost right away, a fellow who was particularly unproductive. Then I met with my new traders to reassure them that I wasn't going to fire anyone else anytime soon. Cerullo heard about my pronouncement.

"What do you mean by anytime soon?" Cerullo demanded. "I expect you to have that desk cleaned up by this summer." He and I then went over each trading position and concluded that of the fourteen traders that I'd inherited from Mullin, twelve would be gone by summer.

RECRUITING CONSUMED A great deal of my time, and right away I needed to hire someone to run my desk when I was away. Already much of the forward recon volume on my desk was handled by my traders; I got used to hearing traders yell over to the Repo desk to ask how much time forward Repo would need to book a recon so that the Strips could be gathered. I found myself managing my position over the phone; I directed traders from London or Tokyo on how to do forward Strips and recons, and how to properly hedge their position. I needed a deputy, someone tough and aggressive, and who knew the Strips business. At the same time, Cerullo was so unhappy with our Treasury bill trader that he insisted I fire him immediately. Treasury bill traders are not powerful figures; T-bills are the shortest of all fixed income instruments, and normally the trader is a low man on the totem pole. As a result, at many firms, the T-bill trader is part of the Repo desk. Cerullo toyed with the idea of giving Brian Finkelstein responsibility for hiring a new T-bill trader, thus putting the trader on our Repo desk. I balked. Finkelstein was a racist; his comments at the diversity workshop were stained on my memory. It was likely that Finkelstein was one of those reporting on me to Mullin and Cerullo. From his desk right behind mine, he could see anyone who approached me and hear my conversations. I intended to run him out of Kidder, not help him consolidate power. Removing Finkelstein was the best means of attacking the racism.

I couldn't look at Finkelstein without glaring. I could never understand why Cerullo felt such affinity for him. Finkelstein was nothing like the people Cerullo usually admired. He was tall, gangly and decidedly nonathletic. When he approached my desk, I stared him down. Finkelstein had made it clear he didn't think blacks were human. Since he was Jewish, my expectations of him had been higher than of other whites, so I was particularly disappointed. I knew that Asians generally didn't like blacks, that Indians didn't like blacks. But Jewish history made it particularly repulsive for a Jew to contribute to the racist dynamic at Kidder, especially when the paranoia centered on black and white dating. Prohibiting race mixing was a Nazi idea. Finkelstein rarely talked to me directly, even though he sat nearby and seemed to have friendships with others on the desk. His reluctance convinced me even further that he was responsible for some of the racial animosity in the office.

I tried to lure a T-bill trader away from Goldman Sachs with the promise that he'd replace Finkelstein. But Cerullo would not back me.

WITH MY MASSIVE trading, I began again to feel the gaps in my desk. I needed more proficient traders. On Wall Street, all my colleagues seemed united in their hatred of one person, a Strips trader at First Boston they called simply the Bitch. Her name was Elizabeth Cavanaugh. I hadn't known her at First Boston, and I first saw her at a broker's dinner. A wisp of a young woman passed me several times, and each time I heard the whispered comment "There's that bitch." Cavanaugh was slender, olive-skinned, with brown eyes and hair cropped in a short, boyish cut. Finally, I asked someone why she was so despised.

"Well, if you make a mistake, any mistake, she rants at you. If you don't pick up the phone after the first or second ring, forget it, she'll rip you a new asshole."

Cerullo had commanded me to clean up my desk by summer, so I decided to start by recruiting Cavanaugh. At first, she refused to set up a meeting with our headhunter. She wasn't interested in Kidder, she said. Finally, she agreed to have lunch with me at a Wall Street restaurant. I offered to meet elsewhere, so her bosses at First Boston wouldn't get wind of it.

"Fuck 'em. They can't fire me. I'm too damn good."

"YOU'RE NEW TO the Strips business, and I understand you've done well. But I've been in this fucking business for twelve years, and I trade all the shit no one wants to trade anymore," Elizabeth explained. She was right. She handled what are called lions, tigers and bears, so named for the complex acronyms of their real titles. Bears referred, for example, to Bonds Earning Accrued Returns. It's a kind of zero coupon that was the original government Strip security. Before 1985, the government didn't strip securities, only private investment banks did. Those Strips are called bears. Between 1980 and 1985, the only Strips that existed were those from private banks. They were worth more, but they were less liquid because they traded "by appointment only." No one kept an inventory of these securities. If a customer wanted to buy a lion, tiger or bear, a trader had to know from whom to get them, and had to be able to make an appointment to get the trade done. As a result, it was a painful way to trade, and few people did it anymore.

Cavanaugh was the master of this game. She'd earned $10 million from lions, tigers and bears for First Boston. At Kidder, Hugh Bush had traded in this area and earned about $300,000. She should have taken home about a million dollars herself, but her total income was $245,000. She didn't work in a high-profile area, and First Boston considered her job as little better than that of a clerk. But she liked First Boston. She knew that people called her a bitch, but she chalked that up in part to her policy against dating traders and brokers. She'd married her personal trainer. She'd grown up in Georgia, and spoke with a deep southern drawl. She wasn't a numbers person, she warned me, but she was very detail-oriented and had a memory like a steel trap.

She knew that people didn't like me, either.

"You came in and started embarrassing people, pushing around the market. Everyone figured it was you that bought all those Strips last September. That was you, wasn't it? I knew if you bought $6 billion in Strips that never appeared on the market, you must be making some money. I have to admire you. If people start calling you names, then you must be doing good. If people don't say anything about you, then you must be no damn good."

By April 1993, I was determined to hire her. She fit perfectly into what I had in mind for the desk. She was very effective at what she did. She didn't care whether people liked her or not. She insisted that people get their work done. We talked a lot about work ethic. She even thought that everyone should be required to work out, that exercise was necessary because trading was such a stressful job.

I began to realize that we shared more than that in common. She was roundly criticized and disliked for traits that in a man were admired. Lots of traders were aggressive, disciplined, control freaks. Cavanaugh was, and so was I. Most of the time, those traders were anointed Big Swinging Dicks. If race was the major factor that kept me from being welcome in that group, then gender was certainly the reason that Cavanaugh was excluded. She was serious about her work, so other traders and brokers were threatened by her. As we talked, I realized I'd rarely had a conversation with someone in my profession who faced the same obstacles. I was candid about what I wanted to accomplish with my desk. I told her: None of my traders have any balls, they don't want to trade size, they're not involved in any auctions, they're cowed by the sales force.

"I have to spend a great deal of my time interviewing, and I need someone I can trust to maintain discipline on the desk. That person has to know that I'm not very popular, so they wouldn't be very popular. It has to be someone who could take the heat. I'm not looking for a person, but for a perfect weapon. I think that's what you are. The perfect weapon, aimed at all the problems I just described and at other issues you don't know about."

I left out my intention of hiring a white woman to sit next to me every day and drive whoever was spying on me crazy.

MEANWHILE, AS I celebrated my ascension into the ranks of management, in the true halls of power, storm clouds gathered. In his diary, which was later submitted as evidence in my case, Richard O'Donnell described a meeting of Kidder's inventory committee. On May 24, 1993, CEO Michael Carpenter, Cerullo, chief financial officer Dick O'Donnell, Equity trading chief Tom Ryan and other Kidder bigwigs got together to discuss the record-level $86 billion in total assets on the consolidated Kidder Peabody balance sheet. O'Donnell reportedly raised the issue of inadequate bank funding for Kidder's level of assets and business activities. Michael Carpenter grew visibly hostile toward O'Donnell. He said he knew nothing about Kidder's funding shortfalls.

O'Donnell pointed out that the funding inadequacy, the financial leverage imbalances and the weak capital structure had been the subject of numerous presentations over the past three years. Carpenter replied that the $500 million needed to meet Repo margin calls the previous week was new. Cerullo explained that he hadn't known until that Friday that there was a funding shortfall caused by his Fixed Income business unit. O'Donnell countered that Cerullo managed the Repo desk. He insisted that the Treasury division could not possibly know all the dynamics of Fixed Income's cash flows.

Carpenter interceded, changing the subject to a review of the pitch for funding from GE. Carpenter acknowledged that Kidder had a severe funding problem. Carpenter said that he wanted Cerullo to reduce Kidder's asset size to an $80 billion consolidated balance sheet by the end of June 1993. Cerullo responded that he did not foresee a decrease in his need for money. He said that even in bad times he must provide liquidity to fixed income markets. He forecast that his need for asset growth would continue for the indefinite future.

O'Donnell warned that even if GE agreed to Kidder's plans for a $2 billion line of credit from Union Bank of Switzerland, Kidder's funding needs would be far from properly met. He pointed out the need for balance, including more bank lines of credit, commercial paper issuance, long-term debt and equity.

Carpenter stated that Kidder had talked to Jack Welch on Friday, May 24. He said that Welch was not concerned about overall Kidder asset size. Welch was concerned with whether Kidder had risk management systems in place to avoid a large hit to P&L, one in the neighborhood of $300 million. Welch was also concerned that conditions at Kidder could result in funding calls on General Electric credit on short notice. Given Welch's view of the world, Carpenter said, the committee should modify its pitch. His diary showed that he ended the meeting by saying he was not worried about the balance sheet review of Kidder Peabody that GE had already initiated.

But three days later, on May 27, 1993, Kidder's Mortgage department reported $70 million in losses. The loss wiped out its earnings for the year. In his diary, O'Donnell wrote that he urged his staff to uncover the reason for the losses. Were they due to stale reporting, sloppy recordkeeping or inaccurate pricing practices? O'Donnell called Kidder's controller, John McDonough, and urged him not to rely on Ed Cerullo or Dave Bernstein to investigate their own division's problems. That wouldn't satisfy him this time, he said. On Sunday, May 30, McDonough reported to O'Donnell that his attempts to get Cerullo involved were disappointing. When he reached Cerullo on Friday, Cerullo had said he was concerned about the losses but did not intend to investigate further. On June 1, O'Donnell met with Carpenter to discuss the Mortgage department's losses. O'Donnell again asked Carpenter for help in gathering all of the facts that led to the losses.

O'Donnell seized on the scandal as an opportunity to invade Fixed Income. The accountants had finally caught up with Vranos and Cerullo. Suspicious of us all, GE ordered an audit of every large trading position. Cerullo directed Bernstein to learn everything there was to know about my trading strategies so the two of them would be prepared when GE's numbers-crunchers arrived.

The crisis with the Mortgage cash cow meant Cerullo was dependent for earnings on my Government desk. We were the only part of Fixed Income that was making money. The bread-and-butter Mortgage area was teetering on the brink of collapse. At the same time, the securities Cavanaugh sold at First Boston were suddenly hot. People were looking for lions, tigers and bears, and we could use the income. I was still trying to get Cerullo to agree to the salary Cavanaugh demanded, and now I was sure she'd be a perfect fit at Kidder. The lions, tigers and bears that she traded were made from thirty-year bonds that were callable—this meant that even though securities were supposed to mature in thirty years, if interest rates were low, the government had a right to cash them in five years ahead of their scheduled maturity date. Lions, tigers and bears had been issued up until 1984. It was now 1993. In other words, the oldest of them was about twenty years from maturity, but could be called in fifteen years. If you could buy the lions, tigers and bears Strips and put back together a bond that matured in fifteen years, it made some very lucrative trades possible. We needed someone who knew where to find these bonds.

I also knew that Cavanaugh could ferret out profitable Strips customers. Her price was a demand that she be paid like a male trader—10 percent of her profits. I set up a meeting for her with Cerullo. When she left, Cerullo was practically gushing.

"That southern drawl! That just kills me every time. Oh, man! She must work out a lot. Did you see her arms? I mean, she's really cut. You know her husband is actually her personal trainer. She's trained for a marathon, and I asked her if she's ever done a triathlon and she's been training for that. Chances are we're probably going to do it together. That is really some woman. Really one impressive woman."

When I saw Cavanaugh again, she was prepared to talk about joining Kidder. But she wanted something that only Cerullo could give her. "Three million up front. One million each year for three years. Guaranteed. Look, I don't want to move. You say you want to bring me out of here. So that's going to cost you. I know I can make $10 million. You say you'll pay me ten percent. Well, I want that million dollars up front for the next three years."

TO LURE CAVANAUGH to Kidder, I told Moishe Benatar and another computer programmer, Andy Kim, to enhance the trading software that Cavanaugh would use. Her system at First Boston could monitor many more securities than ours. The upgrade would bring our analytical techniques into line with what she was used to. Instead, Kim was assigned to another project for Kidder's chief profit and loss accountant, Charles Fiumefreddo. Fiumefreddo instructed Kim to design a program that could identify all forward transactions on the Government Bond desk. As far as Fiumefreddo was concerned, his project was an emergency and took precedent over anything I had in mind. His objective was to help Cerullo in his escalating battle with GE. It was no secret that Jack Welch and senior GE executives were unhappy with Kidder. Kidder was in bad shape, and had been ever since Welch bought it. Welch regretted getting involved with Kidder in the first place; he'd taken over on the eve of Wall Street's collapse, one of the worst times to acquire a financial firm. He'd been sorry ever since, and he let his displeasure show. By spring 1993, he wanted to reduce his involvement. Kidder was under orders to drastically limit the amount of GE's money it used to play the market, and to restrict itself to $500 million. At the moment of the edict, Kidder was using $800 million. To return the other $300 million was bad enough, but for Kidder, GE's overall attitude was even more ominous. Everyone knows you've got to spend money to make money. Kidder could only grow if it could invest more. Now not only was GE refusing to invest further, but it wanted much of its initial stake back, too.

Cerullo wasn't willing to give in immediately. He was convinced there was a way to continue trading at the same volume without GE knowing about it. Fiumefreddo and Bernstein devised a plan for simply reporting less investment to GE. In truth, there were assets on the books that arguably were not GE's. Upper management at Kidder was determined to reduce the balance sheet that GE saw. It looked as if one legal, safe way to do so was to no longer report forward settling transactions as assets to General Electric.

If a trade settled on a forward, or future, date, that meant Kidder was not currently financing the position. In other words, no cash had gone out yet. It was not financed. It was a forward commitment, so why, the reasoning went, report it on the balance sheet if no money was, at the moment, being used to fund it? Kidder could just remove those trades from the list of assets it reported to GE.

Andy Kim had been pulled off all regular duties and assigned the emergency task of writing the software that could isolate those forward transactions from Kidder trades and get them off the books. I was incensed. Asking Benatar and Kim to work on the software for Cavanaugh was the first major order I'd given after replacing Mullin as head of government bond trading the previous month. I was adamant that I be obeyed. People had commonly ignored Mullin in favor of other, external managers. I was determined to put a stop to that. I chastised Kim harshly; then I told Fiumefreddo never to issue orders to my people.

IN MAY, DESPERATE to get his department's revenue back up after the Mortgage desk fiasco, Cerullo decided that Japan was performing poorly. He sent me to Tokyo to shake up the office. As soon as I got back, Cerullo dispatched me to Europe to look into Strips trading in Germany, France and Belgium. Soon I found myself traveling to Europe once a month.

* * *

IN THE SPRING of 1993, immediately after I upbraided him for giving orders to my staff, Fiumefreddo went to Dave Bernstein. By this time, the computer had recorded "time value" profits from forward settling reconstitutions of $56 million. Convinced that it was impossible to make real any of those profits or profits from municipal defeasance trades, he insisted they be removed from the balance sheet. We've got $56 million in profits on the books, he told Bernstein, and all of it is false.

Fiumefreddo's argument revolved around the fact that the "time value" profits calculated by our software were, in fact, "unrealized profits." And he insisted that we could never make them real. It was as if we'd bought a car for $10,000 and realized its parts were worth $13,000. The car was dismantled, the parts stored on a shelf, the inventory value recorded as $13,000. But the $3,000 profit was false because none of the parts had yet been sold. In our case, Fiumefreddo didn't think we could make the profit materialize because we'd sold short, and when it came time to buy our "parts," the profit margin would disappear.

Fiumefreddo's protest landed in Bernstein's lap just weeks after I'd taken over from Mullin, and not long after Bernstein and I met. I was only just understanding how much power he had. Panicked by the news that $56 million had disappeared in a poof, Bernstein summoned me to his office. Fiumefreddo's shadow seemed to linger in the room.

"Now I'm taking his words with a grain of salt," Bernstein said. Fifty-six million is an enormous amount of money. I looked around for Cerullo, surprised that this meeting wasn't in his office. I didn't envy Bernstein having to tell his boss across the hall that he thought a $56 million write-off might be imminent. Bernstein, nervewracked as he was, tried not to overreact. Easygoing Charlie was obviously pissed at me; Bernstein wasn't sure whom to believe. Nevertheless, Fiumefreddo's accusations were so dangerous that Bernstein couldn't ignore them. Fiumefreddo insisted that if a Strip was sold for a forward settlement date and its profit was booked on day one, if we waited until the settlement date to cover our short by buying the Strips, the profit would be wiped out. It wasn't possible, Fiumefreddo complained, to profit from a forward sale of Strips. He'd insisted that all such profits be wiped off our books. I had to prove otherwise to Bernstein. I knew that I already owned the Strips. I owned the $3,000 in car parts. Exasperated, I said, "Dave, this is a no-brainer.

"If I sell something for a forward price of $62, and it's priced today for $60, I can protect the profit by buying the security for $60 today, rather than waiting for its settlement date and buying it for $62 at some time in the future," I explained. "Examine my inventory. If I own the underlying Strips, it means I purchased them in the open market. Therefore, the profits are real. And can and will be realized."

Bernstein was quiet for a moment. "I'm going to have to investigate further to convince myself."

Later I wrote in my diary for May 9, 1993: "Had a brief meeting with David Bernstein who claimed we were booking profits while having significant amounts of negative carry to make up. Clearly he does not understand the simple concept of hedging forward risks. Fium. apparently misinformed him after investigating my trading activity of last week. Municipalities are buying at today's yield for forward settle, so profit is big. Fiumefreddo wants to accrue the profit until settlement date rather than booking it today. Traders want profit today. Surprise, surprise. Benatar says that our profit calculations are correct, it is just priced on a given date. Financing charges cannot be put into our trading system as we would no longer agree with Tandem, the firm's mainframe system, and we would not be able to independently verify our profit and loss. Financing issues are separate from calculation of trading profit. Financing shows up daily in Rizzi's system."

For the next two months, Bernstein, Fiumefreddo, Benatar, McLaughlin and I pored over our forward Strip and defeasance business. Bernstein examined the ledger of all the forward Strip and recon trades that was maintained by the Financing desk. We called it the Red Book because of the color of the cover of the oversize, leatherbound calendar that was kept on the Financing desk. That desk was required to keep a record of the dates when every trade was due to settle, so it could be sure that the requisite amount of Strips or bonds was on hand to complete the trade. Anyone was supposed to be able to access the information at any time, so the ledger was always kept up-to-date and in plain view. Salesmen or traders sometimes had to make split-second decisions to take advantage of market conditions, and disaster could result if only one person was in charge of the ledger and that person went on vacation or stepped away from his or her desk.

Bernstein picked out the longest-maturing reconstitution trade listed in the Red Book and calculated its profits. Since the debate between Fiumefreddo and me began on the day I entered a forward recon for May 5 with a settlement date of October 5, Bernstein chose that trade for his hypothetical tracking. It was my longest outstanding trade at the time, and Bernstein thought it made a good model for his analyses of forward Strips and reconstitutions. He created a spreadsheet on his computer to track the trade. Fiumefreddo and I were at loggerheads, so Bernstein believed he couldn't take either of us at our word. Over and over he questioned me about my hedging techniques for that one transaction. He never seemed happy with my reasoning. First he'd question me; then he'd call Benatar over to my desk and ask him precisely the same questions. Bernstein liked to joke that Benatar was "of the tribe," meaning that they were both Jewish. "He'll give it to me straight," Bernstein added.

Fiumefreddo continued to insist that the forward profits should be erased from the books. He needled Bernstein relentlessly. Each time Fiumefreddo and Bernstein appeared at my elbow, I knew without looking up what would happen. "So what has Charlie come up with this time?"

Bernstein's spreadsheet might have been hypothetical, but the trade he tracked was real. He could watch its progress. Within the first week, he saw that the profit from this trade came true. When the bond settled, the profit would come in, he agreed. At the end of May, I wrote in my electronic diary: "Met with Fium., Bernstein, and Benatar this week for forward trades. Moishe proved that we agree with the Tandem system on P&L. Forward Strips are just like muni defeasance trade, with financing costs showing up on daily financing report, and profit showing on day one."

But it unnerved Bernstein to take credit for all that profit on the first day of the transaction. Isn't there a more conservative way to record these profits? he wanted to know.

Bernstein decided that he could protect us by creating a system in which we didn't chalk up all the future profit from forward trades on the first day. He assigned each forward trade a dummy identification number. Then he assigned each trade a price lower than the price calculated by the computer. That created a buffer, he said. That way, the future profits that we recorded would look lower than the ones we actually expected. At the same time, future profits would be recorded on a day-to-day basis. Instead of entering the whole expected profit onto our books at once (even if it was a reduced dummy profit), we'd enter only the amount generated by the end of each business day.

Benatar and Kim were assigned to reprogram the Government Bond trading computers to handle the dummy identification numbers and prices. Right away, the plan fell apart. In order to reconcile our profit and loss each night, our computer system had to agree with the profit numbers calculated by the Kidder mainframe. If we changed the Government trading system, someone was going to have to change the mainframe also. That system was years old; its software was written in Cobol or some other prehistoric code that no one knew any longer. Kidder had invested $50 million in a replacement system that was not yet on-line. The managers and programmers responsible for the mainframe balked at our plan. Why should we fix that old thing when we have new architecture scheduled to come online in less than a year? they insisted.

We couldn't make a unilateral change to the Government trading system. We couldn't get the mainframe people to go along with us. So the plan to safeguard our profit with dummy identification numbers and prices dissolved. Bernstein and Fiumefreddo settled for establishing specific guidelines for forward settling transactions. Forward Strips or recons must be limited to a three-month horizon. That was okay with me, since a Treasury bond futures contract is usually a three-month instrument. I was still betting on profit from the Fed's reduction of bond auctions using cash bonds versus futures contracts, so the new rule didn't change anything for me. I could still match the horizon of my bet with the horizon of my hedging instrument.

Bernstein and Fiumefreddo also decreed that municipal defeasance trades could be booked only two months forward. The risk with them was greater, since counties and cities can go bankrupt far more easily than the federal government.

There was one other change. Profits were still booked on day one, just as before. But now so were losses. Before, bond traders who had to buy a municipality's bond at a loss wanted their loss booked over time. We couldn't make those adjustments any longer. Bernstein insisted that we take any profit, and any loss, on the first day.

In June 1993, two months after Fiumefreddo's first complaint, Bernstein signed off on my trading strategy.

THAT SUMMER, FIUMEFREDDO'S team decided that it would be beneficial to remove all forward settling trades from Kidder's balance sheet. That way, the balance sheet that GE saw would look low and conservative. This would change the firm's internal accounting procedures. No one informed me of the change. It wasn't the kind of accounting policy that anyone ever discussed with managers at my level. But I'd find out about it in September 1993, as Cerullo and GE battled to the death.

JUST AS BERNSTEIN ended his investigation of my trades, Cerullo won a round with GE. All spring he'd been locked in a heated battle to convince GE to increase our balance sheet. I knew this, even though balance sheets circulated in the senior management loop only. Part of Cerullo's strategy involved encouraging traders to use more assets. The Mortgage desk—after its price mismarking scandal—was doing poorly, and Cerullo desperately needed someone to pick up the slack. He'd ridden the mortgage horse to glory, it had resurrected his entire career, but now it was an old nag. Cerullo needed a new racing pony. In May I'd become the second most-profitable desk; after the Mortgage desk reported its massive loss, I became number one. Immediately after Bernstein approved my trading strategies, Cerullo swung into action. In spite of our clashes over sexuality, in spite of the bitter dispute between me and McKoan, Cerullo encouraged me to increase my trading volume, to use more of the firm's assets.

Early in 1993, I traded with approximately $12 billion worth of Kidder assets. For several months, at Cerullo's insistence, I steadily increased that $12 billion to $30 billion. I barely needed Cerullo's encouragement. I was happy to do it. The huge profits generated by my trades—calculated by our software and recorded onto our books—allowed Cerullo to show impressive earnings to GE. This was his leverage in his quest for a greater commitment of capital from Jack Welch. When I started the push, in May 1993, Kidder's limit as decreed by GE was $50 billion. We habitually ignored that amount and used closer to $80 billion. Ninety percent of that money was borrowed.

Our equity capital—the amount of real cash that Kidder had in the bank—was about $500 million of GE's dollars. We used that cash as collateral for loans. GE insisted that Kidder maintain a leverage (loan to equity) ratio of 100 to 1. That was a reasonable, sound and commonly practiced principle. All of our lenders stipulated that their loans were based on a 100-to-1 leverage.

Thus, Kidder was supposed to operate with $50 billion only, or a hundred times the amount of GE's capital. GE, of course, was liable for those loans. Yet on a day-to-day basis, we were into the market for about $80 billion. We violated not only the GE edict, but the loan agreements with banks. Cerullo had to correct that. Waving the huge profits recorded by my desk under the company's nose, he browbeat GE into increasing its capital commitment to $800 million. Even though the Mortgage desk had stumbled, he argued, 1993 was already a hugely profitable year over 1992, and all because of Joseph Jett's trades.

In June 1993, the same month that Bernstein signed off on my trades, GE agreed to up its ante to $800 million.

CERULLO DECIDED TO lure Cavanaugh to Kidder with a pitch about her career. Money wasn't the only important consideration, he told her. She should come to Kidder because that was best for her future. She stuck to her million-dollar demand. Cerullo wasn't discouraged. He wanted to meet with her again. I was pleased—I wanted Cavanaugh and her accounts on my team—but I wondered: If Cerullo brings her in at a million a year, then what does that say to me? My salary was considerably lower, and I was still angry about the bonus I'd been paid the winter before. I decided to be optimistic: If Cavanaugh got paid a million, then it would create a tide that raised all the boats. When Cavanaugh and Cerullo finally reached an agreement and she accepted Kidder's offer, I also realized I had too many people on my desk. Someone had to go. I sat down with McLaughlin and Unger. I didn't want to fire anyone. I wanted them to leave of their own accord. I tried to be diplomatic.

"I know that we make a damn good team, but the way the structure is here at Kidder, when we do well, I get the lion's share of the money. That's because I'm the one who manages the risk. The rest of you have halfway decent salaries, and a bonus come rain or shine, whereas I can boom-or-bust, depending on whether I generate an income. But in order for any of you to grow, you need to take on greater responsibility, where you are managing the risk, getting the trades done for your own interest. I would suggest that you each begin looking around the Street, see what is available, and tell me what you find."

My Treasury bill trader's position was empty, and I suggested to McLaughlin that he move into it. He wanted to think about it. Unger had heard that the computer programmers were working on modifications for Cavanaugh and became convinced that he was going to lose his job to her. During this period, Bernstein and Fiumefreddo were crawling all over my desk, investigating all my trades. I started marking days on my calendar, with a view toward the day I would have to fire someone to make room for Cavanaugh, and the day that Bernstein and Fiumefreddo finished their investigation.

Then one morning, McLaughlin walked into the office and announced he was resigning to take a job with NationsBank. Salary, $500,000 guaranteed. It was more than I was earning. Suddenly my problem seemed solved—I moved Unger into McLaughlin's job.

Everyone was very happy for McLaughlin, because he'd managed to get over the wall. Ironically, though he was a diligent accountant, McLaughlin had no real interest in trading. He didn't follow news events to stay up on the bond market. But he'd parlayed his connection to my desk into a half-million-dollar-a-year job at NationsBank, which was the best Strips trading institute on the Street. NationsBank believed it had stolen a top trader from Kidder. Sadly, Kevin lasted only a few months in his new job. By that fall, he had left NationsBank.

FINALLY, MY DESK was taking shape the way I wanted. We were making money. In May *The Wall Street Journal* wrote about the Mortgage desk debacle, theorizing that Kidder was a one-horse pony that would buckle with the collapse of the Mortgage desk. Cerullo insisted that he had other strengths. The reporters wanted to talk to people who represented those strengths. Cerullo didn't trust the press, but the *Journal* stories were damaging to Kidder, and Cerullo couldn't pass up a chance to tell the paper it had been wrong. He agreed to let the reporters talk to some of his traders. Before the interview, Cerullo and I had three meetings in which he coached me in what I could and could not say. Under no circumstances was I to give away the size of my position or the size of my profits. I was just supposed to say we were very aggressive in going after customers, and we had 15 percent of total market share in government bond clients. I was supposed to remain anonymous and nameless, Cerullo said, because no one should toot his own horn. Cerullo told the *Journal* reporters that they couldn't ask any questions without him in the room. We fed them pabulum. We each spoke for a few minutes in turn, telling the journalists how great our section was, and then declining to answer any questions.

Cerullo knew what he wanted, and that was full credit for the Fixed Income successes. It was important for the financial and banking world to see Cerullo leading a faceless juggernaut. Cerullo, not Carpenter, not Jett. He was working hard to make Kidder attractive to a foreign bank, but the linchpin in any deal would be the guarantee that he remain to run Kidder under its new ownership. What better way to ensure that than to create the image that Fixed Income was worthless without him. I, however, wanted recognition beyond Kidder. I wanted to make a name in the industry.

Everyone on the Street had long been in awe of Salomon Brothers and its dominance in fixed income. Working as a trader was impressive; it was even more prestigious to work as a trader at Salomon Brothers. Yet we'd surpassed Salomon, and no one really knew of our existence. I wanted it known that when the Federal Reserve Board governors met, I had influence over them. We played an enormous role in the financial markets that were created when the government sold bonds to refinance the national debts of the Third World: bailouts of Mexico, Brazil, Argentina. Yet we were completely unknown. Cerullo wasn't interested in my quest for recognition. Attention was an unnecessary evil. The news media were only interested in problems, and would create them if they didn't exist, he warned me. In the past, news articles about Kidder had only revealed details he didn't want anyone to know. Then questions were asked. At every meeting between Cerullo and GE officials that I attended, the GE people questioned something they'd read in the press. Why did we learn about a $70 billion investment in risky mortgages only in the pages of *Barron's*?, GE officials wanted to know. Shareholders reacted badly to these reports, putting GE on the defensive, confusing and scaring the company's executives, making them combative. Cerullo's explanation was always the same: Reporters wouldn't know a bond if one fell on them. *Barron's* (or the *Times*, or the *Journal*) got it wrong. We don't own $70 billion in mortgages. GE had to trust him, he'd coo, investment banking was not its area of expertise. When they obviously didn't trust him, and sent auditors, Cerullo stonewalled them.

In 1991, there had been a steady drumbeat in *Barron's* and *The Wall Street Journal* about Kidder's high-risk mortgage portfolio and the mercurial Mike Vranos. Vranos was known to jump over desks, lunge at traders, salespeople and furniture, throw telephones and hurl chairs. The press implied that Kidder was inordinately dependent on a manager who acted like a madman, or at least an eccentric. Vranos was strange, but his traders made a lot of money, so they tolerated him. They grew rich through very risky securities. Kidder's CFO, Richard O'Donnell, didn't trust Vranos any more than he trusted Cerullo.

CAVANAUGH REPORTED FOR work on July 7. The new software system was up and running, and in the first couple of months, her performance exceeded expectations. She knew her accounts. Her presence also seemed to lure Cerullo to the desk more frequently. Cavanaugh wasn't pretty in a conventional sense, but she was slender and muscular and in terrific shape. She cursed and swore like a longshoreman, but one with a deep, liquid southern drawl. Cerullo seemed to delight in talking to her about her athletic activity, her workout regimen, her husband's career as a personal trainer.

Her profits removed any doubts I had about accounts, and forever eradicated any hesitation that remained in my aggression against McKoan. I had plenty of proof now that massive trades were possible. I asked Cavanaugh to make a list of accounts that, based on her ten years of experience, she believed we'd overlooked. Instead of going to Cerullo or McKoan to plead for access to the accounts, I called the sales force over to my desk. I didn't have an office, so I handled these conversations on the trading floor.

I looked at one of the salesmen, and then at my list. Did he cover this account? I asked. He did. My tone was sharp and hostile. "You know, for the last six months I've conducted sales giveaways, not just to get you to work, but to put money in your pocket just for making a phone call. Did you know that your account has a portfolio with over $2 billion in Strips, and that the account actively trades that portfolio as much as $500 million each month? That's $15,000 in monthly income if you did the trades. That's $15,000 that you could be earning, but you're not, because you won't make a phone call."

"Oh," the salesman said. "I'll call them right now,"

"No, you won't." I glanced around at my sales staff, who were all listening. My eyes fell on Linda Mead. "I want you to introduce Linda Mead to your account and inform them that Linda will be contacting them for all government securities trades in the future."

MY STRATEGY INFURIATED McKoan. But change sometimes comes only with conflict. I was fed up with the status quo, with being powerless, with our dance of me complaining and McKoan doing little in response. When does protest become appropriate? When does aggression replace protest? When does an all-out assault become the best strategy? I reached that point when I had the ammunition. It was appropriate to use it to assign the accounts to salespeople intent on doing the work. McKoan was satisfied just to coddle the salespeople who were already successful. The only way I could wrest authority for hiring and firing away from McKoan was to show that his performance and leadership were inadequate.

Only once did McKoan agree with my suggestion about reassigning an account. I'd grown concerned about a client based in Atlanta. I very much wanted a black trader named Harry Haigood to handle that customer. But Michael Ricciardi, the East Coast sales manager, didn't think the account was right for Haigood.

"I'm not trying to get into this thing between you and J.J.," Ricciardi told me, bringing up my dispute with McKoan. "I really support what you're trying to do with the government accounts. But I just don't think that a white broker from Georgia wants to be covered by a black salesman. I just don't think that's the right way to go about this."

We looked at each other. I'd first met Ricciardi on the affirmative action team, and I knew he was a native New Yorker who'd been in the class ahead of me at Harvard Business School. We called him Rico for short. My voice rose. "I'd rather have you oppose everything I'm trying to do with the sales force than tell me a black salesman can't handle an account below the Mason-Dixon line."

"These accounts are from the South and I don't think they'd be comfortable talking to Harry," he shouted back.

"The accounts are done over the phone. How the hell are they going to know his color, and what the hell does it matter, a bond is a damn bond!" I stomped away.

MCKOAN MADE IT clear to Cerullo he wasn't happy being usurped by me. The next morning, Cerullo called me into his office.

"I understand you've just become the sales manager."

"If no one is doing the job, someone has to step in."

"Maybe you should at least inform J.J. when you change accounts. And what is it with you and Linda Mead?"

I'd chosen Mead at random; she happened to be sitting in my line of sight when I made the decision to take the account away from McKoan's salesman.

"I just want to make certain that the accounts are being distributed fairly," Cerullo said, flicking a look at me but not holding my gaze.

"I have not distributed any of these accounts. They're all handed out by J.J. I'd like to see them distributed more, if J.J. would get off his duff and make some changes." But I knew what this was really about, and Cerullo didn't disappoint me.

"Well, I just want to make sure that you and Linda maintain a professional relationship."

AT THE BEGINNING of August, my entire trading desk went to dinner with one of the largest government bond brokerages, Cantor Fitzgerald. Since I never encouraged socializing, we'd hadn't gone out together before. At dinner I looked around the table at the team I'd built. For the first time, I didn't feel like I still had something left to do. We were a first-class operation. We had no weak spots. There was no reason why we shouldn't be able to outperform everyone on the Street. As usual, the banter turned to teasing, and someone ridiculed Elizabeth Cavanaugh for once having dated a broker. In the Wall Street hierarchy, brokers were dogs. A lot of them were sleazy. The broker trend of that moment was a good illustration of this: Former or failed models had suddenly turned to brokering. Brokerage firms work on commission, so any advantage helps their business. Brokers often flew traders to Atlantic City in helicopters, treated them to expensive dinners and shows, took them to strip clubs and arranged prostitutes or drugs. The newest gimmick for brokerage firms was to hire models as brokers.

To a trader, however, dating a broker was like dating a used-car salesman. The joke about Cavanaugh was really a putdown, so I spoke up in her defense. Soon after, Cavanaugh got up to leave. She had to drive to the country for the weekend to oversee the construction of her new house. As everyone stood to shake hands and say good-bye, Cavanaugh planted a grateful kiss on me. The table cheered.

I walked into the office the next morning filled with anticipation, expecting Cerullo to spit with rage. Instead, I heard *nothing* about the scene with Cavanaugh. Silence. The other traders on the desk ribbed me good-naturedly for letting her get the better of me, and for once, an encounter with a female co-worker came and went without any overreaction.

A couple of weeks later I flew to California for a golf tournament with our western accounts. I wasn't much of a golfer, but it was what the customers wanted. I played with McKoan, Brian Finkelstein, Michael Ricciardi and four customers. I walked up to the group on the driving range just in time to join a conversation about women. McKoan was the target. The others were teasing him about his latest employee, a raven-haired, dark-eyed beauty who'd been his summer intern. She was supposed to return to New York University at the end of the summer, but McKoan had offered her a job as his personal assistant. "Have you been there yet?" I heard them laugh as I walked up. Finkelstein saw me. "J.J., I think you're too late. I saw her with Rufus downstairs." Rufus was a black salesperson who had just been hired after graduating from Yale. "If he's been there, she won't even be able to feel you," he guffawed as the others bent with laughter.

"What do you think of her?" Finkelstein turned to Ricciardi.

"I wouldn't have that problem, I'm Italian." Ricciardi laughed.

"Yeah, well, I'm Jewish. It's only J.J. who's the little Irishman." He held up his thumb and forefinger, just a couple inches apart. I bent over to place my ball on the tee. The conversation was typical. I wasn't aloof from it, either. Finkelstein said, "J.J., you're lucky Joe Jett hasn't been there yet," and Ricciardi asked, "Hey Joe, what club are you using?"

"A Big Bertha."

"It figures!" They all burst out laughing again. McKoan turned away from the group to line up his shot.

"Leave J.J. alone," Ricciardi said when he caught his breath. "He's always going at it with his wife."

"That may be," Finkelstein countered, "but I don't think she knows it." Their laughter exploded once more. McKoan reddened so deeply the top of his bald pate seemed purple, and he whacked the ball violently. Leaning on my club, I wondered what I could say to defend him or change the subject. I was probably the last person who should speak at the moment, so I backed away and moved to another driving tee.

McKoan was a victim of this stupid "black male sexuality" hangup, too. I thought about his wife. I remembered her telling me how exceptional it was for him to love and adopt her black daughter without hesitation. He hired minority women, and promoted them quickly if they were successful. As I walked across the golf course, I resolved to be less contentious with McKoan. He was an honorable guy. I shouldn't be so combative with him, especially when he had to contend with racists like Finkelstein and Ricciardi giving him a hard time about his wife.

FINKELSTEIN RAN THE Financing desk. His traders were known as Repo traders, for repossession. They sold securities and repossessed them the next day, basically loaning them out for a fee. When a trader owns a bond overnight, he has to borrow money to buy it. Such loans mean interest payments. To reduce that onerous cost, we turned bonds over to Finkelstein's Financing desk, the Financing desk lent the bonds to someone else for a fee, and that fee was applied toward reducing our costs. Often, however, we fought with the Repo desk over the fee because we didn't believe they'd given us our share. Fees that were reported to us as zero would show up on the Repo books as $10. I regularly checked their books, or had Joey-o look at them. When I could prove that the Repo desk was stiffing my traders, I'd demand payment from Finkelstein. He preferred paying to fighting, leaving his traders with less. Several of the Repo traders complained to me privately that Finkelstein didn't pay them enough. They were unhappy. Well, so was I. After the California trip, I decided that Finkelstein had to go. I'd fight racism my way—by stripping the racists of power. With Finkelstein, the first step was to use his traders' displeasure to relieve him of his moneymaking potential. I suggested to Cerullo that all of Finkelstein's traders who were involved in financing government securities should report to me. That was about half of Finkelstein's staff.

"What's with you and Brian?" Cerullo asked.

"Nothing," I lied. Then the truth: "I think his people play a vital role in the development of the Government desk. I think they leave too early and come in too late. I think with discipline they could improve their performance. By putting us under one P&L, we'd be working for one common cause, rather than the continual fighting that we're facing now."

The constant battle over fees was not a great reason to reorganize our areas, but it was good enough.

THE CALIFORNIA JAUNT tripped another wire in me as well. I looked around the trading floor at Kidder with new eyes. I'd been burying all the crap about race, refusing to address it, reluctant to rebel. Now, after being hauled into Cerullo's office to talk about Mead, I was finally getting the message: Kidder Peabody did not consider minorities to be people. I was not a person. Instead, the overwhelming concern seemed to be that I might defile one of the white women around me. This protracted conflict wasn't going to end as long as I was there. I'd told myself before that I didn't need friends at work, and that I didn't care if anyone thought I was scary or aloof. But it hadn't really been true, not until now. Suddenly I realized I didn't like anyone, and I didn't care whether they liked me or not. My only passion was for endurance. I had no intention of leaving, or being driven out, or letting them fire me over some outrageous accusation. I wouldn't make that mistake, even though I had no one to protect me. Chike-Obi had appealed the sexual harassment charges against him to an arbitration panel, and found three middle-aged white men who looked, talked and acted just like Cerullo and the Kidder managers who'd fired him. Not surprisingly, the panel supported the company's decision to let him go. I knew I'd find no allies, either. In my mind there were only three options: quit, comply, or take my accuser's job away from him. The last option became my goal. Cerullo, despite all his racist rhetoric, always rewarded those who made money. That's what he always told me: This racist firm is a meritocracy.

It was war now. Not a game, but war. I challenged everyone in the office with my new mantra. Women who tried to talk to me still heard "discipline must be maintained." But now everyone also got: "What do you think? I'm playing a game?" I'd find a reason to say it several times a day. "This is not a game, this is war. What do you think? I'm playing a game?"

I was very particular about how my traders were approached over the PA system. To avoid confusion, I insisted that inquiries include the bond, the maturity and the yield offering. But people liked shorthand. They'd get on the hoot and holler and ask about a security by referring to its issue date. When I heard that I'd bellow back, "What the fuck? Do you think this is a game? This is a war. What do you mean May 18?" Most of the time I was just angry with people for imprecision that made my job harder. Then I began staging my remarks on the hoot and holler. I'd think about it at the gym before work, where I also drilled myself on preserving the No Women rule. Soon I had no time for my gym friends. I was preparing for battle.

"GET BIGGER.
BE MORE AGGRESSIVE."

AVANAUGH'S TRADING VOLUME was so high that soon she needed an assistant of her own. She hired a young woman named Bernice Rothstein. I continued to dismiss the people that Cerullo and I had agreed needed to go. By September my group was so cohesive, there was no place on earth I'd rather have been. I'd earned $56 million by exploiting the fact that the government had moved to semi-annual bond auctions. Fiumefreddo had challenged my trading strategy, but Cerullo and Bernstein had backed me up. In addition, the largest fixed income bond mutual fund, Pacific Investment Management, had decided to reconstitute every lion, tiger and bear. Only one person in the world knew where to find those bonds, and she was sitting next to me. We were doing everything right.

EVEN THOUGH CERULLO had persuaded Jack Welch to increase GE's investment in Kidder, he didn't rest. To make money you've got to be willing to spend money, and he knew that GE was not. Kidder's Fixed Income area had greater potential than Welch or any of the paper-pushers at GE realized. Cerullo needed a white knight, a rescuer who would take us over, either by buying Kidder's moribund Investment Banking sector, or by dissecting out and buying the Fixed Income department. The trouble was, whoever bought the company or our unit had to be persuaded that Cerullo should remain in charge.

The Fixed Income department generated 110 percent of the firm's net income; the rest of Kidder was worthless. If Jack Welch ever tried to sell Kidder, he'd really only be selling the income-producing area. Kidder's only other valuable asset was its retail distribution network—the brokers who sold to Mops and Pops and other private individuals. That network, part of the Investment Banking arena, was strong, but it wasn't very profitable. Still, it was salvageable. If someone wanted Kidder's Retail Investment unit, they might buy Kidder's entire Investment Banking area. They could get it cheap because it didn't generate any income. They'd probably jettison most of it, like the Mergers and Acquisitions department, and salvage the Retail Investment unit. That kind of merger made sound business strategy.

Cerullo hoped someone agreed. GE was just too stingy. Cerullo felt that Kidder should operate with $2 billion in equity capital from GE, not a paltry $800 million. And he'd hated the fight to increase that figure from $500 million. GE's parsimony meant that Kidder's financial health was always threatened. Short-term loans and bank lines of credit depend on economic ratios within a firm, such as return on assets, asset-to-liability ratios, and the firm's leverage. Because GE was so stingy, Kidder was always nearly in violation of its lending terms. Winning the $800 million only brought Kidder into line, it didn't eliminate the fact that we were always tottering on its edge.

Cerullo and I spoke every other day, often several times a day, throughout the summer of 1993, so I was aware of his concerns. Partly this was because I'd been named desk head. It was also because of his determination to increase our position.

"Get bigger. Be more aggressive." Those words ended all our meetings. By mid-July, we were using over $100 billion.

IN EARLY AUGUST 1993, at the regular Monday morning meeting of desk heads, Cerullo announced that our incredible profits meant our area was carrying the firm. He wanted, he said, to separate the Fixed Income department from the rest of Kidder. Leaning forward, he slid two handouts at each of us. One was a photocopied article from *The Economist* magazine about Deutsche Bank. Another was a similar piece on Crédit Suisse, a bank that owned First Boston. These were our potential suitors, Cerullo said; we should read up on them. We'd never get sufficient capital from GE to grow, so we must find someone else to invest in us, to purchase us from GE and give us the capital that we needed to fund our tremendous growth.

"I intend to go eyeball-to-eyeball with Jack Welch, and make him see reason," Cerullo said. He looked around the room. "Use what you need to."

It wasn't a formal increase of my trading position, but I understood. We had limits; Cerullo wanted us to ignore them and use whatever amount of capital it took to get the job done. My official trading budget had been $16 billion, but by the end of August I'd increased it to $30 billion.

AT THE END of each quarter, Kidder was required to file a report called a Schedule K, detailing its economic health to its parent company. The next quarter end loomed just a few weeks from the date of Cerullo's brinkmanship with Welch. Cerullo had to force Welch's hand before the quarter's end, or GE was going to find out we were wildly overleveraged. At the end of August, Bernstein pulled me aside.

"Listen, you know Ed said he's going eyeball-to-eyeball with Jack Welch? Well, Ed may have just blinked. I may be asking you to reduce your positions, and reduce them pretty sharply. Before the *quarter end*."

I went back to my desk. If Cerullo lost, I'd have to move fast to get my position back below its trading limit of $16 billion. I could wait until I was told, or I could start now. I thought about it. I really had nothing to lose by starting now. It'd be easier to liquidate my position over a month's time rather than over a few days. If it turned out that Cerullo won, I could have my position back up within days. If he lost, I'd score some brownie points by anticipating his difficulty. I couldn't lose by starting now.

I looked at my holdings; this would be simple. Anywhere I was long, meaning any securities I owned, I would sell. Anywhere I was short, meaning bonds that I sold without owning, I would purchase the bonds to cover the short. It would be simple buying and selling of securities on the Street or through customers.

Those were exhilarating days. Bernstein brought me daily reports on Welch's communications with Cerullo. I felt close to the seat of power. I was keenly interested in business policy, corporate politics and Cerullo's maneuvering. I was fascinated with Cerullo's utter disdain for Michael Carpenter. He called Carpenter a "broken toilet of a man." To him, Carpenter was superfluous. He wouldn't help Cerullo in his efforts to get more money from GE, so rumor had it that Cerullo went straight to Welch. I felt that however close to Welch Cerullo had become, then, as Cerullo's biggest earner, I was equally close. It was almost ten years to the day from Welch's visit to the GE plant where I'd worked as a chemical engineer. That day, I'd been ordered to stay out of sight of Neutron Jack. Now my actions directly affected his decision-making process.

By September 11, I'd brought my position down to $10 billion. I had worked maniacally to bring it down from $30 billion, just in case Cerullo lost to Welch. It was done. I could sit back, wipe my brow and consider myself a winner. I told Bernstein what I'd done, explaining my strategy and hope that by acting in advance, we'd be protected. Neither of us saw anything wrong with proactively reducing my position through buying and selling bonds. I even boasted to Bernstein about my initiative.

"I've reduced my position in anticipation of something going wrong. You know, in case Cerullo does blink."

Bernstein smiled. "That's very white of you."

Then the ax fell.

In order to hide assets from GE, Fiumefreddo, Bernstein and Cerullo had changed our accounting system to cloak all the forward settling trades. I had no idea new record-keeping procedures were in place. But they were and, under them, no forward settling trade was allowed to show up on the balance sheet that GE saw. Fiumefreddo had set the new rules in motion in June, after asking Benatar and Kim to change the software we used. Now if a trade settled more than one day into the future, it no longer counted on our balance sheet. If I bought $100 million worth of a security, but the seller was not to deliver the security to me for a week, it would be considered a forward purchase. Under the new accounting procedures, when I looked at my trading position, the computer showed that I owned that $100 million in securities. But when I looked at the firm's balance sheet, it showed something else entirely: I didn't own those securities and wouldn't own them for five working days. In other words, my trading position recorded that I'd spent $100 million, but our firm balance sheet recorded nothing to show for it.

For two weeks, I'd looked only at my trading position, unaware of the new accounting rules. My trading ledger showed that I'd spent $100 million. To hedge that, I had to sell $100 million worth of securities. So I sold. I never looked at the firm's balance sheet. I'd never had to do so in the past, because the two were never different. Until now. I didn't realize that with the new accounting rules, when I spent $100 million on forward settling bonds, I had no bonds to show for it until the day of settlement. That meant, I had no asset to hedge. When I hedged anyway, all I did was create a $100 million imbalance and a new trading position for myself. I hadn't reduced my position at all.

Suddenly I had a huge problem. The timing of my ownership of bonds had become a critical factor. To make the new system work, I had not only to hedge my positions, I had to know the timing of my forward settlement dates, and hedge my positions within those parameters. But there was no way to monitor the timing. So all my efforts to reduce my position had backfired. I spent the first two weeks of September buying and selling bonds I never should have touched. Under the old rules, if I bought $100 million, I could sell $100 million to offset it. I'd be even, regardless of whether the purchase didn't settle for five days. Under the new rules, if I bought $100 million and sold $100 million, I'd be down $100 million. My assets were now a function of time. I created a position where one had not existed.

Of my original $30 billion position, about $24 billion was in forward settling securities that we'd slipped off the balance sheet. So most of my position was directly affected by the new accounting rules. It meant I hadn't helped Cerullo, I'd exacerbated his problem. Bernstein had known what I was doing. I'd flaunted my strategy, and he hadn't suspected that the new accounting system would decimate me. The balance sheets under the new accounting system were reported to only a few people, and Bernstein wasn't one of them. Not only didn't he anticipate the impact, he told Cerullo that I'd reduced my position. Cerullo had even praised me for being a team player and showing leadership.

So when the accountants suggested that my position had, in fact, not gone down at all, Bernstein dismissed them. "I've seen Jett's numbers, and he's down." But the accountants insisted that the balance sheet was being figured in a new way. Their printouts were gospel. Jett's position was not down at all. Panicked, Bernstein pulled me into Cerullo's office. He flew at me in a rage, then turned to Cerullo and said, "Jett just screwed us, saying his position is down and it's not down at all."

"You fucking asshole!" Cerullo screamed at me. We raged at each other full-throttle.

"Fuck that! Look at my numbers! Bernstein's the asshole!" I thrust my accounting reports at Cerullo. They showed that my position was indeed down. Cerullo grabbed the papers and, looking over the numbers, turned on Bernstein and screamed that, yes, now Bernstein was the asshole. Shaking and glaring with rage, I left them shouting at each other. I wanted no part of their ridiculous confrontation. I still didn't know that there was another set of accounting records. Bernstein had seen them in the business unit controller's office, which got them from Accounting. Accounting didn't show those reports to traders. They were so new and so rare that even though Cerullo and Bernstein had sat in the meeting at which the new accounting procedures for balance-sheet assets were announced, they didn't recognize the reports. But Bernstein was pissed and wanted to double-check the numbers.

Two hours later, my phone rang and Bernstein sneered at me again. My numbers were indeed all wrong, he said. "There's a new accounting procedure." I went to his office, where he handed me a report. "These are your numbers as being reported to Accounting." I needn't be privy to how the new numbers were determined, he said. I just needed to know that rather than a position of $10 billion, I was at $29 billion.

We went back to Cerullo's office. The discrepancy between the reports was undeniable, but I thought I knew what had happened. The Accounting department must be a day behind. "They're assholes. It's right there. Here, look, I brought down the position, and here's the proof," I said, once more proffering the reports I'd gotten from the Accounting department. Cerullo looked again at these documents, the familiar papers he'd seen in all his years as a trader. He agreed. Bernstein wasn't satisfied. For two days the three of us fought over the dueling accounting reports. I suspected Bernstein's sources. He was waving around reports I'd never seen before and couldn't pinpoint. On the other hand, I was relying on the same reports that had been crossing my desk every day for years. How could I be sure that the source of these new reports wasn't Fiumefreddo, who had it in for me?

By mid-September 1993, however, Cerullo and Bernstein were convinced that the new accounting procedures had caused my problem. Cerullo called me into his office. Bernstein's numbers are right, he said. He didn't tell me how he knew that; instead, he let me believe that he'd sided with Bernstein. "Don't argue with me, just do what I say! You're wrong, but Bernstein has a solution. Execute what he says."

I was livid, but I knew it was useless. The accounting system could not revert to its traditional methodology because the change in procedures was vital to hiding assets from GE. So the books showed that I had a $30 billion position, even though I knew that if I added up my long and short bonds, they totaled only $10 billion.

Bernstein had won. I was now to follow his instructions as to what trades were done *in my position*! He had wrested control of my desk away from me, and that, I believed, had been the point all along. That he'd accomplished it because of the new accounting methodology was just a fluke. He'd been watching for an opportunity, and one had presented itself. Now I was ordered to take his word for some accounting rules I didn't understand. I'd gone from being a team leader who had solved a problem, to the cause of a problem who insisted that the problem didn't exist.

In his office, Bernstein spoke in spurts, his nervous pauses followed by a rush of words. My position could be genuinely reduced, he explained, by churning my Strips. He told me exactly how many of my Strip holdings I should turn into bonds; then he instructed me to restrip those reconstituted bonds for a forward settlement date beyond our quarter end, which was September 23. GE's was a week after that. I had three weeks to get it done. Bernstein chose this solution because I'd done one- and two-month forward reconstitutions of bonds. For those profits to be real, we immediately had to buy the underlying Strips that comprise the reconstituted bond. However, that left us with a settlement date mismatch. The Strips were bought to settle today, but the bond was reconstituted two months hence. With the change in the accounting rules to ignore all forward settlement trades, the system only saw the Strips that I had purchased to support the future reconstitution. That's all the accountants saw when they looked at my position. So Bernstein's idea was for me to book a reconstitution for today, to make all the Strips the accountants saw disappear and become a bond. Then, since I actually needed those Strips for my original reconstitution, I had to strip the bond I'd just created. But I had to strip it for a future resettlement date.

It was an exhausting manipulation of the accounting system. It left me completely in the dark—I didn't know the rules, didn't even know what my positions were in terms of the settlement dates, didn't know what would settle or unsettle my position. It left me utterly dependent on Bernstein to correct the balance-sheet problem that rose from the decision to juggle forward trades. I began executing trades whose logic was unclear and whose purpose I didn't understand. I couldn't ask that the accounting system revert to its old methods. By now, Kidder was using $125 billion in equity when we were still supposed to be using only $80 billion. Some $40 billion of that was being kept off the books by not recording any forward settling trades. Going back to the old system would return those assets to the balance sheet. GE would instantly see $125 billion instead of $80 billion.

My screwup had jeopardized that scheme. It created another $20 billion position for me. If GE looked at the books at that moment, they'd see $100 billion, and it was my fault. A way had to be found to eliminate that $20 billion from my position. Bernstein's brew of reconstituting bonds, selling them and stripping them again served to take all my Strips off the balance sheet.

LATER THIS WOULD be called phantom trading. Newspaper analyses argued that I sold securities for forward settlement dates without owning them. Thus, the analyses said, on the settlement date I'd had to buy the securities on the open market, for a higher price. The profits I'd expected could never be real, and I'd known that—thus, phantom trades. That would never have happened, the newspapers said, if I had purchased the underlying Strips in the first place.

In truth, I did buy the underlying securities; in fact, I owned tens of billions of dollars in the Strips. But they were removed from the balance sheet by Bernstein's clever trades, for the sole purpose of reporting lower assets to GE. We flipped the Strips so they wouldn't show up on the balance sheet each day. Cerullo was adamant that Kidder grow, but GE was uncomfortable with the risk. Everyone in the firm got in line behind Cerullo, Bernstein and the accountants. All of them agreed that the best way to slip under GE's radar was to leave forward transactions off the books. The solution for my trading position debacle was just a continuation of that scheme. It was a shell game.

RECONSTITUTING A BOND is not as easy as it sounds, and reconstituting $20 billion requires a Herculean effort. To reconstitute a bond, you must have physical possession of a specific number of Strips. To get the Strips we needed in such a short period, we paid their owners exorbitant amounts, losing $2.8 million just in obtaining them. Naturally, this caused a further complication. We did these forward reconstitutions for the sole purpose of generating an up-front profit. Since the forward Strips cost money, that generated an up-front loss. We worked around the clock for three days to prepare the $20 billion reconstitution. We executed one trade, on one day, that left us with a $48 million loss. Since my profits for the year were $70 million, over half were wiped out with one trade I didn't believe I needed to do.

I went ballistic. I argued with Cerullo and Bernstein that the loss should be footed by whoever changed the accounting system without telling us in the first place. They were responsible for the fuckup. My position problem had nothing to do with my trading but everything to do with manipulating the balance sheet to hide assets from GE. "Mortgage securities always traded for forward settlement dates," I thundered. "With the new account-ing system, the Mortgage department's entire balance sheet is wiped out. Violà, the Mortgage department is gone! Hidden! Forty billion in assets just vanish in a poof; an entire block of assets invisible to GE."

That, of course, was the point. My desk would just have to absorb the price. Eighty percent of our profits were wiped out. My traders and I lost $5 million in bonus income.

Cerullo smiled. He'd talk to Mike Vranos about it, he said. Bernstein suggested another accounting adjustment, somewhere down the line. Don't worry about it, he assured me, it'll be fine, we'll do something to take care of it.

IF THE BOOKS could be juggled once, they could be juggled again, as Bern-stein suggested. I asked Joey-o, a former accountant, to work on the prob-lem. I lay awake nights considering approaches. I twisted my trading position into pretzel shapes in my mind, looking for recourse. Eventually, I cobbled together an idea. Since we knew that the forward reconstitutions generated a profit that could be maintained if we purchased the underlying Strips, I suggested that we book a forward recon as far out as they would allow us (at this time, three months) in a security that paid high coupon rates. This would exactly offset the loss we were taking, because the higher the interest, the greater the financial impact of a reconstitution. This should make the entire off-balance-sheet procedure revenue-neutral. We would conduct a series of forward trades, the net impact of which would be zero. It would remove $20 billion in assets from the books and records of the firm. I went to Cerullo and Bernstein with this suggestion. They approved of the idea.

On September 22, 1993, I began a ninety-day reconstitution that would become the final leg of this balance-sheet equation. September 23, the next day, was quarter end. The office erupted in celebration. We'd achieved the impossible, taking the balance sheet from $123 billion on the thirteenth of September to $79 billion on the twenty-third. We'd made $44 billion disappear miraculously in ten days. I personally had made $23 billion disappear in two days.

Bernstein was exuberant; Cerullo was punchy with joy and relief. His giddiness was so vivid I wondered briefly if Welch had threatened to fire him if he couldn't demonstrate control of the balance sheet. Get this thing under $80 billion or you're out of here, I imagined Welch growling. But we hadn't done a damn thing. It was all smoke and mirrors. We'd hoodwinked GE with Bernstein's off-balance-sheet financing. The strategy had been in the works for months, ever since Fiumefreddo angered me back in May when he told Moishe Benatar and Andy Kim to drop everything and work on software that could remove the forward settling trades from the balance sheet. For all those months, everyone in Fixed Income's upper management had been completely involved in this program to hide assets from our parent corporation.

If I hadn't created a sinkhole of quicksand for myself by acting under the old accounting rules, I might have been just as thrilled and exultant as everyone else that we'd pulled it off. Apparently it wasn't illegal. Kidder's in-house counsel had pored over the strategy, I learned later. Together with Bernstein and the accountants, the Kidder lawyers formed the Asset Reduction Task Force. The attorneys analyzed the legal consequences of using forward trades to hide assets, although they called it a "temporary reduction." In their final report they wrote: "KP proposed filings appear appropriate, although undisclosed window dressing could be viewed as 'circumvention' if excessive. Care should be taken not to mislead lenders, counterparties, rating agencies or customers in communications other than the required reports." Kidder didn't report its numbers to the public, but GE did. While Kidder couldn't commit fraud with this off-balance-sheet financing, GE could. General Electric could be accused of falsifying the numbers, and we could be accused of aiding the falsification. The lawyers didn't want the strategy to go on long enough for that to happen.

It was certainly no secret that we'd successfully hidden the forward settling assets, but I was too upset about my lost profits to share in everyone's cheer. Six months later, my displeasure would turn to complete shock once I was fired and everyone in Fixed Income's upper management parroted the same line: "Forward trades?! Whoever heard of those?"

CERULLO HIMSELF HAD wanted the lawyers to evaluate his plan to hide assets from GE. It was his great contingency in his fight with Welch. Their approval provided him with an extra measure of protection in case something went wrong, and he had the power to convince Kidder's lawyers and accountants to accept his strategy. Michael Carpenter, unfortunately, wasn't savvy enough about securities trading to understand what we were doing.

ON SEPTEMBER 23, Cerullo called all his managers into a meeting. I arrived late, as a few others straggled in and while Cerullo asked each person how much money he'd lost and what getting the balance sheet down to $80 million had cost us. Wearily I explained again what we had done. How we'd had to pay nearly $3 million just to buy the Strips for the reconstitutions that eliminated my $30 billion Strip position. How we'd lost $43 million to complete the forward Strips. How we'd covered that with a forward reconstitution three months into the future. How that all meant that, net, we'd taken a $3 million hit. I heard my own voice droning. I was sick of this twisted explanation. It sounded crazy even to me. I didn't want to talk about it anymore.

"Okay," Cerullo said, and turned to Brian Finkelstein. Financing had used forward trades, too, but had taken a smaller hit. His strategy was slightly different, Finkelstein said. He'd appealed to his regular customers, told them, hey, look, we need to get rid of a large number of securities, can you buy them from us? And we'll buy them back from you in a week at such and such a price. No one dared call it parking securities, which is illegal, but it definitely constituted a "buy back, sell back" agreement. On Wall Street it was called window dressing. It wasn't illegal, it was just putting your best face forward. We needed to look better from the outside for only about a week. After GE issued its quarterly report to the public, we could buy back the Financing desk's securities because it would no longer matter how we looked.

ANOTHER PROBLEM AROSE before the end of the week. Bernstein noticed that some of my old trades—ones conducted before the balance-sheet crisis—were scheduled to settle in the week between our quarter end and GE's quarter end.

"Look, we've got a problem. A lot of your trades are going to settle in the next week. If they settle, your balance-sheet assets are going to jump up dramatically. And these people at GE are going to catch on to what we've done. This will look bad for them, and look bad for us." Even though we'd already filed our quarterly report to GE, we knew they could pay us a surprise visit anytime in the next week. They'd almost certainly want to see our numbers again just before they issued theirs. They'd see the discrepancy then. It was critical that our balance sheet remain stable.

"The forward transactions that are due to settle in the next week, do not let them settle," Bernstein said. "Pair them off and roll them forward into next month."

*   *   *

A "PAIR-OFF ROLL-FORWARD" action means to negate an existing trade by executing an opposite trade. For example, to pair off a Strip trade with the Fed that was scheduled to settle on January 1, a trader would choose to put on a reconstitution trade that was scheduled to settle on January 1, too. In my case, it meant writing a settlement ticket and then immediately writing another ticket for a reverse transaction, to roll over the trade.

I should have known that what Bernstein ordered was like telling me to stand on a weight scale while holding a bowling ball. If I threw the ball forward, the scale would register a reduced weight. Everyone would crowd around, congratulating me for losing weight. But that bowling ball is going to land somewhere, and if I catch it, the scale will spike up. So I couldn't catch it and hold on to it. I had to catch it but toss it away again as soon as it brushed my hand. That way, if the weight did jump up at any point, by the time someone turned and asked hey, what was that? the higher numbers would have become a mere shadow that was never really there, just a phantom.

Thus, the trades rolled over from the week of September 23 through 30 became phantom trades. That does not mean they were never conducted. They occurred. There is evidence of them, pieces of paper to prove their existence. But those papers show only traces of the trades. And the results of the trades were rolled over, leaving only a shadow.

CHILDREN LEARN THAT little white lies often lead to larger lies. Lying only creates the need for more lies. This is what we were doing at Kidder. Every crisis sparked another layer of maneuvering and coverup. We were digging ourselves deeper into the hole. I could see that, but I failed to notice that I was being sent down into the pit with the shovel—alone.

TO FOLLOW BERNSTEIN'S instructions, I looked in the Red Book to identify the transactions he was worried about. About forty Strips and recons that were due to settle before September 30 would have caused the balance sheet to increase as much as $10 billion. Instead, those transactions were rolled forward into October, effectively hiding them from the prying eyes of GE.

Early that month, I went to Japan for a couple of weeks, to hire for our Japanese government trading operation. When I returned, Bernstein and Cerullo had won a concession from GE. After they'd brought the balance sheet down to $80 billion, GE declared they didn't have to keep it there every day. GE just wanted to see it back on target by the end of the fourth quarter. GE thought that gave Kidder lots of wiggle room. We knew otherwise. I kept $25 billion off the books, and the Mortgage department kept another $15 billion off the balance sheet. That was our wiggle room, right there.

At the same time, the moribund Mortgage desk suddenly revived. Interest rates were down, and the Mortgage desk needed capital to take advantage of this. It appeared from our balance sheet that there was room to give money to the Mortgage area. But the off-balance-sheet financing hid the fact that there was no money to spare. So Cerullo and Bernstein decided to expand the off-balance-sheet financing, directly contradicting the legal department's warning not to prolong the off-balance-sheet strategy. It also meant that Fixed Income was definitely running two sets of books. We created an entirely new accounting system for reporting to GE. At the same time, I still used the old system on a day-to-day basis. That's because a trader cannot ignore his forward transactions; a trader has to know if he has committed to sell someone something ten days hence. It determines how he manages his risk. Thus, it was impossible for a trader to operate under the accounting system that Kidder used to report to GE. The solution was creating two sets of books.

The lawyers had cautioned Cerullo not to use off-balance-sheet financing on a continuous basis. They neglected to specify at what point it became continuous.

If GE had viewed Kidder as a profitable, going concern, it would have financed it to ensure stability and growth. But Welch decided he was not going to support us. Fixed Income had been profitable for three years and was overtaking other Wall Street investment firms. Cerullo knew that, and so did Bernstein. They knew Kidder had potential. So they scrambled to find a way to grow, to take advantage of the market without stretching the firm too thin. Their creative use of asset reporting danced on the edge of impropriety.

AWAY FROM THE office, things weren't idyllic, either. I had moved from the drug-infested Lower East Side to a two-room hovel in Hell's Kitchen. Friends from the office had visited and teased me about being able to stand in the middle of my tiny bedroom, reach out and touch both walls. My lack of furniture had become a running desk joke. For a long while I hadn't cared because I hadn't spent much time at home. When I did leave the office, I'd just stop at my apartment to change clothes. My closest friend was a broker named Rome Rottura, a Queens native with an intense pride in his Italian heritage. He was one generation removed from the homeland; his mother didn't speak English. Rottura liked to wear lots of gold necklaces; I thought they were tacky and insisted that he remove one or two before we went out to bars and nightclubs. I liked Rottura because he reminded me of myself, before Morgan Stanley. He was a braggart and a live wire who loved to party and chase women. He was two years younger than me, but strangely enough, we were born on the same day. My apartment appalled Rottura. But his reasons had little to do with my day-to-day comfort. If I wanted to pursue women, he explained, I needed a nice place in a good part of town, and a real bed. I wanted to move for another reason— I wanted to live in a neighborhood that would be safe for my parents to visit.

I put off moving because finding a rental apartment in Manhattan is a nightmare for a black man. I called about one place and was told the apartment was "very nice, very clean, good neighbors, no blacks." Another time, when I went to see an apartment, the manager simply slammed the door in my face. In a third place, I was ready to write a $3,000 check for the rent, but the landlord insisted that he had to look at other applications he'd received. None of the rental agents or landlords were ever black. Eventually, I enlisted white friends to act as decoys. They called to enquire about apartments, and even went to look at a few for me. If a place had potential, then I'd check it out.

Finally, a friend found a loft for me in Tribeca. It was a co-op, however, which meant I had to appear before the board for approval. I knew that would never work, so I offered to pay a year's rent up front. The owner insisted on an interview together with the co-op board president. My friend, Janet, who was white, and I decided to go in as a couple. Later we could say we'd broken up. Even so, I expected instant rejection. The landlord was surprised to see me; the real estate agent had shown the apartment to Janet only.

"I hope you don't have a problem with the two of us. We both work on Wall Street. We're very quiet." He didn't look convinced, so I plunged ahead. "Listen, no one in this city wants to rent to someone who is black. If that's the issue, just be straightforward so I don't waste my time. I'll look somewhere else."

He looked startled and started to make excuses when the door to his apartment opened. Another man walked in, followed by a young black woman. The landlord gestured toward the black woman.

"I'd like you to meet my wife," he said. The rent was $3,600, exactly $3,000 more than I was paying in Hell's Kitchen. I moved in at the end of October.

I BOUGHT A bed, a table and a couch. The loft was 2,700 square feet, one huge, open, drafty room with skylights. All my furniture would fit in one corner and I could still Rollerblade around the apartment. My furniture was on order for several months, and when it was finally ready, I couldn't be home to meet the deliverymen. I asked Unger to wait in my empty apartment, but he was busy, too. Cavanaugh volunteered her assistant, Bernice Rothstein, who agreed cheerfully because, she said, she was curious to see a Tribeca loft.

Rothstein was ambitious, but her devotion to her job was subsumed by her wild social life. She burned the candle at both ends, staying out late at clubs and coming to work exhausted. Several weeks after Rothstein helped me with my furniture, Cavanaugh had asked me to speak to her. I told Bernice that she couldn't remain on the Bond desk unless she worked as hard as her colleagues. She worked diligently for a week, then told me that she wanted to take the Series 7 exam. To prepare for the test, Bernice wanted to hire a private tutor, a handsome young man. Another sales assistant had a tutor, and she bragged to Rothstein that she was dating him. I refused to pay for it. "I'm not going to hire a tutor just because you want to work with a good-looking guy. Study, like everyone else."

We hadn't spoken much since that conversation, when, a few weeks later, Cerullo called me into his office. He fumed at me from across his desk. "What is wrong with you people? How many times do I have to tell you?"

Rothstein had complained to the compliance office that she had helped with my furniture, but I wouldn't give her a private tutor. The compliance officer believed that these were firing offenses. She relayed Bernice's complaint to Cerullo. He wasn't going to fire me, he said, but warned, "If you need an errand done, take one of my secretaries in her fifties to do it. Not someone like Bernice, where obvious questions will arise."

Days later, one of McKoan's assistants stopped me in a hallway to discuss coming to work for me. Moments after, Cerullo beckoned me into his office once more. He sat at his tidy desk, his neat hair damp and slicked back.

"I understand you said you were interested in her," he said of the young woman I'd just met in the hall. Somehow he noticed my surprise without meeting my eyes. "Didn't you say you'd like to have an exotic like her? Did you say that to her?"

Nothing of the sort had been part of the hall conversation. In fact, I'd told the woman that I didn't want to hire her because I didn't think she had enough experience.

"I haven't said anything to her. I'm not trying to date her, I have no interest in her."

"Okay, okay, I'm just trying to get you to be careful."

Cerullo's words replayed in my head as I walked away from his office. I had long ago nicknamed the group of women who worked for McKoan as "J.J.'s exotics." He hired pretty, dark-haired women of diverse ethnic backgrounds. I never called the women by that nickname, though. When had I talked about it aloud? Who could have overheard me and reported it to Cerullo?

I'D BEGUN TO feel almost philosophical about the flurry of sex-and-dating lectures, and Cerullo's apparent obsession with black men dallying with white women. I was no longer angry about being chastised for some fantasy threat. Cerullo's fear of me was actually weakness on his part. Now the chats had resumed in rapid succession. The warning about Bernice was followed immediately with the challenge about the "exotic" saleswoman. Just days later, Cerullo summoned me for a third time. The reason was Linda Mead. My sales staff was doing well, Cerullo said, and he'd been looking over my year-end performance evaluations. I'd suggested promotions for half a dozen people, including Elizabeth Cavanaugh, Linda Mead, Joey Ossman, Harry Haigood and Jeff Unger, whose performance had improved at the end of the year.

"I know Linda Mead is number three of your five salespeople," Cerullo began. "What is your relationship with her?"

Now I was angry as much with myself as with Cerullo. I'd been careless. It had been shortsighted to ask Bernice to help with my delivery. It had been stupid to talk to the saleswomen directly about job openings. I'd relaxed some after the hiring of Elizabeth Cavanaugh. Having a white woman trader sit at the next desk meant that people got used to seeing a white woman near me. Cavanaugh had become something of a buffer between me and the other women in the office. I hadn't been diligent, and here was the result: Cerullo was again raising the specter of "black male sexuality" in a rush of complaints, any one of which I knew could be exaggerated into a firing offense.

I answered flippantly, "Linda is a distant third to Bruce Cook. If you think I'm having a relationship with Linda, what in the world do you think is going on with Bruce?"

"I am serious. I am very serious about this. People have asked me about your relationship with Linda. Several people have voiced their concern. We've talked about this before. I'm just asking you directly. I just want reassurance that you're not having a relationship with Linda."

Apparently, he'd heard that Mead had once dated Chike-Obi, and he knew that she and I had danced at an office Christmas party in 1991. I guessed that Cerullo decided that Mead had a thing for black men. Mead was an attractive blonde with waist-length hair. Unfortunately, she had developed the habit of a lot of bright, clever blond women—she played dumb. She wasn't. She had an undergraduate degree in engineering from the University of Chicago, and an MBA. I thought she lacked self-confidence. Maybe she played dumb because men expected that of her. In the office, she spoke in a high, whining voice I never heard her use elsewhere. She told me once that when she acted normal, men were threatened by her, but when she was coquettish and flirty, they fell all over themselves to help her. That may be why she insisted on completing her deals by coming to the desk to hand over her tickets in person. When she bent over to fill out the paperwork, she flung her long hair back so that it flew over the person she was talking to. If she was standing to the left, her hair landed on the seated person's right shoulder. When she did this to me, Cavanaugh would look up and say, "Joseph, are you in there?" Cavanaugh came to refer to this as "being blonded." "Joseph, you've just been blonded," she'd say, when Linda left the desk.

Mead had begun selling bonds for my desk the previous October, and since then she'd made good money. There were five salespeople on my desk, so on average, Linda was involved with every fifth transaction. McKoan was reluctant to give her accounts, however, which held up business if the other salespeople were busy. When I asked McKoan about the delay, he'd inevitably say: "Here we go with this Linda thing again. My salesmen have better things to do than worry about government accounts." My list of accounts that I'd earmarked for my staff annoyed him. Unwisely, I butted heads with McKoan regularly. I was head of a desk, but he was a managing director, and my superior.

Now Cerullo was calling me on the carpet over Mead. I looked straight at him. It was a tactic he didn't like; he rarely looked anyone in the eye himself.

"I'm not having a relationship with Linda. Or anyone else in this office. What I am trying to do is hire a sales force that will concentrate on doing government business and make us the best on Wall Street. That's all."

"That's fine, Joseph. Concerns were raised. I've raised them with you. You've addressed them. Let's go on."

But we didn't. Soon Cerullo was calling me into his office about once a week to query me about Mead. After several of these chats, I muttered my disgust to Cavanaugh, telling her that Cerullo was interfering in my personal life and carrying on about "sexual aggressiveness." She was shocked. "You can date whoever you want to date. Fuck these people! What the hell is wrong with them?" she said loudly, at the desk. There is an informer, I said. Or at least, I thought there was. Someone was keeping tabs on me.

"Boolsheeeyit!!" she exclaimed in her southern drawl. "You have to make clear that your private life is your private life. I can kind of see where they would be concerned if you were doing trades with people just because of their looks or some nonsense like that, but this is just crazy."

IN LONDON THE next week, I had dinner with Jean Joyce, a saleswoman who had become one of my first friends at Kidder. I always felt more relaxed in Europe, and remembering the black musicians and artists who fled the U.S. in the 1930s and 1940s to find acceptance in Paris made me think that's what I needed to do. Just get out of New York altogether.

Over dinner, Jean listened as I chronicled my clashes with Cerullo. Then she told me something I hadn't known. In early 1992, Cerullo had called her from New York asking for details about our friendship.

"He seemed very alarmed and disturbed. I didn't know what to make of it," Jean said. Cerullo told Jean, she said, that he'd received reports that we'd left a bar together. Later, Jean said, she was told Cerullo called others in the London office to ask about my interaction with women there.

On the plane back to New York, I could think of nothing else. Anger and frustration filled me. Now I knew Cerullo's prying into my personal life dated to my very first days at Kidder. It had nothing to do with trying to warn me about what later happened to Mustafa Chike-Obi. And it wasn't restricted to his hauling me onto the carpet in the privacy of his office. He'd been calling all over the world, confronting my friends, undermining me with people who worked for me, spreading doubt and suspicion among my colleagues. It was degrading. And because I hadn't known about it, I'd never defended myself to anyone other than Cerullo. How many of my traders and salespeople believed I'd been accused and reprimanded for actual crimes?

Clearly, Cerullo was collecting information about me. Why? To control me? That made sense in the beginning—when he called London, he was probably looking for leverage against me in his fight with O'Donnell. He'd only hired me to prevent O'Donnell from having an envoy in the Fixed Income area. He wanted to get rid of me as soon as possible, and trumped up charges of sex harassment probably looked like a tidy way to do that. But things were different now. I'd made money, had turned the Government Bond desk around, had proved my worth. The only remaining power struggle was between me and J. J. McKoan, over the sales force and the assignment of accounts, and Cerullo had taken my side on that one. Was he just stockpiling charges against me in case the tables turned again?

As the plane crossed the Atlantic, I spun through every encounter, every lecture, every summons I'd ever received to his office. I recalled all the women's names, the specific accusations, the dates and order in which they happened. I reconstructed each event, struggling to remember if anyone else had been around, who had been nearby or passed within a distance, who had been in the same conferences or meetings. My encounters with women had little common thread, except that each one, no matter how brief or innocuous, was reported to Cerullo. Many of them revolved around saleswomen: Jean, Linda, Anita, and J.J.'s assistant. Saleswomen who worked for McKoan, or assistants and former assistants of his—the "exotics." I sat up in my first-class seat as I said the word to myself. Cerullo's lectures about black male sexuality, about behaving myself, about "warning you people" had come in spurts. Weeks or months of quiet would pass, and then there would suddenly be a cluster of commands to report to his office, one every two or three days for a week or more. What had prompted these spurts? I wondered. My mind raced back over the dates. The lectures cropped up in almost direct correlation to flareups in my fight with McKoan over the sales force. J.J. had won every round until recently, and lulls followed each victory. Whenever there was a lull in my battle with McKoan, there was a lull in the black male sexuality lectures.

Abruptly, a conversation with McKoan flashed through my mind. It had been on the golf course, the same day the other golfers had ridiculed McKoan for struggling to please his wife as her former black lover had. McKoan and I had golfed on alone, and he'd asked me if I'd consider hiring one of his personal assistants.

"I need someone with experience. Give me some of your heavy hitters," I'd said. "I don't need to hire one of your exotics."

I'd been straining to remember when I might have mentioned that nickname aloud. Now I knew. It had been on the golf course. McKoan must have repeated it to Cerullo. Then Cerullo demanded to know if I had my eye on one of the saleswomen—"Didn't you say you'd like to have an exotic like her, did you say that to her?" That confrontation had come between the challenges about Bernice and Linda, and just as I had won a round with McKoan.

It was J.J. who watched me, reported my movements, and exploited Cerullo's paranoia about black men. I knew that as surely and as suddenly as I knew my own name. I'd never suspected him because of his affinity for ethnic women, including his wife and daughter. Because he was the butt of racist jokes himself. Because a man of his sensitivity and intelligence wouldn't dehumanize blacks with absurd and primitive notions about black male sexuality.

It was J.J.

MAN OF THE YEAR

BEFORE I COULD decide what to do with this revelation, my hand was forced. After a recruiting trip to Harvard with Cerullo the next week, I settled into my plane seat to describe to him the London trip. My meetings had been very successful, I was about to hire new traders and I'd talked to banking and treasury officials in Great Britain, Italy, France and Germany about using the Strips market to increase liquidity of their nations' debts. We might be able to get those countries to begin issuing Strips, I told Cerullo, who rode next to me on the flight home. I had a meeting scheduled later that week with the Polish ambassador to the U.S. to discuss using U.S. bonds to relieve the Polish debt.

Cerullo didn't want to talk about any of that.

"You understand that we are going through the entire year-end reviews and promotions. Some of these are very controversial." I decided to joke with him.

"My promotion is controversial?"

"I'm not allowed to talk about whether you're up for promotion or not. I'm not allowed to discuss that directly with you. But I do want to ask you about certain of your nominations. First, Elizabeth. There's some feeling that Elizabeth just started this summer and maybe it's premature to have her up for promotion. How are you two getting along?"

"Brilliantly." My voice was flat.

"What is your relationship with her?"

Any intention I might have had to try to be diplomatic about McKoan evaporated.

"Oh. It's Elizabeth now. Ed, I have to tell you. Every time I come to your office with a request for salespeople or a change in the sales force, J.J., and I know it's J.J., brings up this idea of women I am supposed to be having a relationship with. I want it to end."

Cerullo's voice rose. "Listen, you have to understand that you're probably the second or third most powerful person at the firm, and we just want to make certain that you're not using your position to satisfy your sexual aggression."

Passengers around us stared. I didn't look away from Cerullo.

"This isn't about power. Hell. Everyone on the damn trading floor is using their power to have sex. What about Mel Mullin?" Cerullo knew as well as I did that Mullin was only one of many who had married someone in the office. He waved this argument away.

"I've told you that Kidder is not your typical Wall Street firm. There is a culture here. It may be Wall Street culture that people on trading floors meet, they mix, they marry, but it is Kidder's culture that has concern about the sexually aggressive nature that seems dominant in your race."

Anyone listening might have wondered why I didn't punch him then. I'd long grown used to his words and their impact had dulled. I looked at him. His short, sandy hair was dry for once, but as usual he wouldn't meet my gaze.

"Ed, I don't even think this is about, as you put it, black male sexuality. This issue comes up when I try to get an account changed, when I try to get a salesman hired, when I try to get something done that helps my desk. This is about power."

He dismissed my words. Our plane was making its descent, and I sensed he wanted to end this conversation. "There's competition everywhere. But in my asking you today, this is about a promotional decision that we have to reach in a short period of time." In the airport, Cerullo went straight to a phone and made a restaurant reservation; he wanted to continue discussing job reviews over dinner. In the taxi into Manhattan, we were silent. I was determined not to let the black male sexuality issue be subsumed by a conversation about promotions and performance evaluations. That would validate Cerullo's complaints—and McKoan's. I wasn't going to let him dress up his racist fears in a camouflage of concern about promotions for women on my staff.

As soon as we sat down in the restaurant, I began the conversation where we'd left it when the pilot announced we were ready to land.

"Ed, just think back. I come into your office to complain about an account not being switched. You say you'll talk to J.J. Half an hour later you're calling me in to ask about my relationship with Linda Mead. A week before, I asked about why another account hasn't been moved. You say you'll talk to Rico. Twenty minutes later you call me in and you're asking me about Farita. This happens over and over and over." Farita was one of McKoan's assistants.

McKoan had committed to hiring twenty salespeople by the end of the year, I reminded him. It was already December, and only six had been hired.

"If he can't do his job, then it should fall to me. And those salesmen should report to me."

"I think both you and J.J. are trying to do what is best for the company. J.J. has legitimate concerns about the abuse of power. All I'm asking you to do is be aware. This firm has a culture. It was here long before you and will be here long after you are gone. The culture of the firm will endure."

I wanted to force what I saw as the real issue. I had McKoan up against a wall now. It was time to push my advantage.

"I'm asking you to turn the Government sales force over to me. I tried working with J.J. I'm sick of this bullshit. All we are trying to do is hire the people with the experience to get the job done. That should be all we're doing."

But manipulating Cerullo was never easy.

"I'm sure you and J.J. can work together. I think you both want the same thing, you have the same goals in mind, and all I'm asking you to do is open up the lines of communication. Talk directly to J.J. See if you can reach some accommodation."

EVERY MONDAY MORNING in the Fixed Income area, Cerullo led a managing directors' meeting to review the market. Though not a managing director, I attended as head of the Government Bond desk.

Another of Kidder's arcane traditions dictated that a trader who was leaving the firm didn't take off his suit coat. He'd sit at his desk with it on. I'd seen it happen just before the long-bond and options traders had quit. So the next Monday morning after my dinner with Cerullo, I sat at my desk right before the managing directors' meeting without taking my coat off. Joe Ossman looked me over. I appeared odd, but not just because I had my suit coat on. I hadn't slept all weekend. I'd stayed up through the nights, pacing in my cavernous loft and thinking about what to say to the other managing directors. I sat perfectly still at my desk, staring at Joey-o, waiting for the meeting to begin. I felt nearly feverish.

"War has begun, Joey-o, and I'm going to this meeting and might not be back."

That day's meeting looked to be brief. Cerullo chatted with several people about the markets, and then began to draw the meeting to a close. Did anyone else have anything to say?

"Yes, I do."

Everyone's gaze turned to me. In that second, my tension evaporated and a quiet calm descended. "I'd like the Government sales specialists to report directly to me, and furthermore . . ."

McKoan erupted from his chair, sputtering.

". . . I'd like complete hiring and firing authority for the Government sales staff."

"That's it! I've had it! I'm sick of this guy, I've had it with this guy! He keeps pushing and pushing! First he wants some salesmen, now he wants a sales staff! Why don't you just take away my whole damn sales staff! Get rid of him! Why don't you get rid of him right now!"

Mullin glanced around in shock. I shouted back at McKoan.

"You're sick of it! I'm sick of it! I'm sick of the fact that every time I try to get something done, you bring up the fact of whether I've slept with some goddamned white woman! I just want you to do your job and stop asking about my fucking sex life!"

Everyone looked as if a bomb had just exploded on the table. Cerullo bolted upright. "Okay, hold on! Hold on! Everybody out!" The trading managers scrambled through the door, leaving me, Cerullo, McKoan and Ricciardi in the room. McKoan raged at all of us.

"I can't work with Jett! He's unpleasant, he pushes me around, no one wants to work with him. I want him fired! I want him fired!" he screamed. His large round face was red with fury. "He's totally disrupted life at Kidder. I want him fired!"

I leaned forward, stabbing the air, ignoring Cerullo's pleas for calm.

"Every time I ask for change, someone drags me in and accuses me of fucking some damn white woman. I can't be responsible for your sexual inadequacies and I'm tired of having them thrown in my face."

Cerullo leaped in. "Let's focus on the issue, which is the sales staff." I didn't take my eyes off McKoan.

"Fine. J.J. committed last May to hire twenty people. I recruited and brought them here, only to discover that J.J. doesn't have time to see them."

Cerullo looked at McKoan. "J.J., why not?"

"It's difficult, the people have to be just right. A lot of people have recently left. He's rude, unapproachable, unpleasant. People say hi and he responds with these weird phrases, 'Discipline must be maintained.' What the hell is that? This isn't the army, and it shouldn't be that way. People are afraid of him."

Now Cerullo looked at me. "Yes, people are afraid of you. Do something about it."

The conversation was losing focus, moving away from the real problem—the black sex bullshit. I looked around at all of them.

"You've created the situation where if I talk to anyone, I'm called in for a lecture about my sexuality and charged with sexual harassment."

"Let's not discuss that. Let's focus on the issue, which is the sales staff."

Quickly, Cerullo ordered McKoan, Ricciardi and me to form a task force to hire more salespeople who would report to me. McKoan, he said, would remain in charge of deciding their performance bonus. He directed the two of us to work together to reassign key accounts immediately.

"What about this black male sexuality bullshit?" I repeated. For once, Cerullo looked at me.

"Let's not discuss that. That's not the issue."

ALL THROUGH THAT fall I traveled to Europe and Japan every month. I'd hired three traders in England, and the manager there had begun complaining to Cerullo that I was trying to take over his franchise. Tension seeped into nearly every relationship at work. Tension between me and the London manager, tension between me and McKoan, tension between me and Finkelstein. I wanted complete control—over hiring, over positions in England, over Finkelstein's Financing area, over the Japanese government bond market. I crisscrossed the globe, sometimes twice a month. No longer was I after Finkelstein or any of the other managers. I was after their jobs, yes. But only to consolidate my power base. My real strategy remained to oust Cerullo.

Cerullo was the kingpin, the man sitting on top of the pyramid. However, if you cut off his head, it wouldn't change how things operated. I spent a great deal of time in his office because he wanted to know everything—what trades I was doing, what workout regimen I was following, what women I was pursuing. But he didn't originate trading ideas or strategies. His whole *raison d'être* was supposed to be to lure capital to our desks, but even there he'd proved ineffective. He'd gone eyeball-to-eyeball with Jack Welch, and blinked. When I came along, he'd ruled an empire built completely on the strength of one trading area, the Mortgage desk. The rest of Fixed Income was nonperforming. He wasn't exploiting his resources. Everything outside Mortgage was nonworking, and Cerullo had no idea how to fix it. Fixed Income meant the Mortgage area, which earned a 40 percent return. Everything else was earning 10 percent. Then I'd come along. I'd seen an opportunity when he asked me to abandon O'Donnell. Now I saw another one. J. J. McKoan was in charge of international sales, and I decided we needed someone in charge of international trading. If I could build a broader base of support—one that was global—I'd have an advantage over Cerullo. Cerullo hated travel. He'd been to Japan only once in two years. I'd been four times between May and October. He'd been to London twice in two years; I'd been there five times. Cerullo was intent on his Mortgage desk in New York. While I had a reputation of being tough on my sales force, it was energetic salespeople who'd propelled my appointment to desk head, and now energetic salespeople in London and Tokyo who were clamoring for my leadership.

*   *   *

IN SPITE OF the acrimony and arguments with McKoan and Cerullo, there was no disputing the increasing profits from my desk. Even though Cerullo had been ready to kill me for jeopardizing his scheme to show GE a reduced balance sheet, it was clear to everyone that my numbers in the fall gave Fixed Income its profits for 1993. In November my reward was twofold: Cerullo promoted me to managing director, and nominated me for Kidder's "Man of the Year" award. His recommendation and praise went to Kidder's CEO, Michael Carpenter, who ultimately chose the annual winner. As for my promotion, it didn't change my job responsibilities, but it did mean that I attended more meetings with Cerullo, and it also qualified me for an invitation to the legendary managers' retreat at his place in Vail, Colorado.

I SPENT THE month of December 1993, flying back and forth to Aspen on weekends to brush up on my skiing. As soon as Cerullo invited me to what he affectionately called "Boy's Week" in Vail, I knew I faced a week of grueling skiing. From his relentless conversations about sports, Cerullo knew that I had once studied kung fu, that I lifted weights, played golf and skied. He'd tried to persuade me to join him in his endless preparations for triathlons, but I begged off because I can't swim. In truth, it had been years since I'd skied, though I was once pretty good. When I accepted the invitation to Vail, I knew what I was getting into. Cerullo would turn the weekend into one long competition on the slopes. It wouldn't be fun to strap on skis again. I'd have to arrive in Vail ready to race. Cerullo would run me off the mountain if he could. I couldn't prepare for this in Upstate New York because the snow there is mostly ice. Vail had powder, and I knew enough about skiing to know going from ice to powder meant learning how to ski all over again.

I also felt like I'd devoted enough time doing nothing but work. I spent so much time on planes between New York and London that Cerullo's secretary balked at handling my scheduling as well as his. Finally, I hired my own secretary. At first, she used my Lotus Agenda organizer to schedule my appointments and travel. But I'd gotten into the habit of recording impressions of my meetings and struggles with Fiumefreddo, Bernstein and Cerullo in the agenda, and some of the language was pretty strong. A lot of it was intimate personal opinion, and I'd logged reactions to some of the more sensitive conversations I'd had with Cerullo about "black male sexuality." The new secretary asked me about these entries—it was clear that I'd found the meetings offensive. I didn't want her to see that information, and I didn't want to censor my personal observations. Instead, I told her to stop using my laptop to organize my schedule. I installed a copy of Lotus

Agenda on the computer at her desk, and told her to keep my business schedule on that separate program.

In the aftermath of the managing directors' meeting, the subject of "black male sexuality" seemed to evaporate. For several days, I waited tentatively for the fallout from my screaming match with McKoan. When nothing happened, I began to feel that with my confrontation, I'd quashed the whole racist subject. In fact, I remembered, Cerullo had even refused to admit he'd been concerned about the subject. I began to believe I'd completely destroyed McKoan's leverage against me by exposing him in front of everyone. I expected never to hear about it again.

I was earning great money. I'd accomplished most of what I set out to do. Things were coming together on my desk; the only slight remaining concern was the presence of a few traders and salespeople who had to go. Now it was time to live a little. I decided to start dating seriously, and to devote time to my old hobbies and interests.

Every Thursday night I flew from New York to Aspen. One weekend in early December, I allotted bonuses to my staff. Taking a page from Mel Mullin's book, I hoped that small bonuses would send a message to the people I intended to let go. One of those was a trader who responded to the meager bonus—and the implication of imminent firing—by entering a risky trade into the computer and leaving for home. The risk manager caught it, and chased the trader into the lobby. He refused to return to the office to clear the trade.

"I got fucked out of a bonus and the only way I can make more money is to take on risk. You have any problem with that, go see Jett. He's the one who fucked me."

The risk manager took his problem to Cerullo, who ordered the trader fired. The trader called me in Aspen, panicked and frantic, blaming the risk manager for the problems. He decided to take the two weeks' vacation owed him. Since Cerullo had already fired him, there was little I could do by phone from Aspen. At the end of the month, the trader returned to work. It was Christmas Eve. Cavanaugh pulled me aside.

"Come on, Joseph, don't fire him on Christmas Eve."

"I can't help it. He was fired three weeks ago. Now it's just a matter of him turning up to be told."

ON A FRIDAY in the middle of December, the office buzzed with preparations for a Christmas party. Eager to leave early, the women who worked as data input operators in our back office lobbied for permission to put off the stacks of trading tickets until Monday. They would input all the Strip-recon trades first thing the next week, they promised. Since I was taking so much time off that month—I was in the office only two or three days a week—I could hardly be tough on them. I knew that if we didn't enter the trades into the computer until the next working day, the phantom might leave a bigger trace. If it takes all day to toss the bowling ball away, some of the recording functions at Kidder would actually see it and make note of it. I decided to take a chance, and sent the input operators home early.

On Monday, Bernstein railed at me, livid over a $10 billion spike in my trading position that showed up on the firm's balance sheet. Hours later Cerullo called me into his office and let me have it with both barrels. My excuse—that I had allowed the clerks to leave early to attend the Christmas party—was met with derision.

"You're becoming soft!" Cerullo spat.

Late in the afternoon on December 28 I received a phone call from Bernstein. His voice was a mix of anger and worry.

"Hey there!" I exclaimed. I knew our conversation was being recorded, as all such calls were.

"Hey, tell me something, do you recall the conversation we had where I said, 'The last day, on December twenty-seventh, please don't do trades where you buy next day and sell forward' "?

"No. You said to have nothing settle on December twenty-seventh."

"Well, see, the thing was that, for future quarter ends the thing that you need to be careful of is that one of the quirks of the system is that something that is for regular-day settlement can influence what gets on our balance sheet. So while the rule of thumb generally is, you know, settle long, settle short is the rule to go by. If we have a big position, if, if, if we have regular-way settled things, they often get sort of swept into this convoluted accounting that we use and get counted as part of our balance-sheet obligations. So when we have regular-way buying offset by forward sales that are recorded on the last day of the year, you know, the forward buys get added on the balance sheet, as a regular-way sell—the regular-way buys get added on the balance sheet, the forward sales don't get subtracted from it. So even though your trade date is flat, it can still add a couple of billion to the balance sheet. So we ended up a couple of billion higher in our Strips inventory than I thought we were going to be. So, anyway, I mean, there's not much we can do about it at this point, and, hopefully, we kind of can . . ."

"Well, where did we end up?" I asked.

"What basically happened was that we ended up adding about two billion and change, onto the long position because we have those, you know— several big treasury positions were bought for next-day settlement and sold forward."

I was confused. "Okay, actually, I, I try to . . . I don't see how I could have . . . I, I try to wipe out all trades settling on the twenty-seventh. I do remember you saying try not to . . . I, I thought that just by pairing off everything that was due to, the twenty-seventh that it would wipe away that problem. You are saying that that actually . . ."

"It might have been we have that problem anyway. What you are saying is that the stuff that you were buying . . . You were putting trades on the twenty-seventh . . ."

I interjected, "To pair off stuff that had been put there on the twenty-seventh and before, that is, you know, the future selling, I had future selling dated on the twenty-seventh, so I was trying to, I try to . . . neutralize it. Exactly, neutralize everything on the twenty-seventh. I thought officially nothing would happen. That didn't work, eh?"

"I think I understand where we're at," Bernstein said. "I understand what you're trying to do, but no, you can't do that. Pretty much, the stuff that was going to settle on the twenty-seventh. If you were to put in the forward trade, let's say you had a forward buy that was going to settle on the twenty-seventh . . . If you put in a forward sell, that was going to settle on the twenty-seventh, on December tenth or something, you can pair it off that way, but once you get to the twenty-seventh, you are pretty much screwed."

Baffled, I responded: "I had stuff that was due to settle on the twenty-seventh, sold like a week ago. I put in trades on December twenty-first to sell what I'd bought on December twenty-seventh so that nothing would ever happen."

"Those trades work," Bernstein said.

"Those trades worked?" I was now thoroughly confused.

"I'm talking about . . . I have several billion dollars of trade date December twenty-seventh stuff where you were buying for December twenty-eighth and selling for January. Those are the ones that screwed us."

"Okay, I see. All right, I didn't know that that is the way it worked. Okay. It was my misunderstanding. I try to . . ."

"I don't think that there are going to be any awful repercussions, but you know . . ." Bernstein warned.

"But even with that problem, aren't we way under . . ."

"Look, I'll tell you what the problem is," Beinstein said. "You still made the $14 billion number. You would have been at $11 billion or $12 billion or something. The problem is that when I went home last night, you know, we were like window dressing the Repo books up to the last minute. So I said, 'Well jeez, Joe's not going to be at $14 billion, he's only going to be at $11 or $12 billion.' "

"Oh, no!"

"So, I had Brian Finkelstein's limit higher for the report. I'll tell you frankly just in case there are repercussions, and I don't think it's going to be a big deal, right now the firm is at about $82 billion or so, but from what I get from O'Donnell, I don't think that is a problem. I mean, I think that unlike the third quarter where we really were under the gun to prove that we're not going to use $80 billion, I think that we have, sort of acknowledgment up there that the balance sheet is going to grow. That they are almost comfortable, to show we just have trouble containing ourselves because we are such a high-growth business and all that stuff."

"Yeah!" I responded.

"So, basically I think we may be okay. I think that other thing is that, just between us, you know, it's always the case of the year-end close that there are, you know, five different ledgers going this way or the other which run together."

"Yeah."

"We do our best not to call attention to, you know, the stuff in the Strips book, but just for my own security going forward, let's get these trades done," Bernstein admonished.

"Okay. I got you. While I didn't know, I didn't realize that's what I did. Okay, but I got it. I got you."

We now lived with an almost intolerable degree of tension and paranoia; big brother was watching and might catch us at any moment. Everything we did had to be carefully considered.

IN EARLY JANUARY 1994, my desk threw an end-of-year party. The Government Bond desk finally had a personality. It wasn't just that I paid my traders fairly. In fact, they earned bigger commissions than Cerullo paid me. The Street average was 10 to 12 percent commission; I paid my people that, but earned just 5 percent myself. I suspected that this discrepancy was due to discrimination, but I could never prove it. My traders were happier with me than with Mullin for other reasons, however. Mullin had been a pushover for the sales staff, always willing to execute unprofitable trades if the salespeople insisted. The sales staff didn't care that the traders lost money on a transaction because they earned their commissions anyway. Mullin's traders were used to him waffling under pressure from the sales staff and ordering them to carry out trades that did them no good. I put an end to that, beginning when I worked for Mullin myself. I repeatedly refused to do trades that made no financial sense just to keep the sales staff happy. Later, when I finally took Mullin's job, I stood up to the sales force in a way he never had. My traders saw that I was willing to defend their interests. I insisted that we be given our own specialist sales force, and that those salespeople worked hand in hand to back up my traders. Suddenly the people who worked on the Government desk had a common goal, and they were motivated to make money because they knew I'd keep my word. And I rewarded anyone who showed initiative; I got rid of a lot of deadwood and promoted people who demonstrated a willingness to work. Soon my traders realized that the Government desk was a meritocracy—their jobs depended on their performance, not on how long they'd worked with Mel Mullin.

The culture of the Government desk changed dramatically. No longer a dead end, it became known for offering opportunity. People finally knew it existed. That could not have been said during my first months at Kidder, when I was mistaken for a mailboy one day when I wore a golf shirt to the office.

At the Christmas party, Bernice Rothstein drank far too much. After my toast—"We will destroy our enemies!"—she staggered toward me and Joe Ossman. Joey-o turned to flee, but I grabbed his arm, not willing to be left alone with Rothstein. He reached out and pulled Elizabeth Cavanaugh into the huddle. By the time Rothstein, a little wobbly, spoke to me, the three of us were watching her with wary eyes.

"I just want to thank you for all you've done for me. Especially lecturing everyone to take care of themselves. I've been taking care of myself. I've lost a lot of weight, have you noticed?" She opened the vest of her outfit. She was wearing a blouse underneath. Then she pirouetted and staggered slightly. "And I've really got my legs in shape. I just want to thank you and I've told my father all about you and he's so happy that I'm working for someone who looks out for me and takes care of me and my daddy just wants you to know that he appreciates you looking out for me."

Cavanaugh stepped forward and turned to a salesman, asking him to escort Rothstein home.

AT THE END of 1993, Michael Carpenter announced he'd chosen me as one of four top producers to speak at Kidder's worldwide annual conference. In 1994, the meeting was held at Disney World in Florida.

It'd be my chance to grab some public credit for Fixed Income's success. Cerullo had quashed any efforts I'd made all year to make it known on the Street that ours was a powerhouse desk. He'd carefully controlled all the press coverage of Fixed Income's trading strategies so that neither I nor any of my traders received individual credit for our work. He carefully controlled how much detail of our trading strategy was known beyond our desk. I didn't like any of that. My trades were innovative, brash, daring and very profitable. My team made money in an arena not generally considered to be lucrative. I wanted my professional peers to understand how we did it. I wanted to brag.

I drafted a speech that summed up a three-pronged approach to trading. First, to hire dynamic, determined traders. Second, to shape those traders into a cohesive team—and eliminate differences stemming from racism of sexism along the way. Third, to use that team to make the Government desk more profitable than the Mortgage operation. I intended to explain to the conference that we could reach those profits with Strip and recon forward trades that acted just like municipal defeasance trades.

Cerullo hated my speech. On January 5, I wrote in my electronic diary: "Reviewed speech for Florida with Ed this morning. I did not do a very fluid job on the walkthrough. He wants to throw out the entire talk because we reveal the muni defeasance behavior of the Strip-recon arbitrage and discuss too many specific trading strategies involving the behavior of Strips and the yield curve."

Cerullo refused to let me talk in any detail about the forward recons or the muni defeasance. He didn't think the audience wanted to hear that level of detail, but more important, he forbade me to talk about anything that would give away trading strategies. He didn't want the world to know we made money from forward recons; pretty soon, everyone would be doing it, he said.

As usual, Bernstein delivered Cerullo's decision, calling me at the end of December to tell me that "we'll be making some minor changes to the script."

I had no intention of listening to Bernstein or Cerullo. I chose my own words. I wanted credit for my trades, and the time had come, I decided, to publicly distance myself from Cerullo. I would declare my independence with a message that would sound innocuous to the people at the conference, but would have a very specific meaning to Cerullo, Bernstein, Mullin McKoan and Finkelstein.

On the night of the banquet, as I walked to the podium, I spotted Cerullo and McKoan in the dark auditorium. I wondered where Carpenter sat, and who else might be listening to my speech. I kept my eye on Cerullo as I started talking.

"The U.S. government bond market is the largest securities market in the world," I began. "It is rumored to be the most liquid securities market in the world. However, after Bill Clinton has had his way with it, the liquidity is definitely not what it once was. The government bond market is not one where high profits are never made. It is an ever-changing market. One can never become wed to one's ideas. One must always remain supremely objective, because the government bond market, itself, is supremely objective. It is a market that begs no quarter and gives none. It does not care about anyone's political philosophy, race, color or creed. It is just you, your phone, your abilities against the world. It is the perfect market, in fact."

I looked up and saw Cerullo gesturing at me. I went back to my speech.

"My father often would say to me, relate his own coming-of-age story during the Korean War. Back in 1951, a call went out to integrate the armed services. And my father, at the time, was working as a cook in the army and entertaining the troops by engaging in fisticuffs against all comers each night and making a little money on the side in that fashion.

"Well, when they decided to integrate the troops, they gave him a parachute, told him to pull this cord, threw a rifle in his arm, gave him five good old boys from Georgia and about four other Hispanics who spoke very little English, and parachuted them out on the front line and said, 'Go and destroy your enemy,' and that was pretty much it.

"In that time, he said that he learned one thing above all else, that when you truly begin to live is when your wants and your desires become subservient to what is necessary, when what needs to be done and what I must do, takes precedence over what I want and what I desire."

My voice echoed through the auditorium, and the crowd broke into applause. I looked up again, in time to see Cerullo rise from his seat. McKoan moved with him. Together, they walked out of the auditorium.

I went back to my notes.

"Here, at Kidder, we were in a situation where what we wanted was fine but what needed to be done required some strength and management, real leadership. Kidder had a structural problem for us on the Government area. Kidder, in the Fixed Income side, had long been dominant in the Mortgage area. The Mortgage product leads. It leads the Street. It was necessary for us to develop a government specialist team, to have a group of salesmen who are dedicated to moving the Government product.

"But, as I said to them when we—when we started on that effort, 'It is only in the heat of the crucible that steel is made. It is only when you meet yourself on a dark alley and question your own resolve, question your own ability to take what is weak in you and have it annealed out, no matter how painful that may be, that you are able to become successful.'

"Today, Kidder has become the leading player in stripping and reconstitution of bonds. We have approximately forty percent of the market share of all U.S. government stripping and reconstitution activity, on a month-in, month-out basis. Often, numbers are as high as seventy percent. Our market share, with customer transactions and long maturities has doubled since 1990 to ten plus percent in this last quarter. The quarter before, we were at thirteen percent.

"I am three strong traders and five strong salesmen away from telling you that this year, 1994, I will produce more revenues than Mike Vranos, and I will produce more profit, before bonus and taxes, more than the CMO desk. After bonus? Well, I don't know.

"In order to take what is base and turn it into something noble, you must be willing to apply all pressure to it, to have it go through fire and go through hell and show that it is indeed something worthy of more capital, of more firm commitment, and more of the most important assets, humanity, to any department that we have here.

"Kidder does, indeed, have the resources to be a dominant player in the largest markets in the world. We have the people. We have the leadership to make it so. We have the market knowledge and the attention to detail that is required. We have the discipline. Without discipline, you can do nothing in this world, nothing."

The crowd erupted in cheers and applause that lasted several minutes. Later, Kidder CEO Michael Carpenter lauded me as "the voice of Kidder's future, our present potential." Then he named me Kidder's Man of the Year.

THE FOLLOWING MONDAY I left for London. On Tuesday Cavanaugh called from New York. She was worried, she said. For the last two days,

Bernice Rothstein had been huddled in Cerullo's office for hours at a time. When Cavanaugh tried to ask Rothstein what was going on, Bernice snapped, "I don't have to talk to you!"

I flew back to New York on Wednesday morning and went straight to the office. Cerullo was waiting for me.

"Get your coat and get out of here. Hand in your card. What's wrong with you people? I warned you about this so many times, now look what you've done to me!"

After long interrogations of Rothstein while I was in London, Cerullo had concluded that I had sexually harassed her. He refused to detail the specific charges; the most he would say was that Rothstein had complained that I'd repeatedly harassed her. He wanted me out of the office; I had time enough to hand over my key card and collect my coat. Someone else would clear out my desk.

But Human Resources intervened. Cerullo couldn't fire me without cause; Rothstein's charges had to be investigated. While the inquiry went on, I stopped coming to work early. Rothstein had suddenly developed a noticeable work ethic, and began appearing in the office before most anyone else. I demanded a virtual escort, refusing to be left alone at the desk. I bolted when I saw that she was present alone. Cavanaugh, Joey-o and I were convinced that Rothstein had complained about the Christmas party scene. After several weeks, the Human Resources office determined that they couldn't substantiate a charge of sexual harassment. There was no mention in Rothstein's report of the Christmas party. I guessed she couldn't even remember it. Rothstein's complaint, it turned out, stemmed from two separate incidents: one day when she'd come to work hung over and I'd commented that her eyes were bloodshot, and another day, when she had trouble using a touch-screen computer, I'd told her the problem wasn't the computer, it was her long, lacquered fingernails.

On January 21, the day after Human Resources cleared me of the charges, I waited for Cerullo to arrive at work. I stormed into his office and accused him of trumping up charges with which to fire me, just as he had done to Mustafa Chike-Obi.

"I'm going to stop these trades that do nothing for me but are so critical to your efforts to take this firm independent," I threatened. I didn't care if a boycott would threaten my career. I already knew I wouldn't be at Kidder by the end of the new year, no matter what happened. Why should I stay late every night to work on massively complicated trades when Cerullo had signaled his intention to fire me?

Cerullo shifted gears.

"You're unaware of the sacrifice other people are making for the good of this firm. What we are asking you to do is small. Other people are making significant sacrifices. We are so close now. We're on the verge of independence from GE. This will be a far larger firm with room for everyone. The forward Strips and recons will only go on for two more months.

"Anyway, I invited you to Colorado for Boy's Week. I hope you'll still come."

I GREW MORE suspicious. Sometimes I wondered if I wasn't crazy. In late January, a particularly meek and unproductive saleswoman asked for a private meeting. We met at a restaurant frequented by people from all over Wall Street; I felt safe in the noisy crowd.

"I've been working very hard and I want to keep my job," the saleswoman said. She looked at me intently. Her words sounded too deliberate. "I'll do anything you want, anything at all, to keep my job."

I felt something brush my foot. Was she playing footsie with me, or was I imagining things? Alarm bells went off. It had to be a setup. I almost turned my head to look for McKoan or Cerullo. I cut the rest of dinner short.

Later the same month, another lower-ranked saleswoman applied to me for a job as a government specialist. She was straightforward about her qualifications. "I think I have what it takes, I'm very forceful, and I'd really like to work with you. But I'm not going to sleep with you."

It seemed that everyone presumed I had my way with anyone who worked with me.

AT A BLACK-TIE dinner at the Rainbow Room for new managing directors, Carpenter again praised my speech and asked others to follow my example. The aimless cocktail chatter was punctuated by a warning. A fellow new initiate stepped up to me. "Listen, I just want you to know that a lot of people are still talking about your speech. You've heard Carpenter say that most people loved it. But there are some people, and I mean people really close to you, who apparently are very upset about that speech. I just thought you should know."

"People here?" Cerullo, Ricciardi and McKoan were at the banquet.

"People very close to you."

Later, as we sat at dinner, Cerullo walked up to my table. Eyeing my date, he began asking her pointed questions about how long we'd been in a relationship. I ignored him. Then Michael Carpenter joined our group. He had no interest in Cerullo; they barely acknowledged each other. Carpenter butted into Cerullo's conversation with my date and told her that I was a real up-and-comer, and that he wouldn't be surprised if I were running Kidder someday. Then he turned to me and said he'd heard I played golf. I should give him a call, he said, and we'd play a round.

I'm sure I read no more into his seemingly innocent invitation than anyone else sitting around with their drinks. That was probably a lot. Carpenter had made it known he was one of those who had liked my speech at the worldwide conference. And certainly everyone knew he despised Cerullo. If he was showing deliberate interest in me, it might not be far-fetched to believe he would consider me to replace Cerullo.

GE HAD SWEETENED its relationship with Kidder a little bit more. Welch told Kidder that GE wasn't going to invest more money in Kidder, but it wasn't going to sell Kidder, either. Instead, the chairman was willing to allow Kidder to pursue outside financing. Kidder could use GE's name and credit rating to secure loans from foreign banks. This was manna from heaven to Cerullo; he was being given permission to contact the foreign banks he had long been interested in, to form relationships with them and, he hoped, from there persuade one to buy the Fixed Income department from GE.

The effort to secure a foreign bank loan meant a continuation of the off-balance-sheet financing. We had to convince the foreign banks that we generated profit on only $800 million in equity capital. They wanted proof that we could control the size of our balance sheet. Thus, the so-called phantom trades became all the more important. Since we were wholly owned by GE, we were excluded from the equity markets. Once GE gave us permission to seek outside financing, we had no trouble raising money. Investors were eager to participate in a firm that was earning 30 percent returns. Welch should have seen that, but we were owned by a man who did not understand our industry. Part of the problem was Welch's relationship with Michael Carpenter. They were friends, and Carpenter reported only to Welch. As a result, hard-hitting questions were rarely asked. Carpenter was not an effective leader. He was unable to present Kidder Peabody to Welch as a company with growth potential or as a long-term part of the GE family. He didn't know enough about investment banking to deliver competent information to GE, and the man who did, Cerullo, was his sworn enemy. Cerullo's only victories came when he got through to Welch himself—first when he won an equity increase to $800 million, and then when Welch gave him permission to look for foreign investors. In fact, Carpenter wasn't able to present Kidder to GE at all. Most of what GE executives learned about Kidder they read in *Barron's* and *The Wall Street Journal*.

The off-balance-sheet financing had become a small industry. Hiding the $25 billion from GE generated so many trade tickets that we had to hire four additional data input clerks.

We worked late at night, staying in the office long after dark and long after the Wall Street neighborhood was deserted. It took hours to reconcile all the positions created. I complained bitterly to Cerullo and Bernstein about the bookkeeping nightmare the accounting strategy had caused. Every trade that was due to settle now required three tickets. I could pick up any one and it was representative of all the others—a ticket to roll forward a $5 billion transaction I had initiated weeks before. The first ticket is just to pair off the trade—to catch it and toss it back in the air. When it settles, another ticket is required to strip the bond into its component parts. That, in turn, generates a loss, so a small reconstitution is necessary to offset the loss. A ticket must be filled out for that small recon, too.

All this effort to keep my securities off the books was designed to allow the Mortgage desk to use the funds freed up by hiding assets from GE. This wiggle room existed only because my assets were off the books, and the Mortgage desk happily exploited it. Using $30 billion that I kept off the books, they'd increased Kidder's total position to $110 billion. Restless, my hands tied, I watched as the Mortgage desk made more money, caught up and overtook my desk. We were in competition, and they won. Since their product had a higher profit margin, it made sound business sense for things to work this way, but I hated being in second place. Long workdays, late nights, reams of paperwork—none of it irritated me as much as being in second place.

Mortgage began doing so well that Mondays became their unofficial holiday. At the managing directors' meetings, the Mortgage head gloated over his profits. After the meeting, his traders and salesmen danced around their desks, high-fiving each other and chanting: "The Mortgage Gods are back!!" Peeved, I always reminded them: "The only reason you're making a dime is because of what we're doing over at the Government desk." High, they made a game of it. The Mortgage traders grabbed the PA and announced: "Joe Jett, you're HUGE! You're HUGE!"

It was some consolation—in a way. I was as interested in the money as in the power. If I showed a willingness to sacrifice my personal gain for the good of the company, hopefully my star would be all the more gilded. I thought: I'll just hang on until the books are adjusted. Then I'll bounce back. But that wasn't going to be anytime soon. When Kidder entered negotiations with the foreign banks, Cerullo had to show them what we'd shown GE: that we were in control of our balance sheet. Bernstein broke the news to me.

"I know we told you this would just be until the end of the year, but now we need to keep going, maybe just till the end of February."

"Wait a minute, you told me there wouldn't be any quarter-end requirements for February, that it was just for January, and now you're changing your tune."

"No, no, I know that we committed not to ask you to do anything strange or unusual in February, but Ed is asking if you can reduce a little here or a little there, that you try to do that."

I didn't want to do any trades that would send my sheet up or down; I just wanted to maintain the status quo. But Bernstein insisted that I continue to reduce my position.

We hadn't got the off-balance-sheet strategy down to a science. I relied on my traders to carry out the transactions, and they were not always as meticulous as necessary. In fairness, we were juggling transactions and balance sheets with so many complex and overlapping elements that it was impossible to execute them flawlessly. Time and again our balance sheet spiked. Whenever I was out of the office on recruiting trips, or in Europe, mistakes were made. A balance-sheet spike in January inspired Richard O'Donnell to write a letter to a consortium of European banks, promising that no further spikes would occur, and if they did, he personally would notify Jack Welch. My ass was on the line to Welch.

Throughout January and February, Cerullo negotiated with the European consortium. Most of the winter he spent in Vail, dealing with the foreign bankers by phone, flying back to New York only when meetings were necessary. Bernstein became the de facto head of Fixed Income. If I wandered toward Cerullo's office in search of him, the only person I'd find was Bernstein. Any need had to go through Bernstein.

IN THE FIRST week of February, the office went to Cerullo. His Vail home looked to me like a ski lodge. The enormous house was built of massive honey-colored logs. The living room fireplace was big enough for tall men to walk into. Staghorn furniture with antler armrests and legs, covered with antelope skins, filled the room. The guest bedrooms slept sixteen. The place smelled of money and opulence.

The first morning, Cerullo announced: "Come on, we're going to Dead Man's Run," one of the most difficult ski runs rated "double black diamond." Shaking my head, I donned my ski gear. I knew this was what he had planned. He led us all to the top of the steep, perilous slope and stood, leaning on his poles, looking down the jagged mountainside. "Who's going first?" There was a calculating gleam in his eye. "Go ahead, Joe!"

"It's been a while." There was no other way down from that mountain than to ski, however, so I tucked my poles under my arms in what I hoped was a show of bravado, and whipped down the slope. I went as far as I thought was decent and then looked for a place to stop without falling. I skidded to a halt and then fell. I yelled, "Come on down!" and the others took the plunge. We skied all day, barely stopping to talk. Cerullo pushed everyone relentlessly, and I wondered about the safety of these soft, pudgy Wall Street executives. I also noticed that Cerullo avoided me. We hadn't had a social conversation since we'd argued about the trumped-up sexual harassment charges involving Bernice Rothstein. In midafternoon, Cerullo took us to another double-black-diamond run, where he crashed face forward into the snow. I came up behind him and covered him in powder with a *shush*. "Are you all right?" I asked, as if I cared. Cerullo got up, unhurt.

On the second day, Cerullo chose another treacherous run, only this time he climbed into the ski lift chair with me. As we glided past snow-laden evergreens, he launched into a carefully friendly talk about what I should do to safeguard my money. Don't give any to your relatives, Cerullo warned sagely, and described how he'd once made a gift of money to his sister only to watch her blow it all. Now she was virtually on welfare, he said, but that wasn't his responsibility. He set aside only enough to take care of his father, he told me. The rest of his relatives were on their own. I should do the same.

"Stay high and dry. Keep your money at Kidder," he advised, his breath making tiny clouds in the cold air. I looked around at the stunning scenery, the magnificent snow-topped mountains rising against the blue sky. Cerullo wanted to break the ice between us, but he wasn't taking any chances that our conversation would turn to more substantial, and unpleasant, topics. I said nothing.

By the afternoon of the second day, the extreme ski runs no longer satisfied Cerullo. Now he wanted to race. We trooped back to his house, fetched his long racing skis and then followed him to a race course. Everyone raced, but since Cerullo had the only racing skis, he won virtually every heat. I got the feeling that wasn't unusual. Another feature of Boys' Week at Vail was McKoan's birthday. It fell during the week of the annual retreat, and some kind of party was always planned. The morning of his birthday, McKoan spent breakfast on the phone, calling strip joints to hire a stripper. When he was finished, the others used the phone to call their wives, who themselves were on a parallel retreat on a tropical island. I hadn't realized the depth of the traditions: J.J.'s birthday, the husbands on holiday in the mountains, the wives off together on the beach. These people didn't just work together, their personal lives were interwoven with their professional relationships. I was quite friendly with Elizabeth Cavanaugh and her husband, had spent weekends at their country house and taken dates to dinner with them. But in Vail I saw just what I was up against—or excluded from. I was astounded at how intimate Cerullo and the others were. I sat silently during dinner while they talked about their sex lives, and openly confided troubles with their families or their wives. I had never discussed such intimate details with another guy.

The afternoon of McKoan's birthday, everyone decided to lounge in the Jacuzzi. At first, Cerullo wanted to talk only about each person's musculature. He had a litany of questions for me about my workout and my physique. I'd never been in a Jacuzzi with a bunch of guys, and it wasn't exactly my idea of fun. I just didn't bond with men that way. My discomfort soared when the conversation turned to which bathing suits best revealed certain body parts. When someone started teasing McKoan about his exotic women employees, I leaped at the chance to ask about the stripper. I wanted to talk about something I was comfortable with, not men's bodies. When the Jacuzzi threatened to turn us into prunes, we got out and gathered in the living room and kitchen. I was at the refrigerator, pouring orange juice, when Cerullo walked in.

"So what type of girl did you get?"

"There wasn't much choice. I think she's a big-chested blonde," McKoan replied.

"How big?" someone wanted to know.

Cerullo glanced at McKoan. "Is it a white girl? Did you forget about Joseph?"

McKoan said, "Oh," and then nothing. Cerullo reached for a phone book, asking McKoan what strip club he'd called. I stood perfectly still, drinking my orange juice. Cerullo dialed.

"Do you have any black girls, or any choice at all? We're a mixed group. Just white? Well, we'll have to cancel that then."

I put my empty glass down. Then I walked out of the room.

In lieu of the stripper, Cerullo announced that we would set out for a moonlight cross-country ski expedition. We climbed into cars, drove to a lodge and donned cross-country skis. None of us had ever worn them before. Cerullo, of course, was expert. He skied ahead and waited for us, often at the bottom of a hill, shining his high-powered torch on the inexperienced skiers and laughing riotously at those who stumbled and tumbled down the hills. I don't think I'd ever seen a grown man having so much fun. His glee was child-like. Peals of his laughter rang out in the still darkness. I heard him chuckling ahead of me before I could see him or the fallen person he laughed at. I was determined not to take a single spill, and managed to stay on my skis only with brute force. I popped the ski poles into the ground and mangled them into walking sticks, hobbling down the hills without wiping out. It wasn't skillful or pretty, and I was wet with sweat and exhausted at the bottom of each slope.

Cerullo was on top of the world that night. I don't think his Wall Street accomplishments meant anywhere near as much to him. Trading managers produce no tangible results. They may be kings, but in reality, everyone below them does all the work. With sports, Cerullo could prove to anyone watching that he was still a man.

All week I hardly spoke to Cerullo and not at all to McKoan. Instead, I skied and chatted with managers from our Chicago and Los Angeles offices. I was in Vail for the same reason that I worked with McKoan, Bernstein and Finkelstein—because Cerullo had decreed it. But we never reached any détente. I was acutely aware that this was the group that had demanded my firing. Cerullo wasn't ready to comply, but he did want to put me in my place. To him, the ultimate humiliation any man could face was in failing a test of his physical prowess. He'd invited me to Vail because he'd hoped to plow me into a snowbank.

* * *

THE NEGOTIATIONS WITH the European bank consortium took longer than anyone expected. February flew by. My discomfort, brought on by suspicions at every turn and a restlessness with the trading scheme, was appeased only because I looked forward to my golfing trip with CEO Michael Carpenter. We were to play in the spring, when the weather improved. I was a managing director, and the "Man of the Year" mantle was still fresh. Carpenter had expressed interest in my career, and I began to plan for what that might mean. However, in pursuit of my next job, I took my eye off the current one. I ignored the impact of my personality on people and became even more arrogant. I believed Kidder was a meritocracy, especially because I'd become successful in spite of the racial climate, and I believed that would shield me. More and more, I was away from the office. Developing our European market was essential to me, and I traveled and focused my energies on it. My heart and mind were removed from New York now. No good was going to come to me from that office as currently structured. I had to look for allies and a power base elsewhere. It behooved me to care more about Michael Carpenter now than about Cerullo. I signed up for courses in golf, and over five weeks in February and March, went to Florida twice and South Carolina once to polish my game. I wished I had my grandfather's natural talent for the game. I spent my weekends driving balls across a golf range built on a Tribeca pier, practically frostbitten in freezing winter winds. My absences unnerved Cerullo. He desperately needed our profits to stay high during his delicate negotiations with the consortium. Any time he panicked, my cell phone would ring. Several times I talked to him while standing on a green, golf club in one hand, phone in the other. He whined complaints about my performance.

"You're not making as much money as you did last year!"

It was true, and my absences were partly to blame, but so were market conditions. Yields and interest rates were headed up, so my forward recon strategy was no longer profitable. It just wasn't a good trade anymore. That happened on Wall Street all the time. Without a magic bullet, my profits dropped. But I had trouble finding the enthusiasm to search out another moneymaking strategy because the major reason for my falling profit was Cerullo's off-balance-sheet financing.

Tension was a constant state of affairs in the office. Cerullo and Bernstein were nearly punch-drunk with concern about the balance sheet, and anything seemed to set them off. At the beginning of March, Cerullo chastised me for the crushing load of paperwork I had thrust on the back-office clerks. Bernstein stood by in his office while he fairly hollered at me to do something to lighten the load. The clerks had complained.

"The actual flows are down!" I shouted back. "The paperwork is from all the trades we're doing to keep the assets off the balance sheet!"

In unison Cerullo and Bernstein let out a sigh, and both looked deflated.

Fidgeting, they glanced at each other. Suddenly the air was gone from their criticism. They'd forgotten that the reason for the crisis was of their own making.

"Who complained?"

"Just some people in the back office."

We looked at each other for a moment. "Anything else?" I asked. Bernstein seemed to shrug. I walked out of Cerullo's office and went straight to the clerks. They denied having complained.

I went home to Ohio that week, to meet my newborn niece, and when I returned, Cerullo waited for me with a two-foot stack of computer printouts.

"Do you know that these are all your trades?" he said, his hand resting on the stack. Someone in the back office had complained again, he said tersely.

"The last time you brought this up I asked and nobody was bothered by the amount of paperwork. So what exactly is your complaint? The number of trees? The overtime? They seem to enjoy getting paid double time. Everyone seems to know the reason we're doing these trades is for your consortium of foreign banks. Is that done?"

"We expect it to be signed any day now," Cerullo said. He nodded toward Bernstein, whose ubiquitous presence graced the room. "But Dave here has come up with a way to reduce a lot of this paperwork. A lot of your trades are in the same security. You buy and sell the same security for settlement on different dates. We're just going to collapse all those transactions so that only the final position will show."

"What do you mean, collapse them?"

"If you bought ten thousand on March 8 and sold eight thousand on March 11, we'll just show the net of two thousand and reduce this ream of papers by half."

I still didn't understand why the number of transactions mattered so. "We don't carry pounds of paper around in this office. Isn't it all kept in a computer?"

Cerullo was insistent. "We just need to simplify things. Why don't you talk with Dave about how we can go about simplifying your position."

"Look, what you're talking about seems to have absolutely nothing to do with trading, it appears to have to do with accounting. Is that what you're talking about, accounting adjustments?"

Bernstein nodded vigorously. "Right, accounting adjustments."

"Then why are you talking to me? Why not talk to Joe Ossman?"

I knew what was behind this whole issue. The stack of papers was a canard. Bernstein was a master at creating conflict over innocuous issues, harping on a simple problem until it assumed monumental proportions, dragging other people or departments into the debate. He would force a string of confrontations that turned increasingly bitter and angry until a small dispute took on the scope of a firing offense. This time, I was determined to stop the game before it started. Joey-o was an accountant. Cerullo should put him and Bernstein to work finding a solution for the so-called paperwork problem. Cerullo agreed. But Bernstein wasn't so easily thrown off the scent.

I went to London on another recruiting trip, and Bernstein moved in on my traders. He told Ossman that all forward transactions should be assigned today's price. It would have meant a huge accounting change and a major adjustment in the profit of all the transactions. Joey-o told him: "You can't do that. No one would recognize the trade."

Bernstein wasn't done. He also decided that separate tickets should be written for this new system, a move that would further increase the necessary paperwork. When I got back, Joey-o filled me in. "He tried to shaft you."

Cerullo called us in. He flaunted another large stack of paper.

"Well, I told Joey-o what to do," Bernstein evaded. I erupted.

"We can't do that, it'll have a huge P&L impact, and you're asking us to write additional tickets to aggregate every transaction into one ticket. Your stack of paper will reach the sun. I don't understand what you're trying to do. You say you want to decrease the paperwork and your solution will only increase it."

Cerullo commanded: "Find a solution to this."

Next, Bernstein frightened Cerullo with charges of more losses. We were back in Cerullo's office.

"Dave here is afraid that when we allow your trades to settle you're going to have to write a big check to the Fed." The trades would be returned to the books when the foreign bank loans came through. "Dave is saying because your transactions were booked as much as three months ago when interest rates were much lower, the Feds are not going to accept these securities, they're going to ask you to pay the difference between the sale price three months ago and the sale price today."

I snorted in derision. For the first time, Bernstein claimed there was something fundamentally wrong with my trading. His argument was like saying that if I sold someone a security and the price drops, they could refuse to pay the agreed-upon price and offer me only the current, lower price.

"That's bullshit. Who dreamed this shit up?" I turned to walk out.

"Wait a minute." Cerullo looked at Bernstein. "So, Dave?"

Bernstein studied a sheet of paper he was holding and shrugged. I guffawed and walked out.

The next day, I was back in Cerullo's office again, with Bernstein.

"Okay, Dave says the Fed is not going to ask for a check. But you're going to end up with a reconciliation problem, because you're going to have to reconcile these trades you did three months ago with today's price. So each day, when each trade settles, you're going to have to book a loss."

"What is going on here? First you bring me back here and complain about the height of a stack of papers on your desk. For some reason that becomes the be-all and end-all of our collective lives, the solution for which is to quadruple the size of the stack of papers. And you're more than willing to quadruple it. Now I've come in here two consecutive days with Dave complaining that I'm going to somehow lose money from a perfectly hedged position. Think, gentlemen. If I bought a security that is going to settle at a point in the future, I sold some other security against it. My position is hedged."

Cerullo turned to Bernstein. "Dave?"

Dave had no answer. This time, I didn't leave.

"What is going on here?" Cerullo and Bernstein were silent. They spoke only in order to criticize or charge me. They never gave away any more than they had to. I looked at the two of them and made a decision. Since I was now a managing director, technically I outranked Bernstein. He was still quick to give me orders, though he never did with other managing directors. That was going to end. I'd talk only to Cerullo, and not to or through Bernstein.

"Are you guys done? Because I have to go golfing. I have a big game with Carpenter."

WORK WAS TOTAL war. Everyone wanted me fired. I had no allies, so I hoped to reach *up* to Carpenter. Carpenter hated Cerullo, did not trust the Fixed Income managers, and had little in common with anyone in our area. I hoped to parlay that—and golf—into an alliance that would protect me.

Over Presidents' Day I took a week off and flew to Florida for a five-day golf class with Mike Adams, the golf teacher to the pros. Rome Rottura came, too. Rottura insisted that we had to master golf. We pushed one another's careers. He was in line for a major position as head of a Government desk at a brokerage firm, and he wanted me to do well so I could direct my traders toward his shop. He wanted me to take Cerullo's job almost as much as I did. The five-day course with Mike Adams cost a bundle. We bought the requisite expensive equipment—Big Berthas, chromium alloy clubs, the works. The instructors made videotapes of our golf swings, and we watched the playback to learn from our mistakes. Rottura and I developed a credo: "We need one round of seventy-six, and we'll be set for life."

All week, Cerullo left messages at my hotel room. The balance sheet had spiked again, and he was furious. His anger was steeped in moral outrage that I was playing golf, a game that required no prowess and was the last resort of wimps. He knew that Carpenter was an avid golfer. At the end of March, I took another five-day golf trip to gauge my progress.

By this time, Bernstein's accusations totaled four separate charges, each equally ridiculous in my mind. His claims were nonsense, and I began to feel like he was floundering, powerless against me. He couldn't attack the very concept of my forward trades because he'd spent two months analyzing them the year before, and had signed off on my strategy. Instead, he tried to say there was something amiss with the phantom trades he and Cerullo insisted that my desk do. I knew there was nothing wrong with those trades. I wasn't going to listen to Bernstein's whining anymore.

Throughout the March golf trip, my cell phone seemed to ring every three greens. It was always Cerullo. He was full of complaint, but made no mention of any trading problems.

"I thought you weren't a golfer. I thought you were a man, I thought you played sports that men play."

"You're not as profitable, the whole firm is not as profitable as it was last year."

"I need all my traders to put their nose to the grindstone. We can't live off last year's profits."

"I'm taking karate, and that's a man's sport."

I had a history of weird conversations with Cerullo, and I knew what they meant. He was nervous that I was trying to get in good with Carpenter. Now he wanted to bond with me, too. When I got back from Florida, Cerullo sat down for a long chat about computers he should buy for his children. He left for Vail the next day, and on the same afternoon, Bernstein called my desk.

"I have a problem with your trading. You're going to lose a bundle of money."

"How?"

"You just are. I've called Ed in Vail and told him. I've got him on conference call, so you'd better get back here."

I walked toward Cerullo's office, the irony of being summoned there by Cerullo's disembodied voice not lost on me. Bernstein spoke in a stumbling rush of words laced with long pauses and ums. He reasoned that when a forward trade settled, because the original price was higher than today's price, somebody would be stuck paying the difference. Because we rolled the trades forward, we'd never seen the effect of letting them settle.

"If we let the trades settle, we'll have to pay up," he concluded in a rush.

Cerullo said nothing before I blurted out.

"I'm sick of this asshole. I don't know what you're trying to pull here, Ed, but you'd better find an asshole with a brain to do it. I settled $5 billion in trades yesterday and no one has come to me asking for a check. I'll let every trade that we've kept off the books settle over the next week and if someone shows up asking for a check, send them to me, and I'll write the check out of my own money. I'm sick of you sons of bitches. I've heard all the rumors."

"Calm down, calm down," Cerullo's voice urged. "Nobody's out to get you, Dave is just doing his job."

"Look, this is the same tired bullshit he came up with before. It makes no sense. You know it makes no sense. And I'm sick of answering this asshole's questions."

"So, Dave?"

For once, Bernstein had something to say. "I'm certain, I'm certain if these trades settle, he's going to have to pay up."

I jumped up. "Wait right here." I rushed out of Cerullo's office and fetched the Red Book. Opening it under Bernstein's nose, I ran a finger down the list of forward Strips. Had Bernstein honestly forgotten how the ledger worked? Or was he just on a witch hunt? Each forward Strip transaction was booked as a loss on the day it was conducted, not on the day it settled. I gestured to the list of Strips that had settled that day.

"Where's the demand for the check? Has anybody called you? Has anybody called the back office?"

Bernstein pressed his lips together. No one had asked for a check. My anger became vituperative.

"When is this going to end? Every day this fucking idiot comes up with some stupid new excuse, he doesn't have a goddamned brain in his head." I talked to the air, envisioning Cerullo floating somewhere in the ether. Events were spinning out of control. Either I'd be fired, or I'd spend the rest of my days in an endless round of panicky manipulations. I'd rather be fired, I realized. I was seasoned now. I could look for a more peaceful job elsewhere and not be turned away for having too little experience. I filled my free moments over the next few days putting out feelers at other firms. I wrote about the conference call with Cerullo in my electronic diary.

"Last Tuesday, I was called into Bernstein's office. He had Cerullo on speakerphone. Bernstein claimed that I had been avoiding allowing Strips to settle because if I did I would have to write a very large check to the Fed Reserve Bank. I guess this is his response to my ripping him a new asshole last week. I told him that he was nuts and that we have settled several billion in Strips with the Fed as we reduced inventory for quarter end. I complained to Cerullo that Bernstein was making daily accusations against me and that I was sick of answering them."

ON MARCH 27, Cerullo finally secured the loans from the consortium of European banks. The banks were going to back Kidder Peabody with a $3.7 billion line of credit.

On March 28, flush from victory, Cerullo wasn't at our Monday morning meeting. There was bad news instead. The Mortgage desk announced that their largest customer, Askin Capital, had just gone under. They'd been selling Nuclear Waste mortgage bonds to Askin on credit, essentially bank-rolling Askin for two years. Now they were going to take a huge hit. Cerullo got on a plane and flew back from Vail. While he was en route, Bernstein was seized by another flash of impending disaster. Convinced my position was bound to lose money but unable to reach Cerullo on his plane, Bernstein called Carpenter to warn the CEO that I was about to lose a fortune.

"You called Carpenter?!" I fairly screamed into the phone.

Bernstein was prim. "I'm not going to talk about it. I just wanted to inform you."

Cerullo landed, and I couldn't find out from him what Bernstein's latest charges were, either. He was obsessed with the Askin collapse.

"Listen, this Askin Capital situation has forced us to have as simple and understandable a balance sheet as we can," Cerullo told me. "So I want you to liquidate your position."

CERULLO ORDERED ME to sell all my assets and get rid of the forward transactions on my books. The panic in the office was contagious. I struggled to keep my head. There was some logic to Cerullo's request, after all. Any time someone owes you, as Askin did, then you have credit exposure. Under normal circumstances, I enjoyed the luxury of my credit risk being the federal government. Askin could go under, but the U.S. was not likely to. However, to an outsider—like the European banks in Cerullo's consortium—any credit exposure is a credit risk. All credit exposure is the same. Cerullo's consortium would see only a $300 million credit exposure. They wouldn't stop to consider that $200 million of it was to the federal government. The fact that a major customer was unraveling lent a small amount of logic to Cerullo's move to reduce our exposure across-the-board.

It would also cause a loss. I pointed out to Cerullo that liquidating positions before they matured—before they reached their settlement dates—would cost us money. It's just temporary, Cerullo countered. We have to get the balance sheet down to get the credit risk down. I didn't trust his assurance that the move would be temporary, because I'd long since stopped trusting him at all. Did it even matter? I wondered, because I presumed I was not going to be around for the fallout anyway. I'd already started looking for another job, looking for a way out of the endless recriminations and manipulations. Now I was particularly glad I'd already put out feelers. My interest in my desk was plummeting daily. Because of Askin, Kidder's future was even more dismal. I'd even asked a few traders and salespeople whether they'd come with me if I moved to another firm. My priority was to keep my team together. Cerullo might liquidate my position, but as a trader, I felt unassailable.

Bernstein objected violently to the liquidation plan. We couldn't let the assets reappear on the balance sheet so suddenly, he insisted. Cerullo was unmoved, determined to reduce our exposure. They fought. Finally, they decided to split the difference. We'd do the trades to liquidate the position, Cerullo told me, but not report them until the end of the quarter on Thursday. My head reeled. This strategy was certainly fraudulent somehow. I told Cerullo and Bernstein it was their responsibility.

"I can't have anything to do with this. I'm doing the trades as directed, but if you want these tickets, you come out to my desk and get them. I can't have anything to do with what you do with them."

Thus we began a bizarre system. My total position was about $29 billion, and on March 28, 1994, my desk began systematically liquidating the forward trades. For each transaction, I left the tickets untouched on my desk. Bernstein walked nonchalantly by and picked them up before anyone from the back office made their routine collection rounds. He took the small piles of tickets to his office, where he hid them until Thursday afternoon. I suppose hiding those tickets was a small gesture compared to the months of hiding billions in assets from GE. On Saturday, Bernstein called extra data clerks into work, so they could input all the tickets.

To eliminate my forward transactions, first we paired off all forward settling trades. We had to pair off every transaction with an equal and opposite transaction. The two trades, one the reverse of the other, canceled each other out. Each one also canceled its part of the off-balance-sheet financing. We were throwing the bowling ball back at ourselves. Three days after the European banks okayed Cerullo's loan, the balance sheet exploded, jumping up to its true value of about $30 billion.

The losses from liquidating my position before the trades had matured had to be tremendous, but because Bernstein had hidden the tickets for several days, we didn't know yet what the final figure would be. The first week in April, Cerullo called me into his office. He needed to figure out what we were facing.

"Do you have any idea how much liquidating your position has cost us?"

"You guys took the tickets. I would imagine anywhere from forty to a hundred million."

His hair was damp and his eyes looked watery. He was tired. "Would those losses be real? Would they be permanent?"

"Not if you return my position to me. It's very simple. If I've sold a Strip for a forward settlement date, I have to own the underlying security, so I have to buy it back. But I have to tell you, every day you wait, you're locking in my loss. There should be no loss, but again, it's been a week now."

BERNSTEIN AND FIUMEFREDDO corraled themselves in Cerullo's office for hours at a time. I walked in at one point to hear them discussing my trades. Bernstein offered the same allegation he'd made a year before and that he'd raised again throughout March. There were forward trades, Jett doesn't own the bonds, he's going to lose all the money.

"Let me buy the security today," I interjected.

"We're looking into that," Cerullo said. "Let us do our work. Please leave."

I went downstairs to Moishe Benatar's office. In 1993, he'd discounted Bernstein's complaints, and Cerullo had listened to him. Maybe Cerullo would listen again. I asked Benatar to go upstairs and explain, once more, why Bernstein's charges made no sense.

Benatar never got the chance. Bernstein interrupted him, and Cerullo sent Benatar back to my desk with orders to monitor the trades in my ledger. Make sure there are no forward trades left, Cerullo commanded. The next time I saw Benatar, he was hard at work on his new assignment.

"I think there are four or five more trades in your ledger. I used the computer to track them, and you have four or five you haven't eliminated." He said he wasn't allowed to talk about his conversation with Bernstein and Fiumefreddo, he was just supposed to monitor my ledger.

Alright, I thought, if Cerullo won't let me or Benatar explain, I'd get my message to him another way. I sat down and wrote a detailed memo explaining the math involved in the buying and selling of forward settling bonds. It was the first of almost a dozen such memos I'd send him that week.

THE RUMORS ABOUT me started to affect my ability to walk into a new job. No one was returning my calls. Still, I told my parents I was confident I'd find a new job any day now. When I interviewed a trader from Merrill Lynch whom I was considering hiring for Kidder, he wanted to know why he should work for me if I was about to be fired.

"They say it's the end of the Black Beast of Wall Street."

This was new to me.

"Yeah, you've been the Black Beast for almost a year," he quipped. "I'm not asking for inside information, but when do you think it'll happen? Your firing. There's a dead pool out for the date, and I want to win."

DAYS PASSED, BUT still Kidder did not report our loss. Don't worry, Cerullo told me repeatedly, we just have to make certain of where we stand, but you'll get your position back.

Halfheartedly, I wanted to believe him. We seemed to be slowly changing places. Now that he had the European bank money, Cerullo was calmer. But I felt more agitated. I still didn't know what the loss was from liquidating my position. I grasped at feeble hopes. The Mortgage desk seemed to be unraveling—another of its major customers, Piper Jaffrey, was in serious trouble. If Mortgage was going under, then my desk was Cerullo's only hope. Perhaps that's why he wasn't reporting my losses. At the same time, every day my P&L came back the same: zero, zero, zero, Cerullo was digging us a bigger hole. The transactions had been completed at the end of the quarter and still were unrecorded. D-day must be GE's quarter end, I thought. They couldn't let GE report false numbers. If they did, then they sure as hell couldn't say anything about it afterward. Maybe Cerullo intended to give me back my position. It was all he had without the Mortgage desk.

April 10 arrived. GE reported record profits for its quarter end, even mentioning the continued strength of its brokerage unit, Kidder, Peabody & Co. Now they have no choice, I thought. They have to return my position to me. If they don't they've not only committed fraud—failed to report losses, failed to record them on my balance sheet, failed to report the off-balance-sheet financing—but they'd also be making the losses permanent. I waited.

Four days later, Cerullo called. He was in Michael Carpenter's office. Would I join them to "iron out the remaining issues in the Strips ledger"?

"Is Bernstein going to be there?" I wanted a showdown with Bernstein over the math involved in buying and selling forward securities. I'd like to force him to explain his understanding in front of Carpenter.

"No."

Carpenter was gone. But Richard O'Donnell, Charles Fiumefreddo, Kidder's director of systems development Anthony Colyandro, a lawyer named John Liftin, and the head of Human Resources were arrayed around the room. Suddenly the meeting felt ominous. They asked me to explain my trading.

"Where do you want me to start? What aspect of this is being questioned?"

"The trades that did not settle," Liftin prompted.

So it wasn't the forward settling trades they wondered about. The issue was the phantom trades, the ones Bernstein told me to pair off and roll forward. I began describing the balance-sheet crisis that started in September 1993. Liftin, it turned out, was one of the Kidder attorneys who had advised against continuous off-balance-sheet financing. After I talked for a couple of minutes, Liftin became befuddled, and Cerullo stepped in to explain what his entire Fixed Income department had been doing in September. He took the lead in explaining my trades. I directed most of my conversation at O'Donnell, hoping his distrust of Cerullo would render him sympathetic, or at least, open-minded.

The meeting droned on as Cerullo and I struggled to explain what Fixed Income had been up to for six months, and the others struggled to understand what sounded increasingly like a bizarre shell game. At one point, Liftin sighed for the umpteenth time.

"Well, we're looking at a loss of $200 million."

I was speechless for long seconds. "Two hundred?" I gasped. Our own calculations had come up with an estimate of $110 million. This seemed like the perfect moment to make a case for the return of my position. The only way to offset that loss was to let me earn back the money. I thought my argument was well received. Though weary, no one at the meeting was accusatory or angry, as I'd felt certain they would have been had Bernstein been in the room. We all shook hands at the end.

The next morning I went straight to Cerullo's office. "So, am I still going to get back my position?"

"They haven't decided yet. Just hang tight." On Friday I asked the same question again, and got the same noncommittal answer.

Later that day Elizabeth Cavanaugh invited me to Saturday dinner at her country house in Connecticut. McKoan stood nearby our desk. Anger flared and I impulsively turned to one of the blond saleswomen and asked her if she'd like to be my date for the dinner.

WHEN I CAME home from the gym on Saturday morning, I found a message from Cerullo. He wanted me to come to the office and "put all these trades to rest." I called back but he didn't answer. So I left him a message: "I'm heading up to Connecticut. I'll wait half an hour before leaving. Or we can just meet on Monday."

Over dinner, Elizabeth Cavanaugh was moody. "We should get the hell out of there. Why don't you use my headhunter? His number is on my desk at work." I told her I'd already arranged to meet an attorney to talk about what I should do if Kidder fired me. I wanted to be prepared to demand my severance pay, and I wasn't willing to sign any kind of non-compete pledge or make any promise not to poach any employees.

On my way home, I stopped at the office. The trading floor was quiet and deserted. Cavanaugh's address book was on her desk, as she'd said, and I copied down the name and number of her headhunter. I looked around, then decided to take my laptop and my P&L statements for the last two years as well. The laptop I wanted to take to my meeting with the lawyer; the P&L statements I wanted to show to prospective employers.

THE NEXT MORNING, Sunday, I met with the labor lawyer. In the afternoon, I tried to work. I called my office in Tokyo, but the trader I needed to talk to wasn't in. I called several times, leaving messages each time. His failure to call me back was very unusual. Finally, I called again and told the secretary I wasn't going to hang up until he came to the phone. The trader picked up.

"I can't talk to you, man. Something big is going down, and we've all been told not to talk to you."

*   *   *

A COUPLE OF hours later my buzzer rang. It was a messenger from World Courier. He stepped out of the elevator and gave me an envelope marked BY HAND. I tore it open as my door closed and stood in the foyer reading the terse letter on elegant Kidder stationery. I wasn't surprised. It confirmed what I'd already suspected, and made real what I knew was coming. Ed Cerullo's enormous, looping signature dwarfed the typing on the page. I couldn't help noticing that while Cerullo signed himself, "Very truly yours," there was no greeting before the blunt declaration.

"I have made several attempts to reach you, and, since I am unable to reach you by telephone, I must send this letter to advise you that effective immediately, your employment with Kidder Peabody is terminated."

PART
THREE

"KIDDER REPORTS FRAUD AND OUSTS A TOP TRADER"

'D LEFT ELIZABETH Cavanaugh's house late that Saturday night, sometime after ten, and was in the Kidder office close to midnight. The next day, I'd persuaded a friend to convince a labor lawyer acquaintance to agree to an unusual Sunday morning meeting. But I wasn't the only one who was busy that weekend. I learned later, from press reports, Kidder colleagues and, eventually, GE's lawyers' notes, that as I sat through dinner with Cavanaugh and then met with the lawyer, a whirlwind of activity had set my firing in motion. On Friday Jack Welch rushed to catch a plane. He was headed for a three-day golf weekend with his wife. Then a phone rang, and a tense Michael Carpenter came on the line. The weekend trip evaporated into thin air as Welch shifted into his take-no-prisoners style, stopping just long enough to tell his wife to get off the plane. About the same time, in San Francisco, David Bernstein put down his phone, then picked it up again to book a red-eye flight back to New York. Gary Lynch took calls from GE to accept a special assignment for his law firm from the company. GE and Kidder officials rushed to GE's offices at Rockefeller Center. On Sunday Elizabeth Cavanaugh's phone rang at her new house in Connecticut, and she was ordered back to the city. Joe Ossman and Jeff Unger got the same call. They were all told to get down to the office right away.

Bernstein didn't sleep more than an hour on the overnight flight from California, and he drove into New York from the airport in a panic and bleary-eyed. A dour group of lawyers from Lynch's office waited for him. The sight revived him somewhat, but didn't clear his confusion. The Government desk's position had been under scrutiny for weeks, that much he knew. He'd met with Ed Cerullo, talked repeatedly to Mike Carpenter, argued with me about it himself. Now a phalanx of grim, tense outsiders crawled all over the office. Bernstein didn't know what was going on, and he didn't know what had happened to me. The other Government traders, looking small and frightened, milled around the office, quiet as mice in a tomb. Unger practically whimpered. One by one, they were taken into a back office and questioned. The sessions lasted all day, but no one told them what it all meant. The questions were sometimes clumsy, sometimes went off on tangents that Bernstein thought led nowhere. The Lynch lawyers took notes of everything, sometimes several lawyers writing down what the Kidder employees told them.

The lawyers were not the only ones at work. A score of media advisers churned out paper. Welch himself sat at a computer terminal to write a statement, and he didn't want help. Another statement announcing the hiring of Lynch was prepared. Bernstein and the traders were told to sign documents promising they wouldn't talk to me, or about the case. They were advised of their legal rights. They were informed that some of them were being suspended, and wording of that announcement was worked out. Then it was official—the GE and Kidder team had gathered in a conference room and voted to fire me. The official explanation was fraud. Welch's statement, in his own words, went out: "Having this reprehensible scheme, which violates everything we believe in and stand for, break our more-than-decadelong string of no surprises has us all damn mad." By late Sunday, frazzled, exhausted and overwhelmed, Bernstein understood that a publicity blitz was in motion.

ON MONDAY MORNING, Ed Cerullo walked onto the trading floor at Kidder. The Government Bond area was subdued. Cerullo called everyone together, including Joe Ossman, who later repeated his words to me. Cerullo told everyone that my firing was an isolated event. It wouldn't affect any of them, and hadn't affected any of Kidder's customers, he assured them. "We're a strong company, we're going to move ahead."

Joey-o approached Cerullo. "So, what? Should I get an attorney?"

"Are you trying to say you did something wrong?"

Joey-o wasn't sure. He'd conducted about half of the trades in question, he was the desk accountant, he maintained the profit and loss sheet. From where he stood, if the desk had done something wrong, blame for it might fall on him, too.

"If you've done something wrong, yeah, maybe you should get a lawyer," Cerullo advised him. "If you haven't, I don't think you need a lawyer."

Clearly, the choice was Joey-o's.

Ossman, Unger, Bernstein, and Charles Fiumefreddo were sent to a back office. Elizabeth Cavanaugh stayed at her desk on the trading floor. Officially suspended, the others spent the day mostly playing cards, Bernstein silent and intent on the game, Unger in a quiver of near-tears.

HOURS EARLIER ON Monday morning, I'd opened my eyes as soft gray light filtered through the skylight of my loft. The quiet of dawn felt like the start of any other day, and I got out of bed thinking not about having been fired, but about the overnight markets and whether Cavanaugh, Joey-o and a few other traders would come with me to my next job. Barefoot, I walked in the dark toward the television and switched it on, expecting to hear the early market reports. Instead, I found myself staring at GE's chief financial officer as he told Wall Street that I'd been fired for fictionalizing profits of $350 million. An odd buzz rang in my ears at the sound of my name on television. I sat down, hard, and for the next few hours, roamed through TV channels, listening to increasingly lurid reports of my deception, greed and fraud. Anchormen dissected my life in a surreal monotone. I felt detached; it was my name, surely, but they couldn't possibly be talking about me. I knew they weren't talking about anything real; all of it was trumped up. I shook my head at all the folly, dismissing the reports even before the broadcasts ended. Kidder and Cerullo had aimed too high. This strategy would backfire; none of these charges could be sustained. The reporters kept saying "fraud," and I seized on that word. It was proof of the idiocy of the entire saga. It only showcased Kidder's desperation. It was early yet; as soon as the other traders and managers on the Government Bond desk showed up in the office, the explanation for the $350 million loss would come out. It was simple and obvious, even a cliché. Restless, eager for the wheels of the day to start turning, I reflexively filled time running over the events of the last year in my mind. I could explain what had happened in less than half an hour. There was no way GE or Kidder could keep up this charade.

It was simple. Greed, for money and for power, had driven the managers at Kidder into a scheme to wrest the company away from GE, but the plan was built on a foundation of juggled books, forward trades and doctored balance sheets that simply gave way under its own weight. It was akin to a classic pyramid scheme in which ever-growing deposits are required to support the original investment. In Kidder's case, the deposits took the form of increasingly complicated ruses for creating the impression that the ailing Kidder was instead healthy and viable. Pyramid schemes are illegal, but we broke no laws. Instead, we "window dressed" Kidder's books, a common enough practice at banks and other financial institutions. But we lost our common sense, and the ability to see reality gave way to hubris, competition and internecine warfare among angry, bitter enemies. When the pyramid finally collapsed, we were all left standing in the rubble with hands dirty from grappling to prop it up.

It was simple, I told myself again. Kidder was in terrible shape when I joined the company. Only the Mortgage department made any money. Ed Cerullo ruled that area, and he was an intensely competitive manager who didn't broach any interference from his superiors. They were powerless against him because Jack Welch and GE were unhappy with sickly Kidder and unwilling to invest any more money in the floundering company. Kidder needed Cerullo because he alone made money. Cerullo wasn't as charitable. He didn't tolerate men he thought were Wall Street naïfs, like Jack Welch, or worse, a "broken toilet of a man," like Michael Carpenter. Kidder should be led by a man like him, Cerullo. In the right hands, it had tremendous potential. But those hands had to belong to a man at the top of his game, someone who could run a billion-dollar empire as if it were a triathlon. Carpenter had tried but failed to find a suitor to buy the ailing company. Cerullo desperately sought another parent, a company to buy the Fixed Income department away from GE and free him to run it as he saw fit. But who would buy us? Kidder could attract a buyer only if it earned huge profits. We had to invest. So we spent more than GE allowed, and then had to trick GE into believing that we operated within their guidelines.

The trick was a change in accounting practices that allowed the removal of all forward settling trades from our balance sheet. With that tweak of the books, mortgage assets disappeared from Kidder's reported balance sheet. Sixteen billion in assets vanished. GE never knew we were over budget by $30 billion. Our lenders never knew we were overleveraged and in violation of our loan terms. We juggled our books, and the benefit was twofold. We hid the true balance from GE, while at the same time we showed potential investors the huge profit earned with the illicit $30 billion. Cerullo led the profit charge when he urged his traders to invest $120 billion, far above the $80 billion limit set by Welch.

Then Cerullo went eyeball-to-eyeball with Neutron Jack Welch, and blinked. GE breathed down our necks, on the brink of discovering that we used too much of their money, lied about it and violated our loan terms. We scrambled to return our balance sheet to the level GE thought it had been all along. Frenzied trading brought my position down from $30 billion to $10 billion. Proudly I boasted about the finesse of my trades. But because of the accounting changes, I didn't reduce my balance sheet at all. I only shifted the total around. Apoplectic, Cerullo screamed and raged. We fought viciously, all the anger, hatred and jealousy of the last few years finding vent in a war over the balance sheet. I was not about to have my judgment or loyalty questioned, or to take direction from the two men who had manipulated me with racism. I'd battled with every manager at Kidder—from Mel Mullin to J. J. McKoan, Charles Fiumefreddo and Dave Bernstein—and in those conflicts, my race and my relationships with women at Kidder, white women in particular, had repeatedly been a weapon of last resort against me. I was an outsider, and no amount of success or profitability was going to change that so long as men like Bernstein and Cerullo ran Kidder. I would deal with racism in my own way. I'd oust the racists.

Panic-stricken over the balance sheet, Cerullo and Bernstein devised an emergency strategy to bring my position down temporarily. We churned my Strips until the balance sheet hit our target. We rolled trades over into the next weeks or month. Trades due to settle were allowed to touch down only briefly, leaving only a shadow of themselves, until these phantoms moved $23 billion off the balance sheet in two days.

Giddy with relief, Cerullo submitted to GE the balance sheet it expected to see. Pleased with Cerullo's display of control, GE permitted him to look for outside financing. He spent weeks negotiating with a consortium of European banks for a line of credit. Without an infusion of capital, we couldn't increase our profits or appear healthy and lucrative to potential suitors. GE wouldn't give us that capital, so Cerullo got it from the European banks. Bernstein and Cerullo promised that we'd hide our trading from GE only until the line of credit came through. But just as the European banks approved our credit, Askin Capital collapsed. The Mortgage desk had extended billions to Askin, and Kidder was blindsided by its ruin. With Askin and our other outstanding deals, our liabilities were too numerous. Our risk exposure was monumental. Potential buyers would flee from a company with those burdens and obligations. To preserve the appearance of robustness, Cerullo ordered that we liquidate other positions. We had to reduce our liabilities. Mine went first. Trades with forward settling dates or that had been rolled over to hide assets had to be consummated instantly. We couldn't wait for them to mature. We lost money unloading my position, but beat back rising anxiety by assuring each other that it was only temporary. For the time being, it was more important to show few outstanding liabilities. Afterward, we could earn it all back. I could return my trading position to $30 billion in a snap.

Except that it was too late. The pyramid disintegrated. For months each lie had required another, each juggle of the books mandated further juggling, each churn of bond trades made it necessary to flip other bonds or Strips. For months we'd been flailing away, desperately trying to prop up sections of the pyramid only to see the cracks and decay start elsewhere. Finally, the pyramid collapsed. Cerullo's scheme for Kidder's independence ended in disgrace, humiliation and debt.

At least, I thought it had ended. Watching television on Monday morning, I believed all that remained was for Cerullo, Bernstein and Fiumefreddo to describe what they'd done with themselves each workday over the last year. I was alone in my loft, lost in my own angry explanations of what was happening, creating my own justifications and defenses. Already, across town, GE was shaping an entirely different reality, one bolstered by teams of lawyers, investigators and public relations experts. The collapse of Cerullo's plan did not end the saga. GE was enraged, the authorities were concerned about fraud; I was fired, Bernstein and others were suspended. Kidder might yet be salvaged, and those responsible were determined to see their careers and reputations preserved. GE had issued its quarterly statement in early April, without mentioning the red ink at Kidder. Now it had a huge loss to chalk up; worse, it might be guilty of lying to its shareholders. If Jack Welch hoped to exonerate his company, someone had to pay. GE had to explain to its shareholders how it had been so amateurish and so ignorant in its dealings with Kidder, and it had to explain what—or who—had caused this debacle.

I SPENT THE hours after my firing filled with anger, regret and even embarrassment. Everyone would hear about it, and what my friends and family would learn wasn't pretty. The news reports carried straightforward accounts of GE's version of events. Fraud, phony profits, phantom trades. The language of crime, and none of the reporters or officials said anything to qualify or dispel that impression. Yet nothing illegal had transpired, and no one had been arrested. Ethics had been cast aside, but no one raised questions about that because the scheme to hide assets from GE wasn't part of the public pronouncements. Instead, the spotlight remained narrowly focused on my forward recon trades. Suddenly these trades took on characteristics of evil, not because they were inherently bad, but because GE had the power to confer characteristics to mere transactions. It was a matter of perception. By themselves, the trades had no moral bearing, yet now they were invested with a morality that was broadcast to the whole country. Transactions that were conducted daily without consideration were suddenly unethical because they were conducted to settle in the future. What wrong did this now represent? How did the trade become immoral? At what point did it begin to trouble the conscience? It did none of this, I assured myself, but once a powerful arbiter defines an action as wrong, and then repeats the declaration often enough, it becomes conventional wisdom that it was wrong all along. Soon enough, no explanation is necessary, no a priori reason, no legal standing are required. GE declared that the forward recon trades were wrong simply because that perception served its needs.

In my loft, I talked to myself, to the television, I asked questions of thin air. What about all the documented times that my trading strategy and records had been evaluated? When Cerullo came onto the trading floor and grilled me about the sustainability of my strategy because he had a budget report to write; when Bernstein and Fiumefreddo scoured my books to prepare for the GE audit after GE finally learned that the aged inventory was mispriced; when Bernstein created a spreadsheet and tracked a hypothetical forward trade to find out if the computer's credit of profit was real; when Bernstein and Fiumefreddo dissected my forward trading strategy in order to set up their off-balance-sheet financing scheme and hide assets from GE? How could the mere perception of fraud and evil hold up when all the evidence demonstrated that Fixed Income's senior managers knew all about the forward recons and the off-balance-sheet financing?

No one was talking about that part of the story. No hints of the background events emerged on any of the news stories. Instead, the sketchy accounts hammered home in the headlines that Joseph Jett, head of the Government Bond desk, had acted alone, had kept his fraud completely hidden from Kidder and GE. The damage was internal, GE repeatedly assured the country. No investors lost money. Jett was a lone villain whose scheme was simply to inflate his profits so he could earn a bigger bonus. That was it. Nothing about Cerullo's ambitions to wrest Kidder away from GE, nothing about the balance-sheet duplicity, nothing about the assets hidden from GE, nothing about the computer software that booked forward profits up front, nothing about the liquidation of all my forward settling trades before they could mature but not before the profit had been booked—and shown to our creditors. No other names were mentioned besides mine. Nothing at all.

Dennis Dammerman, GE's chief financial officer, appeared on only one show on Monday morning, but the brief interview, with him looking rumpled and sleepy in a striped sports shirt, was rebroadcast all day. After Dammerman's initial appearance lent GE's full weight to the seriousness of the story, the point man for the scandal became Michael Carpenter. In a dark blue suit, Carpenter appeared on show after show, explaining my duplicity and fraud. Chastened and calm, he spoke in a level voice about Kidder's quick action to accept responsibility for its rogue trader. The damage was real, he acknowledged frankly, but it was contained and immediate steps would be taken—had already been taken—to figure out how Jett had gotten around Kidder's computer system, and to ensure that it never happened again.

"He was perceived as a very successful trader and our management system appeared to show he was managing risk well," Carpenter told one interviewer. Ironic, I thought. That management system included Carpenter himself, who just weeks before had named me "Man of the Year" and told me that he was following my career and liked what he saw. I should have taken a hint from Carpenter's TV performance. It was a gloss on the new reality. In truth, a vast void separated him from our day-to-day operations. He knew nothing about the business of Fixed Income. He and Cerullo openly loathed each other. Few people were further removed from my desk and our trading strategy than Carpenter; yet here he was, calm and confident, proffering explanations as if he alone had the answers to the mystery that everyone craved to solve. Suspicion and fury swelled in me again, and I quashed it with reassurances that Wall Street was simply overreacting. Lots of traders had been involved in disputes with their employers; there were always stories like this one churning through the gossip mill. In spite of the continuing parade of television interviews and reports, the scandal was an arcane development in the cloistered world of Wall Street. Naturally it piqued the interest of the early-morning business news programs, but few people beyond the New York City finance world would care or be concerned with what was going on at Kidder. Ours was one of the last, great gated communities in America.

Then my neighbor called to warn me about the phalanx of photographers and reporters that had assaulted him on our stoop, demanding to know if he were me. The press wanted to find a white man with my name. As soon as I ventured outside, I discovered the horde of journalists, and the day's papers. The saga exploded out of its small box and scattered in every direction. The Kidder story was plastered across the front page of *The New York Times* (KIDDER REPORTS FRAUD AND OUSTS A TOP TRADER) and *The Wall Street Journal* (SAGA OF KIDDER'S JETT: SUDDEN DOWNFALL OF AN AGGRESSIVE WALL STREET TRADER").

Even in my anger and anxiety I'd been overly complacent all morning. The news stories had multiplied while I'd huddled in my loft, each one vying to be more sensational and graphic than the last. Before lunchtime, the story had broken free of the bounds of business news. It was a lot more riveting than that, especially once reporters got a taste of the "color." I came to understand that that usually refers to the descriptive and narrative elements of a news story; in my case, it had a double meaning for reporters, editors and producers, one they were not hesitant to share with their audiences. I was straight from central casting—a black man on Wall Street, rare in itself, a conservative black man, hardworking, aggressive. Throughout the next few weeks, my story would fill talk shows, tabloid television, nightly newscasts and news magazines for hours each day. The reports shared one feature, from *The Wall Street Journal* to trash TV: The stories were breathtaking in their condemnation, and unquestioning in their assumption of my guilt. Quickly it became my story rather than the Kidder story, because quickly it was evident that my eccentricities were much more interesting and easier to write about than the intricacies of government bond trading. *The Boston Globe* summed it up neatly when it wrote "when the press went to work . . . they found an astonishing character." The *Journal* found it newsworthy to report my interest in "the philosophy of Nietzsche to the symphonies of Mahler to the poetry of Lord Byron." Then it called me "a loner and a loser." Finally, the *Journal* wrote about a computer system at work—not the Kidder accounting program that made my trading possible, but rather reports that former co-workers at First Boston had found a list of women and their sexual habits on a computer of mine.

The newspapers loved to quote people who said they knew something about me but refused to give their names. They charged me with spending "two hours a night working out at a gym." I was "rock-jawed" or "mus-

cular" in virtually every article. "Sometimes when angered," colleagues told
a reporter, "he would become very still, then arch his back and let out a
fearsome roar." "He spent long hours in the office and worked with an
intensity that bordered on anger . . . ," co-workers described. "Jett managed
by intimidation. He leaned on people, and could make you feel like dirt,"
another former associate said. One colleague said I once told him I "tried
out to compete on *American Gladiators*." "A smart guy who spent a good
part of the day reading Kung Fu comic books and *Muscle* magazine . . . ,"
an unnamed trader from Morgan Stanley said. "Classmates at Harvard said
they encountered an angry young man"; "While at Harvard, Mr. Jett im-
mersed himself in body building and martial arts. He struck some of his
classmates as theatrical as well as strident about his conservative politics."
Morgan Stanley workers chimed in with reports that in my time there, I
"did not perform well and that he did not have the sophisticated arbitrage
experience he claimed in later job interviews." "Mr. Jett sometimes concealed vital information from other traders," co-workers said, without
detailing what information was withheld, or when. A "strong-willed, ego-
tistical player who believed he could outtrade the market," another unnamed former colleague charged. I almost laughed. Who wasn't, and didn't?
Suddenly, linked with the roaring, the workouts and the oblique references
to race, it was a stigma.

"He has been fired, now he should be thrown in jail. He makes us all
look bad," an unnamed trader told a reporter. The paper printed it; after
all, it was just opinion, even if it was stated only days after my firing, before
I'd spoken publicly, before all the facts were known. Several newspapers
and TV shows even seized on a rumor that my Harvard degree was fake—
until the university announced that I'd completed my degree course work
but had not picked up a diploma because of $4,300 in outstanding fees. I
hadn't even realized I still owed the money. I paid it that month.

I couldn't blame that trader for concluding that I was the devil incarnate.
It wasn't even necessary to read the news stories—the headlines alone were
convincing enough: KIDDER'S PHANTOM-BOND TRADER FAKED PROFITS,
HARVARD MBA; FIRED TRADER HAD SHADY PAST; SMOKE AND MIRRORS
BOND TRADES, WHY DIDN'T KIDDER CATCH ON? WALL STREET SUCCESS
STORY ENDS IN SHAME; KIDDER PEABODY: JETT-LAGGED. "He was one of
Kidder's Wizards, until they drew back the curtain."

When no unnamed colleagues were able to offer explanations, the writers
came up with their own. "Kidder's senior management had no inkling of
the manipulations until two weeks ago . . . ," "The articulate Mr. Jett, a
Mahler-loving aesthete who also let it be known on the floor that he was a
Kung Fu master . . . ," "He was a general, a dictator, and he acted as though
it was beneath him to explain anything to his subordinates, let alone reveal
his strategies . . . ," ". . . after his plummet from grace, a different figure has
emerged . . ."

And then there were the experts, the Wall Street consultants and analysts. "The irony of the Jett scandal is that it seems to be a reflection of both a black man trying too hard to win in the exclusive white world of Wall Street and of a medium-sized firm like Kidder trying too hard to compete with the big global players." Why a black man, not just a man?

The tenor of the stories conveyed the idea that you can take a black man out of the ghetto, but you can't take the ghetto out of the black man. The stories said, beneath the Harvard degree and the Brooks Brothers suits lurks as much reason for fear as with the black teenage gang member on a dark subway platform—muscles, a rock-jawed defiant stare, a willingness to lie, cheat or commit crime to seize more than he deserves.

Even the coach of my high school *Academic Challenge* team took a swipe in an interview with my hometown paper, the Cleveland *Plain Dealer*. "Orlando, frankly, parlayed race and intelligence and grades—the whole thing— and that looked good to MIT," he said. So that was it. I wasn't just a fraud trader, I was a fraud, period. I had "parlayed race," the ultimate con, and duped MIT. Everything I objected to about affirmative action caught up with me in that one sentence.

European papers loved my story, too. The British weighed in with WALL STREET "DICTATOR" HELD SWAY IN FALSE TRADES SCANDAL" in the *Independent*. "The dealer at the centre of the derivatives scam was a domineering martinet, colleagues say." The first paragraph of the story explained that I "routinely threatened those who resisted his will." When people at Morgan Stanley heard of my firing, the paper reported, "a spontaneous cheer rose up from the ranks of his former colleagues."

British papers prided themselves on being free to blatantly tout the fact that I was black, unlike their cowed American counterparts. In an article headlined THE MAN WHO KIDDED KIDDER FOR $350 MILLION," the Sunday *Times* of London wrote: "His exposure as a crook has stirred dark and uncomfortable feelings in a society where racial distrust runs deep. Newspapers desperately try to be politically correct and avoid the slightest whiff of racism. Wall Streeters, normally only too eager to get their names in the papers, have closed up like clams. On this subject nobody wants to be quoted." But the *Times* didn't hesitate to describe me pointedly as "a ferociously ambitious trader who took enormous risks. He was powerfully built, spending hours at the gym pumping weights and practicing Kung Fu. If colleagues challenged his judgement, he would explode with rage. . . ." "The power of the man was hard to ignore," the paper quoted Carpenter as saying.

The free-for-all peaked when CNN's *Inside Business* reporter, Deborah Marchini, breathlessly asked viewers in early May: "How could it have happened? In an industry conditioned to be hypersensitive to potential wrongdoing, how could one young trader rise so fast, make so much, and fool so many? It's the story of Joseph Jett."

She barely paused before rushing on, her story a clip job from newspapers of the last two weeks. Clearly, she believed if the information was in the press, it must be true.

"Denied a degree at Harvard Business School, Jett failed to distinguish himself at two other Wall Street firms before rocketing to the top at Kidder Peabody. At just thirty-six, Jett was a master of the universe, running Kidder's Government trading desk and making millions. But his success was an illusion, a well-orchestrated scam to fake company profits for a fat bonus in return."

Marchini's guests pontificated over what questions the Jett scandal raised on Wall Street. Determined to fix on rogue traders on Wall Street, she got into an argument with Martin Mayer, a financial analyst and writer I'd never seen before.

"Are rogue traders really such an anomaly on Wall Street?"

"This accounting system allowed people to take discounts at profit," Mayer answered. "That is, if you buy a six-month Treasury bill at a four percent annual rate of interest, you pay $98 for it and you get $100 back for it after six months. Their accounting system let them take that as a profit. They did that at Lloyd's of London, too, by the way. That sort of thing is rare simply because such accounting systems are rare. . . ."

"But rogue traders who make big bucks with the firm's capital . . ." Marchini insisted.

"That's not what he was doing," Mayer interrupted. "This is happening, and you also get traders who hide slips in the desk or do the computerized . . ."

"Well, I'm a little confused here," Marchini admitted, "because from everything I've read and heard about this case, it seems that he was reporting at least to his own securities desk, billions of dollars in transactions."

"He was doing something which a well-planned computer system would have run up a flag and said 'Look at what this guy's doing.' . . . This is a problem of the organization of Kidder Peabody."

Another guest added, "I believe this is a trader who, from all that's been described in the press, decided that he would be king of the hill in a way that he could ensure and was within his own control, so I don't see this as much more than . . . an accounting system that didn't catch someone. . . ."

But Marchini wasn't listening. She wanted her original theme to be true.

"Let's take a break right here. When we come back, we'll talk about what, if anything, can or should be done with rogue traders."

FEW LAWYERS WOULD take my call. The ones who agreed to meet me seemed concerned only with money and trading me to GE for a lucrative fee. Kidder and GE boasted that they had promptly reported the scandal to the New York Stock Exchange, the National Association of Securities

Dealers and the Securities and Exchange Commission, and that it stood ready to cooperate fully in any regulatory investigation. In what felt like record time, the NASD demanded that I appear before an arbitration panel two days after my firing. Kidder and GE froze my savings accounts, essentially stealing my money and leaving me broke. Three nights after I was fired, NBC's nightly news program flashed my picture and the name of my hometown on the air. The next evening, two FBI agents assaulted my loft, climbing around on the skylight with guns drawn before warning me not to cooperate with the NASD or the SEC. The days streaked by in a blur of unexpected developments, and I fixed on one goal: hearing from inside Kidder that everything was cleared up. Once Cerullo, Bernstein, McKoan, Fiumefreddo, Cavanaugh, Joey-o and others started talking it would become obvious that I was not a rogue trader intent on fraud. Until then, I drifted along, waiting for events to unfold, for the first time in my adult life almost powerless.

Joey-o and Cavanaugh had met with Gary Lynch, GE's new hired gun. Lynch had worked at the SEC for thirteen years and was its "top cop," or chief enforcement officer, throughout the 1980s, when he made a name for himself as the tough, tenacious prosecutor of a Who's Who of Wall Street crooks. He'd sent Ivan Boesky and Michael Milken, among others, to prison. He prosecuted a deputy secretary of defense and a member of the National Security Council for insider trading. Tall, dapper in suspenders and expensive silk ties, Lynch looked more like an investment banker than a regulator. He went into private practice as a perfectly positioned liaison between bankers, businessmen and his former government colleagues. He'd helped pick his successor at the SEC, William McLucas. McLucas would likely accept Lynch's word as gospel.

GE hired Lynch two days before I was fired, and then rushed to announce that he'd been brought in to investigate what had happened on the Government Bond desk. I took little comfort from that. With GE spending its own money to investigate itself, how impartial could Lynch be? Would he truly have free rein to probe any area, look at any documents, ask any questions? Since the 1980s, new laws and stricter penalties had led regulators to punish management at Wall Street firms for the violations of their employees, and as a result, there had been a boom in the Wall Street investigations industry. Companies routinely spent millions on lawyers, accountants, public relations experts and private investigators. Lynch had five lawyers from his firm working with him, an accounting office, a second law firm and an audit team from GE. Had they all been hired to ensure that GE and Kidder appeared contrite and thus provide them with a bargaining chip when they faced the SEC themselves?

As GE's statement announcing his appointment was passed out, Lynch was sitting down with Ossman and Cavanaugh separately, asking them what they knew about my trading strategy. On the same day I was fired, Lynch had the truth at his fingertips. How long would he keep it to himself?

* * *

BY THE END of the week, my mood began to shift. I wandered my apartment, muttering to myself about defenses. My anger grew as the days passed and the bad press mounted, as the media discovered where my parents lived and began hassling them, and still no explanation or retraction came from GE or Kidder. I could not remain powerless for long, so I stayed up nights plotting revenge. I redoubled my efforts to get a lawyer.

I'd called dozens of attorneys, but only Gustave Newman and Kenneth Warner were willing to take my case without money up front. Newman had defended Robert Altman, the Washington lawyer married to "Wonder Woman" TV actress Lynda Carter, against charges that he'd fronted the Bank of Credit and Commerce International's (BCCI) secret acquisition of American banks. Newman agreed to handle the criminal side of my case. Kenneth Warner took the civil aspects. A consummate outsider, Warner had accepted a fellowship with the Supreme Court of Pakistan right after graduating from Harvard Law School. He spent three years in Asia, studying martial arts, picking up Urdu, Hindi and Japanese, learning to play the sitar and acquiring a taste for wearing Indian garments. He brought all that home to New York and opened a tiny law office over a restaurant in Greenwich Village. Over the years, he'd represented Yankee owner George Steinbrenner in a lawsuit against a star ballplayer, and Frank Sinatra and Liza Minnelli in libel cases. He'd moved up in the world by the time we met, ensconced in offices with a view of Central Park and a staff of fourteen. His taste for independence and reputation for plunging in where others feared to tread suited me perfectly.

As the weeks wore on, Joey-o and I spoke regularly, and I frequently asked him what Bernstein was saying about me. I wanted to know if Bernstein had acknowledged his role. Bernstein had nothing to say. In the Kidder office to which they'd been exiled, he calmly played cards throughout the day, stopping every so often to reassure the whimpering Unger that he shouldn't worry, everything would work out.

Newman didn't like my conversations with Ossman.

"They're going to turn him. Watch out. They're going to turn him and you're going to hear these words come back at you."

I didn't want to hear that. I needed to believe that a simple act of truth from Joey-o would make the whole mess go away.

"Listen, we called him 'true blue.' He's all-American. Just saying the name Joey-o gives me a feeling that he'll be straight. He'll be foursquare and tell the truth." But I was trying to convince myself, too. Niggling doubts tugged at the back of my mind. Why was it taking so long? Why was this investigation still going on?

Elizabeth Cavanaugh remained on the floor as the sole representative of my immediate Strips trading group. United in their dislike of and contempt for me, the other traders and salespeople treated her as an extension of me.

Everyone knew we were friends. Now Cavanaugh alone represented the criminal I'd become. I knew she had the strength of character to stand firm, and I was confident she'd set Kidder straight with her customary defiant bluster. Finally, I couldn't take the suspense any longer, and I called her. When she answered the phone, the fire was gone from her voice. Her tone was hollow, cautious. She kept it brief. When I asked if she was okay, she said only, "I'm hanging in there."

The same day, Cerullo surprised me with a phone call.

"I'm calling to see how you are doing." His voice reverberated from a distance, its tenor altered by the echo of a speakerphone. He'd heard from journalists that I was suicidal, he said. I assured him that that wasn't possible, since I hadn't talked to any reporters. A nervous edge in his voice made me think he wasn't alone in his office. I turned his question back to him.

"How I'm doing? I'm preparing to go to war, are you ready?"

"Well, I just called to see how you're doing."

"Who are these six people? Who are the six people who were suspended? Are you one of them?" I presumed there'd been a meeting and for public relations purposes, Cerullo had been chosen to contact me. This call was probably being taped.

"I can't talk about matters related to Kidder."

"You can at least tell me who these six people are. Who are you trying to drag into this? This is between you and me."

"Listen, I only called to see that you were okay."

"Ed, I can assure you I am preparing for battle."

"That's good. Well, that's all." Cerullo hung up.

A WEEK LATER I rode the subway to the New York Stock Exchange on the morning of my hearing. I expected to walk into a small paneled courtroom with benches, tables for lawyers and a dais for the arbitrators. It was to be my first public appearance, and I imagined I'd step into an oak witness box, place my hand on a Bible and tell my story to the public. Anyone milling around the courtroom or waiting for his or her own hearings could listen to my testimony. Instead, when I arrived, I was directed to a small, closed office. Only NYSE officials were present. Kidder, of course, was a prominent stock exchange member, and I certainly didn't need anyone to tell me what these people probably thought of a corporation the size of General Electric. The New York Stock Exchange serves as Wall Street's ultimate authority, and, as a private trade group, its arbitration processes were put in place to protect its franchise. The system protects those who belong, and affords a neat means of eliminating those who do not. It also serves to cast anyone with a legal dispute into an arena beyond the reaches of the law. Wall Street employees customarily sign arbitration agreements upon accepting a job—a contract that commits the worker to resolve any disputes through industry arbitration and not the courts. As a result, courts generally refuse to accept lawsuits until after the arbitration process has been satisfied. Warner had already warned me that a civil court might refuse to hear my appeal for the release of my bank accounts until after I'd completed the arbitration process, even though the seizure of my money had no basis in law and wasn't part of any contract between me and Kidder. In effect, arbitration employment agreements force Wall Street workers to take disputes to an often biased panel of arbitrators, and deny them access to due process under civil law. Loyalty to the exchange is strong, and members honor a tradition of hiring only those traders who are registered with the organization. I expected the Exchange to cancel my registration, a loss tantamount to being banned on Wall Street. I consoled myself that, as its name suggests, the Exchange concerned itself mainly with stock traders. Since bonds trade through the brokerage market, few bond traders were registered with the Stock Exchange. A banning wouldn't matter. I could still trade bonds—if anyone would hire me.

My appearance before the Exchange was brief. I didn't have a lawyer, I pointed out, so although I was willing to cooperate, it made no sense to start now. Give me a postponement, I asked, so I can find an attorney. I sensed no sympathy or even agreement with the idea that I could hardly answer questions without counsel. The panelists viewed me as hostile and uncooperative. There would be no postponement. This was the hearing, as far as they were concerned. If I refused to speak, so be it. They sent me away to await their ruling.

I HAD TO settle my priorities. Two things concerned me most—bringing my lawyers up to speed on the events at Kidder that led to my firing, and finding a source of income. With no prospects of a job and no access to my savings, I had no money for rent or food, much less to pay the teams of civil and criminal lawyers now working on my behalf. My lawyers both headed offices with teams of attorneys, legal aides, researchers and administrative assistants, and already costs were mounting. In the weeks immediately after I was fired, as my cash on hand dwindled, I discovered several checks for expense account reimbursements. Over the previous year, Kidder had paid me back for travel and other expenses, and I'd simply taken the checks and stuffed them in a desk drawer. Scouring through my apartment, I unearthed reimbursement checks worth about $25,000. It was the only money I had for the next several months. At first, finding a new Wall Street job was not about money, it was about proving that I wasn't a pariah. In fact, I was a pariah, and any hopes I'd had of waltzing into a new position evaporated quickly; after all, people were quoted in the papers saying they thought I should go to jail. They were hardly in a mood to hire me. In an ironic twist, I even approached several of the black-owned investment firms, only to be turned firmly away. Soon I spent so many hours each day huddled with my lawyers, taking a regular job of any kind seemed impossible.

WHEN THE SUBPOENA arrived from the SEC, it left me in a quandary. How should I cooperate with the myriad authorities who suddenly wanted a piece of the Kidder scandal pie? I hadn't had a lawyer when I went before the NYSE; now I was about to appear before the SEC with lawyers who weren't at all familiar with my case. Warner had been handling a lawsuit to free my money from Kidder's freeze, and Newman had been hammering out an agreement with the FBI and the U.S. Attorney's Office, inspired by the skylight raid on my loft. We agreed it would be better for me if the U.S. Attorney's Office led the primary investigation. Any deal with the FBI and the U.S. Attorney's Office would be compromised if I testified to the SEC. In addition, I was convinced the SEC would ultimately do Gary Lynch's bidding, so I couldn't see any reason to cooperate with the commission. By mid-May, I'd agreed to meet with the FBI.

But the SEC subpoena had to be answered. I had to win a delay to give my lawyers time to learn my case. On May 5, I rode an elevator high into the World Trade Center to the offices of the Securities and Exchange Commission. As I waited with Robert Schwartz, one of my attorneys from Newman's office, clerks and lawyers in the fluorescent-lit, featureless office scurried back and forth. Several of them seemed startled to find that the subject of their files and government forms was a black man. Finally, we were ushered into a cluttered conference room, and I glanced in surprise at the group of SEC lawyers. College seniors on a first job interview? I'd met more lawyers in the last month than in my entire previous life, but these attorneys stood out for their youth. They wore bargain-basement suits and expressions of inexperience on their unlined, even pimply faces. In contrast, the lawyers from the U.S. Attorney's Office fit my image of well-educated, articulate, clever litigators. I was beginning to sense the hierarchy in the legal profession. The job of District Attorney or U.S. Attorney is often a stepping-stone to private practice for smart lawyers. The same is not true of those who work for the Securities and Exchange Commission. I came to believe that having a job with the SEC is a good sign that the attorney didn't attend an illustrious law school, graduated in the mediocre ranks of his class or couldn't find a job elsewhere.

Bob Schwartz easily took charge of the meeting.

"We haven't even had a chance to speak to Joseph ourselves. You insisted that we come down here, but we're not prepared to talk. Let's just wait till we've had some time to talk to him."

The young lawyers huddled together, their faces angry.

"We have the power to subpoena. We've subpoenaed your client, and he's going to answer our questions now."

Startled, Schwartz looked at the lawyers for a beat. Their reaction seemed disproportionately angry, I thought. I looked at Schwartz.

"My client wants to cooperate, he's eager to cooperate, but we have to hear his story first." We wanted a postponement, he explained. But the SEC wasn't interested. Schwartz asked for a break to consult with me. If they insisted on questioning me today, he said, then I should give only one answer: the Fifth Amendment. When we sat down again at the conference table, the SEC lawyers pulled out lists of questions. To each, I cited my Fifth Amendment right not to incriminate myself. Each time, Schwartz intoned: "We're eager to cooperate, but we have to talk to our client first, we don't want to sit here and take the Fifth. Can't we just stop this right now?"

The SEC attorneys ignored him, continuing down their list of questions, until one young man stopped abruptly, exasperated.

"Does your client intend to take the Fifth on the remaining questions?" I nodded as Schwartz repeated his request for a delay. That ended the proceedings.

"We'll be in touch sometime in the future."

BAD NEWS CONTINUED to trickle out of GE. Days after firing me, Kidder fired another trader who'd worked for Mel Mullin on charges of concealing losses of $10 million, sparking speculation about "deeper troubles" with supervision at Kidder. GE announced steep cuts into its first-quarter profits because of a $210 million after-tax loss at Kidder, ruining what Welch said would otherwise have been record earnings for the quarter. Then, to top it off, Congress jumped on the bandwagon. Congressman Edward Markey, the Massachusetts Democrat who was chairman of a House subcommittee on finance, demanded that the Securities and Exchange Commission turn over any information on the Kidder scandal to Congress. GE was under the gun.

EVERY TIME I picked up one of New York City's tabloids or turned on a television, I faced stories about myself. Friends and relatives called to tell me of seeing pages of newsprint and hours of TV about me in cities all over the country. I grew weary of reading the same basic explanation of my life: Rogue bond trader whose scheme of phantom trades was intended to post $350 million in phony profit. No matter how many stories I read, they rarely carried any substantial explanation or exploration of my trading strategies. Instead, they were filled with lurid detail about my personality and private life. When reporters did write about or broadcast the financial aspect of my case, the facts and explanations were jangled, contradictory and plain wrong. Few reporters seemed to have a grasp of bond structuring, Strips and reconstitutions, zero coupons, bond trading strategies or the bond market overall. To deflect attention from their ignorance and inability to write a cohesive story, they filled the void with colorful anecdotes about me. Soon I became accustomed to picking up a paper in the morning and reading voices from my childhood, from the plastics plant in Albany, from MIT and Harvard, from every part of my distant past. People I didn't remember, people I would have sworn couldn't possibly remember me, people I thought I'd never see again were quoted in the newspapers with all kinds of insights into my personality and all sorts of convictions that they'd known all along I would end up enmeshed in a scandal at Kidder.

I rarely talked to journalists myself. Photographers still stalked my apartment building and me. I'd wanted to hold a press conference and clear my name, but Newman forbade it. New York's two tabloids, the *Post* and the *Daily News*, were obsessed with details of my private life. The two papers were locked in a perpetual slugfest with each other, and my story was exactly their kind of fodder. They cared not at all about the business or financial aspects of it—the Wall Street angle simply gave them an excuse to run stories every day. The pieces centered almost exclusively on my maverick personality, tastes and habits.

Since the facts of my case would have been too boring and too brief for most newspaper stories, they were used only as a hook for rumor, innuendo, opinion and analysis. Accuracy requirements are eliminated when papers or TV report subjective areas like opinion. Very soon, my trading strategy was not even at issue in most media stories. GE's lawyers had declared me guilty, and that made the charges legitimate to the majority of the press. Later, when Richard Jewell would be hounded as a suspect in the bombing of Atlanta's Olympic Park, editors and journalists all over the country cited the FBI's declaration that he was a suspect as the only thing they needed to legitimize their evisceration of him. The FBI's sloppy accusation exonerated the press from any responsibility whatsoever. In my case, an official statement issued in the name of GE lawyers and distributed by GE's corporate communications office carried the same stamp of credibility for the media. GE charged me with crimes, and that was enough. The press took it from there, assuming that once the official charge was made, their responsibility was to prove I was guilty by virtue of having the proclivities of a fraud and a rogue trader. My private life was portrayed as evidence of a duplicitous nature—a man who has few apparent friends must be a rogue; a black man who dates white women is a pariah; a black man who condemns affirmative action is most certainly a fraud. It was colorful, "independent" proof that I was evil, selfish, antisocial, someone capable of phantom trading, someone who should not have been trusted and could not be trusted now.

Americans have always had a fascination with seeing the mighty fall and the powerful taken down a peg or two. It's a kind of macabre voyeurism.

Anyone who is different stands out anyway, and if they can be punished for their differences, it's all the more entertaining and satisfying. This has gone on particularly intensely since the late 1970s, when, in the aftermath of Watergate and other political scandals, the press began to take it upon itself to investigate every aspect of people's lives. However, Watergate's famous reporting duo made a point of confirming every fact they printed with two on-the-record sources. Those days are gone. Now people like the Eappen family in Boston, whose baby son died in his nanny's care, endure having their every word, action and decision dissected in the press and second-guessed by callers to talk-radio shows who don't even know the family. Character assassination as entertainment has become a norm.

Warner wanted me to hire a public relations specialist. He introduced me to his own PR team, George Sard and Anna Cordasco, at a Japanese restaurant near his office. Cordasco walked up, her eyes widening at the sight of me. She rushed to explain.

"I expected you to be gigantic. I was even afraid of meeting you. We really didn't want to come by. We've read the press and were pretty convinced of your guilt, and we were very surprised that Ken agreed to take your case."

Her reaction didn't surprise me. People expected me to be towering, broad-shouldered and intimidating. In fact, I'm shorter than average, and compactly built, even when bulked up from weight lifting. But my picture had been on TV and in countless newspapers and magazines almost every day for the last weeks. The still photographers who hounded me every time I left my apartment had developed the habit of crouching and kneeling for their photos. They photographed me alone, and in tight focus. If I walked outside in jeans and a sports shirt, the photographers ignored me. Whenever I appeared in a suit, each one would shoot dozens of frames. There was never anyone else or any object in the picture to put my size in context, and when the cameras were pointed up at me from the ground, I appeared immense and menacing. The expression on my face was always grim—in part because I felt grim, but also because it's hard to look pleasant while picking your way through men and women crawling backward at your knees. Now whenever someone new met me for the first time, I anticipated their surprise at discovering that I am five feet eight, that my gaze is level to theirs, that I take up no more space than the average man, that my handshake is with a normal-sized palm.

In spite of my image problem, I didn't want a PR person. The press would run a natural course, and I didn't believe there was much anyone could do to influence it. First they'd condemn and eviscerate, then some reporter somewhere would begin to feel contrary and start to question GE and Kidder. Eventually, someone would investigate my side of the story. Once I started talking publicly, reporters were likely to become curious. I wanted to hold a news conference, to talk to anyone who would listen.

Newman was adamant that none of us talk to the press. He felt so strongly about this that he threatened to leave the case if I decided otherwise. We'd just begun our strategy sessions, and from the first day, Newman and his colleagues had trouble following me. Newman understood that my story was intensely technical, very difficult to explain and even harder to grasp. From the moment I sat down with Newman and his team of lawyers, my explanations of my trading strategy sounded complicated and confusing even to me. They simply didn't lend themselves to sound bites. Newman feared that no reporter would get the story right, and anything incorrect attributed to me in the press could be used by GE as proof of inconsistent statements. He insisted that when I spoke to reporters, I speak only in vague terms. In the end, that only heightened the ambiguity and the intrigue around my case.

As the press coverage spread, it became clear that I had no idea how to market myself for public consumption. GE had a legion of specialists whose sole purpose was to control information and massage the image of its executives, products and business strategies. I could have been a Midwest Boy Scout with the power to heal and raise the dead, and GE's expert PR staff could have made me look evil inside a week.

In the end, I couldn't tell a story that anyone wanted to hear. The press and public were not interested in a tale of finance and business. It bored them. The story was complicated and its plot didn't move forward for months at a time. The main characters all sat in front of computer screens and talked about bond trading. The dialogue was in jargon. My story carried a death-blow: It was technical, complex and boring. People prefer drama, intrigue and larger-than-life personalities. It would take my own lawyers and agents from the FBI and the U.S. Attorney's Office a year to understand what we'd done at Kidder, and not because it was so unusual. Rather, for the average person, including educated lawyers, it was like being dumped into a graduate school course on high finance.

But Cordasco and Sard began to work on me anyway. They were concerned that I conveyed too tough an exterior. I didn't realize, they cautioned me, how hard, how unapproachable and how intimidating I appeared. The simplest things contributed significantly. Don't look people in the eye so intently, Cordasco warned me repeatedly. I'd always believed it was proper to meet someone's gaze, but Cordasco told me that I stared right through others. My direct, intense stare was scary, and unnatural. It made people wonder what I was thinking and convince them that whatever my thoughts were, they couldn't be good. It's unnerving, she told me. She warned me to be brief, consistent and comprehensive when I talked about my trades or Kidder. I was learning that much of my popular image, constructed without any input from me, came from how I looked, moved, my body language, my facial expression. The words I spoke, the content of my message or explanations, were not what impressed reporters, editors or readers, or made me newsworthy. If reporters or the public watched me and felt comfortable, and could say to themselves, "I like him," then they'd decide I was credible. If they didn't like the look of me, then nothing I said would help much. And the decisions were completely out of my control. Reporters have an infinite advantage over their subjects because they decide what the story is about, which questions to ask, how to edit the answers. The profession is invasive. Newman and his PR team wanted me to take control of my own story, to swing as much of that advantage back to me as possible. If the media insisted on portraying me, then it was up to me to win friends and influence people through the image portrayed in the media.

GUS NEWMAN'S LAW firm was small, with offices and conference rooms on the thirty-second floor of a Midtown skyscraper at Third Avenue and Fifty-seventh Street. Large couches filled his roomy corner office, which commanded a sweeping view of the city and the East River. A Hirschfeld drawing of Newman (I always looked for the "Nina") hung on one wall, not far from photos of him defending Floyd Flake, the congressman, and Robert Altman, the attorney for BCCI. On the morning of our first strategy session, we moved into his conference room. Bob Schwartz and John Cuti from Newman's staff sat around the table, opened their pens and fingered their yellow legal pads. Newman settled into a plush chair. Cuti was young; Newman described him as the brightest kid he'd ever met.

"Okay, so how did this off-balance-sheet financing work?"

I leaned forward and rested my forearms on the glossy table.

"Well, first of all, it's important to understand that you have two different inventory numbers. You have trade date inventory, and you have settlement inventory. Now trade date inventory is everything that you've bought or sold no matter when or for what day it has been bought or sold. Everything is added together to give you a gross inventory number. Settlement date inventory on the other hand only looks at what has settled, what you've paid cash for and that is physically in your inventory on a particular settlement day. Now Kidder goes by trade date inventory, and every trader uses trade date inventory, but GE goes by settlement inventory. So the off-balance-sheet financing allows us to show GE a settlement date inventory that is far, far lower than the actual inventory would be."

No one moved. I stopped. They weren't writing. They just stared at me as if I'd spoken in tongues. I started over. In my mind, I could clearly see the information, like a package with a neat ribbon that I just needed to grab and present to my lawyers. But I couldn't reach it. I couldn't bring it out. I'd never before tried to explain my trading strategies to anyone outside Kidder. Even there, I'd mostly had it explained to me by Dave Bernstein. I had no talent for explaining technical concepts to people who didn't immediately grasp them. This had happened before, when I'd tried to explain the mathematics of trading to the uninitiated. Then, as now, I grew frustrated and impatient. Concepts that were self-evident to me went right over their heads. They interrupted me with questions. Soon we were all confused.

Newman had handled the BCCI case, and Schwartz had defended Princeton–Newport Partners when they were embroiled in Michael Milken's scandal. They knew where Wall Street was, and I'd believed they were familiar with securities, even if only junk bonds. Now I could see we were going to have to start from scratch. A remedial course was necessary. I backtracked to the very beginning, Bond Math 101: "A bond is a debt instrument issued by the U.S. government. When someone buys the bond, they're allowing the government to borrow money, and the government agrees to pay interest on this money. They pay the interest twice a year. The amounts of these payments are reflected in the coupon, or the amount of interest."

The arcane minutiae of trading made Newman restless. He didn't seem to believe it was necessary for him to master the mathematics of Wall Street. Instead, he wanted to know how we could disprove Kidder's charges of fraud. From a legal point of view, he said, it was easier to work up strategies to combat the stories of phantom trading. Who was involved in the trades, what were my interactions with my managers, what documents could I produce? I had no documents, only my laptop with its personal organizer into which I'd written brief, diarylike entries. Some were short essays, but the majority were notations of appointments with comments about what had happened at the meetings.

"Okay, so how do we prove there were no phantom trades?" someone asked.

"But there were," I said. The three lawyers looked up suddenly. They seemed to stop breathing. "The phantom trades were conducted to manipulate the balance sheet."

These trades had won me the "Man of the Year" award, I told them. I was proud of them. I'd always been open about my strategy. Confused, all three lawyers had questions. How could I be proud of trades that everyone else used as proof that I was a criminal and pariah? What exactly were these trades?

I SETTLED INTO a new routine. My lawyers needed an intensive explanation of events at Kidder and my trading strategy. So did the FBI. By midsummer, I was meeting several times a week with my own lawyers, then once or twice a week with the FBI and the U.S. Attorney's Office. I spent my days in small offices, repeating technical explanations over and over until my mouth dried and my tongue grew numb. None of the lawyers or investigators had any particular experience in investment, finance or Wall Street.

I remained inept at reducing technical concepts to conversational terms. The sessions were agonizingly slow and repetitive.

Money was becoming more of an issue. I still had no income, and my landlord badgered me about paying my rent. The $25,000 in expense reimbursement checks was quickly disappearing. In mid-May, Warner filed a suit with the New York Supreme Court and the NASD, demanding that Kidder free the nearly $5 million in my bank account, and another $4 million in a deferred compensation package. At the hearing, I found myself in a sea of lawyers. I listened, quiet and still, and made only brief remarks about my innocence. However, it was my first official public appearance, and the first statement of my defense. The lawsuit argued that "the fact that at all times he kept all of his funds at Kidder Peabody provides strong evidence of his own sense of innocence," and asked the court to expedite the NASD arbitration. Lynch was there, too, with an affidavit listing preliminary findings of his investigation. The press seized these hints of the legal battle to come, and the chance to describe me as alone and lonely in the courtroom, no family by my side, dressed in an expensive suit and gold cuff links.

Two weeks later, the court ordered Kidder to release a small portion of my money from a 401K retirement fund. Essentially, the judge had to threaten Kidder: He told the company that he would order an expedited arbitration if the money was not released. Not wanting that, Kidder sent me about $140,000. At that point, I had about $700 of my expense reimbursement checks left. My lawyers got the bulk of the money; I kept $40,000 to live on for the next three years.

It made no sense to remain in my expensive loft. I couldn't afford it anymore, and my neighborhood was crawling with photographers and cameramen and reporters who knew where I lived. On days when I left the house in a baseball cap, jeans and sneakers, the photographers ignored me. The casual clothes bought me some desperately needed privacy. One afternoon, dressed casually, I walked past a photographer who did a slight double-take. For a moment I thought my pseudo-disguise was blown, but after a second's thought, the man didn't raise his camera.

I tried to stay in the loft for a while, paying the rent by selling my furniture and stereo. I posted a FOR SALE notice in the co-op lobby, and neighbors brought friends to see my belongings. I got a fair price for them. I hired a local moving company, fittingly named Man With A Van, to haul away some of my belongings. As the movers loaded their truck, I asked on the spur of the moment whether they had any job openings. A husky mover looked at me. "We always need help," he said finally, apparently deciding I looked as if I could handle the job. Without planning, I stepped into a new life. I'd already stopped socializing; I had no girlfriend and no interest in dating. My social interaction came from meeting with lawyers every morning. Now I added another outlet. At about one o'clock in the afternoon, I made my way to the corner of Canal and Hudson. The truck emblazoned with MAN WITH A VAN rumbled by a few minutes later to collect the guys who'd signed on to the moving crew. I gave the boss a fake name. I didn't want anyone on the job prying into my private life, but mostly I didn't want the fact that I was moving furniture to find its way into the New York *Daily News*. My pseudonym was Frank Arouet, because the crew boss would never connect it to Voltaire's real name, François-Marie Arouet, one of my favorites. I insisted on cash-payment; I didn't trust banks. But the fact that Kidder could claim assets held at BankOne without a court order taught me never to deposit money in a bank under my own name again. In truth, I wasn't a very reliable worker, since I was at the beck and call of my attorneys. After a while, I figured my crew boss had stopped calling me Frank and started referring to me as "the son of a bitch who didn't turn up."

A lot of moving in New York City takes place during odd hours. Man With A Van had many commercial clients, and they didn't like their elevators and hallways cluttered with movers, boxes and dollies during rush hours. Many evenings from dusk through the night hours, I found myself dressed in tattered jeans and a sweatshirt, standing at the aisles or cubicles of a brightly lit office complex not unlike Kidder's trading floor. The empty desks, silent computers and telephones, files and paperwork resonated with the educated professionals who sat in the chairs and conducted business during the day. I was one of them, and this was my world. Yet there I was in the deserted night, an outsider now, sweating and straining to carry their desks, file cabinets and conference tables out of one office and into another.

I worked as a mover as often as I could, then got a job as a delivery man, a personal trainer, and later as a roofer. I took whatever unskilled day work that could be fitted around my meetings with lawyers. The heavy work was cathartic. It kept me out of the house, and the physical strain became a vent for anger and frustration. The leap from heading a fifty-man, worldwide, high-finance operation to loading sofas or stapling tar sheets to roofs was vast. But I never hesitated to take a job. I needed a roof over my head and food on the table, yes, but it was more than that. I'd worked since I was in grade school. I carried my own weight in the world, and believed there was no time that exempted a man from that responsibility, no situation in which labor could not be exchanged for the right to take up space in the world. Work was an asset that never expired, never lost its value. In my gloom, I sometimes called my father, and he'd tell me: "Take a couple hours off. Relax. Then get your butt back to work."

Even so, I couldn't afford the exorbitant rent in Tribeca any longer. My landlord wanted me out as soon as he was able to rent the apartment to someone else. In September I moved into a cheap, one-room, railroad tenement in the East Village. It had a toilet and sink, but no bath tub. I showered at my health club every day.

Anyway, it wouldn't be for long. My fight with GE and Kidder would turn a corner soon, because I knew they could never make their charges stick. Soon the press would begin to investigate. I had tremendous confidence in my friend, Elizabeth Cavanaugh, and in Joe Ossman. The truth would out. It would be impossible for these accusations to last very long.

But by summer, the initial accusations of fraud, trades Kidder knew nothing about and phony profits, began to morph into more insidious charges. GE and Kidder officials insisted that no one at Kidder had understood my deliberately obtuse trading strategies, but they hadn't been stupidly blind to the dangers. It was just that when they asked me to account for my strategies, I rebuffed them with threats, with scary and intimidating behavior. I was a thug, they explained, ruthless and chilling in my treatment of subordinates and managers alike. Their latest arguments transformed me from a rogue trader acting in secret to an office menace who prevented interference by threatening my co-workers' physical safety.

Then the investigation took a truly ugly turn.

When GE's lawyers and auditors questioned J. J. McKoan, he told them that both Elizabeth Cavanaugh and Linda Mead were my lovers. He knew this because he'd long suspected me of offering preferential prices to Mead's customers, then paying her a larger sales credit than other salespeople. Suddenly Cavanaugh and Mead found themselves grilled about their sex lives before rooms full of suited men. I heard about this from a broker I'd worked with.

"Apparently, they've nailed Elizabeth for having an affair with you. It's all over the Street."

I knew this would traumatize Cavanaugh. Happily married, she had always taken a principled stand against dating brokers, traders or anyone else she worked with. She'd always insisted on being treated and paid like a man. She'd refused to dress sexy or act coy, strategies many women on Wall Street adopted to get their jobs done. Cavanaugh had worked hard to ensure that her gender had nothing to do with her success. Now, at the end of the day, to have her entire career dismissed as the result of an extramarital affair with her boss had to be galling, insulting and frustrating for her.

The auditors decided the only way to determine whether Mead and I were lovers was to conduct a full-blown investigation of every trade she'd made. They drew up nearly one hundred graphs of her trades, searching for a pattern of preferential treatment.

It was all too much for Elizabeth Cavanaugh. Her Steel Magnolia exterior had been kicked until dented, and she caved. In near tears, she left the Kidder Peabody building on a weekday afternoon. As she got outside, she pulled her cell phone from her bag and dialed my number. When I picked up the phone, I heard her voice cracking with anger against the backdrop of street noises.

"You've ruined everyone's life, and I have only one thing to say to you. Nigger, I hope you go to jail. Have a good life."

The phone clicked off. I never heard from Cavanaugh again.

*   *   *

I SPOKE TO Joey-o a few days later. "You know, it's weird, there are all these reporters looking for information." I hoped he'd take the hint and talk to the press himself. He had common sense, and good instincts for the right action at the right time. For the first time, however, Joey-o sounded evasive.

"Yeah, they're everywhere. It's crazy."

I told him about Cavanaugh's phone call. He replied with another description of how Unger had spent his day, crying and lamenting, "How am I going to get out of this, how am I going to get out of this?"

I jumped at that.

"Joey-o, just tell the truth. All of you, tell the truth and we'll be back trading in a week."

I knew I'd never go back to Kidder, but if I were exonerated I could get a job and take my traders with me. Wall Street was skeptical about the Kidder and GE claims that none of my managers had known what I was doing with $30 billion. If Ossman told the Street that Bernstein had ordered those trades, we'd suffer no long-term harm.

I didn't know that Cavanaugh and Ossman had already made those statements, but that it hadn't mattered because it wasn't the truth that Gary Lynch and GE wanted to hear.

IN LATE MAY, the pressure on GE found a form. A group of GE shareholders filed a class-action suit against Kidder Peabody, charging that they'd overpaid for stock that fell when Kidder's crisis became public. The suit also named me, Michael Carpenter and Richard O'Donnell.

At the end of June, GE forced Carpenter out of his job. He'd spent the first months of the scandal insisting that it could have happened anywhere. "There is no system in the world that cannot be beaten by somebody that is determined to game it," he said in one interview, but as Wall Street grew increasingly skeptical over Kidder's claims of ignorance, Carpenter himself became a liability. Axing him might restore investor and customer confidence. Soon GE was backing away from most of Kidder's managers. Just before Carpenter's resignation, *The Wall Street Journal* reported that Lynch's team had targeted Mel Mullin for investigation. Then in July, three years after the Hamptons pool party at Mullin's expansive beach house, events caught up with Ed Cerullo. He'd been on a hot seat of his own all summer as more people expressed incredulity at the idea that he'd been in the dark about his own Government desk. Now rumors circulated that the Lynch investigation report blamed Cerullo, along with other Kidder managers, for failing to supervise my trades. Cerullo's initial press had been good—early newspaper stories had quoted other Wall Street managers praising Cerullo as one of the best traders on the Street—but then reports emerged about another occasion when Cerullo was accused of lax supervision. One of his traders at Kidder had resigned in 1991 after being accused of exploiting a mortgage pricing error by First Boston. Cerullo had denied knowledge of the incident, but the trader said later that "Cerullo was aware of all aspects regarding the mispricing of the securities, including the fact that I had alerted First Boston to their error. He approved of and encouraged me to do the trade." The NYSE agreed that Cerullo bore some responsibility, and it censured and fined him $5,000. Now Lynch was saying it had happened again. For GE and Kidder, reaction to the unpublished Lynch report was obvious—get rid of Cerullo. The official explanation offered that Cerullo had resigned over the continuing poor performance of the Mortgage department. He left Kidder with $7 million in severance. Internal GE memos made it clear that Welch decided to cut Cerullo loose as soon as he found out about the off-balance-sheet financing scheme.

Now that Cerullo was at the center of the wrath of GE's edgy, unhappy shareholders and executives, he ended his public silence, and moved to get his story out before the Lynch report was released. The day after he resigned, he sat for interviews in the office of a New York PR firm. I read them closely in the next day's *New York Times*. Still under scrutiny from the New York Stock Exchange and the U.S. Attorney's Office, he insisted that he'd always monitored my trading, but was a captive to internal Kidder audit reports that never indicated any problems. He wanted full credit for being the first person to uncover my trading scheme. Uncharacteristically woeful, he said, "If I need to fall on my sword, fine. I'm not smart enough to comprehend all the bad things that people can do." And he was bitter.

"Somehow to single out one supervisor as singularly responsible for a department with seven hundred or eight hundred people, $100 billion in assets and $20 billion in daily transactions and earnings of $1 billion is totally unrealistic," he said.

As far as I was concerned, Cerullo hardly had reason to complain. There were no charges or investigations against him, no slander in the press, no confiscation of his money. He was free to fade away, retreating again into silence with his multimillion-dollar golden parachute.

IN CONTRAST, GEORGE Sard, my lawyer's brother-in-law and PR person, decided to blanket the media with profiles of me. Interviews were set up with *Esquire* magazine, *The New York Times*, *New York* magazine and *The Wall Street Journal*. Sard believed that only *Journal* reporters were knowledgeable enough to handle my story. He fed information to a writer named Mike Siconolfi about Kidder's weak Mortgage department. However, business writers are not investigative reporters. They may have enough technical expertise in an area like finance to write competently about bond trading, but they lack the experience, outlook and skills to initiate an investigation of legal charges, political scandal or corporate intrigue. They lack the skepticism of political reporters. Only later would I understand that investigative reporting was a specialized aspect of journalism, one rarely practiced by business writers and not sought after by business editors. Instead, they concerned themselves with daily news stories based on information gathered through conventional channels. They liked official statements and press releases from corporate communications offices. They were loath to question the veracity or motivation of large, established companies or their senior executives. Sometimes the naïveté surprised me. I remember one legendary financial writer telling me: "You're sincere, I know, but I spoke to Gary Lynch. He worked for the government. He wouldn't lie."

In spite of Sard's efforts, Siconolfi's piece on me read like a regurgitation of all the GE and Kidder press releases. Gradually, the press began to lose interest in my case. The blitz of tabloid stories had numbed even the hardiest readers of the *Post* and *Daily News*. The papers had written enough stories about the Black Brute of Wall Street, roaring, quoting Nietzsche and threatening co-workers with barbells. Apparently there was nothing left to write about. Once the dry, boring details of the case began to emerge, coverage evaporated. No one was interested in a nerdy guy who'd lost his job in interoffice politicking over an arcane, stultifying bond futures trading strategy. The writers and reporters would have had to work entirely too hard to figure out the financial aspect—and for what? So that editors could bury their stories on a back page, and so readers would skip over them because they were dull? I know about profit and loss. There was simply no return for the investment on accurate stories about my life.

On August 3, Mel Mullin was fired. He'd maintained that he was unaware of my trading, he had never looked into my strategies, had never been asked about them and, in fact, was disinterested in the whole subject. He was let go summarily, and denied his $2.7 million deferred compensation.

The next day, Gary Lynch released his report. In my lawyer's office, I read silently through the ninety-page dossier. It was the whitewash that we had expected, exonerating Kidder management and blaming me alone. After a three-month investigation, the Lynch team asserted that the entire Kidder fiasco was the work of one rogue trader. I scoured the report looking desperately for statements from Elizabeth Cavanaugh, Joe Ossman, Moishe Benatar or Jeff Unger. They were barely mentioned. Unbelievable as that sounded, it wasn't the most outrageous part of the report. That honor went to the report's announcement that I'd acted entirely alone, and had concealed my every move. With a jolt I read that I'd started cheating in November 1991, just a few months after coming to work at Kidder, and that's how I vaulted to the top government trading job.

It wasn't a report as much as a prosecutorial brief. It shined a harsh light on Fixed Income management, too. Lynch minced no words in blaming three people who'd already been swept out of Kidder—Cerullo, Mullin and Carpenter—for a complete breakdown in supervision. Their "lax supervision," "missed opportunities" and "poor judgment" meant that "for over two years . . . they never understood Jett's daily trading activity or the source of his apparent profitability." Lynch tore into Cerullo for keeping the discovery of my trades to himself for weeks.

The next day, Kidder demoted Dave Bernstein for not catching on to the trading strategy, either.

ALSO IN AUGUST, I heard from my friend Rome Rottura. Things had gone bad for him, too. He'd been in line for a new job, and when I was fired, his connection to me was too strong for his new employer to ignore. The offer was retracted. I asked whether he'd talked to Joey-o or Jeff Unger.

"Word on the Street is, you're finished. Listen, Joe, no one's going to stand up for a dead nigger."

I'D BEEN MEETING with Justice Department officials since May. Andy Bingaman, an FBI agent who was also an accountant, brought two lawyers from the U.S. Attorney's Office, Howard Heisse and Reid Figel. Both agencies were part of the Justice Department. Heisse, the head of the Securities Fraud division, played the good attorney; Figel, his assistant, was the bad guy. Heisse asked his questions pleasantly; Figel immediately challenged my answers. Bob Schwartz and John Cuti sat in each session with me.

The U.S. Attorney's Office had no love lost for me or anyone on Wall Street. Their interest in my case stemmed from their interest in any high-profile case, especially one that might bring down a group of wealthy Wall Street financiers in a take-no-prisoners city like New York. A high-profile case virtually guarantees low-paid city, state or federal lawyers an entrée into the lucrative world of private practice. Thus, the agencies vied for a piece of the Kidder story. If they could indict several people, they'd win press coverage, and create opportunities for themselves. They wanted me to cooperate with them not just because they believed I wouldn't get a fair hearing at the SEC, but because of their own interests as well. They were also pragmatists. The two U.S. Attorney lawyers didn't believe one person could have been responsible for everything that had gone wrong at Kidder. And that made the difference for me. The SEC and the NASD, with encouragement from Gary Lynch, wanted to bring down only me. The U.S. Attorney's Office, however, was eager to bring me down as well as the rest of Kidder management.

For the first half-dozen sessions, we talked only about my trading strategies. We met twice a week in the FBI offices at 26 Federal Plaza. The FBI agents were always cordial, treating me as prime witness rather than prime suspect. I sat in the stuffy, unventilated room and talked, and Bingaman, Heisse and Figel asked questions. The overwhelming feature of each session was the painfully slow and stultifying progress we made in covering Kidder's trading and balance-sheet strategies. The sessions were held mostly in the morning, and we drank gallons of coffee to keep going. I had no documents, no tapes, no papers to prove anything I said. I just told my story. Over and over I repeated the foundations of my trades, the technical aspects of the strategy, the basic chronology of events.

A couple of weeks into the session, Figel leaned back and looked at me. "It's interesting," he said, "that all your supporters are women."

Tell us about your relationships at Kidder, the FBI agent and lawyers asked. Mead, Cavanaugh, Day? Soon it seemed that a significant part of each session was devoted to leading questions about the women at work. I hoped that stoic answers would deter them, but a few days later we spent an entire morning session discussing Linda Mead. I said nothing as I walked out of the meeting room, but the irony of the situation filled my mind: Here I am, accused of a huge financial fraud, and all anyone is interested in is who I may have slept with. Was this going to turn into a witch-hunt of women? Would anyone who had worked with or near me, like Mead, end up being fired and publicly humiliated just for being a woman? Then one morning I got a call from one of my oldest female friends. Andy Bingaman and two other FBI agents had arrived at her apartment and questioned her for an hour the previous night, and their interest focused on what she called "pillow talk and lover's confessions." At the next FBI session, I pulled my lawyers aside and complained. This whole line of questioning made me bitter. Kidder had already grilled Mead about her interaction with me, and now the U.S. Attorney's Office was asking my old friend the same questions. The sessions were becoming a replay of Cerullo's lectures about black male sexuality.

At the beginning of the next meeting, Schwartz asked me to step out of the room, and the two teams of lawyers had a long conversation about why my sex life had become a priority over the trades in question. The sex questions stopped after that, and discussion of the trading strategies resumed center court. Bingaman, the FBI accountant, relaxed and asked fewer questions; he seemed to grasp the trading principles. Soon he took fewer notes, and sometimes flicked his eyes impatiently at the two lawyers when they asked rudimentary questions for the umpteenth time. Bingaman believed me, I decided.

In the middle of the Justice Department investigation, Heisse got a long-sought better job in private industry. One day he was gone, and Figel was promoted to chief investigator. Figel, who'd played the bad guy, was skeptical, and once Heisse's good-guy persona was eliminated, the questioning took on a hostile tone. All along, the two investigators had talked with Kidder. They'd been up front with me about their constant contact with my old employer; as they'd questioned me, they also questioned Kidder officials. Now Figel confronted me with evidence he'd gotten from Kidder. He came to each session armed with new allegations from Kidder and demanding my explanation. The confrontations were often dramatic. It became clear that after sessions with me, Figel would take my words to Kidder and demand that they answer my allegations. Then he'd turn around and bring their explanations to me to disprove. I'd offer my explanation, and Figel would drop the next "gotcha" from Kidder. Soon he came to our sessions with large placards, graphic diagrams and multicolored flip charts, all diagramming my trades, all provided by Kidder. I walked into our sessions and Figel would point to a huge poster and say, "Explain that!"

I could always explain whatever challenge Kidder presented. Kidder had no proof, no documents of any charges. It had only theories, claims and counterclaims of what I'd been doing on my trading desk, and the insistence that the firm had been in the dark the whole time. Never at a loss for words, I'd approach the board or poster and offer my explanation; Figel would mull it over, and then next time there would either be a counterresponse from Kidder, or a new charge altogether. It was a good sign that I was never empty-handed. Figel had to see that I was sure of my trades, that there was nothing I'd done that I wouldn't hesitate to do again. But I often felt that Figel was conducting a trial right there in that room. The message was loud and clear: If Figel ever presented me with an allegation I could not explain, he'd leap at the chance to say, "That's it, we've got him." I couldn't let that happen.

IN OCTOBER, AFTER three weeks of abrupt and furious negotiation, GE sold Kidder to the PaineWebber Group. GE badly wanted to unload Kidder, and once it was gone, wanted nothing more to do with it. The company refused to pay for the severance costs of hundreds of Kidder employees who stood to lose their jobs. In a terse memo, Kidder advised its workers that they'd get two weeks' severance for each year worked, and warned them that "time spent looking for a job should be done during nonbusiness hours." Hundreds of people stood to lose their jobs, because PaineWebber wanted only parts of Kidder. As I read news accounts of the deal, I wondered if the irony was apparent to Cerullo. After all, he'd hoped another firm would buy the Fixed Income department. Now it had happened, but as punishment for Kidder bringing nothing but embarrassment and few profits to GE. Jack Welch had spent $650 million on 80 percent of Kidder in 1986, and then dumped another $1.4 billion into the ailing company, to little benefit. Welch, notorious for not tolerating poor performance, had never liked the company, never liked the investment banking world. Eventually, neither would PaineWebber. It ultimately dismantled Kidder, and even jettisoned the venerable, old southern name that Cerullo had cared about so much.

I heard that GE committed to find new jobs for Jeff Unger and Joe

Ossman. It was important to keep them happy. But Unger, already at the end of his rope, filed a lawsuit against Kidder instead.

THE NYSE BANNED me in December, citing my refusal seven months earlier to testify before its Enforcement division. I was banished from trading securities or working for any member of the exchange. A two-hundred-word story hit page 15 of the D section of *The New York Times*. I wondered why it rated even that much attention. It was hardly newsworthy.

In late 1994 and early 1995, my sessions with the U.S. Attorney's Office and FBI grew more infrequent. Increasingly frustrated, Figel dug for information from both me and Kidder, but GE stalled on giving him original material. It insisted on providing him with graphics and charts prepared by its people. Figel wanted the raw data so he could interpret them himself. Instead, he got mind-boggling statistical correlations prepared just for him. When Figel refused to accept the prepackaged data, he waited weeks for Kidder to relay the material he requested.

Figel and I often argued. It was clear that many of the concepts behind our trades, the balance sheet we tried to protect and the profits we calculated and recorded, were represented by numbers too huge for Figel to comprehend. Anyone who has never worked with billions of dollars still has a genuine appreciation of money. By August, Figel had started trying to create his own charts to establish whether the phantom trades had kept my position off the Kidder balance sheet. He wanted me to prove the effect the trades would have on each day's inventory. I'd told Figel that my trades were intended to be revenue-neutral; Kidder countered that by their calculations, the $1.7 trillion in trades had generated $170 million in profit. One morning in Figel's office, I calculated the trades again, and arrived at a $12 million profit. I looked at Figel, triumphant. He snapped at me.

"Twelve isn't zero, it's an awful lot of money."

I stared at him, considering the nuance.

"With trades this large, Reid, that's slippage."

The frustration was corrosive, and Figel often lost his temper with me. More weeks of grappling with meaningless numbers passed, and by February, Figel was almost overwhelmed by the competing arguments and counterarguments for every little point from me and Kidder. Finally, he literally threw up his hands.

"Why doesn't anyone support you? Why doesn't anyone back up your story?"

"What about Joey-o?" I still believed that Ossman had to have told Kidder officials, the FBI and the NASD about our trading strategy. Once again I told Figel that Ossman had often been sitting in front of his computer when Dave Bernstein walked onto the trading floor and pressured me to get the trades done.

"No one else supports you!" Figel yelled now. "If everything you say is true, then how come no one else is standing up for you?" I rose from my seat and shouted, "No one's going to stand up for a dead nigger!" The words hit Figel like a blow, and his face contorted in distaste, then anger. He didn't like racist epithets. It was the same point that Rome Rottura had made the previous summer, only now I believed it myself. I couldn't count on Joey-o or anyone to stand up for me.

Bob Schwartz literally dragged me from the room, saying, "Listen to me! You've kept your cool throughout this difficult ordeal for months. If Figel wants to put you on the stand to testify against Kidder, he must have confidence that you're not some hothead who's going to lose his composure on the stand. You don't need a race card, you haven't needed one your whole life. You've done well, so work with Figel and soon he will begin giving us documents from Kidder that will help prove your innocence and send Cerullo to jail."

IN FEBRUARY 1995, Nicholas Leeson fled Barings PLC in Singapore, the 232-year-old British investment bank that had financed the Louisiana Purchase and served as investment adviser to the Queen of England. Leeson was on the run from a trading scandal that ultimately cost $1.3 billion, the demise of Barings, and his freedom. Arrested in Frankfurt, Germany, Leeson confessed, was extradited and sentenced to six and a half years in a Singapore prison. His drama revived press interest in the outrages of rogue traders. My name still had brand-name appeal, evidently—anyone who covered the growing Leeson scandal cited me as America's homegrown version of the same criminal.

The same month, an episode of the hit television show *Law & Order* had a plot involving a hotshot Wall Street bond trader. The protagonist was a black man who objected to affirmative action and refused to identify his race on job applications, was the son of a conservative father, a loner whose favorite philosopher was Nietzsche, and a stern, driven man who refused to dress down on casual Fridays because people would mistake him for a mailboy. The black man had an affair with a white woman in his investment firm, conjured a scheme of fraudulent trades, and then murdered his boss to cover it up. Of course, when the cops caught him and the lawyers convicted him, he cynically shouted that racism had caused his downfall.

It didn't escape my notice that the show appeared on NBC, the network owned by GE.

IN MARCH THE Securities and Exchange Commission notified my attorneys that they were considering formal charges of fraud. Galvanized by the success of our sessions with the FBI and U.S. Attorney's Office, Gus Newman invited the SEC to join our discussions. The commission sent attorneys and trading examiners to eight of my sessions with the FBI between March and July. One of the commission officials was a young Asian woman, a researcher and analyst with a technical background. For the first time, I found myself talking to someone who instinctively grasped the principles under discussion. At a glance she understood Figel's array of charts and graphs. The other commission investigators were the same young, inexperienced lawyers who seemed to have fallen into government service as a sinecure for life. Often they failed to follow the conversation between me and Figel; they'd suddenly ask questions that were off the subject entirely. They never made commonsense extrapolations. They lacked basic math, finance and trading concepts. I wanted to retrace my steps through Bond Math 101, but the SEC lawyers were impatient and uninterested. They didn't seem to have time or inclination for independent investigations, either; they always appeared armed with whatever material the Lynch team had provided. I grew increasingly suspicious that they were merely front men for Lynch's, and GE's, agenda. At our first meeting, they scattered when I came into the room. Whenever we got together, they congregated in an opposite corner and frequently turned their backs on the rest of us. Finally, before the third session, Bob Schwartz asked me to step out of the room, and explained that we felt that their body language and behavior indicated a predisposition against me. It seemed to indicate an unwillingness to give me a fair hearing, he said. The SEC lawyers assured him that was not so, but their mannerisms never really changed.

Soon a rift among the SEC officials emerged. The Asian woman started answering some of her colleagues' more obtuse questions before I could. When she explained my point to her colleagues, she appeared exasperated that they seemed to be ignoring the obvious. They yelled at her to let me answer the questions. I sensed that the technical analyst believed me, but the SEC attorneys wanted a case to prosecute. Did they have their eye on a prominent trial that might lead to a good job at a private law firm? The animosity grew until finally the young woman approached me and John Cuti as we headed for lunch. She said that because of the difference in opinion among the SEC staff, she wanted her regional director to join the next session. This struck me and my lawyers as a good sign—the regional director was willing to mediate among his own people by hearing me for himself. At the next session, the SEC regional director, Dick Walker, attended. Before I could start my explanation, Reid Figel began describing his view of what had happened at Kidder. As I sat quietly listening, it dawned on me that he believed in my innocence. Occasionally, I offered a broader explanation, but for the most part I listened as my pleasure and satisfaction grew. When the meeting ended, I walked out, elated. The U.S. Attorney was definitely on my side, I thought. Now the SEC regional director had been brought in because half the SEC was on my side, too. It wasn't unreasonable to hope that the entire investigation was going to be dropped.

I called my parents and told them that it would all be over any day now. I spoke too soon. A few weeks later, my hopes were dashed when we walked into another session with the U.S. Attorney's Office and one of the SEC lawyers casually remarked, "Oh, by the way, we've already decided to bring charges." I stopped, shocked, and my lawyers stared at him.

"Well, you shouldn't come to these meetings with the U.S. Attorney anymore," Cuti said. "It's unethical if you're charging him."

Essentially, the SEC had been spying. They'd used my willingness to let them listen in and even participate to lay the groundwork for their case. I'd refused to talk to GE or Kidder lawyers, for obvious reasons. Now the SEC was telling me that, in fact, it was my adversary, too, after it was too late to reconsider my cooperation with them.

SO NOW WE knew—the SEC planned to charge me. It just wasn't official yet. In August Kenneth Warner brought a securities law specialist into my case. The lawyer had participated in some of our early exploratory meetings, but had dropped out when he realized he wouldn't get paid. Now he was back, touting his connections with the SEC's chief enforcement officer (and Lynch's successor), William McLucas. He could arrange a meeting, maybe make these charges go away. "Let me do the talking," he said. When the meeting opened, I heard him begin to describe the vast imbalance between the punishments meted out to Cerullo and others, and to me.

"The others at Kidder pleaded no contest and got $40,000 slaps on the wrist, and yet here you are, pursuing someone who is doubtless the most prominent minority on Wall Street. You seem to be wanting to drive him off Wall Street," he said, as I stared, incredulous. "Is this what we're about? We should be trying to encourage blacks to come to Wall Street, we should ensure equal treatment. If the others are getting slaps on the wrist, he should be facing a similar punishment."

His appalling plan was to bargain with the SEC for a lower sentence because I was black. We'd never discussed anything like this. But he'd read the Lynch report and accepted that I was guilty. As he droned on in comfortable tones, he said not a word about my innocence. Instead, he laid out his race-based plea for leniency. Don't punish Jett because he's black, he almost said. No way, I thought, there's no way I'm having any of that. Incensed, I pointedly ignored my own lawyer. I looked directly at McLucas.

"I'm surprised you're trying to charge me, given the evidence you've got from listening to eight sessions of me talking to the U.S. Attorney. There are facts here. Very evident facts. Whether I'm black or I'm white, they're very clear."

I looked over at the SEC regional director, Dick Walker. He'd come to one of our last sessions to hear me for himself. I'm innocent and this man knows it, I told McLucas. At that Walker turned beet red and screeched at everyone in the room.

"He's trying to pull the wool over your eyes! He's very smart! Don't listen, just don't listen!" Fury filled his face. My lawyer, John Cuti, gaped at him and later called him "apoplectic." "Berserk" was the word that crossed my mind. He continued screaming at McLucas about ignoring what I said, as if I were some sort of siren, whose voice should not be listened to.

After that, I insisted that the securities law specialist leave my case. I didn't want anything to do with begging for favors because I was black. Bob Schwartz and John Cuti agreed, and the guy disappeared from the scene.

THE MEETINGS WITH the FBI and U.S. Attorney's Office kept up into the fall of 1995, even though they were fewer and farther in between. I now had cases pending against me at the NASD and the SEC, as well as the unofficial Justice Department investigation and my own sessions with my lawyers. My days were filled with a mind-numbing and endless procession of discussions of my Kidder work. We hadn't been able to talk to anyone at Kidder. Cerullo, Bernstein, Mullin, McKoan, even Joey-o and Elizabeth, had signed agreements forbidding them from any contact or cooperation with me. In addition, we'd had no access to any Kidder records or documents. All I had were the handful of P&L sheets and my laptop computer that I'd grabbed on the way out of the office that last Saturday night before I was fired. I could—and did—talk until I was dizzy about my trades, but the FBI, the NASD and the SEC all wanted to know what paperwork, what documentation could I show to prove my claim? Even my own lawyers wanted proof. But I had none, and no access to any. I knew this made everyone skeptical. The idea that proof was beyond my reach implied that it didn't exist.

Ken Warner spent months on legal maneuvering to force Kidder and GE to grant us access to records, and finally, in November 1995, the NASD ordered them to grant us discovery. Overnight, my life changed. I stopped working as a mover and roofer, and became my own unpaid legal aide. The documents Kidder was forced to turn over were limited, but I pored over each one with intensity and scrutiny. And it paid off. I struck the first mother lode when I came across several memos written by Kidder's internal lawyers after they reviewed the use of forward trades to reduce the balance sheet.

In September 1993, Kidder's internal counsel formed a "balance-sheet reduction task force" to review the legality of Fixed Income's balance-sheet reduction effort. In a memo entitled "balance-sheet expectations," they wrote:

Balance sheet will go down about $15 billion. $12 billion temporary use of off-balance-sheet instruments. Significantly $8.5 billion of reduction will be temporary.

Baseline imperatives: 1. No parking practices; no implied or explicit commitments; no side deals. 2. All accounting practices mandated by GAAP. No changes in accounting policy involved.

Key issue: readers of third-quarter 1993 financial ports may not realize that balance sheet is expected to climb $15 billion in October. Should they be informed?

Kidder issues: (Kidder Peabody aider and abider to General Electric fraud?). If there is a pattern of large balance-sheet fluctuation obviously managed solely for reporting purposes, at some point the SEC may view Kidder Peabody's procedures as circumventions.

The attorneys reached the following conclusions:

1. Avoiding any indicia of parking is essential as is continuing Peat Marwick approval under GAAP.
2. Kidder Peabody proposed filings appear appropriate, although on disclose window dressing could be viewed as circumventions if excessive.
3. Care should be taken not to mislead lenders, counterparties, rating agencies or customers in communications other than the required reports.
4. General Electric's proposed 10-Q intent 8 filings appear appropriate but General Electric may need to consider generalized disclosure in response to some items especially on 10 K. Accordingly Kidder Peabody should ensure that General Electric officers are adequately informed.
5. Reinflation of Kidder Peabody's balance sheet between September 23rd and General Electric's filing of 10Q on September 30th: MUST BE AVOIDED! Deadline 45 days after quarter end.

The document re-created the litany of warnings that Dave Bernstein had given me throughout the 1993 and 1994 off-balance-sheet financing effort. Here was proof that Kidder's attorneys had reviewed and okayed my transactions.

Then, at last, I found the smoking gun. In a folder containing Bernstein's computer records was a sheet bearing the calculation of the profit from a forward reconstitution that Bernstein had done in May 1993 while questioning me about the possibility of false profits in my Strips trading ledger. Attached to it was the spreadsheet that Bernstein had created to calculate the profits behavior of my furthest reaching forward recons. Attached to this tabulation sheet was another spreadsheet on which Bernstein had calculated the effect of financing cost on the ultimate profit from that same forward reconstitution.

Armed with just these two documents, Gus Newman asked for a meeting with the U.S. Attorney. The discovery process had begun, he informed them, and we already had evidence that precluded any successful criminal case. The U.S. Attorney's Office would never win. Newman reminded them that a criminal case would be tried in front of a jury. And that he was willing to work without money.

Weeks later, the U.S. Attorney's Office informed me that I was "not a target," official Justice Department jargon for the subject of an open investigation. "You're not a target, we're just asking you to give us information. We'll let you know if you ever become a target."

But I knew that anything I said in my sessions with them could be admissible in court. I wanted official notification—a letter, a notice—that my case was closed. The government lawyers dragged their feet. No letter was forthcoming, and weeks passed without another session. We'd met twenty-five times over the last year and a half. Finally, in November John Cuti called Figel and asked when we would see the U.S. Attorney or the FBI again.

"Let me know if you ever get married. You can invite me to the wedding."

FREED FROM THE Justice Department and the threat of criminal charges, I now had time to go through the hundreds of boxes of discovery documents. I spent all winter indoors, hunched over a conference table at Davis Polk & Wardwell, leafing through thousands of pages of reports, notes and depositions. My back ached and my eyes would sting by the end of the day. I went hours with no fresh air, without moving, with only a brief break in the downstairs cafeteria. Kidder had insisted that I look at the documents at Davis Polk, their law firm on Lexington and Forty-fifth Street. Over five hundred boxes filled that conference room, and I was warned to look only. Discovery was granted only for the documents Kidder deemed directly relevant to me. A paralegal was assigned to sit in the room and keep an eye on me. I brought my own paralegal, so the two could watch each other watching me. I arrived each morning as soon as the firm opened at 8:30, and stayed until they sent their paralegal home—usually about eight at night. Technically, I could copy documents. But I quickly learned that when I asked to photocopy a specific item, a Kidder lawyer seized it, pored over it, declared it protected under attorney-client privilege, and refused to return it. We didn't have time to protest or appeal. My efforts made their job easier. There were simply too many documents for anyone to rifle through; they waited for me to flag something as interesting or worthwhile, and then simply commandeered it. Soon I took to transcribing documents. I grew friendly with the young black woman paralegal that Kidder's attorneys had assigned the tedious task of sitting with me each day. Even though we both knew she wasn't supposed to, she sometimes made copies for me.

Every evening, after ten or twelve hours of hunting through paperwork, I spent half the night writing long memos to my lawyers about the pertinence of what I'd found.

My lawyers and I also did other basic research. I knew that Kidder had changed the accounting system it used to calculate the way profits and losses from Strip and recon transactions were recorded. Accountants changed systems all the time; a trader like me had nothing to do with those policies and procedures. Kidder made its changes retroactive, however, and that caused a large write-off of previously declared profits in my trading ledger. This sort of thing had happened before on Wall Street, I knew. But in those cases, the companies had announced losses due to accounting adjustments. No one had been blamed for fraud or asked to return bonuses or pay fines because of suddenly disallowed profits. I set out to find evidence of the losses. As it turned out, there were plenty of recent examples. In 1987, Bankers Trust wrote off $80 million from options positions that had been wrongly valued by the company's accountants. AIG Financial Products wrote off approximately $90 million on misvalued swap contracts that had been written by a former Columbia University professor of business. Metallgesellschaft employed trading strategies for commodities futures contracts devised by a former member of the President's Council of Economic Advisers and ended up taking a $1.3 billion loss because the holdings had been misvalued. Even after I was fired, in February 1995, Salomon Brothers announced a list of write-offs—$510 million of interest misclassified as trading profits, $194 million of unreconciled balances, $23 million for ledger problems, $35 million for nonexistent profits going back to 1988. In all these cases, the constantly changing world of financial accounting practices was responsible for the losses. Except at Kidder. In my case, GE refused to take responsibility for the changes and the resulting losses. For the first time in any investment firm, the past profits were suddenly called false and fraudulent, and I was the criminal who surreptitiously and deviously used the old accounting system to create them.

Shortly, my lawyers and I learned that the shareholders who had filed a class-action suit against Kidder had won discovery rights, too, and theirs were broader than ours. They had the right to look at documents covering all of Kidder's operations. Warner asked the shareholders' attorneys to request documents for us; they agreed and soon began sending them to our office. Everything was stamped with inventory numbers indicating it had come from Kidder. Now, however, we had even more paperwork to wade through. There would never be enough time to examine everything before the SEC or NASD hearings began. Both were slated for sometime that summer. I worked virtually alone. We had no money to pay anyone to help with document searches. Many evenings alone in my lawyers' offices, I felt overwhelmed with hopelessness. The task was Sisyphean. There was just no way to complete it all before the hearings began.

The SEC said it wanted to begin hearings in February, sparking a crisis in my lawyers' offices. None of my principal attorneys were free in February, not Gus Newman, Bob Schwartz or Ken Warner. For a time, it looked as it only John Cuti would be available. We pleaded for a delay, but Kidder objected to every appeal. It wanted to rush me to trial before we'd gone through all the documents. Kidder and GE knew I'd left Kidder empty-handed. I knew the evidence was in those boxes. We were now in a battle over the time needed to find it.

Then everything changed when the SEC learned that I'd been receiving documents from the lawyers representing GE shareholders. Even the commission's mediocre lawyers knew this was a wrench in their case. Now it was their turn to want a delay. The SEC lawyers had relied on Gary Lynch's team to provide them with documents. Suddenly the young lawyers at the SEC wanted to conduct their own discovery. For that they they needed more time. Miraculously, a postponement easily materialized. The trial was put off until May.

I still disparaged the SEC lawyers as incompetent and unmotivated. They had obtained a mere twenty-seven boxes of records from Kidder, while Kidder had confronted me with more than five hundred boxes of pertinent information. There was only one item that the SEC lawyers had that Kidder had not provided: telephone audiotapes recorded from my desk at Kidder. On a trading floor, where transactions valued in the billions of dollars occur each day, the taping of voice and telephone conversations is absolutely necessary to resolve disputes that arise from oral agreements. Once the SEC had those tapes, they were legally required to turn them over to us, too. Until then, Gary Lynch had provided us with only transcripts of these calls. Once we had the tapes, too, we discovered that the Kidder transcripts were laced with inaccuracies. Lynch's transcribers seemed to substitute different words and phrases wherever Kidder employees made damning statements. I supposed the Lynch team hoped we'd accept the transcripts and not bother to listen to the tapes. They underestimated my resolve.

Most of the calls were between me and traders, or between me and David Bernstein. I desperately wanted the tapes of my calls with Cerullo, but those had mysteriously disappeared. No tapes of me talking to Cerullo existed anywhere, Kidder said. On the other hand, there were plenty of recordings of Bernstein's calls—he'd been suspended and placed under GE suspicion. And there were endless spools of tape-recorded conversations among me, Joe Ossman, Jeff Unger and Elizabeth Cavanaugh.

ANOTHER CRITICAL PIECE of evidence disappeared, too. We learned that GE had dismantled the computer system that ran the Government Trader, the program written by Moishe Benatar, Andy Kim and Mel Mullin specifically to expand the settlement dates that we could input when conducting trades. The Government Trader made forward Strips and recons possible, and was the very program that booked the profit from those trades up front. GE had the computers and software in its possession, but now acknowledged that they'd all been destroyed. Yet everyone knew the software was a central, important factor in our case. Certainly, the program could have been preserved on at least one desktop computer so investigating authorities could see how it worked. I knew that if I'd had the program in my possession and had obliterated it, GE and Kidder would have screamed "destruction of evidence." As it was, GE was unapologetic about erasing every trace of the software that had created this whole debacle.

IN JANUARY 1996, the SEC filed its official charges, and out of the blue I heard from Mel Mullin for the first time in two years. Would I be interested in preparing a joint defense? his lawyers asked mine. Kidder had fired Mullin and confiscated $2.7 million of his deferred income. The SEC charged him with failure to supervise, and he sued Kidder to get his money back. The FBI and SEC had deposed him, and he'd insisted that he'd been unaware of my trading strategy, that he'd never looked closely at my trades, had never asked about them. I knew better. But unlike the others at Kidder, Mullin was now on the outside. Cerullo had been allowed to resign with a multimillion-dollar severance package. Mullin was fighting for his $2.7 million, and he was refusing to settle with the SEC. Though I was wary, I realized his interests dovetailed with mine—if I were innocent, then he was innocent of failure to supervise. Even so, I worried that Mullin had been sent to spy on me, to check out my defense and report back to Kidder and GE. At the very least, Mullin's lawyers were going to play both sides against the middle, and use that leverage to extricate their client.

I had to get what I could from Mullin in the meantime. What was he prepared to do to help me?

Mullin came to Newman's office on a cold day in early February. He looked thinner than I remembered. Settling into a chair, he broke the ice with complaints about the disparity in the way Kidder had treated him and Cerullo. He was still angry that he'd been summarily fired, not allowed to retire like Cerullo. He was unhappy about the way some of his longtime employees had been treated, too. Moishe Benatar was his friend, Mullin said, and he hadn't been able to find work since Kidder went out of business. Everywhere he went, Benatar was tainted by his connection to our desk.

One of my lawyers interrupted. "Let's begin with the facts, and see where the areas of agreement exist between Mr. Mullin and Joseph," he said. I wanted Mullin to acknowledge what had happened. There was plenty he could contribute if he told the truth. He knew about the intense oversight my desk had been subjected to as far back as 1992, when Cerullo blasted us for not performing well in my first weeks on the job. He was there for the scrutiny after we started earning money. He knew that Hugh Bush had plagued me with criticism of my trading practices. Bush had let it be known he was prepared to testify that he'd raised flags about my trading in 1992. But I'd heard that Mullin had been telling people that Bush had never questioned my trades; Bush and I simply clashed personally, he said.

I knew Mullin—when he lied, he grew ashamed and wouldn't look anyone in the eye. Now he was locked into his story that he'd known nothing about my trades. How could he change the statements that were in his depositions? What was he willing to do to help me?

Mullin got up and wrote an equation on an erasable board set up in the room: "c + P = Bond + Acc." It meant Strip coupon plus Strip principal equals a bond plus accrued interest. He proposed a hypothetical bond that paid $6 in interest each year, or $1 every two months. If we executed a recon with a settlement date two months forward, the bond would have a forward price for the coupons and principal of $101. Mullin claimed that the Kidder system failed to properly add the accrued interest of $1 to the calculation, resulting in the posting of $1 in unrealized profit. He claimed that this $1 profit should not have been posted at all. He went on to say that if this recon was done in isolation that the $1 in profit would dissipate to zero as the accrued interest on the bond accumulated each day.

I interjected. In isolation, the profit would dissipate not because of the posting of accrued interest, I said, but rather because the recon would establish a short position in the Strip coupons and principal that would eat away the $1 in profit. "This negative accretion is the only effect that a trader would see."

Mullin agreed. The lawyers sat silently, heads bobbing between Mullin and me. We agreed that in isolation, a Strip or recon done for a forward settlement would result in the exchange of cash equivalents at the Fed with no opportunity for profit or loss.

"But this would never happen," I explained, "because the Fed requires physical delivery of the Strip coupons and principal to make the exchange. At the moment I make the commitment to execute the exchange at a future date with the Fed, the system would show me short the Strips that comprised the bond." Kidder's computer system treated a recon as a sale of Strips and purchase of a bond. "I'm obligated to purchase these Strips to make delivery to the Fed. If I purchased the Strip coupons and principals at today's price of $100 and held them until the delivery date there could be no loss of the $1 profit, negative accretion would not, could not, be obtained from a covered short Strip position.

Mullin thought about this while the lawyers waited. He agreed, but added: "For large recons the purchase of the Strips would expose you to market risk. In short, a recon maintains a risk-neutral position, the short position in the Strips is balanced by the long position in the bond. When you cover the short position in the Strips through purchases in the open market, you're left with only an unbalanced long position in the bond."

The lawyers looked dazed, but Mullin and I didn't help them out. Kidder would never allow an unbalanced long position in the bond for extended periods of time, Mullin said; I agreed.

"But do you agree that if I bought a bond, that is, took a long position in a bond, and offset the purchase by the sale of a futures contract that I would have eliminated market risk? That I'd realize all profits if cost of carry were positive?"

Mullin said yes, he agreed with that scenario.

"Well, that's precisely how I reduced the market risk of the bond position generated by the forward recon, by selling a futures contract."

"But are you balancing the future purchase of the bond imbedded in the forward recon with a sale of a future commitment to deliver a bond?"

"Yes, precisely." I said.

"Well, I see no problem with that."

Warner perked up. "So this was a legitimate trading strategy?" He leaned toward Mullin.

"It's a reasonable trading strategy that any expert would attest to."

My relief was brief. He was still insisting that he hadn't known about my strategy. The Lynch report made no mention of this strategy, either, Mullin said.

"Well, this was the whole reason for my huge short position in futures contracts," I said with some exasperation. Mullin laughed.

"I remember it well. I had to liquidate that massive position."

Warner wanted Mullin to explain how Kidder's computer system made my trading strategy possible. Trades with corporate settlement dates—five days out—were certainly legitimate, Mullin assured him, even Strip and recon trades with the Fed. This corresponded with what we knew the SEC Enforcement division had decided about forward trades. After a two-year study of accounting procedures during which it consulted with GE's corporate audit staff and Kidder's lawyers, the Enforcement division reported that if a trader arranged for a reconstitution to take place tomorrow, it was called a "regular way trade." On page 2 of its report, the division said: "This type of delivery instruction resulted in a next day exchange of securities with the Fed and thus would not have distorted Kidder's books and records." A next-day settlement was the proper way to conduct such a trade, the SEC ruled. Yet we knew that the SEC and the Lynch report charged that any trades done more than one business day forward were fraudulent. Now Mullin was saying there was nothing fraudulent about trades done for corporate settlement. What was the technical difference between next-day, or "regular way" trades, five-day forward trades, and any other forward trades, Warner wanted to know.

"If it is legitimate up to the fifth day, what changes on the sixth day to make it illegitimate?"

Mullin stammered, but couldn't explain why there should be any difference. Even I didn't understand his convoluted evasions. Over the next hours and days, I gradually came to trust him, in no small part because he acknowledged that during his time as my manager, he felt I'd been underpaid. My bonus should have been higher, he said, because my profits were real. If he would make that statement, Kidder would be forced to argue that only my post-1993 trades were questionable. After all, Mullin had designed the computer system, and he'd taught me his trading techniques. Now he was vouchsafing the forward trading strategy, declaring that it had resulted in real profits.

IN JANUARY 1996, when the SEC officially announced its charges against me, the news splashed across newspapers and TV. My story had faded from the front pages. Few people knew where the NASD investigation stood. Fewer still realized that the FBI and U.S. Attorney's Office had dropped any consideration of criminal charges against me. Now the SEC revived interest in my fate. Little surprised me anymore. Considered objectively, the SEC decision made political sense. Wall Street needed to see the SEC weigh in on such a notorious case. GE and what was left of Kidder Peabody needed the official stamp of the SEC. The commission could hardly ignore such a high-profile case; its *raison d'être* was to pursue scandals like Kidder's losses. And, last but not least, the public needed to hear that the SEC was putting on a trial.

The SEC chose to prosecute me through its administrative law process. I'd read enough histories and analyses of the SEC to know that wasn't good. The SEC could have chosen a six-member panel or even a jury to consider my case. Instead, it decided to send me before a lone commission employee called an administrative law judge. Under procedure for such a hearing, the burden of innocence falls upon the accused more heavily than anywhere else in the American judicial system. Only when its case was weak, when it didn't believe it could win in front of a panel or jury, did the commission resort to a solitary judge. The SEC enjoyed a nearly 95 percent conviction rate. It was reluctant to jeopardize that.

Though the charges were not unexpected, the implication was devastating nevertheless. Gus Newman wouldn't represent me; he was committed to another trial. Bob Schwartz was also already committed to other trials. I was distraught. I'd spent nearly every day for over a year with Newman or someone in his office, and it had taken painstaking hours to bring them up to speed on my trades. Newman and Schwartz had participated in the meetings with the FBI and U.S. Attorney's Office; they knew my case backward and forward, and were comfortable with me and convinced of my innocence. Now, on the eve of my hearings, I was robbed of my most knowledgeable attorneys. I'd have to rely on my civil lawyer, Ken Warner. I'd hardly spoken to Warner. He knew very little detail of my case, barely more than what he'd read in the papers. I respected and liked him, but I sensed his assumption that it didn't matter whether I was innocent or guilty, only that we had a strategy to get me off. Yet I knew I was innocent and wanted a most forceful defense.

In addition, three weeks before the trial was set to begin, the SEC announced a major change in the way it viewed "regular way" trades. In a two-year study of GE and Kidder trades, the SEC had originally found that a reconstitution that was arranged to take place tomorrow was called a "regular way" trade and declared that "this type of delivery instruction resulted in a next day exchange of securities with the Fed and thus would not have distorted Kidder's books and records." The definition gave sanction to the concept of forward recons with the Fed. It declared that such forward trades left no distortion on Kidder's books. Now, suddenly, the SEC reversed itself. The SEC's new position was that "regular way" trades generated false profits, too. Two years after I was fired, months after deciding that forward trades were legitimate, and just weeks before my trial, the SEC changed its definition of acceptable accounting procedures.

I felt frantic, cut loose. There was nothing to do but start over. We began legal cram-sessions that lasted late into the night after I spent each day rummaging through boxes of discovery documents. All of us were edgy and tired. Warner was now my lead attorney, and he had to get up to speed. He was uneasy with the technical aspect of the trades. He wasn't comfortable we could win on the technical merits. He wanted to focus not on the trades but on evidence that showed that other people knew about them.

"You're not accused of losing money. There's no law against losing money. You're accused of fraud, that all these managers didn't know what you were doing. We have to show that they did know. Let's concentrate our energies there."

I opposed this approach so vehemently that I became emotional. Warner and I quarreled heatedly, sometimes at the top of our lungs. I was desperate to argue that I wouldn't have lost a cent if Cerullo had not forced me to liquidate my inventory. I wanted the case debated on the numbers, on the technical merits. I didn't want to get up in front of a roomful of Wall Street lawyers and government bureaucrats and rest my fate on their sense of camaraderie with me. I couldn't win an argument that relied on them looking at me and seeing a person they liked. I'm black. Inherently, I had less credibility. I doubted the ability of the judge to listen to me, then listen to Cerullo, Bernstein and the others, and pick me over them. Regardless of what I said. I'd be better off showing that no money would have been lost had Cerullo and Bernstein simply left me alone. That was math. That was hard science. It was cold, hard numbers, far more compelling than a hope that the judge would believe me over them.

The SEC judge was a new appointee, a middle-aged white woman named Carol Fox-Foelak. She'd just taken her job at the SEC, after years as an administrative law judge at the Social Security Administration. I imagined what her experience and outlook must be. At Social Security, she likely saw only minorities who lived at the low end of the economic and education scale, and was most familiar feeling somehow separate and different from them. I wanted to give her the opportunity to say: "I'm not saying I believe Joseph Jett, it's just that the numbers show he would not have lost the money, so therefore, he's innocent."

But that would require her to understand the trades. As far as we knew, she had no business, financial or investment background whatever. Mine was to be her very first case since coming over from Social Security. For that reason, Warner insisted that the test of my integrity and innocence would not be made with long arguments about the veracity of my trading scheme. He reminded me that I'd spent thousands of hours trying to explain basic Wall Street trading and mathematical principles to inexperienced lawyers and investigators. The burden of proof was not in teaching judges, lawyers and investigators to master the intricacies of trading. Warner believed it didn't matter whether my strategies were plausible or profitable, or whether they behaved the way the computer predicted. My case boiled down to two simple elements: Were my trades legal, and did Kidder management know about them?

I almost cried in frustration. If I couldn't make him understand, what chance did I have with the judge?

Finally, Warner said, "Let's just see how it goes."

THE SEC TRIAL

T HE ENTRANCE TO Carol Fox-Foelak's courtroom was through a side door. The judge's L-shaped bench sat to its left, facing into the room. Tables for lawyers faced the bench, and between them on the far wall stood six or eight chairs that would have served the jury had there been one. When I walked into the room just before one o'clock in the afternoon of May 20, 1996, and sat at my table, I guessed we faced east. We weren't far from New York City Hall. The SEC team occupied a big table nearest the judge's bench, and our table sat behind theirs. Behind us, three or four paralegals had chairs, and spectator seats filled the rest of the room.

Reporters and a sketch artist sat in the jury chairs. A sketch of me sitting at our defense table appeared on CNN that night, and Warner later got the artist to give it to him. It hangs on his office wall, a drawing of him perpetually orating and me forever sitting behind him. The television cameras waited for me as I arrived, and I stopped to say that I had no hope of a fair hearing in this one-judge kangaroo court. My only hope was that this sham trial wouldn't take place behind closed doors. I knew we had found devastating evidence among the Kidder tapes, spreadsheets, letters and reports. The media had to take notice. The television cameras and their bright lights were a welcome sight for once. But George Sard, Warner's public relations specialist, was crestfallen. He saw only who wasn't there. No one had come from *The Wall Street Journal*. The paper had tormented me when my story first broke, but now, apparently, they weren't interested. And without their interest, I was cut off from one important avenue of justice.

I sat at the defense table, despondent. Guilty as charged, and the hearing hadn't even started. Was GE behind this? Did Jack Welch and his conglomerate exert so much power that they could silence the press? Sard went to the telephone; when he came back, he offered lame explanations. *The Wall Street Journal* said it hadn't been aware of the trial schedule, but they'd try to send someone. This was going to be a public relations battle more than anything else. I couldn't prove my suspicions, but it seemed impossible for *The Wall Street Journal* to ignore my trial without malice aforethought. Had Jack Welch picked up the phone to the *Journal's* executive editor, or had a lazy reporter simply told his editor my trial wasn't important? The *Journal* had wielded its powerful pen against me for months, it had written about me as it had about Michael Milken. Ignoring me now was tantamount to ignoring the Milken trial. I just couldn't believe it was happenstance.

CNBC, the major business network that broke my story in April 1994, with its early morning interview of Dennis Dammerman, sent no one, either. GE owned CNBC. CourtTV, which had televised virtually every sexual harassment case on Wall Street in recent years, sent no one. GE owned CourtTV. Was I facing a planned news blackout?

"OKAY," JUDGE FOX-FOELAK said; "this is a hearing in the matter of Orlando Joseph Jett and Melvin Mullin, administrative proceeding number 3-8919. And, Mr. Mullin, I have been informed, has reached a settlement with the commission, so this hearing will involve Mr. Jett only."

She looked up at the four SEC lawyers and my four attorneys. We knew already that Mel Mullin had finally cut his deal with Kidder and the SEC, just the day before. His lawyers had exploited the leverage he gained against Kidder by preparing a joint defense with me. GE didn't want him taking the stand on my behalf. He'd gotten back his $2.7 million in deferred income, and worked out a deal with the SEC on the charges of failing to supervise me. Mullin was off the hook. He paid a $25,000 fine and accepted a three-month suspension from trading. A final irony came from the fact that when we'd asked for a delay in the SEC trial, Mullin had objected. The SEC had sided with Mullin and denied our request. Now he wasn't even here. He still had to testify when called. But I had no idea what he had promised Kidder he would say.

The SEC lead attorney, Jonathan Gottlieb, got up. Gottlieb was a very young lawyer with watery blue eyes and an uncertain demeanor. As he began his opening statement, the SEC's more senior attorney, a woman named Petra Tasheff, sat silently with her hands folded in her lap.

"Good afternoon, Your Honor," Gottlieb began. "This case is about using fraud to, first, survive and then dominate the world at Kidder Peabody. As we proceed in this case, we will see how the Respondent, Orlando Joseph Jett, devised and utilized a false profit scheme during his employment at Kidder, during the period between July 1991 and April 1994.

"The evidence will show that Mr. Jett implemented this false profit scheme in a measured, incremental progression which, in combination with the force of his personality, and loose supervision, allowed him to perpetuate the scheme for more than two years. Mr. Jett's fraud created the appearance of profits which were not real. False profits which concealed real trading losses and allowed the Respondent to, first, keep his job, then earn promotions, awards and procure millions of dollars in personal compensation; that was, until Kidder unscrambled Jett's trading, and concluded that the profits were not real. As a result of Respondent Jett's fraud, Kidder's parent, the General Electric Company, had to take a $210 million charge against its 1994 first-quarter earnings.

"The evidence will show that Mr. Jett's explanations do not make sense, are internally inconsistent and ignore several bond trading tenets, which had to be known by an individual with Mr. Jett's education and background."

When Gottlieb finished, Warner asked for a short break. On the table in front of Warner lay the Red Book, my trading desk leatherbound ledger. He left it there when he stood to speak after the recess.

"Your Honor, Joseph Jett committed no fraud and he did nothing wrong, absolutely nothing. He acted openly, honestly and innocently. He didn't win any popularity contests at Kidder Peabody. That is for sure, and that is a big reason why he is here. But Mr. Jett did not conceal anything from anybody. He didn't deceive or defraud anyone.

"And that is what I would like to talk to Your Honor about now. Why the facts show openness and honesty on Mr. Jett's part, not fraud," Warner continued. "Now, this case involves an accusation of fraud, Your Honor, but it lacks the critical elements of fraud—concealment and control. Mr. Jett concealed nothing. Every trade he entered, every one was listed in Kidder's records, which produced multiple reports explicitly recording forward settling trades. No trade tickets were destroyed. No transaction entries were changed, and no trades were diverted to hidden accounts."

He turned toward the defense table.

"Mr. Jett also kept a separate book, in addition to all the computer entries, listing all of the trades that are now being challenged as false and deceptive, Strips and recons settling more than one day forward. This is the book right here, Your Honor." Warner paused. "And if I may hand it up, I just wanted to make a reference to a page or two? May I do that? As you can see, Your Honor, this so-called Red Book got its name from its bright, red cover, and it was used exclusively for listing Strips and recons, nothing else but that. Now, I ask Your Honor, would a trader, intent on fraud and concealment, keep a book like this the way he did, right out in the open, listing everything? I say never.

"And how about the entries in the book? Wouldn't you expect a trader, intent on fraud, to maintain strict control over the book, if he kept it at all, writing in it just himself? But is that what Mr. Jett did? Not only is that not what he did, he did the opposite. Most of the entries in this book were put in by somebody else. For example, if Your Honor takes the 1993 book, going to March 4, which is page 63, you can see, right at the top of March 4, the word 'recon,' and that is Mr. Jett's somewhat distinctive handwriting compared to the other handwriting that is in the book.

"But the main point is that this book, this bright, red, big-as-life book, which sat there on Mr. Jett's desk, contained all the information that he supposedly was concealing."

THE SEC'S FIRST witness was supposed to be Charles Fiumefreddo, followed in rapid succession by David Bernstein, Elizabeth Cavanaugh, Jeff Unger, Joe Ossman and Moishe Benatar. Plainly, the commission wanted to get its toughest witnesses on the stand quickly, to exploit the short time that we'd had to get ready. I'd spent two nights sleeping on the couch in Warner's office so we could prepare round-the-clock for Fiumefreddo's testimony.

Then the "midnight miracle" destroyed all of the SEC's best-laid plans. And, I believed, most of its case against me.

As my SEC hearing opened, a federal judge in another courtroom ruled that the shareholders who had sued GE could not be denied the notes, depositions and documents underlying the Gary Lynch report. Kidder and GE had fought for two years to suppress those notes, arguing that the attorney-client privilege protected Lynch's research and investigation documents. Ultimately, the federal judge decided that the Lynch report was not a legal document, but a public relations chronicle. Therefore, no attorney-client privilege applied. The shareholders were entitled to see what Lynch had used in his investigation. That meant the same documents could be turned over to me and my lawyers.

Both sides now knew that new material was about to come raining down on us. The SEC grew suddenly cautious and reserved about its witness schedule; it wanted to pull back on its plan for full-speed-ahead testimony from Fiumefreddo, Bernstein, Cavanaugh, Unger and Ossman. None of us had copies of the notes yet. As we waited for them the tension was like that between two ticket holders vying for a million-dollar lottery. Someone might win big, but someone else was going to find himself a loser. I could barely sit still and calm through the first days of the hearing, so eager was I to bolt the courtroom and run to my lawyers' offices to read the Lynch notes. I knew with absolute certainty that Lynch's team had covered up the truth. The notes would prove it.

The SEC shuffled its witness list, opting for more predictable testimony on the day of the hearing. Instead of Fiumefreddo, it called its trading analyst and examiner. When the woman took the stand, I was surprised to see it wasn't the young Asian who had sat in on my sessions with the Justice Department. Instead, Michele Rebhandl was sworn in. I'd seen her at one of the U.S. Attorney sessions. She had been assigned to analyze my trades and determine whether or not they generated real profits. Rebhandl was questioned by a small, elderly SEC attorney named Ellen Hersch. Hersch was not one of the SEC's heavy hitters, so throughout the trial she handled peripheral witnesses. Now, because of the juggling of Fiumefreddo's testimony, Rebhandl and Hersch were thrust, unprepared, into the spotlight.

"Because the volume of transactions that occurred were so large, we had to do a sampling of transactions to review, because we couldn't look at everything," Rebhandl explained. She'd decided to focus on the forward reconstitutions in the G-1, or Government desk, ledger, she said. That was another name for the Red Book.

"Why did you pick this particular type of transaction?" Hersch asked.

"We believed that the forward reconstitutions were the ones which generated the false profits."

I looked at Warner. Hersch accused me of false trades, but what she'd said was that she'd found the forward recons in the Red Book, the G-1 ledger. Where anyone could see them, right? For several hours, Hersch led her through an arcane accounting of how the trades broke down. Rebhandl probably hadn't ever testified before, and she quickly grew confused, stumbling over an explanation of how she decided the profits were false. It wasn't her idea, she insisted, but rather the direction of her supervisors. They'd told her to examine the forward recons in my book because they generated false profits, and she'd simply accepted that as fact. She'd counted any forward recon booked to settle for a day or more in the future. Not surprisingly for a government clerk, it took her a year and half to assemble and analyze twenty-two trades.

The mundane testimony left my head heavy. The room was hot. The lawyers frequently suspended their questioning to argue with each other and the judge. When they resumed, most of the questions were stultifyingly dull, especially to me, because they covered ground that was well known. Rebhandl talked about the mechanics of how a transaction was recorded on the trading ticket and then entered into the Daily Transaction Journal, the Position and Profit Report No. 2 (PPR-2) and the Fixed Income Daily report. What had she found in these reports, where did the profit show, how were the trades entered? The questions droned on. My head felt heavy with sleep. Rebhandl wasn't doing much better. In court with us that day was a fraud investigator named Ernie Ten Eyck, whom we'd hired to testify as an expert witness. He spent much of the morning writing quick notes to Warner about Rebhandl's testimony. Only he seemed to enjoy her testimony.

On cross-examination, Warner walked up to Rebhandl with several reports. He wanted her to show where she'd found false profits. She couldn't pinpoint any in the mass of papers he offered her.

"So we've looked at the Daily Transaction Journal. It's not there. Let's look at the PPR-2. Can you show me where it is on the PPR-2?"

Rebhandl shuffled papers. Warner leaned in.

"Was I correct in understanding your testimony before to be that you were showing the effect of a forward settling recon on the numbers?"

"We were showing that it did affect the numbers."

Warner tried again.

"I'm asking you to show Judge Fox-Foelak where the profit is that affected this report, coming from the forward settling recon. Can you identify the profit on this forward settling recon? And you said no with respect to the Daily Transaction Journal. Then please show it to us on the daily PPR-2."

Rebhandl paged through the reports. Warner pointed to bond index numbers, and they confused each other over which part of the bond they were discussing.

"So my question is, can you tell us, on this page, can you show us the profit impact from this forward settling recon?"

The young woman looked at him. "No."

Exasperated, the SEC lawyer objected. Warner was badgering Rebhandl, asking the same question four times. But she couldn't point to the false profits on any of the reports she said she'd used to analyze my trades. As the lawyers argued back and forth, I wondered what had become of the Asian analyst. Why wasn't she testifying against me? She had attended all the sessions and had demonstrated technical knowledge far beyond confused Rebhandl. I turned in my chair and saw her sitting in the audience. Our eyes met and she rolled her eyes in mock disbelief, then smiled. Had she refused to testify against me?

Finally, Warner turned back to the witness.

"Well, is there any of these paths to the focus report that will enable you to tell Judge Fox-Foelak whether this forward settling recon added nothing, added something plus, added something minus? Is there any number that you can identify here as being connected specifically with that transaction?"

"Not specific numbers, no."

"Okay. So would you agree with me, Ms. Rebhandl, that test trade number one does not trace and identify the specific profit or loss impact on the profit and loss in the Fixed Income Daily?"

"I can't give you a specific number of the impact on the P&L, no."

"Now, I could go through all twenty-two trades and ask you these same questions, but would your answers be the same?"

"Yes," Rebhandl said. "Yes. The methodology was the same."

She also admitted that figures in twenty-one of the twenty-two trades did not match, and that Kidder failed to provide more data when she asked for them.

I felt embarrassed for Rebhandl. She was just a government clerk. She admitted it had taken her a year and a half to analyze twenty-two trades. Now she couldn't pick out any fraudulent transactions, she couldn't identify where the money had came from. Warner hammered at her: "Do you think this firm was due for some investigation? Isn't the SEC supposed to know about these things? Aren't you supposed to investigate these things?"

BOXES OF NOTES from Gary Lynch's investigation arrived at Warner's law firm in midafternoon. We raced back to the office, almost giddy with anticipation, and carried the boxes into our "war" room. For the rest of the day, I rarely left the conference table. We dug through the boxes, drunk on adrenaline, reading and gasping and exclaiming at the accounts given Lynch and his people by Charles Fiumefreddo, David Bernstein, Joe Ossman, Jeff Unger, Elizabeth Cavanaugh, Linda Mead. They were all there. Lynch had questioned and deposed all of them, some more than once. Bernstein had six sessions with Lynch's people. Hundreds of pages of handwritten scrawl, much of it in the writing of a variety of lawyers, filled the boxes. I couldn't read them fast enough. When I picked up one page, my eyes would fall on another and I'd be torn over which one to read first. My mind picked out names like beacons—Bernstein, Cavanaugh, Ossman. My eyes jumped to dates, noting when the interviews and depositions had taken place: April 1993, May 1993. More than two years before, most of them.

As I read, my mood swung wildly. Anger vied with disappointment. I didn't think I had any illusions left to shatter, but I felt a searing disillusionment. All the people I'd respected, the people I'd defended as "true blue," straightforward, no-nonsense—every last one of them had betrayed me and themselves. It was all there in the handwritten Lynch notes.

Thunderstruck, I dropped the notes, and pawed through the SEC depositions from Fiumefreddo, Cavanaugh and the others. Then I stopped. We had to organize our research somehow. Warner, John Cuti, another lawyer named Lew Fischbein and myself, each grabbed a different witness's deposition. Depositions are legal testimony, and as we read them, we realized that Joey-o, Cavanaugh and the others had each denied any knowledge of my forward trades or their profit impact. That was in direct contradiction to what they'd told the Lynch investigators. We shouted and high-fived: if any of them testified now, we could prove their depositions were perjury by confronting them with the Gary Lynch notes. I almost wanted to jump with joy at the thought of destroying GE's case with the very evidence it had sought to hide. It was over! It was over!

A press conference seemed like a great idea. But George Sard felt that only newspapers could devote the space to a Lynch cover-up. Television wasn't an option, since forty-second sound bites on network news wouldn't convey the impact of what we'd found. But Sard thought perhaps *60 Minutes* or another news magazine show might be interested. He left to work the phones.

I went back to the scrawled Lynch notes, picking up a piece of paper with comments about an April 1993 interview with Elizabeth Cavanaugh. Suddenly I could almost feel the weight of sadness in the paper in my hand. In the first days after my firing, as Cavanaugh was left working on the trading floor alone and Ossman and Unger were sent to play cards in a back room with Bernstein, my traders had tried to tell the truth. In the weeks that I waited and hoped, convinced absolutely that once Cavanaugh and Joey-o started talking about our daily routines it would become clear that everyone in Fixed Income knew about my trading strategy, they'd been called one by one into an office to confront Gary Lynch. The scrawled notes proved that initially, at least, they each had told of the forward re-constitutions, the front-end recording of unrealized profits, the phantom trades, the off-balance-sheet financing scheme. Evidently those were not the answers that Lynch and his team wanted to hear. Slowly, over the next days and weeks, the accounts in the notes changed. Joey-o, Cavanaugh and Unger modified their stories. I could only imagine the pressure on them—those were the days during which Unger whimpered endlessly about getting out of this mess, and the time that Cavanaugh and Linda Mead were accused of having sex with me. So they all caved.

The sky through Warner's windows was black. It was well past midnight. I looked at the boxes around me, thinking I'd always remember this moment as the "midnight miracle." I heard Cuti and Fischbein wondering aloud if Fiumefreddo would dare show his face on the witness stand. The SEC lawyers must be looking over these notes about now, too. Surely they'd be just as shocked to discover that Gary Lynch, their venerable ex-head of Enforcement, had suppressed evidence. My lawyers started shuffling off to find places to sleep. I held on to the Cavanaugh notes. I looked at the papers again. April 18, 1993, the day of my dismissal, Lynch wrote down what Cavanaugh told him:

Cavanaugh was aware that Jett did large forward trades and at one time thought it was based on a decision by Jett and Bernstein to have Jett's large positions off the books. By the end of the first quarter of 1994 she had heard they were taking off positions by putting on Strips and recons for forward settlement dates. Cavanaugh didn't know how that would be done and would not know how to do it. However, that is what she had heard. She also heard that there was a similar effort by Jett and Bernstein in December.

Cavanaugh asserted that as far as she is aware forward Strip and recon trading has been done since she arrived at Kidder. She does not know how to do such trading and has never participated in it but she understands that it has been done. She also recalls forward Strip trading had been done at Smith Barney when she was there. Cavanaugh also recalls that First Boston did forward trading with the Fed but it was probably for settlement in 2 or 5 days.

I looked at the next pages, dated three weeks later, May 9, 1994. Lynch interviewed Cavanaugh again, asking her the same questions.

Cavanaugh was adamant she was not aware that Jett was doing forward transactions although she was aware that Bernstein and Jett were having conversation about getting Jett's position down. She had heard from Joe that he was asked to reduce his position by quarter end, but had no idea how that was to be accomplished.

If I remembered correctly, it was right after that that Cavanaugh had called to say, "Nigger, I hope you go to jail."

But Cavanaugh had tried to tell the truth, at least on April 18. Her words that day exonerated me, not only because she seconded my explanation that Bernstein oversaw the forward Strips and reconstitutions, but she also made it clear that every Strips desk on Wall Street did similar trades. But in the ensuing days, Lynch robbed Cavanaugh of her self-worth, her pride, her ability to stand on her own—he accused Cavanaugh of being my lover and helped her be ostracized by everyone at Kidder.

The Cavanaugh notes left me profoundly sad for my onetime friend. It was late, I was tired, and the euphoria of the "midnight miracle" was waning. To revive myself, I picked up the Lynch notes taken during the questioning of J. J. McKoan. If I ever had any doubt that he was the one who'd reported to Cerullo every time I passed a white woman in the hall at Kidder, the proof was now in my hands. I read through the most bizarre account of office politics I'd ever seen. It was dated May 20, 1993.

Rumors About Mead: The first rumor McKoan heard was about Linda Mead being involved with a man named Mustafa Chike-Obi, a trader who was formerly head of the Mortgage Collateral area, Chike-Obi was fired a few years ago due to a sexual harassment charge. There were rumors of Mead and Chike-Obi having had a personal relationship when they worked together at Goldman. However, Mead was hired as a trainee at Kidder, so she was not in a position to benefit from any favors from Chike-Obi.

Jett Gets His Own Sales Team: Mead eventually became a salesperson. When Jett started his zero activity, he wanted a specialized government sales force. A short list of salespeople for Strips (and also some coupons) was put together. Mead was put on the list because she was seen as intelligent, aggressive and in need of the client base. Bruce Cook was also on the short list and was the senior point person. In addition, Garrett McDaniel, Harry Haigood and Andrew Lazar were also on the list. All five of these salespeople reported to

Michael Ricciardi, McKoan's senior Eastern sales manager at the time. In order to develop a client base for these salespeople, McKoan and Ricciardi focused on the largest STRIP clients and took them away from other salespeople at Kidder. Other salespeople could trade in Strips if they had an account that wanted to do so, but salespeople on Jett's short list did most of the Strips trading. The group was set up in the first quarter of 1993, or the end of 1992, and soon started doing a lot of business.

Sales Credits: The normal sales credit on a Strips trade is 1/32. So for every $1 million in bonds, the sales credit is $312.50. Kidder's payout to the salesperson is 10% of the sales credit. Jett actually had a policy that for large or new trades, he would pay four times the sales credit, or 4/32. A trader has such discretion to pay more or less than the sales credit. The mechanics are that the salesperson writes up a sales ticket. The trader clocks it and puts on a sales credit. At the end of the month, the system pays out 10% of the sales credit. Three or four of the salespeople in Jett's group became significant producers.

Initial Rumors About Jett and Mead: There were rumors about Jett and Mead being involved in a personal relationship. Mead became successful over a relatively short period of time, so it was difficult to tell if people were just being jealous. If the rumors were true, however, it would have presented a conflict of interest. McKoan is not sure if there is any firm policy against having a personal relationship when one person is in a position to influence the compensation of another, but it is at least troubling. McKoan and Brian Finkelstein brought the rumors to the attention of Ed Cerullo. Jett denied everything. So McKoan and Ricciardi decided to keep an eye on things. In order to do so, they monitored the trades for size, to see whether they were suitable for the client. However, it was difficult to tell whether Jett was being excessive, because of his discretion over the sales credit. Ricciardi, McKoan's East Coast sales manager, was the direct supervisor. If Ricciardi or McKoan had a suspicion, they would have to ask Jett to explain the sales credit. They did have those dialogues with Jett, and he would deny it. On several occasions, Cerullo explained to Jett that it looked bad. Ricciardi left about three weeks ago for Citibank, and his position is as yet unfilled.

Juicing Rumors: After the Jett affair became known, Jack Pascal, a senior salesperson in a Japanese group, came to McKoan and said that he and others thought that McKoan should investigate whether Jett and Mead were having an affair, and whether he was juicing Mead's credit. Pascal did not tell McKoan who reported rumors to him. No examples were provided; it was just hearsay. In addition, some salespeople talked to Brian Finkelstein. Again, it is difficult to determine the truth of the allegations, because of people's envy, but McKoan has not heard any complaining about any of the other salespeople in Strips (none of the other salespeople were women). The first time McKoan heard of the juicing rumors was after Jett left, perhaps in the middle of April. Mead's profits are very large, but the profits are large for all of the members of Jett's sales force. Bruce Cook is the largest producer, and Mead is the second largest. For *example, the total number of gross sales credits that the five salespeople have earned from year to date, from which they will receive one-tenth, is the following: $5.8 million to Cook, $3.79 million to Mead, $2.97 million to Haigood, $2.7 million to Lazar, and $2.0 million to McDaniel. These credits include all kinds of governments, but at least 80% of these salespeople's business was Strips. Mead is the tenth biggest producer domestically. To determine if this resulted from any unusual favoritism, however, McKoan needs to go through each trade. These numbers have now dropped off dramatically, but the desk changed a lot prior to Jett's departure, because a lot of other traders left. In addition, investors are not very active when rates rise. Aetna was Mead's largest account. Lazar covered Aetna for coupons, while Mead covered Aetna for Strips. However, most of Aetna's activity was in Strips. McKoan has not heard that Jett favored Aetna at the expense, for instance, of Met Life, but McKoan has not looked in detail at whether Jett was giving preferential treatment to Aetna as opposed to other customers. In any event, it is difficult to determine the truth of the allegations because Jett could always say that he particularly needed those bonds at those times.*

Mead has not been confronted because Toni LaBelle told McKoan not to confront her. McKoan ordered all of Mead's trades examined going back to June. On these reports, "10M" is the New York office, and 1137111 is Mead's RR number. The reports go by day.

Jett's P&L: Jett's P&L is affected by the sales credit. Traders do get charged for the sales credits they assign, because 10% of the sales credit gets taken out of the trader's P&L. Cerullo likes to see about .8 or .6 in gross sales credit to P&L. However, Jett was generating so much profit, he could afford to pay a lot of sales credits. In addition, since Jett's P&L is charged for the net amount of the sales credit, Jett could have juiced Mead's numbers at a substantial benefit to her, but not at a substantial loss to him, because double sales credit to her is only 10% of the total amount. In other words, a $100,000 charge to Jett, from Mead making 1/10 of 1/32, is a lot to Mead, but not a lot to Jett. In addition, it has even less of an effect on Jett, because his P&L is not directly tied to his compensation.

Other Rumors About Jett and Cavanaugh: McKoan has also heard a rumor about Jett and Elizabeth Cavanaugh. One of the traders, Nick Corcoran, who hated Jett from day one, told Brian Finkelstein that he saw them kissing in a bar. McKoan heard of this in perhaps April. There was also an allegation that Jett had a one evening fling with Jean Joyce, one of McKoan's salespeople from London when she was in New York in the beginning of 1992. Joyce has now left the firm. She only indirectly did business with Jett, because she reported to a trader who reported to Jett.

McKoan and Jett: McKoan probably dealt with Jett more than anyone else because they had a lot of run-ins on trading/sales issues. There were often situations that McKoan needed to bring to Jett's attention, including how he treated people and verbally abused them. McKoan did not see Jett's P&L, al-

though he could have if he had wanted to. McKoan was not aware that Jett was doing forward transactions with the Fed.

I stared at the papers in my hands. Three managing directors and one executive managing director who for over two years had professed to know nothing about my trading with $30 billion of GE's assets had found time to closely monitor my relationships with white women. Three executives who had claimed abject ignorance of my trading strategy still found time and interest for sick, pernicious attention to my relationships.

Even if I'd had a relationship with any of the women in question, would it have warranted persecution of them and me from our superiors? I glanced through the notes again. McKoan even said he didn't know Kidder policy toward office romance. He had to know that Mel Mullin had married an employee, promoted her and governed her bonus. He had to have heard that there were seven married couples on the trading floor, three of which included husbands who determined their wives' bonuses. He certainly knew that dating was rampant on the trading floor. But he didn't care about any of those couples, because they were all the same race. His objections had nothing to do with business conflict of interest, or trading improprieties. It had everything to do with race.

I HANDED THE McKoan notes to Warner, and he passed me Linda Mead's. I wasn't sure I could read any more about the Lynch sex inquisition. The interviews with Mead started on June 10, 1994. Her comments made it clear that she was deeply affected by the rumors and gossip about a relationship between us. They had ruined our friendship, and clearly Mead felt they'd ruined her career.

Mead graduated from Dickinson College in 1986, worked for Goldman Sachs. In the beginning of 1993, management at Kidder decided to focus more on government issues, an area in which Joe Jett worked. Since she started work at Kidder, Mead had worked with Jett on a small STRIP account for a dealer. Generally, traders do not like dealer accounts, especially small ones, that go through salespersons since the trade could have been done directly on the trading computer screens. Nonetheless, she believed that Jett thought she was diligent. She got involved in Strips as a way of getting more business. Outside of a professional setting, Mead claimed to have had very little social interaction with Jett. At work, she and Jett communicated a lot through the "squawk box," although she could not see Jett too well from where she sat. Socially, Mead does not spend her free time with Kidder colleagues and was not as close to them as she had been to her former co-workers at Goldman Sachs. On the evening of Kidder's Christmas party in 1991, many people went out afterwards to a bar. Mead said she was surprised to see Jett at the bar, but she stressed that she had not gone there with Jett, and she did not speak to him. The only other occasion where Mead and Jett saw each other socially occurred on Jett's last weekend at Kidder. On Friday afternoon April 15, Elizabeth Cavanaugh, another Strips trader, invited Mead to see her new Connecticut home on Saturday evening. Although Mead, who is originally from Connecticut and whose parents still live there, had no plans to be in Connecticut that weekend, she accepted the invitation. Cavanaugh said Jett would be there as well, but Mead claims she definitely did not want to be set up with Jett on a blind date, and she made that clear to Cavanaugh. Jett and Mead arranged to drive up from Manhattan together in a car Jett rented for the trip. Mead reports that Jett claimed to have spent the day doing laundry. During the drive, Mead talked about a race she had run that morning. At one point while watching a movie Jett had placed his hand on her knee, but that was all that had ever happened between them. Mead also asked Jett about rumors in the market about an investigation by the Fed into Jett's activities. Mead had heard about these rumors from several people during the week. Jett gave her a "vague answer" that essentially dismissed the rumors and dispelled Mead's concerns. At the previous weekly meeting, held on Tuesday or Wednesday at 4:30 P.M. or 5:00 P.M., Jett acknowledged the rumors and told all of the government salespersons and traders that he was surprised people wasted their time talking about this sort of stuff.

The Lynch notes also made it clear that Charles Fiumefreddo held a unique vision of his participation in the May 1993 review of my trades. He claimed to Lynch at first that he had not participated in the investigation. The notes showed that Dave Bernstein said that he had. Lynch's people confronted Bernstein and Fiumefreddo with a copy of my electronic diary, and in particular an entry I'd made complaining that Fiumefreddo couldn't understand my explanations. Suddenly both modified their recollections. First, the notes showed, they said they had questioned the legitimacy of profits. Bernstein insisted that Fiumefreddo had approached him claiming that all my profits were false; then they told of investigating and finding not false profits but accelerated profits. Confronted with Bernstein's testimony, Fiumefreddo then admitted he had participated in the audit, but now claimed only to examine the balance-sheet implications. He'd participated only because he was trying to get some software written. Lynch's notes recorded that Fiumefreddo said that he had no interest in my desk's profit and loss. Gary Lynch was incredulous—wasn't Fiumefreddo Kidder's chief profit and loss accountant? "Yeah, but that doesn't mean I had any interest in Joe Jett's profits."

Finally, Fiumefreddo insisted that he'd raised questions about my forward settling trades in June 1993, and warned of a possible $56 million write-off. From what I read in the notes, I believed Lynch next virtually accused Fiumefreddo of lying. I hoped we could ask him. Charles Fiumefreddo was scheduled to take the stand on behalf of the SEC the next morning.

I looked at my watch. It was almost five A.M. I kept reading. Sometime later, a hand shook me awake; it was nearly eight. I dashed to my apartment to change into a fresh suit and tie. The morning's *New York Post* carried a headline about Michele Rebhandl's failure to point to any profit impact from her analysis of my forward recons. It was the first headline that made me smile: BOMBSHELL. Suddenly we seemed to be winning the public relations war. *Good Morning America* asked me to appear on its broadcast. CNN invited me on the air. *USA Today* wrote a Moneyline cover story. I was thrilled. Network television meant the general public had heard about my case.

I wanted all this newfound press attention to focus on the impact of the Lynch notes. Sard had been unable to interest any of the major newspapers or *60 Minutes* in the story. Anna Cordasco ushered me from reporter to reporter for interviews, and I tried to explain that we had evidence from the Lynch notes proving that GE was the true fraud in this case. Charles Fiumefreddo, the star SEC witness who was scheduled to take the stand, was about to perjure himself, I said. After my last interview, with the British newspaper *The Guardian*, I walked into the courtroom to find the entire SEC staff missing. They'd asked Judge Fox-Foelak for a ten-minute delay to the proceedings. The delay stretched to a half hour. Finally, one of the SEC examiners in the gallery told us that the SEC attorneys were huddled upstairs with Fiumefreddo, reviewing his testimony.

"They may not put him on the stand," John Cuti warned.

"They have to put him on the stand," I snarled. The thirty-minute delay stretched into two hours. At 11:00, Cordasco rushed in. "Ladies and gentlemen, Charlie Fiumefreddo has left the building!"

Warner and Cuti high-fived each other, and our paralegals jumped up and down with joy. The SEC attorneys shuffled back into the courtroom. They looked sour and tense. The SEC, they announced, would not be calling Charles Fiumefreddo, Elizabeth Cavanaugh, Jeff Unger, Joe Ossman, Kevin McLaughlin or Hugh Bush to the witness stand after all. All of those witnesses were officially removed from the SEC's roster. As my lawyers celebrated, I was livid. I felt cheated. The very people who were closest to my trading strategy and most knowledgeable about events on the Strips desk would now never testify. We'd never be able to ask them about their contradictory statements and lies. We wouldn't have the chance to present those facts to the judge and into the record. The SEC had made its problem disappear just like Cerullo had made me disappear when I proved a threat to him. "Missing witnesses," I was told they are called in the legal profession—witnesses who are promised but who are never delivered. Was I supposed to be satisfied with that? Warner assured me that the judge would draw an adverse inference in my favor from the failure of these SEC witnesses to take the stand.

However, an adverse inference didn't do my reputation much good, or help my public relations battle. The SEC's withdrawal of witnesses simply confused the reporters in the courtroom. They needed to hear about Lynch's cover-up from my former colleagues. I wanted Warner to call Fiumefreddo and the others. If the SEC wouldn't put them on the stand, then we would. The idea left Warner aghast. Every single one of these people had refused to answer our repeated phone calls and requests to meet. They'd all signed agreements with GE, we'd heard, that they'd have to return their bonuses if they didn't cooperate with GE's lawyers. Their legal fees were being paid by GE. They could only be hostile witnesses, Warner said. And what was the point of calling witnesses who will certainly be impeached? If they told the truth now, the SEC lawyers could simply point out that they'd perjured themselves once, why wouldn't they do it again? I didn't care if they were exposed as unreliable and liars, I wanted to use them to illustrate the Lynch cover-up.

"What about Elizabeth?" I asked Warner.

"Joseph, I hate to tell you this, but if someone tells you 'nigger, I hope you go to jail,' she may take the opportunity to fulfill her expressed hopes. There is a likelihood that she will say that her original testimony was the lie."

FIUMEFREDDO'S SPOT ON the witness stand was filled with Anthony Colyandro, director of systems development at Kidder, who testified about the company's computer programs. He described how input operators used tickets, blotter entries and sometimes wire-transfer paperwork to input trades into the computer.

"The input screen would have information that was required to process a transaction. And it would be things like the side of the trade, buy or sell, the number of bonds, the description of the bond or the Cusip number, the customer account number. And possibly any delivery instructions that would be different from the ones that reside on a file. Any sales credit that was to be paid to the broker, and that type of information."

The SEC lawyer, Kay Lackey, asked whether traders "would they enter information, for instance, on trade date?"

"Oh yes," Colyandro said. "Trade date, settlement date. If it was different than—the system would come up with a specific trade date and settlement date. If you were going to vary from that, you would have to indicate."

"How often would the input operators input this data about specific trades into the computer?"

"All day. All day long. We processed about, on the government side, about anywhere between twelve thousand and fifteen thousand transactions a day."

The system had a security program, called Safeguard, that prevented anyone tampering with the data, Colyandro said. He spent hours describing how the Kidder computers interfaced with one another, and the myriad figures, reports and data streams that resulted. When John Cuti got up to cross-examine Colyandro, the systems manager said the Strip and recon accounts had been opened in 1987.

"Do you know when Mr. Jett started at Kidder?"

"Nineteen ninety-one, I believe."

"Okay. It's a fact then that these accounts for stripping and reconning were at place at Kidder before Mr. Jett started there."

"That's correct."

WE SPENT THE next night searching for the Lynch notes from David Bernstein's interviews. We knew he'd met with Lynch's people on six different occasions. There was still a chance the SEC might call him to the witness stand.

I was scheduled to testify the next morning, so John Cuti occasionally threw mock questions at me as we worked our way through the boxes of Lynch papers. It was hardly necessary. After my twenty-five sessions with the U.S. Attorney's Office, I'd been over the same ground so many times that none of us had any concerns about challenges from the SEC. Instead, we concentrated on preparing me to explain the trades to a layman—the judge. I was still certain Fox-Foelak didn't know a bond from a rooster. But by 11:00, I couldn't keep my eyes open any longer.

Feeling bleary-eyed and exhausted that Thursday morning, I took the stand shortly after nine, prepared to spend the morning explaining my trading strategy. But Petra Tasheff didn't want to ask me about the technicalities of my trades. Pulling out a chart with numbers and dollar signs, she plunged immediately into hostile questions about my finances. She'd discovered an array of things I'd spent money on in the last couple of years; now she went through each item. She almost seemed to gloat, and I quickly realized she believed she had evidence of my motive for fraud: lavish living. But she hadn't done as much homework as she'd thought. I'd spent little of the money on myself. Right after she began her questioning, Tasheff pointed to her chart, where "kitchen design" was written. What about these decorating bills? she demanded. A new kitchen for my parents, I said. Tasheff hesitated slightly, then recovered and asked about a series of checks to educational funds and banks; I'd paid off student loans for my brother and sister-in-law, I explained. She demanded to know why I'd written a check for $100,000 just before I was fired. I told her the money was the down payment on a Manhattan condo I'd tried to buy. The deal fell through when I lost my job. I also lost the entire $100,000 down payment, I said. She asked about a *USA Today* article that said I'd given my parents over $2 million. The article was wrong, and coincidentally, that morning the paper had printed a correction. Tasheff hadn't noticed it. In truth, I'd dispersed my 1993 after-tax bonus to my parents and siblings. I hadn't kept a penny of it.

I could see the discomfort grow on her face. She wasn't well prepared. Papers were missing, and she spent a lot of time rifling through documents. She didn't adjust when her line of questioning faltered. She had a list of things to ask, and she stuck to it doggedly. Thus, she proved beyond a shadow of a doubt that I supported my parents and that my family spent a lot of money on education. I wasn't sure from her expression whether she thought she'd made a point in showing that money was the motive for my alleged crimes. Mostly she just looked confused.

If Tasheff realized her attack had backfired, she concealed it with more hostility. She shifted gears, asking about trading principles in great detail. Her tone was abrupt, hostile, and she phrased questions just vaguely enough that I had to ask her to repeat them. She mocked me for not being able to answer. Then she demanded only yes or no answers. But often her questions were imprecise, and I had to ask the judge for permission to elaborate. More than once Tasheff tried to stop me, until the judge intervened.

"Okay, okay. Both of you, I am interested in building a record. It's true you are entitled to a yes or no answer, but I want to hear the rest of it."

When I explained the conditions of the market that led to various trading strategies in 1992 and 1993, Tasheff grew livid. She demanded that the answer be stricken from the record because all she'd wanted was a yes or a no. Fox-Foelak refused. "Counsel, he certainly answered that question in the affirmative. His testimony will not be stricken. Keep going."

The SEC hoped that courtroom rules would shut me up. Tasheff referred to my answers as "speeches." "I object to speeches, Your Honor," she spat. I sat stiffly in my seat, trying to control my anger, trying not to stare holes through Tasheff's skull. I was twenty pounds lighter than I'd been two years before, and my clothes hung loosely from me. I tried to remember what my lawyers had advised me about appearing menacing. But it was difficult as I felt my anger grow.

Tasheff moved on to settlement dates, her questions harping on the fact that in my early years at Kidder, I'd only booked trades for five to seven days in the future. When I explained that the computer only allowed such inputs, she grew irritated at "another speech." She repeated: Wasn't it true that I'd only booked forward by five to seven days?

"I would use whatever settlement date my customers demanded."

"Okay. Eventually, after you had been at Kidder for a while, you started entering forward reconstitutions for much longer periods of time, isn't that correct?"

"Yes. There came a time in, I believe, as a fully developed strategy, 1993, where forward reconstitutions were the focal point of our trading strategy." I explained that after we got new computers, we could input any settlement date we wanted for customer trades, and for Strips and recons.

"But in any event, your Government Trader system did not enter reconstitutions for forward settlement automatically; you had to take a specific action to make that happen, correct?"

"Yes." I wasn't sure where she was going with this. I explained how the system worked. Tasheff stared at me silently, impatient again. "So is your answer, Mr. Jett, that yes, you knew the Government Trader system would record an automatic profit every time you touched the screen for a forward reconstitution?"

"I would not call the profit automatic for the same reasons that any Strip or reconstitution, the action in and of itself is not what makes the profit, it is the market activity that the trader takes that creates the opportunity to make the profit."

"Well, you knew that every time you did a forward recon there would be a positive P&L impact, didn't you? Yes or no, Mr. Jett?"

I started to explain, then stopped. "For the same reasons as before, I will answer no. There is not an automatic impact."

She persisted, anyway, insisting that I could see the profit from forward recons just by looking at my computer screen. But I knew that the system never isolated the effect of one Strip or recon. I sensed what Tasheff was getting at—she wanted me to say that I'd known I was supposed to discount any profits posted by the computer for forward settling recons.

"Mullin told you early on in your tenure at Kidder that there could be a distortion to the P&L figures of the firm if traders didn't adjust the prices on forward settling trades, correct, Mr. Jett?"

"I saw that in his deposition statement, but I don't recall him ever saying that to me."

She insisted that I'd known all along I was supposed to discount the profit generated by the computer. I shot back with an explanation of the two-month review with Bernstein and Fiumefreddo in 1993 of how we should handle profits from forward Strips, recons and municipal defeasance trades.

"It was an exhaustive review and at the end it was determined that we would continue to post profits on day one, and also if there were a loss we would continue to post a loss on day one, so, yes, that is something that caused a great deal of management investigation and management discussion and we reached a decision and I adhered to that decision throughout my period at Kidder."

Tasheff wasn't interested. Her tone was severe, her face pinched.

"I'm going to ask you to listen to the question once again, Mr. Jett, and see if you can answer this question. You didn't adjust the prices when you ordered forward reconstitutions, did you?"

"We did not enter in adjustments for forward trades of any kind."

She paused slightly. "And you didn't take any other steps to prevent a P&L distortion from occurring through entering forward reconstitutions, did you?"

Warner objected to this question, but the judge overruled him. I repeated my explanation that the 1993 review had determined how we handled forward profits.

"There was no policy at Kidder that asked for a trader to make adjustments because of his forward trades. Normally, a trader would—I always found it to be the case that traders whenever they lost money would seek to make an adjustment. When they made money, no adjustment was ever requested."

Tasheff let my words linger for a while, shuffling papers and making ready to change the subject. She wanted, she said finally, to talk about me personally. She made it sound as if the idea were distasteful to her. Why didn't I like Hugh Bush, Kevin McLaughlin or the business controllers group? Why did I have such a harsh regard for their work ethic? I glared at her, wanting desperately to quip that as a government lawyer, she probably had no concept of discipline, either. We spent nearly half an hour going over why I disparaged David Bernstein. Tasheff fixated on the fact that in September 1993, when Bernstein had asked me to reduce my position, I'd called him an idiot. I said I thought it was an idiotic idea. To Tasheff, it painted a picture of me as contemptuous of everyone at Kidder. It wasn't far from the truth. I thought angrily of McKoan, Cerullo, Finkelstein and Ricciardi.

Then she turned to a copy of my diary. She saw it as evidence that I was a brute, after all. Tasheff scoured for passages in which I was judgmental and called people names. She took particular delight in asking me to read a passage where I'd written that I'd "ripped Bernstein a new asshole." Did Tasheff really not know that traders commonly swore and cursed on the trading floor, and talked trash like this to each other? I was hardly unique. But in her eagerness to demonstrate that I was as evil and intimidating as I'd been portrayed in the press, she ordered me to read passages of my electronic diary into the record. The SEC had always challenged the veracity of the diary. Kidder and GE had flat-out said that the diary was bogus. Both had fought to keep it out of the official record. I'd given it to the Justice Department and wanted the SEC judge to have it, too, because in it I had written that I'd cursed Bernstein because he was investigating my trading strategy.

Throughout the questioning, I faced the spectator seats in the courtroom. Tasheff's back was to the gallery most of the time, so she didn't see the frequent apoplectic look on the faces of Kidder's lawyers. They gesticulated, whispered frequently, wrote furious notes. Sometimes I could even hear their sighs or gasps in response to Tasheff's clumsy questions. Later a friend, who'd been in the audience for part of the day, told me the Kidder lawyer next to her muttered, "They're blowing it, they're blowing it." This offered me little comfort—if I was going to lose to a foregone conclusion, I wanted at least to lose to a worthy adversary.

Suddenly Tasheff stopped and looked at me. "Mr. Jett, you're thirty-eight years old, right?" I nodded. Did I want to work again as a government securities trader? she asked carefully.

"And if you got that other job, you would try to use forward reconstitutions in your trading strategy, wouldn't you?"

I waited. "I've just had two years of my life ripped from me apparently all due to a reconstitution trade that was done to settle more than one day in the future. Two years of my life gone. I don't believe that is justified at all. Would I risk that, risk this happening to me again? No, I would not."

WE ADJOURNED FOR lunch. As we left the courtroom, GE's lawyers crowded around Tasheff, apparently upset at the direction of my testimony. After that, I thought the easy camaraderie between the GE lawyers and the SEC attorneys vanished.

After lunch, Warner let Tasheff's mistake of the morning fly back into her face. He submitted my entire electronic diary as evidence. Tasheff leapted out of her seat to object—the diary had "many, many, perhaps hundreds of entries of double and triple hearsay comments in them," she cried, but it was too late. Her flamboyant gesture in asking me to read the passage I'd written about "ripping a new asshole" for Bernstein had put my diary into the record. Up until then, the SEC had succeeded in keeping most of it out of court. Tasheff struggled valiantly to prevent Warner's request. The better part of the afternoon passed with Tasheff arguing about my personal diary versus my secretary's copy, how the organizer divided entries, what kind of printout was available. It was useless and a waste of time, but Tasheff's sloppiness forced us to endure it. At one point, Warner asked me to read from the diary. Tasheff jumped up.

"Your Honor, I object. There is no purpose for Mr. Jett to read from a diary. He can testify about what his knowledge is today, but there is no point in him going back and reading from a document."

I gaped at her in astonishment; so did a lot of others. She hadn't thought of that argument when she asked me to read it for her that morning. The judge must have realized it, too, because she let me read the entry from May 1993.

" 'Met with Fium.,' that's Charlie Fiumefreddo, 'Bernstein, Benatar this week on former trades. Moishe proved that we agree with Tandem system on P&L. Forward Strips are just like muni defeasance trade, with financing costs showing up on a daily financing report and profit showing on day 1 in Tandem. Bernstein okay on muni for two months forward and Strip recon three months forward."

I knew why Tasheff was so angry. The entries clearly stated that Fiumefreddo, Bernstein, Mullin, Benatar and others had discussed my trading strategy with me for a year before I was fired. Her carelessness meant we could finally introduce the entries that the SEC, Kidder and GE had fought to exclude.

* * *

WHEN WARNER GOT up to question me, he picked up the Red Book. Handing the original to Judge Fox-Foelak, he gave me a copy of a page from May 1993. He wanted me explain how trades were recorded.

"All right. First, whenever we did a Strip or a recon, at this time in May of '93 the Government Trading system was capable of printing out a trade ticket that showed the particulars of the trade. This trade ticket would be given to the back office. Someone would come by, sort of circulate around the room every hour or so, would pick up the ticket, take it to the ticket input clerks who would input all of the relevant information. Either the original ticket or a copy of it would then be returned to the Government trading desk. Normally, it would go to a trader who worked for me, named Jeff Unger, and he would just place it on top of his desk. Thereafter, either Jeff, Joe Ossman or one of the trading assistants would take the ticket, and I shouldn't say just those four, either those categories of people, people who worked on my desk or very often people who worked on the Repo desk, Jim Rizzi or Richie Lafergola, would come over, take the ticket over to Jim Rizzi's desk where the Red Book was actually held. They would take the trade ticket, go to the settlement date of the trade, and then . . ."

I looked down at the copy of the page I held.

"If we start on the very first entry, at the top of the page?" The trade date and the settlement dates were entered. "Next to that are the three letters 'RCN' which stand for recon, and I think it was actually Jim Rizzi who would always use that abbreviation. Next to that it says '$104 million,' which shows the size of the trade. To the right of that, I think you can see the '5525' that's written there? That is almost always, invariably, written by either Jim Rizzi or Richie Lafergola, indicating to them the amount of Strip coupons needed to complete the transaction, the number of Strips that had to be either purchased or needed to be kept for delivery to the Fed.

"Trade date, the settlement date, whether it is Strip or recon, the size of the total transaction, the coupon of the bond of interest and the maturity date of the bond of interest."

Judge Fox-Foelak was looking at the original Red Book. "So on the date a trade was made that was supposed to settle on May 3, for example, the first one indicated is apparently March 2. On March 2 would the person turn to the May 3 page and write all this down? That's what you're saying?"

"Precisely."

Warner spoke up. "And I think you said that this was kept on Jim Rizzi's desk?"

"Yes. It was kept on Jim Rizzi's desk, either on his desk, or occasionally it would be on Richie Lafergola's desk, who sat right next to him, and the two of them were responsible for the financing of the zero-coupon securities."

"Where was the book kept? Was it out in the open, or somewhere else?"

"Just right on top of their desks."

"So it was accessible and available to everyone? And visible to everyone? Throughout the day?"

"Yes. Quite. Throughout the day, throughout the years."

MY STAR TURN on the witness stand had brought the press out of the woodwork, and afterward everyone wanted to interview me. The CNN reporter said, "You seemed to be coaching her," when he asked me about Tasheff. I bit back the urge to say I'd imagined myself like George Bush during one of the presidential debates, when he'd said, "Let me help you there." It was exhilarating to feel I'd won, but I was also disappointed that the questioning hadn't been tougher. I'd wanted the hard questions about my trades, but they hadn't come up. Instead, too much time had been wasted on an effort to paint me as angry, hate-filled and menacing, spending money heedlessly, calling Bernstein names, and hiding behind the Fifth Amendment.

THE LAST WEEK in May, the SEC called Brian Novotny, a Kidder staff accountant responsible for confirming the computer-generated profit and loss reports with traders. Every morning, Novotny collected a four-foot-high stack of trading report printouts from the computer room. He'd break down the reports and arrange them so he could compare them to different trading desks. He compiled one sheet, called a PPR summary report, and carried it to the trading floor. The summary showed trading profit and loss positions on a daily basis, and by month. He also used separate reports that listed futures, daily, month-to-date and year-to-date profit and loss, and trading positions. It took Novotny until about 11:00 each morning to compile his summaries. Then he carried them to the assistant traders on each desk. In my case, that had been Joey-o. Novotny and Joey-o double-checked figures in over half a dozen ledgers on my desk. Joey-o was once a profit and loss accountant, too, so he was familiar with the checking-out process. Novotny usually gave Joey-o the computer printout with futures numbers written on it by Novotny and showing a net-to-date daily, month-to-date and year-to-date number, and he would put a check mark by each one after inspecting them. The numbers were seldom out of synch. Novotny told Fox-Foelak that our desk numbers "agreed probably ninety percent of the time" with his computer printouts. He said he was never told to make any adjustments for future trades in our ledgers.

Even though he came to the desk every day, I didn't know Novotny well. I'd talked to him once when he applied for a job as Canadian bond trader. He'd struck me as smart, likable and keenly interested in bond trading. He was curious about our work, and had told Lynch's investigators that he often asked Joey-o about our trading strategy. So in court I was surprised to hear him deny it.

"With respect to the government—the zero-coupon desk, the Strips desk, you dealt, for the most part, with Joe Ossman?"

"Correct."

"And if you recall, do you recall asking Joe Ossman about every third day how the Strips desk was making money?"

"That is incorrect."

"Do you recall being interviewed by lawyers from Davis Polk in June 1994? Do you recall making the statement that every third day or so Novotny would ask Ossman how Jett was making his money?"

"That statement I do not remember making. No. I don't remember the question but I'll say I don't remember making that statement there, no."

John Cuti looked sideways at him. "Are you saying you didn't make the statement or you don't recall making the statement?"

"I'm saying I don't recall making the statement."

Cuti changed the subject.

"Let me ask you this. On that same occasion, when you were interviewed by Davis Polk, do you recall telling lawyers for Davis Polk the following, quote, 'The highest level of detail is provided in the TJ, or Transaction Journal. The TJ shows every trade that had been made the prior day by ledger and by issue.' Do you recall saying that?"

Novotny wasn't sure. But he agreed that the Daily Transaction Journal was sent each day to each trading desk.

"The clerk would get it."

"The clerk on the trading desk?"

"Yeah. Well, they were off the trading desk but the traders' clerk, let's say. Yeah, they got a copy every day."

"Okay. And Joseph Jett never told you not to bring the Transaction Journal out to the clerk, did he?"

The question confused Novotny.

"To anyone in particular? I wasn't told by Joe not to do anything."

MULLIN FOLLOWED BRIAN Novotny the next day. I knew he wouldn't say definitively that he'd known about and approved of my trades; his deal with Kidder surely prevented that. But the SEC expected him to offer an opinion on my trading practices, and I had little hope he'd keep the promises made to my lawyers and tell the judge that my trades were logical and technically feasible. Mullin, alone, looked nervous. Denise wasn't with him. He glanced once at me and then quickly away. For the rest of the day, his eyes never rested on me for more than a second. I tried to catch his eye, however. I expected the worst from him—a complete betrayal—and I wanted him to know it from my hard stare.

At first, Mullin described the Government desk operation, and how he ran it when he'd headed it. Every day he read the Fixed Income Daily report for its information on trading, interest, profit and loss, inventory levels, sales credits generated by the traders, and the like. He also reviewed the Inventory Control report every day, which showed how capital use and inventory kept up with company guidelines. He described meeting with traders on a regular basis to observe the types of customer business they did, how they hedged their position, what opportunities they were finding in the market, where the firm was competitive and where it was not. He warned his traders, he said, about occasional distortions to the profitability.

"What was your impression as to how well known it was on a desk that the forward settlement trades required an accounting adjustment?" Petra Tasheff wanted to know.

"I thought it was pretty well known."

When I was first hired, Mullin said, I was a cautious trader, still learning and not very profitable. So at the end of my first year, he gave me a $5,000 bonus "that was really meant as a kick to get started and become more profitable.

"I know at some point we discussed that the levels had to grow beyond the levels that we had earned in previous years and at some point in the next few months I had hoped we'd get to a running rate of about a million dollars a month in profitability."

After that, Mullin said, my profitability grew. By the end of 1992, my customer business nearly quadrupled. By June 1992, Mullin recommended a raise and promotion, because he thought I had "a very thorough understanding of the market and I thought he worked very hard with the traders in his group and with the salespeople in the firm in developing a growing business." By the fall, my performance was "outstanding," he said. He liked what he saw in the Fixed Income Daily report, and decided to give me a $2 million bonus.

"Did you receive any reports that showed profitability on a per-transaction basis?" Tasheff wanted to know.

"No, I did not."

Next, Tasheff asked what I was like to work with.

"Well, over time he became very hard on those that he felt weren't working hard enough, weren't smart enough, weren't aggressive enough in pursuing their business. And became difficult with some people."

"Can you give us an example?" Tasheff was eager, but Mullin didn't take the bait.

"None comes to mind. No particular example. It was more a general approach to the people he felt weren't working hard enough or weren't producing for his group."

He could have been describing Cerullo or Bernstein. I was glad.

From 1991 to 1993, Mullin said we talked about stripping and reconning two or three times a week, usually as our computer system showed us opportunities. He said we never talked about settlement dates.

"Do you know of any reason, Mr. Mullin, to do a reconstitution of a bond for further forward than five business days?"

"Not offhand."

He hadn't told me to do recons for settlement more than five days in the future, he said, and never had any idea whether I was doing it anyway. He only heard about them when asked to help liquidate my position in April 1994. That's when he learned that the Red Book was a list of forward settling reconstitutions. Fox-Foelak was confused. She asked Mullin if a trade date was June 1 and the bond had a coupon of June 1 and December 1, and a settlement date was input as December 1, would the computer show a profit of six months' interest?

"That's essentially correct."

When John Cuti questioned him, Mullin described the trading tickets just as Novotny had, with their trade dates and settlement dates written in, and the confirmation that was sent to the Fed for every Strip and recon.

"I assumed confirms were sent down on every transaction," he added.

He talked about coming out to my desk to look at my screen and discuss trades. The Red Book was always available for him to look at, though he denied checking it or reviewing my trade tickets.

"I didn't have the ability on my screen to see individual trades, only net position, totals by issue. But I would come and look at his screen periodically and talk about trades."

"And sometimes you'd point out perhaps an attractive trade that he might have missed and you'd show him how to catch it next time and so on?"

"Or he might explain that it wasn't really doable in the marketplace, but we discussed items that showed up on the screen."

"Okay. Now, would you also sort of look over the trades that he was doing from time to time, not just that you'd come in and look at his screen?"

"Well, as we were talking, he would from time to time be entering a trade into the system. I didn't specifically look over the trade tickets."

"Okay. I think you've once mentioned that Mr. Jett kept a blotter. I think that was the term you used. All of the traders have a blotter on the desk in front of them where they hand-wrote their transactions. Okay. And Mr. Jett did that, too?"

"Yes."

"And you would look at that from time to time?"

The Red Book was always available for him to look at, Mullin said, though he denied checking it or reviewing my trade tickets.

"And you never told Mr. Jett, did you, that he was prohibited from booking a forward recon beyond that period?"

"No. We never discussed it."

"And, in fact, isn't it true, Mr. Mullin, there's nothing per se wrong with booking a recon more than five days forward? Nothing per se wrong."

"I don't see anything per se wrong."

MULLIN TOLD KEN Warner that Bernstein had asked him in August or September 1993 about my forward trades. "There was some point where he asked me. I'm not certain of the exact time." But Mullin remembered asking Bernstein why he was curious.

"What did he say?" Warner asked. "He did say Mr. Jett had the transactions booked?"

"Yeah. He didn't say specifically what he was doing or what his concerns were. My impression was that it was not a major issue and that when I asked him about it, he essentially said, 'It's nothing to be concerned about right now.' "

The same comments were in Mullin's notes with Lynch's investigators. Right after I was fired, he'd told them that Bernstein had said he was reviewing the forward recon trades. Lynch's team had asked Mullin to review my trading profits in 1992. Mullin told Cerullo what he'd found.

"Well, the profits as reported on the Fixed Income Daily in 1992 at Kidder were approximately $27.5 million and my calculation showed that in reality they were closer to $29 million."

Warner knew what that meant. Mullin believed the profits were real enough and that I "actually should have gotten a higher bonus, right?"

"Yes."

With that, Mullin sanctified everything I'd done in 1991 and 1992, gutting the SEC's argument that my entire career at Kidder was a fraud. Certainly, Mullin hadn't said what he'd promised me before his settlement with Kidder. He left the stand without looking at me. I couldn't help saying to one of the GE attorneys, "So was it worth $2.7 million?" GE had literally paid for Mullin's favorable testimony with his settlement. He'd helped me, but not as much as I knew he could have.

THE NEXT MORNING, May 30, a Thursday, Edward Cerullo walked into Fox-Foelak's courtroom. He wouldn't look at me. Two years had passed since I'd last seen him, and he looked gaunt and ashen. Though it was late spring, he didn't appear to have been outside very much. And his customarily damp hair was neat and dry. He'd aged, or perhaps the grimaces on his face simply made the lines deeper and more pronounced. I didn't try to speak to him as he was swallowed up in the crowd of suited lawyers. Fifteen of us squeezed into the hearing room—Judge Fox-Foelak, five lawyers from the SEC Broker-Dealer Enforcement division, two lawyers for Kidder, Cerullo and his personal attorney, my four lawyers and me. Since he was not a party to the suit between me and the SEC, Cerullo had been subpoenaed. As a result, Tasheff, dour as usual, seemed to treat Cerullo almost as if his appearance were an unforgivable inconvenience. Her questions were brief, to the point, in her usual unemotional manner. She started abruptly.

"During the time that you were supervising Mr. Jett, did you believe that you had an understanding of how he was making money on his trading? Could you tell the court what your understanding was?"

Cerullo's voice was calm. "It was my understanding and belief that Mr. Jett was making money trading Strips as well as the long-bond position and the Government department at Kidder, making markets for customers, and stripping and reconstituting bonds."

By the time Tasheff asked whether he'd known before March 1994 that I was doing forward settling Strips and reconstitutions, Cerullo was confident.

"Absolutely did not."

"Before March of 1994, did Mr. Jett or anyone else tell you that Mr. Jett was using forward settling reconstitutions to generate profit?"

"No one."

But he had watched my progress, Cerullo said. Mel Mullin had liked me, he recalled.

"Did Mr. Mullin discuss Mr. Jett's performance as a trader with you?"

"He did. More than once. He was cautious about his early performance but optimistic."

"Do you recall knowing what Mr. Jett's early performance was in terms of profitability?"

"I believe that it was not profitable." But that changed, Cerullo said. Though he only ran into me on the trading floor once or twice a week, he kept an eye on my profit and loss reports, heard positive feedback about me and got good reports from Mullin, who, Cerullo said, "was encouraged by Mr. Jett's improved performance and quite optimistic about his future." That optimism led to my promotion to head of the Government desk.

Tasheff skipped around in her questions, jumping from subject to subject, and covering broad spans of time. As I listened, I thought how unhappy Mullin would be to hear Cerullo testify that his praise of me was used to usurp him. After my promotion to Mullin's job, Cerullo had more contact with me, he told the courtroom, since I attended the same Monday morning sales meeting, and the Fixed Income management committee meeting. At the latter, Cerullo testified, we conducted quarterly and often monthly financial reviews of the department. We also had more frequent discussions about routine business of the day.

"I believed that he brought a seriousness of purpose to his effort, a discipline. In general terms, that's how I would characterize it."

"In 1993, did you feel like you could trust Mr. Jett?"

"Yes, I did." His confidence came, in part, from reading about my trading activity in the Fixed Income Daily report and risk-management reports, he said.

"Did these reports identify profits from forward reconstitutions with the Fed?"

"They did not."

With no suspicions about me, Cerullo recommended me for the "Man of the Year" award, coaching me for less than ten minutes about the speech I would give in Florida. Forward recons never came up in that conversation, he insisted.

"Are you sure about that?"

"Absolutely."

Tasheff skipped to another subject, asking Cerullo when he first suspected my trades were a problem. Dave Bernstein first alerted him to the forward recons, Cerullo answered. He'd asked Bernstein and the risk manager, Barry Finer, to investigate my trades, and Bernstein had come back with good news and bad news. The bad news was that Bernstein had found large positions in my ledger that he didn't understand and could not make sense of. But there was no financial impact, he said. That was the good news.

"I, at that point, engaged Mr. Jett for an explanation of these entries and directed Bernstein to further his research into the implications of these on the books and records of the firm and his understanding of them. Mr. Bernstein did report back to me at several points in time with a revised understanding of these positions and their implications. As Mr. Bernstein revised his understanding of the implications of these transactions, it became clear to me that neither he nor I within Fixed Income had the resources to understand the full impact of what was going on. It was just too complicated."

Cerullo's tone was dry and bored, even rehearsed.

"Mr. Bernstein revised his opinion that there was a financial implication, however modest. He then revised his opinion that there was a potentially significant financial implication. I shared each of those understandings with Mr. Carpenter, but by the third time, when Mr. Bernstein suggested there was a financial implication that was significant, that is when I instructed Mr. Carpenter that we really needed more resources, and he then contacted Mr. O'Donnell, who was the chief financial officer, who put together a team of people from the Accounting department, the Operations department, the Systems department to come to an understanding of these forward trades and their implications."

With Carpenter's forces in place, investigating my trades became a full-time, round-the-clock project, Cerullo testified.

"The financial analysts, the various accountants, the controllers of the firm had different understandings at different points of time, different theses as to what their implication was. At some points in time, they thought they had significant loss implications for the firm. At other times, they thought they did not. While they were doing their research, we were forcing Joseph to bring his position down, and as he did that, losses were being generated in his trading account that grew. And what became clear to me, listening to the accountants over time make different postulates and then unable to prove them, and seeing the growing loss in Mr. Jett's ledger, was there was one thing that was real and only one thing that was real. That this was a growing loss and that it was real to the firm and it needed to be recognized and dealt with."

So he ordered me to reduce my position, he said. I sat still, acutely aware that he wasn't mentioning the European banks, the quarter-end balance sheet, or the collapse of Askin. His only reason was management concern. Any trade with a March settlement date had to be consummated, he said. No rolling them forward; just take them off the books, Cerullo testified. Trades with farther forward settling dates had to have an equal and opposite transaction entered into the ledger so they would cancel out the far-dated trades. When he asked me to justify the trades, Cerullo said, I told him that a back-office bottleneck had forced me to defer trades with the Fed. The back office couldn't keep up with my volume, so I'd postponed settlement of the trades by rolling them forward, he added.

Sitting in the courtroom, I stared hard at Cerullo. I almost felt I could will him to remember the heated arguments we'd had about the two-foot stack of computer printouts, and his demand that I do something to reduce the paperwork load. Now he was testifying that I'd ginned up a back-office bottleneck? My eyes bored into him, but he never looked at me.

Then, Cerullo added, I'd explained that Bernstein had ordered the trades to reduce the balance sheet.

"I believe that Mr. Bernstein reacted in a fashion of being flabbergasted. Denied that that was the case."

"Okay. Had you ever told Mr. Jett, 'I want you to do forward reconstitutions or Strips with the Fed in order to reduce the balance sheet'?"

"Never conceived of the notion, let alone instructed him to do it."

"Okay. Did you ever instruct anyone else, Mr. Bernstein or anyone else, to tell Mr. Jett to use forward recons with the Fed or forward Strips with the Fed to reduce the balance sheet?"

"I did not. There came a point in time when Mr. Jett shared with me the fact that in an effort to reduce the balance sheet he lost money. And he didn't feel that was justified. And in an effort to recapture that money, he had entered forward recons with the Fed. I was left flabbergasted, devastated. I became nauseous. It was clear to me for the first time that he had acknowledged he knew what he was doing and why he was doing it."

"Did you have any discussions with Mr. Jett regarding whether the forward transactions with the Fed had any P&L effect?"

"More than once. Excepting the last conversation I've shared with you, he denied financial implications to these—he denied the financial loss that we were looking at in the ledger as he was removing his positions from the balance sheets of the firm." But the loss became real, Cerullo said, after he ordered Bernstein and Finer to execute my position, because I'd refused to bring it down myself. By then, he said, the total loss was $300 million.

Cerullo paused, and I thought he looked even more pale.

"I was devastated. At some point in time in April, it became clear that Mr. Jett's entire existence at Kidder was a lie. His entire performance at Kidder was deceptive. His every—his entire trading performance, the P&L performance that he registered, was simply an accounting fraud. That there was no substance to it at all. It was a function of these journal entries, these forward entries with the Fed, and that there was no economic or market substance to it, or reality to it."

Tasheff looked at him.

"When you were discussing with Mr. Jett his use of forward recons with the Fed, did he ever say to you, 'Ed, I told you about these things a long time ago. What are you doing asking me about them now?' or words to that effect?"

"Never, not once."

AFTER A TEN-MINUTE break, Ken Warner addressed Cerullo.

"Well, Mr. Cerullo, you made some pretty extreme statements, didn't you, during your direct testimony about the lie that was embodied in Mr. Jett's trading?"

Cerullo's Kidder lawyer was on her feet. It was the first objection of the day, but she'd follow it with dozens more, virtually all of them overruled by the judge.

"Objection, Your Honor. His testimony is what it is. He doesn't need to now testify about what his testimony was."

"Well, let me ask you . . . after your discovery of everything, you realized that Mr. Jett's customer trading was all a lie. Is that it? Is that what I heard you say? It was all a lie?"

Cerullo shifted his gaze away.

"Mr. Jett's customer trading was not the basis of his profitability that was reported to me."

Warner moved slowly.

"When you were testifying on direct, you had some big words for all these things, like it was a lie, it had no substance, it was all a fake, it was a fraud. You got nauseous. Were you nauseous about his customer trading when you looked back on it?"

"I was very nauseous of the substance of what Mr. Jett's presence at

Kidder was about. And it was about a fraud. I was nauseous that it was a diversion for the substance of what Mr. Jett was about at Kidder Peabody."

"But isn't it a fact, Mr. Cerullo, that in 1992 Mr. Jett's customer trading was $87 billion, even by the admissions of Kidder? Isn't that a fact? You do acknowledge, don't you, Mr. Cerullo, that Mr. Jett's customer trading increased every year from 1992 to 1993 and into 1994? Isn't that a fact?"

"The facts that I do know—"

"Is that a fact, Mr. Cerullo? Yes or no, if you know?"

"I believe that may be true." Cerullo's confidence dissipated. I recognized the telltale signs of anxiety. He wouldn't meet Warner's eyes. He launched his argument just as he'd done dozens of times in his office.

"But I do—I'd like to explain what I mean by customer business when I make that affirmation, Your Honor. That Mr. Jett's customer trading in 1993 lost Kidder Peabody approximately $10 million—in '92, lost Kidder Peabody approximately $10 million of real money. In 1993, Mr. Jett's real customer trading that you're speaking about lost Kidder Peabody about $50 million of real money. That those real losses, that real customer trading, was then covered up by this other scheme."

Warner stuck to his original point. "But isn't it a fact that even by Kidder's own admission, Mr. Jett made profits—had profitable trades that generated real money of over $500 million, isn't that true?"

Cerullo insisted that he'd never seen reports attributing profit to me. It would become a theme for the day. Over and over, Cerullo repeated that he'd never seen reports, never talked to anyone about my trading strategy, never asked questions or raised suspicions. His lack of curiosity or awareness meant he didn't know the answers to most of Warner's questions, either. My lawyer changed tack.

"You wanted the Fixed Income department to be successful, right? And isn't it fact, Mr. Cerullo, that you were particularly motivated to feel that way in 1991 because in 1990, you almost got fired by Kidder, isn't that true?"

Cerullo looked directly at Warner in surprise.

"That's new to me." His voice was testy.

"Nobody told you about it? Are you aware of the fact that Kidder went so far as to draw up a whole plan in which your severance was set forth and that the amount that you would get if you were terminated as of July 1, 1990, was outlined? Do you know that Kidder Peabody management had felt that you had put everybody through an agonizing 1989 bonus process in which they felt that you were excessively greedy? Do you know that?"

"I'm not aware of that."

"Are you aware of the fact that Kidder Peabody management in its personnel reports about you said that you were excessively controlling and tyrannical and difficult with the people that worked for you?"

"I'm not aware of that and I don't believe that to be true."

Warner handed Cerullo his Kidder personnel file. The lawyers jumped up to argue. I watched Cerullo, who looked completely taken aback. I could see he was on edge, growing more defensive as he sat and listened to the lawyers and the judge. He still wouldn't look at me. Warner persevered.

"Does it refresh your recollection, after looking at this document, that Kidder Peabody in 1990 was considering your discharge for various qualities of management and other characteristics that they found unacceptable?"

"I have never never been aware of, informed of, directly or indirectly, that Kidder at any point in time considered releasing me." Cerullo looked shell shocked. His anger was fermenting. He didn't like being challenged publicly. And another setback was on its way.

"Now, Mr. Cerullo, in an effort to make the Fixed Income department successful, would you agree that one way to do it is—how can I say?—run a tight ship, keep performance standards high, supervise people properly? In fact, Mr. Cerullo, you've had problems in the past about proper supervision, haven't you?"

"Not apart from this case."

"Oh? Do you remember somebody by the name of Ira Sapperstein? And was Ira Sapperstein prior to the time of this case somebody who was under your supervision?"

The judge looked over.

"Counsel, would you explain where you're going with this?"

"The relevance is this, Your Honor. That Mr. Cerullo was previously involved prior to this in an incident in which he was blamed for the lack of supervision. And I want to show that having had that experience, he certainly didn't want to have it again. And we don't believe that he did have it again."

Warner continued, describing Mr. Sapperstein as someone who reported to Cerullo.

"Isn't it a fact that Mr. Sapperstein was charged with improprieties in connection with trading activities? And he was charged with improprieties at a time that he was working in your department, correct? And, in fact, you were sanctioned for lack of supervision in connection with that matter, isn't that so?"

To Warner, the relevance was obvious. Cerullo had been sanctioned for screwing up once before. "It happened prior to 1991, didn't it? And am I correct, Mr. Cerullo, that you did not want anything like that to happen again?"

"Yes."

Warner looked back at the counsel table, then down at some papers. He'd made notes about several memos Cerullo had written to Michael Carpenter about supervisory procedures in Fixed Income. In the memo, Cerullo suggested that all trading tickets should be reviewed. He'd recommended greater oversight of precisely the kind of tickets that I'd filled out during my years at Kidder. Yet now he claimed to have had no interest in them. Warner looked at Cerullo.

"And the other tickets you know listed trade date and settlement date, correct?"

"I believe they would."

"Well, from your answer am I to understand that you've never looked at an order ticket?"

Cerullo raised his voice. "No. I've never looked at one of Mr. Jett's order tickets."

"And so during Mr. Jett's tenure, had you looked at even one of those order tickets embodying a forward transaction with the Fed, you would have seen it right there, isn't that so?"

"Possible." I watched him, looking as if he was about to lose his cool. Cerullo was not accustomed to having his decisions or actions questioned. The resentment was clear on his face. Warner was implying that the facts were not as Cerullo stated them, and that, I knew, was an affront to Cerullo. He didn't want to be asked follow-up questions, when he'd already made his statement. I'd seen him react that way at work countless times. It was no different now on the witness stand, except that at work, everyone backed down. Warner didn't.

"But you never did it even once."

"That's correct."

Warner still had the Red Book on his table. He turned to it now.

"Have you heard about the Red Book? And you realize, don't you, that had you looked at even one page of that book, you would have understood that Mr. Jett was doing forward Strips and recons, isn't that so?"

Again, Cerullo didn't know.

"I haven't closely examined the Red Book so I can't say that's the case."

After that, Warner asked about the "Man of the Year" award. Warner wanted Cerullo to explain why he'd censured my speech. "And, in fact, you mentioned earlier that Mr. Jett was supposed to give an acceptance speech. Isn't it a fact that you questioned whether he should give that speech because you wanted to avoid disclosing any trading strategies?"

Cerullo bit his words defensively. Angry, he stabbed at the air between him and Warner.

"I never questioned whether he should give that speech, number one. I questioned the appropriateness of one trading strategy. It was articulated because of its technical detail, the inappropriateness to the audience that was being addressed. And that trading strategy that I questioned had to do with municipalities. It had nothing to do with forwards with the Fed."

Warner bit back.

"It had to do with the means by which profits are made in dealing with municipalities, isn't that so? And it has to do in part with the way in which it's possible to take a trading advantage, and I use that term not in any pejorative sense, a trading advantage of municipalities to make profit, isn't that right? And it wasn't a technicality of that that you did not want disclosed. It was the profitability of it, isn't that right, and the way in which it could be done?"

"No, that's not right."

"Well, Mr. Cerullo, Mr. Carpenter has said that you questioned whether Mr. Jett should give a speech at the Boca convention because you, quote, 'Generally preferred avoiding public discussion of trading strategies or profitability of particular areas.' That was said by Mr. Carpenter."

Warner's point was that Cerullo had been secretive about the municipal defeasance and forward recon trading strategies that I'd wanted to mention in my speech. I was proud of the strategy I'd developed after discovering that Kidder's computer booked forward profits for the two trades the same way. But Cerullo had told me not to mention it. Now he flatly denied the conversation. He explained muni defeasance trades to the judge. Warner waited, nodding.

"Uh-huh. And that comes about because Kidder is able to take advantage in municipal defeasance transactions of the time factor of money and the cost of carry, isn't that right?"

Cerullo balked at this description, but Warner pressed him. Finally, Cerullo answered.

"A municipal defeasance, you're talking about a transaction that's booked forward, that's correct."

"Okay. And we're talking about a transaction in which, for example, the sale of Strips is booked forward. That means—"

"No. We're talking about a transaction in which Kidder Peabody sells to a real counterparty a transaction with a forward settlement date. . . . In any forward settling transaction, there is an element of interest earned and cost of carry."

From my seat, I wanted to interject my own question—wasn't Cerullo saying, in effect, that he was aware of my forward settling transactions? But Warner moved on, asking about the Mortgage department's profitability in 1993.

"And in the Mortgage area, do you recall an incident in 1993 where inventory had to be revalued? Was there a revaluation of inventory that caught your attention in 1993?"

"I don't know," Cerullo answered. I sat back in frustration. This was the very inventory that had raised O'Donnell's ire in 1991, the same mortgages that O'Donnell had finally proved were mispriced. Cerullo had lived for two years with that aged inventory hanging over his head, and now he maintained that he couldn't remember? Hoping for better responses, Warner asked about my profitability in 1992. He handed Cerullo copies of a profit report called the Government Daily. The copies covered December

1992 to December 1993. Cerullo agreed that my desk earned less than $5 million in 1990, a pitiful number, and shot up to $15 million in my first year. Nineteen ninety-two was a banner year for the Government Bond desk.

"I believed that Joe's performance was outstanding," Cerullo said.

"Now, you testified earlier that what caused you to become interested in looking into Mr. Jett's trading was that the profits in 1994 seemed too high, is that right? And you were concerned that Mr. Jett, at least you testified to this earlier, that you were concerned that Mr. Jett might be taking some unacceptable risks?" He shuffled through summaries from the G-1 ledger that detailed month-by-month trading profits, interest, the year-to-date for trading and the year-to-date for interest earned. In 1994, my profit had been $8.5 million in January and $3.8 million in February.

"Now, when was it that you got worried about this profitability? Was it January or was it February or was it March?"

Cerullo didn't want to look at the profit columns. Instead, he pointed at the interest column. Warner seized on that, asking him what the interest was for my trading ledger for January of 1994? He had to ask four times before Cerullo would answer.

"What's listed here in January of '94, a net interest number of $27.3 million? And that's a plus $27.3 million, right?"

"That's correct."

"And that represents real dollars, right? That's real money. You were talking this morning about false and everything's a lie, but the fact is that $27.3 million is real cash, isn't it? Yes or no?"

Kidder's lawyer spoke up. "If you know."

Warner glanced at her, then back at Cerullo, who stared fixedly at the papers in his hand. I could hear my heartbeat, and perhaps Cerullo's, too.

"You don't know? Do you know, Mr. Cerullo?"

"I'm not certain."

"Are you serious?"

The room was silent and suddenly hot. Cerullo glanced at him, then away. He tried to answer.

"I'm serious because you've taken—you have taken an accounting convention and tried to apply it to a trading notion and created an extremely distorted view of the reality of the activity."

"Mr. Cerullo—"

"This is an accounting convention."

"Kidder has taken an accounting convention and tried to apply it to Mr. Jett's ledger and called him a fraud. So please allow me to ask you—"

Tasheff spoke up. "This is argumentative."

"I withdraw it, Your Honor," Warner said, with a look of disbelief at Cerullo. But then he asked the same question again, flustering Cerullo. His anger evaporated now.

"I'm not in a—I'm not an accountant and I'm not in a position to represent what Kidder's books and records represented."

"I see. So that would you agree, Mr. Cerullo, that if one is not an accountant, one could not be held for interpreting accounting documents?"

"I believe that the third column—I believe that the column represents trading and interest, was purported to represent the economic activity of Mr. Jett for the period of time of his tenure. And that those numbers were fraudulent."

"I know. We've heard that. But it turns out that you don't even understand what one of the numbers in there is, right?"

Cerullo didn't look up.

"No. I understand what trading and interest is, sir."

"Okay. So tell me whether interest is real money."

"You're trying to apply convention that I cannot affirm for you. It would be misleading."

"What's the convention? That interest is real money?"

"This is an accounting convention."

"You mean this isn't real at all, none of it? Nothing's real."

"No, no, I didn't say that. They're your words."

Warner sighed perceptibly.

"All right. How about February? Is that going to be the same answer? For February of 1994, there's $26.2 million in Mr. Jett's interest column, and it's a plus, isn't that right? But you're not able to say whether that $26.2 million is real either—"

"That's right." Their voices rose, battling over each other.

"—because it's an accounting convention?"

"Mr. Jett had fraudulent entries—"

"I know. But don't—"

"—into his trading ledger—"

"—keep repeating that."

"—which generated accrued interest numbers, which ran through the accounting system, and I'm not, based on this, going to opine how they came out in this digest."

Warner fingered some papers.

"So, of the total in the interest column for January and for February, we have a total interest to Kidder of more than $50 million, right? And, in fact, it was true, wasn't it, that Mr. Jett had very substantial long positions, real long positions that were generating money, right? I know you're claiming about the false profits and you've already said that, but I am saying to you, isn't it a fact that Mr. Jett had real long positions there?"

"I believe that in addition to unreal positions, Mr. Jett did have some real positions in his ledger."

"And I'm trying to talk about that for a moment. And I'm asking you among those real positions, he had positions that generated for January and February of 1994 over $50 million of interest for Kidder, isn't that right?"

"I don't know whether the real positions were generating those accounting figures or the fake positions were generating those accounting numbers. I am unable to make that determination."

Warner changed tack once more.

"Would you agree that the dispute over Mr. Jett's positions involves unsettled positions?"

Tasheff spoke up. "Objection as to what dispute he's talking about."

Warner cocked an eyebrow at her.

"Well, why we're here," he said with a sour face. "It's about unsettled positions, right?"

He turned his back on her and faced the judge.

"This witness has said that my client's whole career was a fraud and that he had false profits, and I'd like to explore that with him, and I'd like to ask him whether the allegation of false profits that he was making concerns unsettled positions."

"Forward dated unsettled positions," Cerullo stated.

"That's right. And let's just clarify for the court what an unsettled position is. Let's take first, settled. A settled position would be that a transaction is booked to take place, and then if it's the same day, it's settled that day. And if it's another day, it's settled on whatever day it is that the transaction—I'll use the word 'closes.' "

Cerullo said, "Settlement refers to the exchange of money for security."

Warner went on, sounding like a man who had spent his entire life on Wall Street. "Now, an unsettled position is a position, let's say, that is booked forward and has not yet reached the point of settlement."

"In the context of which we're talking about today, yes." Cerullo went on. "It's because what I've been trying to suggest to you whether a security transaction is settled or unsettled, with the passage of time, there is an interest calculation, there is an interest accretion, and there is a cost-to-carry accretion. We all know that there are some real positions in here that were recorded. We all know that there were some unreal positions, and some fraudulent positions here recorded by Kidder Peabody."

"We don't all know that, Mr. Cerullo," Warner said quietly. Cerullo rushed on.

"And I cannot affirm for you the details of what's listed here in month-to-date interest. I don't know whether they were the result of Jett's real activity or of his fraudulent activity."

Warner waited until he finished.

"So, you were testifying this morning, making all kinds of claims against Mr. Jett as to what he did or didn't do, but in fact you can't tell us, looking at these numbers, what they actually mean."

Fury flashed in Cerullo's eyes.

"No, sir."

*　*　*

CERULLO CALMED HIMSELF. For the next hour, as Warner jumped from subject to subject, Cerullo stuck to one theme—denial. First, he denied that Bernstein had told him about the inquiry into my trades he and Fiume-freddo were doing.

"No, sir. I don't believe that to be the case." My hand itched to smack the tabletop, hard. Cerullo damn well knew that GE had been breathing down our necks about the aged mortgage inventory loss, and had ordered an investigation of all our major trading positions. I knew Cerullo had dispatched Bernstein and Fiumefreddo to make themselves quick experts on my desk operations so they could handle GE's questions.

"You know that Mr. Bernstein has said that he came to see you on that subject during that period, do you know that?"

"I can't say that I do, no."

I stared at Cerullo, believing now that he'd deny anything. But then he admitted knowing that my profitability came from customer business and muni defeasance trades. Thus, Warner realized Cerullo had to know of my other profit areas as well.

"And isn't it also true that he explained his profitability by referring to stripping and reconning transactions?"

"Yes, it is."

"And isn't it also true that he explained his profitability by referring to what might be called market inefficiencies and price differentials in Strips versus bonds versus futures prices, he referred to those?"

"Yes, that's possible."

My stomach felt empty and I looked up, realizing the morning had passed. It was lunchtime, and everyone agreed to take a break. Warner asked the judge to remind Cerullo that he couldn't talk to anyone about his testimony during lunch. Tasheff interjected.

"I don't plan on talking to Mr. Cerullo, but I don't think he can be limited from talking to his own counsel."

Fox-Foelak and Warner looked at her sharply.

"Yes, he can," the judge admonished.

"Most definitely," Warner added. I watched Tasheff, now wondering if she really knew anything at all about trial procedure. Warner must have had the same thought because he started to explain, under the guise of talking to the judge.

"I think, Your Honor, during cross-examination, he can definitely be limited to talking to anyone, as Your Honor directs, so that he does not discuss his testimony during cross-examination. It is a standard ruling that's given, and during cross he can talk to his counsel about other things but not about his testimony." He paused, without looking at Tasheff. "So I'd ask Your Honor to give that standard ruling in this case."

Tasheff looked confused. "Your Honor, he's not a party in this proceeding."

"It doesn't matter. It relates to all witnesses," Warner said. His tone was gentler now.

Tasheff stuttered at the judge.

"Well, I just think—he's here under subpoena. He's not here, you know, voluntarily. He shouldn't be restricted, I don't think, in his comings and goings beyond to give his testimony under oath when he's in the court-room."

Warner waited for her to finish.

"He's not restricted in his comings and goings. He should be restricted, as virtually all witnesses are restricted during cross-examination, from dis-cussing his testimony."

I watched, fascinated. I'd seen enough courtroom drama on TV and in the movies to know protocols that seemed to baffle the SEC lawyers and judge. Warner went on with his lesson.

"Mr. Cerullo's counsel may have entered an appearance, and possibly if Your Honor permitted him, to object or whatever, but that is not the same thing as conferring with and assisting the witness in preparation of testi-mony."

The judge looked at Cerullo.

"All right. Don't confer with your counsel in reference to what you've already testified to, but certainly you may continue to talk to them about this matter in general."

"OKAY," WARNER SAID after lunch, "what do the position limits repre-sent?" He was ready to establish that Cerullo had trusted and relied on me so much that he'd frequently increased my spending limits. My limit was $8 billion.

"And, in fact, every single month he exceeded them, correct? And Barry Finer, whether you remember it—do you remember Barry Finer coming to you about this and saying, 'Joe Jett's past his guidelines'?" Finer was the risk manager.

"Barry Finer and I had continual dialogue on guidelines for everybody," Cerullo said tightly. "Joe Jett would have been one of those individuals."

"Okay. Now, in response to the first quarter and Mr. Jett's trading, your decision was to increase his guidelines, correct, by fifty percent?" Warner asked. "So the end result was that in 1993, you doubled Mr. Jett's position limits. Did you make your best effort to look into the nature of Mr. Jett's business, his transactions, how he was making money—"

"I believe I did."

Warner's tone remained unchanged.

"Okay. Now, in fact, Mr. Cerullo, you were watching Mr. Jett's activities so carefully during 1993 that you even were aware of who he was dating, isn't that right?"

Cerullo started—"I'm sorry. Excuse me?"—and Tasheff jumped up, crying, "Objection, relevance!"

Fox-Foelak looked bewildered. "Counsel, could you explain the relevance?"

"Well, it's relevant to the extent to which they were monitoring everything Mr. Jett did, including his dating. It's so, isn't it? You made it your business also to know about whether Mr. Jett was dating any particular people at the firm."

"Same objection," Tasheff interjected.

"Overruled."

Cerullo glanced around.

"That's not correct."

"Well, do you know a woman named Linda Mead? And you know that she worked at the firm, right?"

"I did."

"Okay. And it was brought to your attention that Mr. Jett might have gone out with Linda Mead, isn't that so?"

"That's correct."

"And who brought that to your attention?"

"I do not recall."

"Well, suppose I mention the name J. J. McKoan. Does that ring a bell?"

"That's possible, but I do not recall."

"Okay. And how about Brian Finkelstein?"

"That's possible, but I do not recall whether—"

Warner cut him off with questions about McKoan's and Finkelstein's titles.

"Okay. And you've said that it's possible that both of these men may have brought the dating with Linda Mead to your attention."

"That's correct."

"So you were available then to receive that information, correct?"

"I was available to all my reports for anything they wanted to bring to my attention. Or thought worthy of bringing to my attention."

Warner looked directly at Cerullo, who stared back.

"And they had reason to believe that if dating practices were something that they wanted to report, that they could go to you about it and not, for example, Human Resources or anyone else, right?"

"Objection. Calls for speculation," Tasheff cried.

The judge looked at Warner. "Counsel, haven't you gone far enough with this?"

"Did you receive reports about any other dates that Mr. Jett may have had at the firm?"

"I do not recall."

"It's possible though, right?"

"I don't recall."

Warner let the words hang for a moment, then abruptly changed the subject. "Now, by the way, what is a basis trade?" I felt my fists unclench. I hoped Warner had made the point that Cerullo was inordinately aware of everything that went on in our office at Kidder. We had decided not to bring up the black male sexuality discussions, because I knew that the minute race was introduced into the proceedings, that's all anyone would hear from that day forward. I knew the press would leap on the idea that a black man was "playing the race card," and the media would report nothing else from the hearings. We had to hope that the judge would realize that if Cerullo paid such close attention to who I dated, then he must have paid close attention to how I managed $30 billion.

From a distance, I heard Cerullo and Warner agree that an example of a basis trade could be a long bond position and a short futures position. Cerullo said he knew that I had a large position in futures.

"You didn't tell Mr. Jett that he should stop trading in futures, right? Or having basis trades, correct?"

"We're talking about real Strips and recons with real counterparties now?" Cerullo said with a sneer. Warner ignored him.

"I'm saying at the end of '92, when you looked back, he had made forty plus million dollars. That had been a big accomplishment, right? And he got a bonus that you approved, correct? So when you were looking back over that year and at the good accomplishment, you wondered, didn't you, whether this would be able to continue?"

He had wondered, Cerullo acknowledged, so he'd talked to me and looked at reports to understand my transactions. Warner wanted to know about those reports. One was the Daily Transaction Journal, which lists each transaction.

"It's available to you if you'd asked for it?"

"I believe it would have been."

"Okay. And was there also a report called the PPR-2, the Position and Profit Report Number Two?"

"I do not know."

Warner pressed him. The PPR-2 was a commonplace document at Kidder. Everyone else who'd testified had no trouble remembering or identifying the PPR-2. Wasn't it true that there were reports for the asking that listed Mr. Jett's trades and the profits associated with them? Cerullo grew frustrated.

"Sir, the reports that Kidder generated on a daily basis could fill tractor trailers. I received reports that were purported to be correct. I believed to be correct. That provided me a digestible understanding of his activity on a daily basis."

"Okay. But now can you answer my question? Was there a report available to you for the asking had you asked at Kidder that would have listed Mr. Jett's transactions and the profits associated with them?"

"I do not know," said the former executive managing director of Fixed Income. •

"Okay. Did you ever ask for such a report?"

"I did not."

"Did you ever say to Mr. Bernstein during 1993, 'Could you go in and kind of look at the nuts and bolts of what Mr. Jett is doing and give me a report. I'd like to see how during the first six months of last year got doubled, or more'? Did you say that to Mr. Bernstein at any time during 1993?"

"In substance, yes."

Warner kept going. "Uh-huh. And what was your understanding as to what Mr. Bernstein looked at when he was doing these nuts-and-bolts analyses?"

"Sir, I suspect he used different resources at different times. I could not tell you."

"And was it your understanding that he was looking at records? Not just going around and talking to people, but looking at records?"

"Sir, I don't recall." Cerullo's voice was tight, his face still, his tone formal.

The subject changed again. Didn't every Wall Street manager fear that if he lost a hot trader, the trader might take his secrets to success with him? Warner wanted to know.

"Were you satisfied that your understanding of his trading activities would enable you or your department to make some reasonable approximation of his performance if he left?"

"I believed that at the time, yes."

Warner glanced at me.

"You didn't believe that you had the people, meaning you didn't believe that there was anybody at Mr. Jett's desk who would have been able to step into his shoes, correct?"

"Not immediately. That's correct."

EVERYONE IN THE courtroom looked tired and uncomfortable. Cerullo's and Warner's voices waned. Warner went back to my $8 billion position limit. "Now, we were talking about how Mr. Jett exceeded the guidelines month by month in 1993, but although that happened most of the time, there came a point in 1993, didn't there, where he didn't exceed them at all? In fact, he went under them by some considerable amount, correct?"

Cerullo shifted in his chair. "That's correct." Warner pulled out a Kidder graph and asked Cerullo to read figures showing that my position limits were at $16 million in August, but I used only $14.9 million, and in September, only $9.7 million.

"Isn't it a fact that during the last—well, during the last quarter, which would be the last three months, but starting in September also of 1993, that Kidder engaged in a balance-sheet reduction program?"

Cerullo chose his words carefully.

"From time to time, Kidder had targets for balance sheet. They tended to coincide with quarter statements."

"Well, from time to time, that's true, but at the end of 1993, it was a serious concerted effort for an extended period of time, isn't that true?"

"I hesitate to affirm your characterization," Cerullo said stiffly. "All financial institutions have year-end balance-sheet targets. Kidder was no different than any other. And in 1993, Kidder did have a year-end balance-sheet target. That's correct."

"Okay. But with respect to this particular target, you wanted it to be higher than it ended up being, isn't that right?"

"That is correct."

"And what did you want it to be?"

"I don't recall the precise number."

"But you do recall that the target ended up being $80 billion, right?"

"I do not recall that precisely." Cerullo's voice was flat. I squirmed in my seat. After all the energy, anxiety and effort that went into those balance-sheet figures month after month, how could Cerullo say this? Those numbers were burned into his heart and mind in the days we scrambled to meet GE's balance-sheet demand. In those days, we talked about $80 billion and breathed—it was the same reflex. I looked at Warner, willing him to force the truth out of Cerullo.

"But does that ring a bell? Does that sound like that's approximately what it was?"

"I would not dispute—I have no basis for disputing that."

"Okay. And, in fact, you went to Jack Welch to argue your case, didn't you?"

"I don't believe that's the case."

I stared at Cerullo. Was he going to say next that Bernstein had lied when he told me that Cerullo was going eyeball-to-eyeball with Welch?

"Well, you attempted to go to Jack Welch anyway, didn't you?"

"That's definitely not the case. I argued against every balance-sheet target Kidder had. I don't believe I ever took an initiative to contact anyone aside from Michael Carpenter. He was chief executive officer at Kidder Peabody."

"Now, the balance-sheet target was set by General Electric, right?"

"I do not know."

"General Electric is the parent company of Kidder, right?" At that moment, it wouldn't have surprised me to hear Cerullo say he didn't know that, either.

"That is correct."

"What's your understanding of who set that target?"

"I don't know."

At this point, I would have given anything for a jury. No reasonable person would believe any of Cerullo's testimony after this. How could he expect anyone to accept that as the head of Fixed Income, he had no idea who set his investment budget? Warner handed Cerullo a report from an inventory committee meeting dated September 7, 1993. It started with a reference to a prior meeting. They all began that way. This one noted that at the August 30 meeting, they'd discussed the fact that the balance sheet had increased to $98.6 billion.

"Of course, that was beyond the target, right? The $80 billion target."

"I don't recall what the target was at that time."

The report said: "Mr. Carpenter reemphasized that the September quarter-end balance sheet was not to exceed $80 billion." The minutes also indicated that Cerullo reviewed the Fixed Income balance sheets and a plan to reduce assets by quarter end. The next report, from September 13, referred to the same discussion.

"This package discusses the plan that you outlined to reduce the balance sheet, correct?" Warner asked. "At the September 7 meeting then, Mr. Cerullo, you had outlined your plan to reduce the Fixed Income's balance sheet from $90 billion—maybe it's $90.2 billion, but it's ninety something billion—to $73.8 billion, right? Okay. And you said that these reductions will be achieved by moving assets off the balance sheet, such as by doing trades with forward settlements and reducing the amount of Repos outstanding, correct?"

"That is correct."

"And, in fact, isn't it true, Mr. Cerullo, that you had been informed that Mr. Jett was using forward settling trades to reduce the balance sheet?"

"I was informed that he was using forward settling trades. I was not informed he was using forwards with the Fed."

"At September 13, again, the balance-sheet reduction was discussed. And, in fact, it kept being discussed, right? That meeting and the next one and constantly it was discussed."

"I would not be surprised, but, you know—"

"Because that's how important it was, right?"

"I have no reason to dispute that."

Warner wanted Cerullo to look at a Kidder chart. Cerullo agreed that it showed total assets of the firm from March to September 1993.

"Now, in fact, the inventory committee reached a consensus that the transactions that were going to be employed to reduce the balance sheet were not unusual in the ordinary course of Kidder's business, right?"

"I believe that to be the case."

Warner moved on to another graph that showed that the Kidder balance sheet dropped from $99 billion to $75 billion at the end of September.

"And September 27 was pretty much around the end of the quarter, right?"

"I would believe that to be the case."

Now Warner asked him to look at a January 17, 1994, report from the inventory committee, this one with a sheet called the Weekly Balance Sheet Highlights. It chronicled notable highlights from the balance sheet and references to other accounting adjustments.

"And these adjustments are part of what is meant to explain the balance-sheet change that's listed at the top, which here shows January 6, 1994, $103 billion, and January 13, 1994, $110 billion." Warner pointed to each item and Cerullo followed on a copy he held. "So there was an increase of about $7 billion. And on this balance-sheet page, am I correct in saying that it shows a variance of about $7 billion from the January 6 balance sheet to the January 13 balance sheet, right? And down at the bottom on this page is part of the explanation for this variance, correct? And what it says is under 'Other accounting adjustments,' 'Disallowance of, quote, nonregular way, close quote, increased by 5.789.' "

The number meant $5.789 billion.

"Now, a nonregular-way transaction in Strips means a transaction that is more than next-day settlement, farther forward than next-day settlement, correct?"

"I would believe that to be the case."

Warner had made his point. Billions of dollars in Strips and nonregular-way transactions were used to reduce the balance sheet. He turned back to Cerullo. "Well, you saw those numbers at the time, right?" Cerullo punted again.

"There are times that my activities took me out of the office and out of the country and I can't say that I saw these numbers."

Warner hardly looked up. "Uh-huh. Well, you were aware during this period and before that there were billions and billions of dollars, Strip and recon, nonregular-way transactions that were on the books, right?"

Again, Cerullo didn't know about anything, even billions in trades.

"I was unaware of these transactions. They were not discussed at any inventory committee meetings I attended, nor were they brought to my attention by anyone at any meetings that I was absent from."

Warner handed him the January 31 report.

"First of all, the Balance Sheet Highlights indicates that the balance sheet took a massive change, right? And there it refers to a balance-sheet change of $30 billion in the course of one week, right?"

"That's correct."

"And at the bottom of the Highlights page it says, doesn't it, that the nonregular-way sales decreased by $24 billion. Now, is it your testimony then that you attended this meeting and that $24 billion highlight was never discussed and never noticed by you?"

Cerullo seemed to struggle for a satisfactory answer.

"Sir, to suggest that that was a highlight in this package is a very extreme mischaracterization. As I mentioned earlier, you are pulling pages that are buried in a two-inch-thick packet of documents and numbers. And this was certainly not something that was highlighted. I'll tell you it was not something that was focused on. It was not something that was brought to my attention at that meeting, before that meeting, or after that meeting by anyone on my staff or anyone in the firm." He was right that these reports could fill a dump truck. But did he really run his department in such a hands-off manner?

"You would agree, wouldn't you, Mr. Cerullo, that this $30 billion balance-sheet reduction was certainly a matter that the inventory committee was giving some attention to, wouldn't you? And as a matter of fact, during 1994, Kidder Peabody was conducting negotiations with a bank for a revolving line of credit, wasn't it?"

"I believe that to be true." His manner hinted that it might have been something he'd once heard a rumor about.

"And the bank was the Union Bank of Switzerland, right?"

"I believe that to be true."

"And it was important for the firm, in order to present the best financial picture, to have its balance sheet in its best possible condition for presentation to the bank and review by the bank, right?"

"I cannot affirm the statement you've just made."

Warner found it hard to believe that if a company was applying for a line of credit, a bank wouldn't be interested in its balance sheet. Cerullo insisted on ignorance.

"I don't know what the Union Bank of Switzerland was interested in."

"Am I correct that the revolving line of credit that was being sought was $2.5 billion?"

Cerullo claimed not to remember the numbers bandied about in the weeks of meetings he conducted from Vail.

"You can't even make an educated recollection on that? You just have a complete blank on what that amount is?"

"I do not recall the size of the line that was being negotiated."

I LOOKED AT Warner for signs of exasperation, but his face was impassive. He went back to the disallowance of sales. He read from January 24 inventory committee minutes: "Review of the balance sheet of Kidder disclosed that total assets had decreased $29.9 billion.

"And then it talks about a decrease of $23.6 billion in Fixed Income inventory and other things as accounting for the change. Right? So at the inventory committee meeting, however big or small this package of material was, the inventory committee was discussing not only the size of the balance sheet but what caused it to change, correct?"

Tasheff jumped up to object again, demanding to know why Warner was asking all these questions and sending Warner into an angry denunciation. He couldn't ask two questions in a row, he complained. He looked at the judge.

"The point is that the balance sheet was a central focus for Kidder Peabody. Obviously it was discussed at inventory committee meetings, as it's clear from the records. Sometimes explicitly clear from the records and other times implicitly clear, that there are a host of references to the nonregular-way sales in repeated balance sheets, in repeated inventory committee minutes, including this one that I'm holding now, and in many, many others. And there are obvious discussions referred to right in the text as to reasons for the change. And for Ms. Tasheff to keep jumping up and saying every time that this is irrelevant I think only becomes a situation of protesting too much, because it's obvious that from the face of these records that these matters were addressed and discussed and focused on." He turned back to Cerullo. "At the January 31, 1994, meeting, wasn't the reason for the balance-sheet change discussed."

"I do not recall."

Warner nodded toward the report that Cerullo held, asking him to read aloud from it.

"A decrease of $23.6 billion in Fixed Income inventory and a decrease of $5 billion in reverse and securities borrowed accounted for the change."

On another page, the report cites over $9.5 billion in nonregular-way sales of Strips.

"And that was never discussed?"

"I believe that to be true."

"By the way, you know what 'pair-offs' are, right?" Warner changed the subject again.

"I believe so."

"Okay. And did you know that pair-offs were being used in connection with the balance-sheet reduction efforts that were going on?"

"I can't say that I do," Cerullo snapped.

"Well, didn't Mr. Bernstein bring to your attention that Mr. Jett was using pair-offs during this balance-sheet reduction period?"

"I can't say that he did."

"But, again, are you saying he didn't, or you just don't recollect one way or the other?" Warner reached for a stack of papers.

"I do not recall him bringing that to my attention."

Warner then pulled out the February 22 meeting minutes, and pointed to a notation that fluctuation in the size of the balance sheet had been discussed.

"And as a matter of fact, Mr. Cerullo, with respect to the issue of balance-sheet fluctuations, have you ever heard the term 'spikes'?"

"Prior to the investigation, I do not recall having heard the term."

Warner pulled out a copy of a memo.

"Do you recognize that as the memo that you asked Mr. Bernstein to write in February of '94 to Mr. O'Donnell, the CFO?"

"I do not recall, but I would not dispute it."

Warner asked Cerullo to read from the end of the memo.

" 'Accounting adjustments. As our balance sheet has grown, we have seen progressively larger adjustments for forward transactions and for trade date/ settlement date mismatches. Though we would attempt to manage these adjustments at the end of the reporting period, they can cause significant intra-quarter spikes.' "

"Spikes," Warner repeated. "And 'spikes' is in quotes, right? So you were familiar with that expression, right?"

"I do not recall."

I shook my head slightly, to myself. So far, Cerullo's testimony had been one long memory loss. He wasn't prepared to take responsibility for a thing. Now Warner wanted to ask him about his own profits. He pointed out that my 1993 trades accounted for 27 percent of Fixed Income's profits.

"When your bonus was set for 1993, it was set in part in reliance on the profits reported from Mr. Jett's ledger, correct?"

Cerullo claimed he didn't know. He never thought about my profits in connection to his own bonus, he insisted.

"Uh-huh," Warner said with skepticism. "Well, you did focus from time to time on what the factors were that would influence the amount of that bonus, didn't you?"

"My focus was to try to run the most effective department and business that I could," Cerullo said importantly.

"Right. But every once in a while you probably did give some thought to how much you'd be paid, right?"

Cerullo had earned a $600,000 annual salary from 1991 to 1993. The rest of his money came from discretionary bonuses.

"And to whatever extent Mr. Jett's reported profits contributed to a better showing for the Fixed Income department, that was a better chance for you to get a higher bonus, correct?"

"I would believe that to be true."

"Now, during 1990, that was before Mr. Jett came—during 1990, you received a bonus of $2.4 million, right?"

"I do not recall."

I looked at my hands, almost embarrassed at the pinched, unflinching expression on Cerullo's face. Who honestly didn't remember how much money he earned?

"During 1991, Mr. Jett was there just a short time and nothing much was done, you received a bonus of $6.4 million, correct?"

"I do not recall."

"During 1992, that was when Mr. Jett had a total $30 million for that year, you received a bonus of $11.4 million, is that right?"

"I believe that to be true."

"And during 1993, you received a bonus of $15.4 million, correct?"

"I believe that to be true."

"Now, you have not been required to return any portion of the $15.4

million bonus and $600,000 salary that you received in 1993, isn't that true?"

"That's true. I have not been required to give anything back." Cerullo's voice rose, and he snapped to attention. "Voluntarily I instructed my attorneys, when I severed my relationship with Kidder Peabody—"

Warner cut him off. "Could we just get a yes or no answer, Mr. Cerullo? The answer is yes, you've not given it back. It is a fact that you have not returned to Kidder any portion of your compensation of $16 million that you received in '93 nor any portion of the $12 million that you received in 1992, nor any portion of the $7 million that you received in 1991—"

"No, sir," Cerullo said, looking directly at him. "That's incorrect, and it's not what I testified to. You asked me if I had been required to return any monies, to that I said, no, I had not. I attempted to follow up with the explanation that when I resigned from Kidder Peabody, I instructed my attorneys that I did not want to have benefited from Mr. Jett's scheme in any way, shape or form, nor appear to have benefited. And on that basis, instructed my attorney to come to a settlement with Kidder Peabody addressing the substantial deferred compensation I had built up at Kidder Peabody over my fifteen-year career there. And we made an adjustment accordingly."

Warner pulled out another sheet. It was a Kidder employee profile for Cerullo, and it included his earnings.

"Well, let's take a look at them. Let's start with 1993. It shows a salary of $600,000. That was your base salary, right? Then it shows a total bonus of $15.4 million. If you add those two, it comes to $16 million. Now, there's also a deferred bonus. And that number is not included in the $16 million. So then you're saying that your total compensation received for 1993 was $12 million received, plus a deferred component of $4 million, is that right?"

Cerullo had been paid $12 million, with another $4 million placed in investment accounts in his name. Some of that money he could touch, some he could not.

"So my first question then to you is this. Isn't it correct that you have not returned to Kidder Peabody any of the compensation that you have received from Kidder Peabody?"

Cerullo faced the judge. He argued that the deferred compensation had been turned over to him, even though he did not receive the money in hand. He got regular reports of the investment activity, he argued. So the $4 million was already his. And that money he had ordered his lawyers to arrange to return to Kidder.

Warner knew, however, that Kidder by-laws stipulated that anyone who quit was entitled only to the vested portion of his deferred bonus. In Cerullo's case, that worked out to $2.4 million. But his golden parachute had been $7.5 million. He pressed this point with Cerullo, but Tasheff objected to his questions. Warner looked at Fox-Foelak.

"Had he resigned, he would have received $2.4 million. Instead, what he worked out with Kidder was a severance deal in which he received $7.5 million. Now, these are all matters of fact and record. And that is the testimony that I'm trying to bring out and I've now been reduced to announcing it myself because I keep getting interrupted by Ms. Tasheff, but at least it's better to come out in some way or other than not to come out at all."

He paused, and I felt the air in the room expand. Tasheff had just let Warner make the point that Cerullo, at least, had been skilled enough to avoid. He moved on. He was closing in on Cerullo, getting ready to finish.

"Okay. Now, you have testified here, Mr. Cerullo, that prior to March of 1994, you were not aware of Mr. Jett's forward trades with the Fed, correct?"

"That's correct."

"In fact, though, isn't it true that Mr. O'Donnell, the CFO at Kidder, in the early part of April or the very latter part of March of 1994, asked you about that at an inventory committee meeting at Kidder? And isn't it a fact that when Mr. O'Donnell asked you whether you had previously been aware of Mr. Jett's forward trades with the Fed, that you didn't answer him, did you? You sat there silently and said nothing. Correct?"

"I don't recall the conversation or exchange or reference."

Warner was already pulling out another document.

"Let me read to you from page 413 of Mr. O'Donnell's deposition at line 17. 'Were there any conversations—Yes. Did you ask Cerullo whether he was previously aware if Jett had forward trades with the Fed prior to March 29, 1994? Answer: Yes. Question: You asked him that question? Answer: Yes. Question: And what did Cerullo say? Answer: He didn't answer me.' "

Warner looked up from the deposition.

"Now, those were the questions that were asked and answered of Mr. O'Donnell. And does that refresh your recollection that Mr. O'Donnell asked you very specifically, 'Did you authorize them?' And you didn't say to him, 'No, I didn't authorize them.' You said absolutely nothing, isn't that right?"

"No, sir. I do not recall that exchange."

"You don't deny that that is the case; you just don't recall? Is that your testimony?"

"I don't recall that exchange."

Warner waved the deposition in the air.

"Does this refresh your recollection? Page 414 of Mr. O'Donnell's deposition, line 3 . . ."

Tasheff said weakly, "Your Honor—"

"It's only three lines," Warner assured her. "This is from page 414, line 3. 'Question: Can you put it into context of what subject was dealt with after you posed that question? Answer: We were discussing the progress at the point in time with the Strips investigation. I raised the issue. I said, quote, 'One thing that is still very confusing to me is did you authorize these trades,' because it was becoming increasingly difficult for me to see how sixty thousand trades got transacted in his business unit by a trader who worked directly for him, who he promoted, who he nominated for Man of the Year, who he gave a $9 million bonus, who he considered to be an absolute superstar, how could those trades go through without his knowledge or authorization? So that was the question that I had, but he did not answer it, and Carpenter didn't make him answer it.' "

Warner paused.

"Now, does that help you to remember that it was very much that question asked, and you did not answer it?"

"No, sir. I don't remember that question."

Warner looked at him.

"I have no further questions."

EXULTANT, I SNATCHED a glance at the reporters in the courtroom. They looked interested and engaged for the first time in a while. Cerullo had hung himself. Was there anything he didn't know or didn't remember? Almost gleefully, I ran through his litany of denials. Cerullo said he'd known nothing about forward recon trades, and that no one had told him of them. He denied warning me against mentioning them in my "Man of the Year" speech, even though Carpenter had confirmed it. He denied telling me to conduct forward recons to reduce the balance sheet. He didn't know he'd almost been fired for greed and excessive tyranny, even though it was in his personnel file. He wrote memos to Carpenter urging a policy of checking trading tickets, but insisted he never looked at a single one of mine. He never looked at the Red Book, the Government bond desk ledger, either. He saw the risk management reports and the Fixed Income Daily reports, but neither gave him a hint of forward recons. He admitted he didn't understand the figures in the Government-1 ledger—was the money real or not? He didn't know about the Position and Profit Report No. 2. He never asked to see the Daily Transaction Journal. He didn't know if there was a report available that listed my trades and profits. He couldn't say when he first became suspicious of my trades. He had no memory of the May and June 1993 investigations by Bernstein and Fiumefreddo. He could not remember the loss booked over the aged mortgage inventory. He couldn't remember who brought him tales of a relationship between me and Linda Mead—and he couldn't recall any other reports about me and other women. He couldn't remember when Bernstein reviewed my trading activity, and couldn't say for sure what sources Bernstein looked at. He couldn't remember that our balance-sheet target had been $80 billion. He denied talking to Welch about increasing it. He couldn't say who had authority for setting the limit. He never saw reports of the billions in Strip and recon nonregular-way transactions that were on our books. He had no idea what Union Bank of Switzerland wanted from Kidder, and he couldn't remember what size line of credit Kidder wanted from Union Bank of Switzerland. He didn't know about pair-offs. He'd never heard about "spiking" the balance sheet. He didn't remember a Bernstein memo to O'Donnell about spikes. He couldn't remember his own bonus in 1990, 1991, 1992 or 1993. He denied sitting in silence when O'Donnell asked if he'd known about the forward recon trades before March, despite Carpenter's deposition that it had happened.

The list was dizzying. Tasheff tried to redirect, but her questions were dry and feeble. She asked tepidly whether Cerullo had ever tried to hide information from O'Donnell, and then she went over his golden parachute package again. But it was over. There was little she could do to repair the damage from Cerullo's testimony.

THE FEW REPORTERS in attendance picked up on Warner's question about whether Cerullo had known who I was dating. After the session, they wanted to know why Warner had asked Cerullo about my dating habits.

"There was a racist atmosphere at Kidder," Warner told them. Within hours, the lead of the Associated Press wire story highlighted the news that Joseph Jett had charged Kidder with racism. The next morning, a headline screamed from the pages of the New York *Daily News*: JETT CLAIMS RACISM!

Immediately, I knew that if race were introduced into the hearings, it would be the only aspect of my case that got any attention. Cerullo would fade away, his Milquetoast demeanor and stultifying testimony no competition for the sensational double-whammy of race and sex. Everything we compelled him to admit, every fact establishing his complicity or responsibility for the trading strategy would be completely lost in the commotion. Little of his other testimony would make it into the papers. My chances for a fair hearing would fade, too. In my experience, when race is on the table, credibility with whites is lost. Too many people think race is exploited as an excuse for a legitimate failing. Racism at Kidder was not the only point. Racism existed in the extreme. But I'd persevered in my work, progressed through the ranks, and succeeded as a trader and manager. Along the way I'd fought battles for power, and my enemies had stabbed me in the back with any number of daggers, one of which was race. We all tried to find weapons to use against each other. In my case, J. J. McKoan found the volatile combination of race and sex to be a perfect weapon in his plotting against me. But it wasn't the reason I'd lost my job. It wasn't the reason for the campaign to blame Kidder's demise on me alone. I refused to stand up before America—black and white—and claim I was fired because Kidder managers didn't like the color of my skin. That wasn't proof that I'd been wronged. I insisted on standing up and staying I'd been fired because my managers were duplicitous and greedy, because the trading scheme they'd engineered, directed and supervised had backfired on all of us. I wanted the world to know that a man had been unjustly accused and slandered for specific reasons, not that a black man had been wronged just because he was black.

If I had any doubts about the overwhelming distraction of sex and race, they were dispelled when I sat down to talk with a *Wall Street Journal* reporter named Laura Cohen. After a long discussion of my job at Kidder, Cohen mentioned that she'd spoken to my old landlord. He'd told her that I was frequently in the company of beautiful women, most of whom were white. Did I care to comment on that?

"This is crazy," I said. "I've been accused of stealing $350 million, yet every which way I turn people are only obsessed with the women I've dated. All white men have fixation on black men having sex with white women."

Picking up the *Journal* days later, I read the quote from me near the top of the story: "White men have a fixation on black men having sex with white women." The piece read as if that was my answer to the accusations of rogue trading. I dropped the paper with a mix of fury and aggravation. I wouldn't let my entire struggle against GE and Kidder sink under titillation over black men having sex with white women. The *Journal* interview was the first time I'd mentioned race to a reporter, and it was the last for quite a while.

CERULLO'S TESTIMONY WAS followed by one of our witnesses, Kidder Peabody's lead auditor, Jack Capocci. Capocci had guided the six-hundred-hour audit of the zero-coupon trading desk, and he'd written the report of its findings. Capocci now worked in Hong Kong, so he had to testify over the phone. Warner faxed him a copy of the audit report and, together with the judge, half a dozen lawyers and me, crowded around a ceiling speakerphone in an office adjacent to the courtroom.

John Cuti asked Capocci about the audit report's findings on profit potential from arbitrage, which took "advantage of price differences [arbitrage], between the strippable bond and the portfolio comprising its Strips." Capocci had examined Strip and recon trades, done for "proprietary trading only," his report said. As the international phone line crackled, Cuti asked Capocci to look at a page from my trading ledger that was included in his report.

"Okay. Now, the next entry there in that column, 'Institutional and proprietary trading,' there, you see 'reconstitution,' right? Do you see that? Hello? Hello? Hello?"

Silence reverberated from Hong Kong, and for a second we thought the line had gone dead. But Capocci was still there, apparently speechless. His own handwriting showed he'd noted the trades that Kidder and GE said I'd concealed. Cuti repeated himself.

"Do you see 'reconstitution'?"

"Yes," Capocci finally answered.

"And then there's a brief description of what that means, which is 'putting together a previously stripped bond,' right?"

"That's what's stated there, yes."

"Okay. Now, from the column we talked about earlier under 'trading strategy,' this reconstitution activity is described as 'proprietary trading only,' right?" Again, Capocci seemed unable to hear well, so Cuti repeated the question. "Well, if you look under the 'trading strategy' columns, under the column labeled 'Desk,' immediately following the paragraph which describes the Strip-recon arbitrage, there's a notation that this is 'proprietary trading only,' isn't that right?"

"I see that, yes."

Capocci sounded uneasy and launched into a digression about institutional customers and brokers, and broker's brokers. Cuti, exasperated, waited until he finished and then went back to the ledger page and asked Capocci if the document we all looked at was prepared by auditors that he'd supervised, from discussions with members of the Government desk and reviews of desk documents. It was, Capocci acknowledged.

"Okay. I'm asking you what's here. 'Reconstitution,' right?"

"Right."

"And then it says, 'Hedged with financial futures, Treasury bonds,' do you see that? Immediately below 'reconstitution.' "

Capocci struggled to find his place in the document.

"Does seeing this entry here immediately beneath 'reconstitution' refresh your recollection that you were told that financial futures were used to hedge Mr. Jett's proprietary trading?"

"I don't recall."

"You see immediately beneath 'hedged with financial futures,' 'arbitrage profit,' right?"

"Right."

"And we've already been through the fact that you were told that arbitrage profit came from stripping and reconstitution, isn't that right?"

"Right."

"And then immediately below that, there's a notation, 'twenty to thirty percent forward transactions [greater than five days to settlement date]; one to three months.' You see that, right?"

"Yes."

"Do you recall Mr. Jett telling you or hearing from another auditor that they were told by Mr. Jett that his reconstitution and Strips trades were done for forward settlement?"

Like everyone else, Capocci had one answer: "I don't recall."

*　　*　　*

ON JUNE 3, Bernstein took the stand, and remained there for three days. The SEC spent the entire first day questioning him. His testimony followed the same themes as Cerullo's and Mullin's—and sharpened the focus on the SEC's strategy. Listening to Cerullo, Bernstein and Mullin, it seemed impossible that I'd traded forward recons in secret. For two weeks, lawyers from both sides had asked them, plus a motley array of accountants, trading examiners, systems analysts, and market experts, about a litany of daily reports, computer records, profit and loss statements, inventory committee meetings, trading reviews, phone calls and casual conversations. The trades were simply too big to believe that no one knew a thing about them. Instead, the SEC tried to draw a finer distinction, to let Cerullo, Mullin and Bernstein say they'd known about my forward recon trades, they'd just never known that there were any profit implications. None of them had ever heard of booking profits up front for forward recons as was done with muni defeasance trades. My trades, in and of themselves, were not wrong. In fact, Kidder's managers had innocently used those trades to help master their balance sheet. They didn't know there would be a profit problem; when I saw it, I hid it from them. This was a fallback position: They went from not knowing anything about my trades, to knowing only part of the truth.

Bernstein opened his testimony by saying that in 1993, only about 10 percent of his time was spent monitoring government securities trading. Weeks went by without him stopping by the Government desk, he said. But in May, he admitted, Fiumefreddo had told him about my forward trades.

"He explained that he was undertaking a project where he was attempting to identify forward positions so that they could be segregated and not considered as part of the balance sheet for accounting reporting purposes, and was trying to get the necessary resources to prepare a report which would clearly identify these forward trades."

Bernstein and Fiumefreddo talked about the plan several times, until finally they discussed how the trades might affect my profits. Bernstein worried that unless an accounting adjustment were made, "it was possible to record either a profit or a loss that was really a creation of the fact that the market assigned a different price to forward trades than to spot trades, you know, rather than an actual economic profit."

He and Fiumefreddo had talked to me about it, "mostly in late May of '93," in three or four meetings over a week. He said we talked on the trading floor, for about ten minutes each time.

"I guess before the first conversation with Joe, you know, just sort of eyeballing it, it looked like we were recording the purchase of a bond and the sale of Strips, so it looked like some sort of reconstitution trade, but, you know, I didn't really know what it was. I couldn't tell who the counterparty was, and that was part of the conversation we had with Joe."

"And what did Joe say about what these forwards were when you went to speak to him?" the SEC lawyer, Bruce Newman, asked.

"Joe explained that they were forward reconstitution trades done with the Federal Reserve."

Newman wanted to know what I'd told Bernstein about the profits of these forward reconstitutions; he answered that I'd assured him there was no up-front profit, but then he admitted he was still confused. So he wrote a memo to reassure himself that he'd understood me. It was now Exhibit 79, and Newman pulled it out.

Bernstein read his own writing: " 'Though the sum of the extended trade prices of the Strips will exceed the extended trade price of the bond [by an amount equal to the bond's accrued interest], the reconstitution does not result in a, quote, automatic, unquote, profit.' "

Bernstein believed that this memo exonerated him. He even insisted that he'd shown it to me and I'd signed off on it. I never saw any such paper, and it didn't have my signature on it. Newman wanted to know where it had come from, his computer or a typewriter. No such file was found on his computer hard drive. No disk copy existed of it, unlike the Excel spreadsheets he had used to calculate profits from my forward trades.

The Lynch notes were full of contradictory statements from Bernstein. Also, Kidder had preserved hours of Bernstein's taped telephone conversations. I believed that Cerullo, Kidder and GE originally intended to bring down Bernstein, so they'd collected evidence against him. However, he could also bring down Cerullo, so in the end, they left him alone. But the notes, tapes and evidence were still around. And the Lynch notes made it clear at least to me that he'd lied about many parts of his story.

He called me Joe throughout his testimony, even though Newman kept making pointed references to Joseph Jett. Bernstein just thought of me as Joe. He had none of Cerullo's hesitation about discussing the pair-offs, rollovers or balance-sheet spikes. He'd first heard of them near the end of 1993, when Kidder managers tried to keep track of its year-end budget.

"After some study, it was determined that the pair-off/roll-forward mechanism, when it was performed in such a way so that one leg, for instance, the pair-off, was done for regular-way settlement, next-day settlement, and the other leg was done for forward settlement, that even though that pair of trades was intended to offset each other and not affect the firm's economic position, if you will, that in fact the balance-sheet accounting methodology that we used eliminated forward trades from the balance sheet but kept regular-way trades on the balance sheet."

He denied understanding the purpose of the pair-off trades. By February and March of 1994, he'd grown worried about my trades, and wrote a note to himself to discuss with Cerullo "a large number of forward trades which will never settle." That led to the heated arguments between us as Bernstein kept revising his analysis of my trading position. He admitted as much— that I hadn't agreed with his figures or his interpretations. Then he said that I had complained about back-office backlogs, and that was a reason for the rolling over. He agreed that Cerullo and he decided to pair-off my trades as a recourse. He admitted that I was upset about this.

"Well, this was I guess a day or two afterwards, and he was rather upset, expressed to Ed the fact that he didn't initially understand exactly what the nature of eliminating these trades was, but that in fact rather than eliminating paperwork, they were generating additional paperwork . . . and he was rather adamant that we not do any further reduction to the forward positions."

By March, Cerullo and Bernstein had called in Carpenter and grilled me nearly every day about my trades. That's when, Bernstein testified, I'd said that the forward trading pattern that included the pair-off and roll-forward-type high-volume trades that had become so prevalent, was in fact initiated at the end of the third quarter as a balance-sheet reduction tactic.

THE NEXT MORNING, Warner stood up to cross-examine Bernstein, and wanted to go back to the memo Bernstein wrote himself to explain that my forward reconstitutions booked no up-front profit. Bernstein's greatest problem was the Lynch notes. He'd made inconsistent statements, even asking the Lynch investigators at one point, "Kidder can't deny that a hundred plus people knew that forward trades with the Fed took place. Issue is if I had P&L effect." Warner wanted Bernstein to name those hundred people. Bernstein also said he'd told the Lynch investigators that he'd shown me the memo. But no notes about that existed in the Lynch papers. It was hard to believe Bernstein would never mention this critical memo to Lynch.

"Six interviews, never asked you specific questions about that?" Warner asked.

Bernstein acknowledged that forward settling trades were not unheard of in government securities, and that unless an accounting adjustment was made, there would be an inevitable profit or loss impact. It wasn't written policy, he admitted, but traders at Kidder understood this in general. His testimony contradicted Fiumefreddo's, who had said he hadn't known of any unofficial policy that adjustments had to be taken for forward trades.

Warner spent the next hours quizzing Bernstein about the effort to reduce the balance sheet. Bernstein had told Lynch's investigators that he "didn't care" how I got my position down, as long as the balance sheet was reduced before GE's quarter end.

"Isn't it also true that Mr. Cerullo told you of the need to keep the balance sheet smooth in 1994 because of the ongoing financing negotiations with the Union Bank of Switzerland syndicate?"

"Yeah. Ed—I don't know if I'd say it exactly the way you said it, but Ed did express the fact that the inventory committee felt that there shouldn't be abrupt changes in balance-sheet level."

Later, Warner went back to the pair-off trades.

"It's correct, isn't it, Mr. Bernstein, that if the timing of a pair-off is not correct, then it could end up having assets recorded on the balance sheet, isn't that so? And that was a topic that you talked to Mr. Jett about more than once, right?"

"Yes."

Then Warner asked Bernstein about the $27 million in interest, the money Cerullo hadn't been able to say was real or not. Bernstein knew better.

"So my question, Mr. Bernstein, is the $27.3 million number which is positive interest on settled inventory, that is real dollars that come to the firm, correct?"

"Yes."

TOWARD THE END of the afternoon, Warner zeroed in on the notes from Bernstein's meetings with Lynch investigators. The Lynch papers indicated that Bernstein had told the investigators from the outset that Kidder had blown the 1993 review of my trades.

"I remember trying to express to them . . . that there is a hypothetical line of questioning that we could have pursued that would have allowed us to find the distortion sooner, but that we didn't do that, and that didn't necessarily mean that we had been wrong or unprofessional or somehow, you know, not doing our jobs by doing that, but simply that we had not hit upon that line of questioning that would have revealed the P&L distortion to us earlier."

Warner looked at his copy of the Lynch notes.

"My first question to you is with respect to the phrase which is quoted in the Davis Polk notes, 'We blew it'—are you denying having said that, or are you saying you don't recall if you said that?"

"Well, I tried to explain . . . the context. . . . That's all. There's nothing more I can say."

The afternoon passed in a long, detailed discussion with Bernstein about what he had said to me in May 1993 about my trades. Warner questioned him over and over about what he'd asked me—had he "blown it," had he not asked the "right question," what would the right question have been, should he have understood differently from the questions that were asked? They went around and around the subject until I hoped it was apparent to everyone that the conversation in May had come to the clear conclusion that my profits were real.

The Lynch notes clearly recorded Bernstein as saying after that audit that "C.F. decided that the trades were not false profits, just accelerated profits." C.F. was Charles Fiumefreddo.

Sitting at the defense table, I felt sure that Warner had proved that Bernstein and Fiumefreddo okayed my trades in 1993. But just like Cerullo,

Bernstein stuck by his story, however absurd it sounded in light of the evidence.

WARNER PUSHED THE button on a tape player, and Bernstein's disembodied voice filled the courtroom. "Obviously we try not to draw attention to the stuff in the Strips book," he said to me in this taped conversation. "But for my security, get these trades done." The sound switched off.

"What did you mean by that?" Warner asked Bernstein.

"I don't remember what I was referring to."

On another tape, Bernstein warned me to buckle down and get more efficient. "You are becoming conspicuous." On a third tape, he assured me that "I know we committed to not ask you to do anything strange or unusual with the balance sheet, but this is Ed's parting shot." After he clicked off, my voice is heard, lingering on the line, swearing.

Warner looked at Bernstein.

"It sounds like you want Jett to do some kind of trades and he doesn't want to do them."

ONLY ONE OF my direct employees took the stand during my trial. None of my Strips traders would respond to inquiries from my attorneys. But Richard Ward, who had traded the five-year Treasury bond sector at Kidder Peabody for twelve years, agreed to help us.

The trial had begun with the SEC and Kidder taking the position that no managers were aware that I had conducted forward Strip and reconstitution trades. In the Lynch notes, Bernstein was recorded as exclaiming that Cerullo couldn't deny that one hundred plus people knew of the forward trades. This had forced the SEC to acknowledge that the trades were known. Instead, they then contended that the profit impact of the trades was unclear.

But this had also been debunked. Bernstein's spreadsheet with hand calculation of the profit from a forward reconstitution had shown that Kidder management was aware of the profit impact from the trades. So aware, in fact, that they could calculate the profit from looking at any single trade ticket for a forward Strip or recon.

After that, the SEC fell back to a final position. It held that the profit from a forward trade should be adjusted downward to eliminate the time-related profit embedded in the trade. Since I had failed to do so, they claimed my actions were fraudulent on that basis alone.

Richard Ward testified that he and every other Kidder trader was prohibited by the accounting staff from making profit adjustments for forward settling trades. Ward could not recall (as I did) whether it was Charles Fiumefreddo who had put this policy in place.

The SEC made no effort to rebut Richard Ward's testimony.

As the trial drew to a close, the SEC seemed to have no basis for their accusations against me.

My final day on the witness stand before the SEC was a complete shock both to me and to General Electric's lawyers. Ken Warner questioned me, tying together the numerous threads of testimony and physical evidence presented. My direct testimony took all morning; at 2:00 P.M. we broke for a lunch recess. Then the SEC attorneys had their final opportunity to cross-examine me. I took the stand at 2:45 P.M. The SEC attorney asked a few brief questions, then stated, "Nothing further, Your Honor." Bewildered, I looked at the clock. It was 3:07 P.M.

We packed up our stacks of documents, spoke briefly to some reporters and walked into the hallway only to be greeted by Larry Portnoy, one of GE's attorneys. He raced down the hall at full gallop.

"What happened?" he hailed us breathlessly.

"It's over," John Cuti replied.

"What! The cross is over!" He looked at his watch, incredulous. "Oh my God!" He raised his hand to his head in disbelief.

"Larry, they had nothing. You have nothing," Cuti scolded him.

"Just you wait!" he retorted. "When you go against us you won't be dealing with amateurs anymore."

Cuti and I took seats on some hallway benches as General Electric's lawyers gathered in an angry huddle. They denounced the SEC attorneys as rank amateurs who had completely failed in their efforts to prove me guilty of fraud. Cuti and I chuckled as one of the GE attorney's blurted loudly enough to be overheard. "They didn't even ask him!" in response to Portnoy's probing.

WITHOUT A JURY, it wasn't a matter of days or weeks until the verdict came back. We didn't go out for lunch or home for the weekend to wait for a ruling. Instead, as I understood the SEC's regulations, Judge Fox-Foelak had sixty days to rule once the case was officially closed. When we left the courtroom after twenty days of hearings, the case was far from closed. My press got better: At the end of the hearings, the *New York Post* had proclaimed JETT LOOKS LIKE HE'S IN THE CLEAR, and *Business Week* magazine carried a headline that asked, DID JETT COMMIT FRAUD? DON'T BET ON IT. Those stories were heartening. The SEC trail had exposed what had really happened at Kidder, and I began to believe that others were now changing their minds about me. How could the judge not see it the same way? I just had to wait for her verdict.

I had no way of knowing it when the hearings were over, but Fox-Foelak wouldn't close my case for a year and five months. The hearings ended in June 1996, but the case remained officially open until November 1997. First, Fox-Foelak allowed the SEC six months to prepare a written brief.

My lawyers then requested the opportunity to counter with a brief of their own. For months, attorneys on both sides asked to submit new documents and evidence. Not all of it was accepted. When one side made a request, the other side came back with a petition of its own. Every step took months to prepare and complete. In the meantime, the clock that counted down the deadline for my verdict stopped ticking.

JUSTICE DELAYED, JUSTICE DENIED

T

HE END OF the SEC hearings didn't mean I had a break. In the final week of a hot July, barely a month after the last SEC session, the whole exercise started over again, this time when the National Association of Securities Dealers convened its arbitration panel. I had sued Kidder Peabody for the return of my assets, and I'd gone to court to force the arbitration process to be moved from the New York Stock Exchange to the NASD. An arbitration panel at the exchange was made up of three representatives from within the financial community. That meant, technically, that Kidder Peabody employees could sit on my panel. I didn't like that idea. Procedure at the NASD, on the other hand, required that the three-person arbitration panel include two individuals from outside the financial industry. I thought my chance of a fair hearing would be better at the NASD.

This trial would prove far different from the near kangaroo court setting of the SEC hearing. First, the SEC had chosen to have the case overseen by a new judge. Fox-Foelak had heard only one previous SEC case and had yet to render a single decision. Fox-Foelak also admittedly knew little of the highly complex securities and trading stratagems that were at issue. Finally, it seemed to me that the SEC judge had been uncomfortable with the rules of law and evidence. At one point, she declared that a witness's current recollection outweighed a taped telephone conversation made two years previously, and also outweighed contemporaneous notes taken two years earlier by the witness's own attorney.

In direct contrast, the NASD, mindful of the tremendous press attention given to the case, had created a blue-ribbon panel of arbitrators to oversee and rule on the matter. The arbitrators averaged twelve years of experience in handling arbitration procedures. In addition to the tremendous legal experience that was shared among the panel members, the chief arbitrator was also an accounting professor at Fordham University. He was able to ask incisive technical questions of both myself and General Electric's expert witness. Here at last I was able to present a technical defense of my trading strategy.

General Electric's attorneys were at a great advantage. They had sat through the entire SEC hearing and knew and had studied every piece of evidence and all of my testimony. They were also aware of the severe weaknesses of the SEC case. Therefore they sought to widen their net. The SEC case had been about fraud, a difficult charge to prove. The General Electric attorneys charged me with three violations: fraud, undue enrichment, breach of duty. They claimed that they would prove me guilty of fraud; but even if the panelists did not believe me to be guilty of fraud, they should at least find me guilty of undue enrichment. Undue enrichment meant that the money that I had been paid, I had not earned. The General Electric attorneys also claimed that even if the panelists did not find me guilty of undue enrichment; they should at least find me guilty of disloyalty. After all, Kidder Peabody no longer existed and I, in their opinion, was the primary cause for its demise.

General Electric's lead attorney told the arbitration panel of two men and one woman that "this case, when you boiled it all down, is about the difference between reality and make believe. Joseph Jett created a world of make-believe transactions. They're called forward reconstitutions or recons, and as we will learn as we go through the case, those make-believe transactions resulted in vast make-believe profits on the books of Kidder Peabody." He sounded just like Gottlieb at the SEC—with one exception. He also made the argument that General Electric did not have to prove me guilty of fraud in order to win the case; they simply had to prove me guilty of disloyalty. My lawyers stopped the proceedings, surprised and curious: Was GE officially dropping its accusation of fraud in favor of a charge of disloyalty? The GE attorneys consulted. No, they said, they wanted to accuse me of both. They demanded $82 million in payback and penalties. GE knew its case had been damaged at the SEC. Its witness list was devastated. Its experts had trouble pinpointing fraudulent trades in Kidder's books. As a result, GE called only five witnesses, and fought to prevent the NASD arbitrators from reviewing transcripts of the SEC hearing.

With that we were off and running again. For the next five months, I spent nearly three days of each week in a hearing room at NASD offices on Whitehall Street, listening to an identical parade of witnesses repeat everything they'd told the SEC. But this time things were different. The three NASD panelists were the cream of the crop. They knew finance and trading. The hearing was halted on several occasions so that the chief arbitrator could check his trading positions with his broker. The panelists were not prepared to accept nonsensical arguments.

General Electric called their expert witness. They used the same person who had appeared before the SEC. This surprised me. The fellow was a risk manager, not a trader. He had an accounting background, not a technical one.

By the end of the trial, it was clear from the arbitrators' questions that they did not believe me guilty of fraud. What was at issue to them was whether the money I had earned had been real. In a virtual one-on-one contest against General Electric's expert witness, I had to prove the technical merits of my trading strategy. I felt I'd been born for this fight. It was certainly the fight for which I had yearned. I covered blackboards with equations and graphs depicting my trading strategy. I detailed how I had sought in 1992 to take advantage of the steepening yield curve by shorting long-dated Strips and holding bonds and short-dated Strips against them in a relative value trade. I showed how the forward recons in 1993 had allowed me to establish a long position in the treasury bond basis. I described how the Clinton administration's move to semiannual rather than quarterly bond auctions created a long bond basis opportunity that had enriched Kidder Peabody during 1993. My arguments were technical. This was math. This was the numbers. It did not matter that I was black and my opponents white and backed by the most powerful and most highly capitalized company in the free world.

Numbers do not lie. They do not care about a person's race, color, sex or creed. They demand no quarter, and they give none.

GE's expert witness described a trading strategy that he thought would be profitable. I criticized his strategy and pronounced that had he followed it he would have been unemployed like many others who had opposed me while I was trading. I was back in my element, supremely confident and overbold. Yes, I knew that I could lose, but both I and the General Electric attorneys would know that I had been right. Time and again, Ken Warner or Gustave Newman sought to rein me in. But with each question from the panelists, I grew more confident. They understood the math. They understood.

General Electric countered with their accountant. He offered no proof, but simply claimed that I had not taken everything into account and therefore my argument was fraudulent.

In December, just over three weeks after the NASD hearings ended, I got a call from a paralegal in Ken Warner's office.

"Joseph!" she said breathlessly. "You won!"

I was puzzled, not even sure who I was talking to. "Won what?"

"The NASD ruling!"

I thought she was joking.

"No, I'm not! You won the NASD ruling! Listen!" And she held her receiver up in the air; in the background I could hear everyone in the office shouting, "Joseph, you won!"

I laughed. The NASD arbitrators had met one time to consider my case, and had immediately rejected Kidder's charge that I had engaged in "fraud, breach of duty and unjust enrichment." They threw out Kidder's $82 million claim against me. I was innocent of fraud; more important, the experts had determined that the money I made was real. Instead, the three panelists ordered Kidder to return $5 million in my brokerage account, including giving me immediate access to $1 million. The NASD did not order Kidder to pay my legal costs, as I'd wanted; instead, the panel denied the application "without prejudice," and never explained why. But that meant I could go to a second round of arbitration.

I couldn't help but feel vindicated. Finally, I could call my parents with some good news. Mops was overcome. All the bad press in Cleveland, especially the stories about my personal life and the rumors that I hadn't really graduated from Harvard, had worn my mother down. She needed to hear I'd been exonerated. Two down—the Justice Department and the NASD—and one to go—the SEC. I'd been right about the shift in attitude toward me and my experience at Kidder. All it took was exposure—of the events at Kidder, of the Fixed Income ledgers and computer printouts, of the testimony of people I'd worked with. A momentum was building now that the authorities, the press and the public could hear the other side of the story. I took the measure of the New York newspaper headlines once again, and they were gratifying: JETT SCORES AGAINST KIDDER, PEABODY; FORMER BOND TRADER WINS ROUND AGAINST KIDDER; PAYBACK TIME FOR ACCUSED TRADER.

IN APRIL 1997, GE lawyers from Davis, Polk & Wardwell, Gary Lynch's firm, contacted my attorneys. Robert Wise, the trial attorney who'd led the NASD case against me, was curious: Did I have any settlement terms? Even though we'd won at the NASD, he said casually, it wasn't likely to go so well with the SEC. It might be in my best interest to settle the whole thing, reasonably. My lawyers and I did not know if he was asking officially on behalf of GE, or just putting out feelers of his own. But I was dead certain about my terms: a full return of my assets, payment of all my legal fees and a public apology from Jack Welch.

FOR A YEAR after the NASD ruling, the SEC was silent. Judge Fox-Foelak established a timetable for each side to submit its legal briefs, and from the outset she gave the SEC six months. I believed she realized the media headlines were favorable to me, and wanted to issue her ruling only after all the attention died down. I continued to live at ground zero, unable to clear my name or rehabilitate my reputation and find a new job on Wall Street, and unable, really, to go forward with my own plans and personal life until the case was finally resolved.

I'd moved from my Tribeca loft in the fall of 1994 to a cheap, squalid apartment between avenues A and B. The long, railroad apartment was only about nine feet wide, and it didn't have a shower or bathtub. I washed up every day at the New York Health and Racquet Club. But I couldn't afford even such a crummy apartment on my own, and shared the tiny place with an artist who painted ugly abstract canvases, changed his name frequently and complained incessantly about his inability to meet anyone special. A lot of his friends were boy-girls. He was furious with me for installing an additional phone line under his name, but I was afraid to list it under mine. I kept the TV tuned to CNN whenever I was in the apartment, just to discourage conversation with my roommate.

I kept my suits at a friend's house in Brooklyn, so it was sometimes difficult to get to my lawyers in a hurry. But I didn't want to walk around in Greenwich Village in a suit, and end up with reporters staking out my new home. As a consequence, I was often late for meetings with my attorneys. Finally, I realized I had to rent a locker at the health club, and I stored a suit, ties and three shirts there. I'd arrive at the club in jeans and a baseball cap turned backward, and leave suited up as Joe Jett.

In February 1995, a good friend who continually house- and dog-sat for people who were out of town moved into an apartment belonging to a man who was leaving the country for the rest of the year. My friend introduced me as an aspiring actor and dancer, and I moved into the apartment to house-sit. It was just a few blocks up Avenue A, and I stayed there most of the year, vacating only when the owner returned for brief visits from Europe. I thought I was completely incognito until one day a neighbor said, "I saw you on TV the other day, it looks like people are at least willing to hear your side."

Throughout 1995 and 1996, to make ends meet I took on an assortment of odd jobs—moving furniture, construction (I turned down only one job, because it was asbestos removal), roofing on Lower East Side apartment buildings, pulling wires at the new Kinko's copy center, building high-end personal computers (I can slap together a computer from its component parts in a few minutes) and selling them at the @Cafe in the East Village.

The currency of the East Village is food stamps, and I discovered that a robust underground economy is entirely based on this illegal tender. Food stamps could be converted into cash at the local corner market. I learned this after the IRS seized my checking account in June 1995, claiming that I owed taxes on the money that was frozen in the Kidder account. The IRS wiped out what money I had left. So I worked for cash, and sold computers for cash and food stamps. I lost money when I exchanged the food stamps, but though I was willing to take on any work to survive, there was no way in hell I was going to stand in a grocery store line and actually buy food with food stamps.

Since I had no housing costs, I used the money I earned to rent one air-conditioned room in a Midtown apartment, which I converted into an office for my fledgling investment business. I traded money held in my Kidder account, tracking the market and identifying profitable opportunities with computer-generated technical analysis. I generated a 43 percent rate of return. I just couldn't touch any of the capital or the profit.

Around Thanksgiving 1997, nearly a year after the NASD ruling cleared me of fraud charges, Judge Fox-Foelak of the SEC finally put an end to any further modifications or additions to the case against me and closed the file. After months of silence, it seemed as if now something might happen. Suspense returned to my life. The judge had sixty days to rule, but technically she could rule anytime before that. I'd spent over three years living at ground zero, and I was sick of it. Now, for the first time, it seemed as if I might finally see an end to it all.

If I felt sorry for myself, that attitude dissipated when I went home to Ohio at Christmas. When I talked to my childhood friend Harold Massey, I heard of too many classmates whose fates had been far worse than mine. Kids who grew up and went to jail. High school classmates who now dealt drugs from their hardworking parents' homes. A former friend who was arrested for selling drugs because he used his two-year-old daughter as a "courier" and stashed drugs in her diaper. Another friend who did time for statutory rape. A friend across the street who was on trial for killing a policeman.

My father had taught my brother, sister and me to resist those temptations—just as many other parents in our neighborhood taught their children. They taught us to be proud and to stand up for ourselves, our race, for what we believed in. I was more than willing to fight Kidder and GE. I was more than willing to take my chances with the SEC. I was determined to survive, and not through the art of compromise. Too many of my former friends and neighbors had gone that route. They had barely survived, and there was no quality to their lives. Sometimes I wonder if that isn't the most insidious legacy of slavery. Slaves couldn't fight back, and they couldn't escape through dying. In order to survive, they simply existed. Too many of their descendants simply exist in the same way; and have made too many compromises for that survival. And that often leaves blacks and the black community with little self-respect. I couldn't go that route.

My old friends told me I'd become more approachable than when I worked at Kidder. That surprised me. I didn't think I was softer or gentler. I thought I was harder. If I hadn't become harder I wouldn't have survived the years of accusations. I never tried to be likable. I just did what I had to do. The managers at Kidder were competitive, back-stabbing and often overt racists. I couldn't like them at any time. Instead, I did what I thought made an effective leader—in part because of my philosophy about leadership, but also because no one at Kidder had endeared themselves to me as human beings. Even J. J. McKoan, whom I originally respected for his tolerance and apparent fairness, turned out to be hateful. I was an outsider at Kidder, and I still felt like an outsider at home. From the time I'd left Wickliffe, Ohio, through the years at MIT, Harvard and on Wall Street, I'd been the ultimate outsider. I'd chosen that life. I wanted to be a fierce individualist. I drove myself hard. I craved recognition and accomplishment. When Kidder, Peabody & Co. accused me of orchestrating a $350 million fraud, I became even more isolated. Now I was weary of the battle and the isolation.

After Christmas, I went back to New York, began writing a book about my experiences, and increased my efforts to start a hedge fund. I craved normalcy and routine. The following April, the fourth anniversary of my firing, came and went with no word from the SEC. I still spoke to my lawyers about Kidder and the SEC trial. But the sixty days passed, then became 120. My lawyers and Wall Street experts began advising me that rather than rule against the Street and jeopardize its high conviction rate, the SEC would simply let my case lapse. Taxpayers had paid millions for the investigation and the trial, with no payoff for anyone. I knew now that there would never be a Perry Mason moment when a jury foreman stood up and said, "Your Honor, we the jury, find the defendant, Joseph Jett, not guilty." I'd never see a front-page headline in *The Wall Street Journal*: SEC FINDS JETT INNOCENT. Too many people and entities inside the financial community had too much at stake to see me exonerated, and too many people outside Wall Street just didn't care enough anymore. So there was no pressure or incentive to resolve my case. I'd have to be satisfied with what I'd already gained. The Justice Department had found no grounds for criminal fraud. The NASD had ruled no evidence of civil fraud and ordered my money returned to me. Taking those facts and the evidence at its own trial, the blundering denials and the "truckloads" of documents, the SEC couldn't rule in favor of GE. But I knew the commission wasn't about to set any precedents with a ruling in my favor, either. So the SEC was following the Golden Rule: With nothing nice to say, it wasn't saying anything at all. It looked like it would simply let the statute of limitations on my case expire rather than rule. Four years after my firing, I gave up waiting for the SEC to rule.

My goal now was to regain control over my life. To take it back from Kidder, GE and the press. When life turns on a dime, you don't know it at the time. For me, the change swooped down during the week I was fired. I thought my personal formidability, my confidence in myself, my determination to win the political battles I'd been fighting with Cerullo, and my personal financial resources were enough to get me through this skirmish with Kidder and Cerullo. However, I totally underestimated the battlefield. GE weighed in, and threw all of its power, influence and clout into the battle. Suddenly I was fighting on a national scale, before a tabloid press, and a huge, powerful publicity machine that spoke for an entrenched establishment corporation and that controlled a television network. I began the week that I was fired with a small strategy to defy Cerullo and Kidder Peabody by taking my staff to another investment banking firm, and ended five days later with my money confiscated, the FBI investigating me, my picture on national television and the label "fraud" synonymous with my name. Not even a full week had gone by and I had not spoken publicly. Only one side of the case had been heard. It didn't matter. I was squashed in the popular publicity machinery.

My recovery from that public character assassination was slow. Press coverage of the SEC trial had been very favorable. At the trial's end, the New York *Post*, which had initially branded me a rogue trader, proclaimed my innocence with the headline: JETT LOOKS IN THE CLEAR. Although the trial had been ignored by *The Wall Street Journal* and *The New York Times*, the rank-and-file of New York City began pulling for me. I was hailed on the street by people of all races and ethnicities with the thumbs-up sign and requests for financial advice. Beginning in early 1997, after the NASD decision, several university graduate business schools invited me to participate in case studies of my story. At some schools the classes of graduate students were divided, half playing the role of Kidder Peabody, half playing my part. Students at New York University and University of Michigan at Ann Arbor dissected the case and then grilled me afterward.

My outspoken opposition to affirmative action led to several appearances on nationally syndicated cable talk-show programs alongside black business, political and media leaders. We talked not about Kidder, but about the black community. The PBS program *Crossing the Line*, emceed by comedian Jackie Mason and famed attorney Raoul Felder, invited me to debate the Reverend Al Sharpton and Professor Lionel Jeffries on the future of blacks in the next millennium. Neither Reverend Sharpton or Professor Jeffries showed up, so I debated New York Councilman Adam Clayton Powell III instead. My plain-spoken rejection of the virulent anti-Semitism that has poisoned the rhetoric of many of today's most prominent black leaders took the audience by surprise. I argued that for blacks to progress in the next millennium from their current position as low man on the totem pole, dependency on the federal government whether by welfare or affirmative action must end. I said the popular words of dependency uttered by most black religious leaders must be replaced with words of discipline, self-reliance, hard work and self-respect. I warned that the black man was in danger of becoming the ultimate herd animal following blindly behind the latest religious zealot spewing anti-Semitism. We black men have become sheep when we need to become lions, I declared. Black culture is becoming a dangerous monolith unwilling to abide independent thought. Free thinkers are derided as Uncle Toms, or worse. But I would not be silenced.

I gave numerous talks to junior high and high school students in Pennsylvania, New York, Connecticut and New Jersey, offering encouragement to accomplished black students who found themselves derided for acting white. In no-holds-barred conversations, I warned them against the self-destructive aspects of the current black culture and told them of their sacred responsibility to redefine what is black. I told them that it is not enough to simply survive, they must be warriors and leaders. If those of us who have the ability to lead do not lead, I said, then the black man will go the way of the Indian.

Despite my unconventional and outspoken views, I was asked to host a talk-show radio program on a predominantly black station. In the summer of 1998, the organizers of the Million Youth March held in Harlem asked me to address the crowd. "We do not think that you are an Uncle Tom, Mr. Jett. You just march to that different drummer," one of them explained.

In April 1998 I joined a panel discussion on PBS entitled: *The Kingpins of Finance*. I shared the podium with Wall Street notables Muriel Seibert and Morton Davis. I also appeared several times on the *Cavuto Business Report* on Fox to discuss the financial markets. I had gone from Wall Street outcast to Wall Street celebrity. The General Electric–owned CNBC invited me to appear on their program. When I asked why the invite, the producer intoned "ratings."

Wall Street professionals from across the globe have called to express interest in my fledgling hedge fund; major Wall Street houses have expressed interest in clearing my trades. My long battle to clear my name was not yet won, but the tide was surely turning.

But I couldn't say how my story ended. It simply didn't have a tidy Hollywood ending. The SEC case still floated around, frustratingly unfinished. I had to decide whether to sue GE or Kidder for legal fees. Another round of depositions, investigations and hearings, covering the same ground I'd been talking about incessantly for four years, didn't appeal to me. My lawyers were eager to sue for legal fees, and convinced they could win, but I wondered at the sanity of spending years running up additional legal fees just trying to recover the old ones. I'd already handed nearly $4 million to attorneys. Most of the money the NASD ordered Kidder to release never found its way into my pocket. Certainly, I wanted my money back, but I also wanted my life back. I'd grown sick to death of hearings, depositions, lawyers. How much longer would this go on? Yet if I gave up now, would it be tantamount to letting GE win? It knew that with its expansive legal team and limitless budget, it could string out litigation until I was old and gray. It didn't matter that the Justice Department and the NASD both said I'd committed no fraud. It didn't matter that the SEC appeared unwilling to take a stand.

I was still living in a small East Village apartment, and in July I took a break to meet my parents in Upstate New York. They'd traveled across the country by train with my sister and her family, stopping at various places along the way to visit family. They ended their trip at the home of my sister's in-laws, where I joined them for a long weekend. It was a relief to get out of the hot city in the summer. I talked with my parents and sister about my case a little, but we didn't dwell on it because I was convinced the SEC was not going to rule. Instead, I told them about my plans for a new business, describing the companies I was modeling my hedge fund after and some of the quirky people I'd interviewed to possibly work for me. I explained that I was setting up the fund as an international business, so I wouldn't have to worry about the SEC. But I spent most of the warm, sunny days playing with my three-year-old niece and her seven-month-old baby sister. I hadn't seen the new baby since shortly after she was born.

On Monday morning, I went with my family to Penn Station in New York City, where they all boarded a train bound for Detroit. They planned to attend a family reunion, and then head to my sister's home in Los Angeles. As soon as their train pulled out of the station, I crossed Manhattan for a meeting with a group of computer programmers who had spent five years developing software at one of Wall Street's best-performing hedge funds. The programmers had contacted me when they decided to break away from the fund and set up their own business. They were frustrated that the traders at their fund got all the credit, and the bulk of the income, for the computer programs they'd created. The group included two new partners, a postdoctoral fellow at Carnegie Mellon University and a research scientist at Sandia National Labs in New Mexico. They told me they had backers for their own fund, but they didn't want to relinquish managerial control or ownership of the artificial intelligence–based software they'd developed. Could I help them raise capital so they could start their business but remain independent? It was exactly the kind of project I was interested in. Their business proposal—and their idea of a utopian work environment—intrigued me, and we talked for several hours.

The next morning, I was still excited about this new business idea, and I got up early to research its potential. I spent the morning examining market analytics programs used to guide investment decisions. When my rumbling stomach prompted me to get some lunch, I looked at a clock and was surprised to see that it was nearly one-thirty in the afternoon. I hadn't talked to anyone or checked my voice-mail all day, so I picked up the phone and dialed my office for messages. I was intrigued to hear a recording from Lew Fischbein, a lawyer in Ken Warner's firm. I hadn't heard his voice in quite a while. His message surprised me even more.

"Joseph, we've just received the SEC decision and I want to get it to you," Fischbein said. My full attention focused on his next words. There'd been no warning that Judge Fox-Foelak was about to issue a ruling. Fischbein's voice was steady.

"As expected, she found against you," he continued, "but she only found against you on a books and records violations and not on the real serious matter of securities fraud, where she said that this case did not involve the purchase or sale of securities. Nevertheless, she does find in her apparently twisted view that you intended to commit fraud. So I'm sorry. Obviously it's not unexpected. But give me a call, I know you've been moving around and I need to know how best to get a copy of the decision to you."

I clicked off the line. An image of Judge Fox-Foelak filled my mind, but it wasn't the one of her sitting behind the judge's bench. Instead, I found myself remembering a day in the courthouse lobby when she'd tried to pass through a security checkpoint. The guards had insisted on inspecting her purse, and she'd taken umbrage. I'd watched as she shouted, "I'm a judge! I'm a judge! I'm a judge!" at them. For some reason, this scene came to mind now. I sat near the phone, quiet for a few minutes, wondering how she'd found me guilty if she'd cleared me of fraud. How had she found me guilty when the NASD had cleared me and the charges against me there had been much broader than at the SEC? I should have been exultant, I should have cheered and danced around the apartment. Fox-Foelak had said it herself—no fraud, according to Fischbein. That's what the whole, miserable case had been about, what every moment of public humiliation had been over, what had led to the loss of friends, my career and nearly $6 million. Now I'd won. Even the SEC judge had refused to go along with the script written by the SEC Enforcement division. I knew I should have felt ecstatic and vindicated. But in her back-handed verdict, Fox-Foelak had ruled that my trades were not fraudulent because, as trades conducted with the federal government, they didn't involve the purchase or sale of any security. Then she'd insisted that I'd had every intention of defrauding Kidder, and fined me for the lesser crime of a books and records violation.

How could she have ruled against me at all? My lawyers had presented the same case to a blue-ribbon arbitration panel at the National Association of Securities Dealers, where the charges against me had been much broader, and they'd cleared me of fraud. Had Fox-Foelak decided that I had to be guilty of something, so she'd picked the only remaining possibility, books and records violations? Warner and my other lawyers had reassured me that such a charge wasn't even under consideration, since Kidder, Peabody & Co. had never been accused of books and records violations.

Instinctively, I picked up the phone and dialed my parents' cell-phone number. The last thing I wanted was for someone at the family reunion picnic in Detroit to click on CNN and then run to Mops and Pops with this bolt from the blue. I knew that my relatives would be asking about me, and my parents were feeling good about my case after the Justice Department and NASD findings. This would be a setback, and I didn't want them to hear about it from someone else in the middle of a party. There was no answer on their cell phone.

I dialed again, this time reaching Lew Fischbein at Coblence & Warner. Ken Warner was on vacation in France, but Fischbein got hold of him for a three-way conference call.

"It's weird!" Fischbein said. He was the only one of us with a copy of the judge's decision. "She finds him innocent of securities fraud. In fact, she argues that the case is not in connection with the purchase or sale of securities. I'm still reading, but she doesn't seem to accuse Joseph of lying. She just says that the facts indicate intent to commit fraud."

Long distance, I heard Warner sputter, "What?"

"Well, she says that it's based on her interpretation of the facts. Oh!" Fischbein suddenly exclaimed and stopped. "Joseph. I forgot the penalties. She orders disgorgement of $8.2 million and a fine of $200,000. And you have to write the check within twenty-one days."

The three-way line was silent for a moment.

"I don't even have a checking account," I said finally.

Fischbein was still reading. The judge also banned me indefinitely from the securities industry. "Actually, the order becomes final if no one petitions the commission within twenty-one days."

Warner spoke up. "I should put together a statement saying that we intend to appeal. Are you going to make a statement, Joseph?"

My mind was elsewhere. "What happened to all the evidence we presented?"

"Joseph," Fischbein said, "it's fifty-five pages and I just got it. All I can tell you is that I see the words 'irrelevant' and 'gave no value to' wherever our position is discussed. She just put blinders on."

So my account had meant nothing. The Red Book, the phone tapes, Bernstein's spreadsheet, the Lynch notes meant nothing. I slumped in my seat and let out a long breath. Why was I surprised? I hadn't lied or committed fraud, but she'd declared that I intended to do both.

By late afternoon, the ruling had generated a frenzy of media attention. I was thrown back in time to four years earlier. It had been months since reporters hounded me, and months since I'd seen my picture on television. The SEC decision revived the attention. Phones rang off the hook at Coblence & Warner with reporters and TV correspondents wanting my reaction. A stream of bulletins came across the news wires, and my story once again made the nightly television news. Some of the coverage declared that I had been found innocent of fraud, some of it emphasized that I'd been found guilty of books and records violations and fined. The verdict could be viewed as clearing me—as evidenced by a *Wall Street Journal* headline that said, KIDDER'S JETT IS SANCTIONED BUT CLEARED OF FRAUD—or as condemning me, an opinion voiced by Gary Lynch, who told reporters that "it's a complete rejection of the Jett defense." That afternoon, I sat through quite a few conference calls with lawyers and advisers, and finally agreed to appear on several television business shows. On the air, I tried to explain that I felt vindicated over the fraud charges, but was outraged at the verdict on the books and records violations. I hadn't even read the full ruling yet.

Later that day I finally reached my parents. "Listen up, Mops and Pops. The SEC has found me guilty of books and records violations and ordered me to pay $8.4 million total."

Mops was shocked. "But how could they when that arbitration panel said you were innocent of far less serious offenses?"

"I don't know how, Mops." I knew I sounded bitter, and I didn't want to upset her. So I tried to soften the blow. "They were GE's last hope of avoiding a cataclysmic slander suit and they came through for them. Early indications are that she just refused to even consider most of our evidence. Hey, look, it's a kangaroo court. We knew that going in. They convict ninety-five percent of the people they try."

"You be sure to tell people that," Mops said. She genuinely believed that would do the trick. I didn't share her conviction.

TWO DAYS AFTER the ruling, I went to Warner's office and picked up a copy of Judge Fox-Foelak's decision. I got on a train bound for Philadelphia to visit friends and spent the entire trip reading the ruling.

After declaring our evidence to be irrelevant—the Lynch notes, my electronic diary, Kidder's internal audit, Bernstein's calculations of reconstitution profit, Mullin's testimony that I was underpaid, and the withdrawal of many of the SEC's witnesses before they testified because their early statements to Lynch contradicted their later depositions (the judge said my attorneys could just as easily have called them)—Fox-Foelak was able to ignore evidence that other people at Kidder knew about my trading strategy. It didn't matter, the judge declared, because she agreed that I'd told everyone at Kidder the truth about my trades. Though I'd explained my strategy openly and often, Fox-Foelak decided that I was aware that no one I spoke to could completely understand what I was talking about or the profit implications of my trades. Since I knew that, she said, my actions carried an intent to defraud Kidder, Peabody & Co.

As Fox-Foelak saw it, Kidder's books and records were erroneous because only I understood that the books and records were wrong. I spoke the truth freely because I knew that no one else understood it. I recognized the computer glitch that made posting profit from forward reconstitutions possible, but no one else understood the implications of this. Further, I knew that Cerullo, Mullin, Bernstein and the auditors didn't understand any of it, and I failed to correct or enlighten them. I exploited their ignorance. My having told the truth about my trades was no defense, Fox-Foelak declared. I was guilty of intent to defraud, even without any evidence of concealment.

Yet I committed no fraud.

"Mr. Jett's actions did not violate the antifraud provisions because they were not in connection with the purchase or sale of any security within the meaning of the securities laws," Judge Fox-Foelak wrote. Apparently, she came to this conclusion because forward recons of Treasury bonds did not become real until the bond was actually, physically delivered to the Federal Reserve. The Fed would not process Strips or recons without the bond in hand. Any bond entered into the computer for a forward settlement date had yet to be delivered to the Fed. Yet Strips and recons always took a couple of days to settle, so the trader had time to gather the securities. Nevertheless, Fox-Foelak determined that these were not real trades.

But I was still guilty of exploiting "an anomaly in Kidder's software, in the manner of a pyramid scheme, that credited him on Kidder's books with enormous, but illusory, profits. He did this with an intent to defraud."

Cerullo, Bernstein and the others were blameless, Fox-Foelak said, because they "did not affirmatively approve" of my trading strategy. "The evidence shows only that Kidder failed to follow up" when doubts about the strategy were raised. Her finding was in keeping with the SEC's charges of failure to supervise against Cerullo and Mullin.

Incongruously, she did agree that my forward reconstitution strategy could be profitable, and she dismissed the SEC Division of Enforcement's charge that a forward Strip or recon is in itself wrong or immoral. She found that booking a forward recon was a valid trade, but declared that I knew that the profit opportunity from such trades was "rather small." So she pronounced it wrong of me to pursue the strategy and allow large profits to be booked based on it. She held that booking the profit from a recon was a books and records violation that I had committed thousands of times.

This reasoning dumbfounded me. She admitted that my trading strategy was valid and could generate profit. She believed that the profit potential was small. Yet she was penalizing me for using the same strategy to make a huge profit instead? She did not say my trades were illegal—just too profitable. Yet where was the SEC's case if the trades themselves were not invalid or illegal?

Warner told me he'd never seen a verdict in which the accused was found honest and aboveboard but guilty nevertheless. He knew I was determined to appeal, but he couldn't help me. He couldn't afford to represent me anymore. His decision wasn't a surprise. We'd been talking about the cost of appeals and further arbitration to force GE to pay my legal bills for the last couple of years. We both had long known that Coblence & Warner couldn't work for free. An appeal of Fox-Foelak's ruling would cost several hundred thousand dollars, and as a practical matter I wouldn't be able to sue for attorneys' fees until after those appeals were concluded. Warner told me he'd go ahead with the appeal if I could raise the money from friends or family. But he didn't have a choice, he said. My bank accounts were empty, the money released by Kidder had already paid past-due legal bills, and no more money was forthcoming. Coblence & Warner had achieved its original goal of defending me against charges of fraud. It no longer made financial sense for the firm to represent me further. If I wanted to appeal Fox-Foelak's ruling, I was on my own.

So I set to work on my petition. It was supposed to be submitted along with a bond worth 10 percent of my penalties—in my case, an $800,000 bond. I didn't have that money; I worked on my petition, hoping I'd get the bond requirement waived later. I had twenty-one days to prepare a legal document detailing my objections to the ruling and my reasons for wanting it overturned. I knew that if I lost to the SEC, I could appeal that decision to the federal circuit court of appeals. The petition had to cover all the bases that would be scrutinized by either authority. I worked by myself, struggling to word the petition to reflect the right tone of legalese.

My arguments seemed obvious to me: The SEC's five commissioners should overturn the guilty verdict on books and records violations for the simple fact that "the SEC Division of Enforcement failed to ever charge Kidder Peabody or anyone else with any violation per se of any books and records rules in connection with this case. . . . Therefore there is no primary violation that Mr. Jett could have caused or aided or abetted." I also pointed out that "it is noteworthy that this decision invokes a completely new argument for Jett's guilt than was proposed by the Division. The Division claimed that entry of a forward Strip or recon was in itself fraudulent and was the grounds for the books and records violation. This [judge's] decision is in agreement with common sense and the testimony of Mel Mullin finds nothing per se wrong with forward Strips and reconstitutions. . . ."

I also wanted the commissioners to know that the judge's ruling "finds that Jett made no misrepresentations and finds no evidence of concealment or dishonesty. The Decision breaks new ground in establishing a policy in which being honest is held to be no defense . . . never before has someone who followed the bookkeeping procedures of the firm been found guilty of books and records violations. It is never asserted that Jett did anything other than follow the bookkeeping procedures as he was taught."

I pointed out that GE had dismantled the computer software that we used for our trades without letting the SEC or the judge take a look at it. Yet Judge Fox-Foelak "makes no adverse inference from the destruction" of the program. If the software had been in my hands and I'd "willfully destroyed it, we are certain that an adverse inference would have been forthcoming." I also argued that Fox-Foelak shouldn't have ignored evidence, including "the Lynch notes, the Jett diary, the Strip and recon trade tickets, Bernstein's calculation of profit from a forward recon, and the audit report." She also failed to consider that "any manager has only to review one Strip or recon trade ticket to know every detail that is claimed to be concealed. Every manager on Wall Street must, as due diligence demands, review the trade tickets of traders that report to him. It is the first requisite of management. The managers all by simply denying doing this most fundamental aspect of management create this fantasy world in which Jett trades over $1.76 trillion in securities with no one knowing."

Part of my petition pointed out critical errors Fox-Foelak made in her ruling. She misunderstood how the Government Trader software worked, largely because she never saw it and relied on a GE accountant to describe it to her. They got it wrong, and thus so did she. I also challenged a chart included in the ruling that purported to lay out my trading strategy. The chart was unintelligible to me; Fox-Foelak simply got my strategy all wrong.

"The Decision has concluded as Mullin testified that there is nothing wrong with forward settlement of Strips and recons and that sound reasons exist for them," I wrote in my petition. "It is extremely prejudicial to conclude that when Jett does what is logical and reasonable even in the opinions embodied in the Decision that he is engaged in fraudulent behavior. Jett is held guilty for not crusading for a change in accounting policy; for not 'disabusing' the firm's accountants of their own accounting policy. Jett was a trader not an accountant, not an auditor, nor a business unit controller. A blue-ribbon panel of NASD arbitrators ruled that Jett was not even guilty of disloyalty because he always followed the rules as set out to him by his managers and acted in the best interest of his firm."

In the end, I listed eighty-six objections to Fox-Foelak's verdict. My petition had to be as broad and as complete as possible, because only the findings listed as objectionable would be considered by the SEC commissioners and later, if necessary, by the circuit court of appeals. It took me the full twenty-one days of round-the-clock effort to put the petition together, and I barely got it into the mail before the deadline. I took off for Philadelphia to visit friends and recuperate from those intense three weeks. Right after I arrived, Warner called to tell me that I'd sent the petition to the wrong office. I had to send two copies, one to Fox-Foelak and one to the SEC's Division of Enforcement. I had to rush back to Manhattan so the petition would carry a New York postmark, to satisfy the further arcane requirements of the SEC.

I KNEW THAT Fox-Foelak's decision surprised many people on Wall Street. Virtually everyone expected a foregone conclusion when investigators in the SEC's Division of Enforcement declared me guilty of fraud and demanded $22 million in fines and restitution. Everyone understood that the hearings were simply part of a formula to be followed, and that the judges traditionally rubber-stamped the Division of Enforcement's conclusions. No one expected Fox-Foelak to break away from the mold, least of all the Division of Enforcement.

Officials there weren't at all happy with their judge. Apparently, they expected Fox-Foelak to go along with the script. On the day of the verdict, one of them told *The Wall Street Journal* that finding no fraud "was obviously not adequate." The ruling was a technicality, they said. A more serious punishment was appropriate, they argued. They were not consoled when Gary Lynch called the verdict "a major victory for the commission staff." They thought the judge had failed to censure me not only for the forward recon strategy, but for other trades that lost money as well. Probably they expected me to be pleased with Fox-Foelak's ruling, but I, too, was unhappy. I'd had unshaken faith in the strength of the evidence that demonstrated that Cerullo, Bernstein, Mullin and others understood and endorsed my trading strategy. I was not willing to accept partial victory. I wanted to be cleared of everything—not just fraud, but any idea that I'd duped or misled anyone at Kidder. As I worked on my petition, it never occurred to me that the Division of Enforcement was working on an appeal of its own. Yet both of us raced to complete the paperwork within the twenty-one allotted days. A few weeks after Fox-Foelak's ruling, the Division of Enforcement announced it was taking the unusual step of asking the SEC's five commissioners to set aside the verdict in favor of the original complaint of securities fraud and a request for fines and restitution totaling $22 million.

MEDIA ATTENTION AFTER the SEC verdict was like a quick-burning firecracker on the Fourth of July. For several days, there was a flurry of desperate attention to my case, with editors and TV producers battling to speak to me and have me appear on their programs. Then, as abruptly and quickly as it began, it was over. I was left in the quiet after the storm, trying again to put my life in order. After everything, I was three "no fraud" verdicts wiser, nearly $6 million poorer and on my own even more than the day I was fired. What had it gotten me? What did GE earn from it? Had any of it saved Kidder? Certainly not. The venerable old southern firm finally went down, and not because of me. It never recovered from the 1987 market crash, and made one bad business decision after another in the years it had left. Had my case taught Wall Street a lesson? Not that I could see—new forms of risky trading emerged every day, and forward reconstitutions still went on. Was GE better off? Perhaps. It had averted a major fraud lawsuit of its own. But it, too, was mired in an ongoing legal battle with me. I was determined to push my appeal through the long and arduous legal process. I was determined to clear my name completely and revive the career I'd lost. I'd missed some of my most productive years in the best investment economy in recent history. Vindication from the Justice Department, the NASD, and even the SEC hadn't changed the fact that Wall Street didn't trust me. Investor confidence is everything in that business. I battled that distrust every day, trying to find investors for my hedge fund. I'd lost more than a job, though. People I'd cared about, trusted and considered friends disappeared from my life. One called me "nigger" as she went. I haven't spoken to any of them since, and have no idea what has become of them. I am remembered on Wall Street, however. Friends tell me that when my story comes up, other people often still say: "Whatever happened to him? Isn't he in jail now?"

I couldn't say where anyone was. Cerullo, I knew, had retired with $7.5 million in severance pay, his huge house in Vail and whatever riches he'd put away over the years. He paid a $50,000 SEC fine and was suspended for a year. Beyond that, he'd vanished. I'd heard that Mike Vranos had started a hedge fund. Mullin was reportedly hoping to start one, too, but every time I heard about him, he hadn't gotten around to it, and seemed to be in semi-retirement. Bernstein had become a consultant. I never heard a word about Charles Fiumefreddo after that day at the SEC hearing when his name was withdrawn from the witness list and one of my advisers announced: "Ladies and gentlemen, Charlie Fiumefreddo has left the building!"

I hadn't talked to any of them, didn't know where they lived, or whether they'd resumed working. They disappeared into the woodwork, silent behind a cadre of Kidder and GE lawyers who didn't want them talking to the press or the public.

After calling me a few times to tell me that gossip and inquiry about her sex life had ruined her career, Linda Mead disappeared. I heard she couldn't find a job for a year, and when she finally did land a position, she left it shortly after the *Law & Order* episode portraying the devious black trader-murderer who slept with a white woman colleague. The black character was clearly supposed to be me, and everyone on the Street who gossiped about the sordid details of my case knew the white woman was supposed to be Mead.

Someone told me that Elizabeth Cavanaugh moved home to the South, and went back to working in finance. I heard that Jeff Unger moved to Cleveland and found work at a small securities firm. Joey-o tried to get a job with Mike Vranos's new hedge fund, but I never learned how it worked out. My old friend Rome Rottura finally wrote me a letter, two or three years after he stopped speaking to me, but I never answered him.

Cerullo and the other managers disappeared with their millions, their careers over but their anonymity intact, their names, faces and reputations unknown to the media or the public. Cavanaugh, Mead, Unger and Ossman were less lucky. They were younger, with their most productive professional years still ahead of them, and their careers were destroyed. For Cavanaugh and Mead, their personal lives were savaged as well. I didn't need to talk to them to understand they felt their lives had been trashed as badly as mine. But they, too, faded away, became anonymous and eventually uncon-nected with the Kidder scandal.

As for GE, my lawyers told its lawyers that I would settle the SEC charges with them only in return for a full public apology from Jack Welch.

I never heard from them again.

ACKNOWLEDGMENTS

No one asks to be robbed of their reputation or to have their good name sullied and to be denounced as a criminal. It is an unpleasant ordeal. It is also a challenge. When all except your family have turned their backs on you and all that you had has been taken from you, you must reach within yourself. How many of us know if there is anything there to draw upon? Few people are granted the opportunity to truly see what they are made of, to be tested by fire before the world. My wealth was not in my bank account. It was within me. It took my adversaries to drill this home to me. Thank you, Jack Welch, the lawyers of General Electric and my co-workers at Kidder Peabody. I have swallowed your poison and it has made me stronger.

I must first thank my literary agent, Suzanne Gluck, without whom this book wouldn't be possible. She believed in this project and made it happen, opening doors that had already slammed shut.

Thanks also to my editor, Henry Ferris, who had the daring to present my views on the black experience in an uncompromised fashion during a time when blacks are expected to merely toe the line. And thanks to my publisher, William Morrow, for supporting this effort when others dared not.

A very special thanks belongs to my cowriter, Sabra Chartrand, who has taken the arcana of Wall Street high finance and made it accessible to readers. Thank you for your patience and tenacity. I could never have accomplished this without you. I promise to be no stranger to controversy and with any luck we will do this again.

Early on in this ordeal I nearly despaired that the world would have any inkling of my perspective of the events that this book chronicles. I became convinced that there is no free press in this country, that corporate interests like General Electric, which owns NBC, CNBC and Court TV, can, through strength of ownership or advertising dollars, effectively control what is reported and what is declared truth.

In fact, among this nation's journalists, reporters and publishers there still exist those rare people who possess the courage to take on the corporate interests in their dedication to present the facts and both sides of controversial issues. This book exists because of them. So thanks go to Neil Cavuto, Paul Tharp, Peter Richmond, Saul Hansell, John Crudele, Gary Weiss, Susan Orenstein, Tom Lowry, Michelle Kurland of BBC Educational TV and Ed Bradley of *60 Minutes*.

Thanks also to Jackie Mason and Raoul Felder and their PBS series, *Crossing the Line*, for believing in me.

Thanks also to my attorneys, Gus Newman, Ken Warner, John Cuti, Lew Fischbein and Robert Schwartz, and the firms of Coblence & Warner and Newman & Schwartz, who went $6 million in the hole on my behalf. Anna Cordasco and George Sard restored my name, and that is truly priceless.

And thanks most of all to her I call simply The Baby, for enduring my tremendous melancholy and outrageous mirth. Truly when I walked alone on high mountains for whom did I seek if not you.

INDEX